Gifts
of
Sight

Bruce Shields

WESTBOW
P R E S S
A DIVISION OF THOMAS NELSON

ISBN: 978-1-4497-7094-5 (e)
ISBN: 978-1-4497-7095-2 (sc)
ISBN: 978-1-4497-7096-9 (hc)

Library of Congress Control Number: 2012918844

WestBow Press books may be ordered through booksellers or by contacting:

WestBow Press
A Division of Thomas Nelson
1663 Liberty Drive
Bloomington, IN 47403
www.westbowpress.com
1-(866) 928-1240

Printed in the United States of America

WestBow Press rev. date: 11/9/2012

To the memory of
My Mother
Who taught me to love beauty
and to remember the source from which it comes

Table of Contents

Prologue

A cold morning rain is pattering gently against our cabin windows. The weathered oak table before me is bare, save for two old friends: a large mug of steaming hot coffee and an empty pad of yellow writing paper.

The rain began before dawn and now filters out much of the early morning light. Across the valley, the next ridge of mountains is a misty blue-green silhouette against the pale gray sky. As the eye traces down the mountain slopes, blue hues give way to deepening shades of green, until they reach the verdant valley floor far below. Down there, lights are beginning to twinkle through the treetops, and threads of smoke are rising from hidden chimneys, heralding the start of a new day. Overhead, low clouds drift lazily in and out of the valley gaps. White and willowy, they impart a smoky appearance, from whence these old Smoky Mountains derived their name.

My eyes linger for a moment on this tranquil scene before rising slowly up the mountain toward our cabin. Outcroppings of stone and large ever-greens come increasingly into focus, until just outside my window every needle of every pine bough is clearly visible. Droplets of rainwater hang from the tip of each needle and seem to shiver in the morning cold.

Inside the cabin, there is still a morning chill in the air, and it feels good to wrap my hands around the coffee mug for a little added warmth. This old mug, with its warming contents, has been my companion for over half a century, bringing warmth to my body and to my soul. It was there when I first contemplated the miracle—and it was there when I aspired to join those who devoted their lives to understanding and preserving that miracle. It has been with me throughout the journey—through my good fortunes and my failures. And it is with me even now, as I marvel for the umpteenth time at what I have just witnessed outside our cabin window: the miracle—the mystery—the gift of sight.

—

It begins, of course, with light.

High above the heavy, gray clouds, blanketing the Smoky Mountains on this rainy morning, the sun is shining—shining as it has for eons—a mystery in itself. Rays of that sunlight are piercing the clouds and the rain and touching the blue-green mountains—touching every tree, every branch, every leaf and needle, every droplet of rainwater. Some of the light is absorbed and some is reflected. Like the effect of a pebble, when it is tossed into a still pond, the reflected light expands outward in concentric circles across the valley and far beyond. And, like the expanding ripples on the surface of the water, the expanding circles of light represent waves of what scientists call electromagnetic radiation. The waves differ according to the distance from one crest to the next, called a wavelength, and there is an enormous spectrum of these wavelengths, all traveling through space at the same speed (186,000 miles per second). Within this spectrum of wavelengths, there is a very narrow band that can be perceived by our eyes—the visible light. Different wavelengths within the visual spectrum impart a sense of color to our sight from the objects that reflect those wavelengths—the gray stones on the mountain slopes, the brown tree trunks, the green leaves, the clear droplets of rainwater. When light passes through a prism, it separates into all the component colors, which we can see on a wall—or in the sky, when sunlight passes through raindrops to create a rainbow.

So, at any moment, we are surrounded by millions upon millions of different wavelengths of electromagnetic radiation, moving in all directions at once in seeming chaos. And that is where the miracle of sight really begins. Some of the visible light, making its way across the valley from the blue-green mountains, enters the windows of our cabin and the windows of my eyes, called the cornea. These clear, dome-shaped windows in the front of our eyes not only help protect the delicate structures inside, but also begin the process of converting the seemingly chaotic visible wavelengths into meaningful, focused light. Inside the eye, the partially focused light passes through another window, called the pupil, which is the opening in the iris, or colored part of our eyes, similar to the diaphragm of a camera. Behind the pupil, light next passes through a lens, like the lens of the camera, bringing it to pinpoint focus (albeit with the help of glasses for many of us) on a structure in the back of the eye called the retina, which is analogous to the film of the camera (for those who can remember what cameras were like in the pre-digital age). Amazingly, light coming from a vast landscape that is miles across is now focused in the back of the eye on structures that are only a few millimeters in diameter. It is in the tissue-paper-thin retina that light energy is converted into neural impulses, which travel through a series of nerves (kind of like electricity in a wire), to the command center for vision in the very back of the brain. And it is here, in a part of our brain called the occipital lobes—about as far from the eyes as you can get—that the miracle of sight really happens. From light high in the heavens and a myriad of reflected wavelengths, the complex visual pathway within my eyes and through my brain ends in something that causes me to be conscious of the vast panorama of beauty that is surrounding me—the blue-green mountains, the verdant valley floor, the drifting clouds, the rocks and trees, the droplets of rainwater.

It was my great privilege, for nearly a half century, to study this miracle—this gift of sight—trying to better understand it and doing my best to help preserve it. For we know that not everyone shares equally in the gift. And it is the very wonder of the miracle that makes it so bitter, so overwhelming, for those who are deprived of enjoying it to the fullest. At any point along our amazing visual pathway, from the very front of the eyes to the very back of the brain, there are literally thousands of things that can go wrong at any time in our lives. Many people lose their sight late in life, depriving them of the anticipated joys of the "golden years": those exotic trips we had always planned to take—the books that piled up over the years, which we would get to one day—the grandchildren, who we simply wanted to watch grow up. It is like gazing at the beauty of a sunset as it fades into the dark of night, but knowing that the dawn will never come. Others are robbed of good sight in the prime of their lives, leaving them only to remember what was and to wonder what might have been. And then there are those whose visual system fails to develop properly at birth or early childhood, and who never fully experience the joy of sight. For them, there may not even be the memory of a sunset.

I was not only privileged to work with some of these people with impaired vision, doing what I could to help them preserve their precious gift of sight, but to do so within the academic environment of two of the world's finest universities—Duke and Yale. Doctors who choose a career in academic medicine have the opportunity not only to care for patients, but also to touch a larger portion of our society through research and education. When my wife, Sharon, and I first came to Duke University, in Durham, North Carolina, for my residency training in ophthalmology, we assumed that we would eventually return to our home state of Oklahoma, where I would establish a private practice, and we would raise a family and enjoy a quiet life. But something unexpected happened rather early in my years at Duke—I became captivated by the excitement in being a part of the constantly changing face of medicine. For me, these changes meant new knowledge about the miracle of sight, a better understanding of the diseases that affect it, and especially new and better ways to diagnose and treat sight-threatening disorders. And I soon realized that I wanted to be a part of it. One night Sharon and I sat down and discussed this possible change in our life's plans. She knew it would mean a different life than we had envisioned—I would be away from home more often with work and travel, we would have to live on a more modest income, and we would not be returning to our family and friends and that quiet life back in Oklahoma. However, Sharon not only agreed that I should give academic medicine a try, but also strongly encouraged me to pursue my dreams, and in the decades that followed, I don't believe either of us ever regretted that decision.

Two good fortunes came our way during the residency years at Duke that would advance my career. The department was expanding their faculty, and I was offered a teaching position after completing my formal training. This led to the second boon, which was the opportunity to spend a brief time in Boston studying the complex group of eye disorders, called glaucoma, at the Massachusetts Eye and Ear Infirmary, a teaching hospital of Harvard University. At that time, the "Mass Eye and Ear" was one of the leading glaucoma centers in the world, and I was in awe of the storied history of the institution and of the giants of our profession who still walked the hallowed halls. The research of these internationally renowned professors, with whom I had the privilege to study glaucoma, literally revolutionized the way we were treating our patients. I looked forward to returning to Duke Eye Center as the "head" (actually the only member) of our fledgling glaucoma section, and making my own mark in eye research.

As it turned out, my contributions to research were modest (at best), but I soon became aware of another joy of academic medicine for which I did seem to have some aptitude—education. I enjoyed teaching young students and doctors as we saw patients together in the clinic and worked together in the operating room. I also enjoyed giving them lectures, as well as traveling to speak at meetings around the country and abroad. But what I discovered I enjoyed the most was writing, and it was here that I seemed to find my place in academic medicine and my greatest opportunity to contribute to my profession. And it was also here that I found the fulfillment of a lifelong fascination with the lure of the empty page—and it is for that reason that my other companion on the weathered oak table in our cabin this rainy morning is the empty pad of yellow writing paper.

———

I have long felt that the empty page represents the epitome of opportunity. So many treasures in our world began with the blank page in front of the master. How many great works of literature, enduring musical compositions, or masterpieces of art began with a sketch or an outline on the waiting page? It is truly the material beginning from which dreams move toward reality.

Since childhood, I have been captivated by the sense of excitement when I sit before a blank sheet of paper, pencil in hand, wondering if this may be the page on which something of value will materialize. Of course, I have long since reconciled myself to the notion that, for most of us, greatness will never appear on our pages. But still there is the opportunity for personal satisfaction and enjoyment, and quite possibly for touching at least one life: a well-written letter to a loved one, who is far away; a poem for a friend, or maybe that only I will read; a drawing for the sole delight of a grandchild.

I realize that I am exposing myself as one of the pre-cyber generation, although I suspect the day will come for me too when the empty page will be replaced by the empty computer screen, as it already has for so many young writers and artists. In fact, my laptop is close by, and I will eventually be transferring my handwritten words to it. But for the moment, my empty page and a pencil still provide the best and most exciting way for me to begin the journey of converting dreams to reality.

———

The events that allowed me to satisfy the lure of the empty page in my medical practice (and which, in truth, opened the door to an unanticipated and immensely fulfilling career in academic medicine) began with a series of lectures on glaucoma that I prepared during my time at Harvard and presented to our residents and medical students when I returned to Duke. I included a printed outline with each lecture, and was surprised to learn that some of the residents were saving them in binders for future reference. They eventually suggested that I consider publishing the outlines in a more formal format to be used by residents and students at other universities. This thought had never occurred to me. There were already several outstanding books on glaucoma—written by the current giants of our profession—and I doubted that many people would pay attention to yet another one, especially one written by a virtual unknown in the field. But the residents finally convinced me that a focused study guide in a simple outline format would serve a need for students and young doctors who were beginning the study of glaucoma. Furthermore, since my research didn't seem to be going anywhere, it seemed reasonable to focus my academic efforts more on education, especially within the sphere of writing. So, with my faithful coffee mug and many pads of empty writing paper, I spent the next two years attempting to write a book. Then came the rejections.

There were a large number of medical publishers in the world at that time, and I thought I had been rejected by all of them. But one day, just as I was about to give up on the dream of becoming a published author, a call came from the distinguished publishing company, Williams & Wilkins in Baltimore, informing me that they were willing to take a chance on this unknown writer. And so it was that I joined the ranks of medical authors.

I wrote the entire book with pencils on countless pads of yellow writing paper. The publisher had given me an advance on royalties, which allowed me to hire a typist to convert my handwritten pages into about two thousand sheets of double-spaced text, which would be condensed into a book of 540 pages. This was before the days of word processors, and the typist used a conventional typewriter to laboriously type and retype each page as I pored through them with corrections. I was also able to hire a young man to help with my library searches, which consisted of going to the medical school library at Duke and finding and making copies of the thousands of reference articles that I wove into the book. Untold evenings and weekends were spent with these articles spread all over the floor of my study at home as I tried to organize them into paragraphs that flowed and made sense. The illustrations in the book were all line drawings by an excellent medical illustrator at Duke, who was also a friend and member of our church.

The publishers had invited me to Baltimore to hand deliver my manuscript and meet with the staff who would be turning the text into a book. Sharon and I decided that this would be a good trip for the whole family, and so with our young children, Sarah and John, in the backseat of our station wagon and my manuscript safely stowed with the luggage, we set out for Baltimore. As we approached the outskirts of the city, one of their worst rainstorms in years was raging. The wind was approaching gale force, pounding rain against our car so hard that I could barely see the lights of the car in front of us. To add to our predicament, I managed to get us totally lost. I think we drove over the Francis Scott Key Bridge at least three times as I watched our gas gauge approaching empty. The mood in the car was becoming very somber and tense, and with my family in peril, I am ashamed to admit that my overwhelming thought at that moment was of my manuscript (the only copy I had) being blown all over Baltimore, should we have a wreck. But we finally made it to our hotel, and the next day dawned bright and beautiful. I drove to the Williams & Wilkins headquarters while Sharon and the children swam in the hotel pool.

Upon my arrival, I was taken to a large conference room, surrounded by bookshelves with hundreds of volumes. They explained that all the books were their publications, arranged in chronological order, from the very first book at one end to the most recent at the other, and I couldn't resist imagining my book taking its place with these decades of venerable textbooks. After meeting with the production staff, who reviewed the process involved in bringing a book to market, I was taken across town to their printing house. In striking contrast to the quiet and orderly headquarters that we had just left, I now stepped into a huge, noisy building that seemed a bit chaotic with many different activities all going on at once. The smell of ink and paper brought back memories and emotions from my days, long ago, when I had worked briefly at our hometown newspaper, although it was obvious that printing techniques had changed dramatically since then. Now using offset methods (so I was told), original copy was transferred directly to enormous sheets of paper with multiple pages that would subsequently be cut into their component parts and bound into books. The times had changed, but it was no less thrilling than in my boyhood days when I had watched our newspaper go to press, except that now I was really a part of it.

Since the intent was to provide a simple guide to help students learn the basic aspects of glaucoma, the book was entitled *A Study Guide for Glaucoma* and was organized in a modification of my original outline form. During the long hours of writing the book, I often wondered if anyone would ever read it, much less find any value in it. I consoled myself with the thought that, even if no one read my book, the effort of writing it would not have been in vain, because of the knowledge that I would gain in the process. But when the book was finally released, the reception it received and the impact that it had on the rest of my career was far beyond anything I could ever have dared to imagine.

I suppose it was my appreciation for the difficulty that some people, like me, have in learning that led to a writing style that others found to be helpful. Learning had never come easily for me. But when the light finally came on, and I was able to grasp a new piece of knowledge, I couldn't resist the temptation to share it with others. And because I was a slow learner, I tended to explain things in simple, concise terms, which some readers seemed to appreciate. Whatever it was, I was grateful and humbled when my first book received generous reviews and Williams & Wilkins asked me to consider writing a second edition to keep up with the rapidly changing knowledge in the field. With the success of the first edition, the name of the subsequent editions was changed to *Textbook of Glaucoma* and the format was upgraded to that of a more traditional medical textbook with photographic illustrations, along with the previous line drawings, and much more attractive covers.

Over the course of the next two decades, the book underwent three more editions and was translated into five additional languages. In the year 2000, it was included among "One Hundred Important Ophthalmology Books of the Twentieth Century." By now, we had moved from Duke to Yale University, where I had more responsibilities and felt it was time to pass the work of writing subsequent editions to the next generation. My partner and close friend at Duke, Dr. Rand Allingham, kindly agreed to be the managing author and, along with several of my colleagues and past students, wrote the fifth and sixth editions, which I consider to be the best yet. We are still with the same publisher, although with the numerous mergers of medical publishers over the years, it is now called Lippincott Williams & Wilkins.

And so it was that the lure of the empty page opened up a new and wonderful world for me in academic medicine. The success of the *Textbook* led to opportunities to author and edit several additional books with valued colleagues and to write chapters in other books and scientific papers in professional journals. It also led to more invitations to speak at meetings nationally and internationally, with the chance to visit new places, meet new people, and share new knowledge. As I traveled around the world, speaking at medical meetings, it was humbling but gratifying to be in some remote part of the world and have doctors tell me they used my books and ask me to autograph their copy. But the greatest joy of my academic-related travels was the friendships that were forged with the world leaders in our profession, many of whom remain my dearest friends to this day.

Throughout my years at Duke and Yale, I had the privilege of working with brilliant leaders in the medical profession and also with remarkably talented students and young doctors, who were clearly the brightest and best in our profession. The greatest joy in my career was working and learning with these young people, many of whom have gone on to become leaders of our profession and remain cherished friends. They were truly remarkable people, having trained at the most distinguished universities, with impeccable credentials in their scholarly achievements, as well as in research, athletics, music and every other imaginable endeavor. And yet they looked up to me as their teacher, simply because I happened to have written some books and was fortunate to receive the recognition that followed. Of course, it might never have happened without the Duke residents who encouraged me to pursue this path, and I will always be grateful to them and for the opportunities that writing and teaching gave me to work with such fine people and to touch the largest number of lives through the doctors who used my books to help their patients. And yet, as the years passed, I began to sense a growing uneasiness that something was missing in my desire to fulfill the lure of the empty page.

—

The problem with medical writing is that very little of it has lasting value. What is accepted today as fact or the appropriate way to treat a disease may be found tomorrow to be incorrect or to yield to newer, better treatments. I enjoy collecting old medical books and occasionally find myself chuckling at something that was once accepted as gospel and is now clearly known to be false. But then uneasiness creeps in as I realize that the same thing will eventually happen to my books—in fact, it already has. Medical technology advances so rapidly that it is virtually impossible to get a book into print before some aspects of it have been replaced by newer knowledge. This is why medical textbooks must constantly be updated with new editions. But it is unsettling to think that the labor of one's professional life will one day amount to, at most, nothing more than decaying pages on a dusty shelf.

And so, as I enter the eighth decade of my life, with my medical career behind me, I find that the desire to fill the empty page with something of lasting value is even more unquenchable than it was in the days of my youth. But then, as with every aspiring writer, the seminal question arises—what to write? What do I know beyond the technical aspects of my profession? As I tussled with this question for many years, I gradually began to realize that, yes, there is something else beyond the treatment of disease that I have learned in my practice—something that may be even more important than the scientific knowledge that I have been fortunate enough to acquire and share.

Physicians have a unique opportunity to enter intimately into the lives of their patients, sharing their joy of good health and all life's blessings as well as their heartaches of affliction and loss. As I cared for my patients over the years, I had the privilege of meeting many people with remarkable courage, who faced incredible hardship, either because of their own personal illness or that of a loved one, and yet lived their lives with hope and dignity, with good cheer and a sturdy attitude, with an approach to life that embodies lessons for all of us. While I was trying to preserve their gift of sight, they were giving me a gift of even greater value. And, just as I once had an overwhelming desire to share scientific knowledge with others, I now yearn to share some of the lessons gained from these very special people.

And so it is that I am sitting in our cabin on this rainy morning with my two old friends—the large mug of steaming hot coffee and the empty pad of yellow writing paper—once again attempting to write a book. But, unlike my other books, this one is not about scientific knowledge for the well-being of our patients. Rather, it is about knowledge that I have received from my patients by observing the ways in which they lived their lives. Many of their stories are inspiring, some are humorous, some poignant, and some heartbreaking, but I believe that each offers lessons for living that can benefit us all.

The names of many of the patients in these stories have been changed to protect their privacy. In a few cases, I have also taken the poetic license of altering the facts of the story, either to further protect the privacy of my patients or to fill in gaps where my knowledge of their story is incomplete. What I have attempted to portray most accurately, however, is the essence of their stories and the lessons that I have learned from them.

These stories, then, are not so much about the miracle of sight, as precious as that is, but rather about a vision that transcends the physical realm. They are stories about a vision that allows us to see beauty where others may see only wretchedness, to know peace in the midst of chaos, to see the power of love when hate seems so strong, to see hope in the midst of despair, and to know, even in our loneliest hour, that we are never alone. These are some of the inspirations that I have received in observing the lives of my patients. And I hope that in reading their stories, you too will be touched by their gifts of sight.

Ω

1.

George Johnston

"**W**hich is better now, Mr. Johnston? One? Or two?"

The old man's frail body shook as though with a foreboding chill. How could they hold him responsible for such a decision? A decision that could so totally affect the rest of his life—indeed, that could mean the difference between his life and his death.

In the small, dark room, with its eerie silence his inquisitors waited for his answer. Could they hear the pounding of his heart or his strident breathing? With cold and clammy hands, he held tightly to the arms of his chair to steady his tremor. He feared that, even if he could discern the correct answer, he would be unable to say it. At that moment, he had never felt so alone—not since the day when his dear Margaret had left him.

—

George and Margaret Johnston had not been blessed with children, but they had been blessed with each other. Neither could quite recall when they first met—somewhere back in the shadowy memories of bygone youth, where reality and fantasy tend to blur. Long before they had first spoken, they had been very much aware of each other. Perhaps it was because each reflected the other—the timidity, the pain in social encounters, the loneliness.

Neither possessed any remarkable physical attributes—each a little below average height and slightly built, hair that was medium brown and

1

seemed to receive minimal attention, faces that were pleasant enough but without memorable features and that rarely showed any expression, as though afraid to be acknowledged and wanting only to blend into the crowd. But their eyes told a different story. In them dwelt the same plea as in every child: I am special; I want to be understood; I want to be loved.

It was their eyes that first met, and for many years that was the only way they communicated. Their parents belonged to the same Baptist church, but they lived in different parts of town, and so, during their elementary school years, they only saw each other on Sundays and Wednesday evenings. They secretly longed for those times of the week, even though they were too shy ever to speak to each other.

When they graduated to junior high school, they were thrilled to finally be attending the same school, and even more so to find that they had some classes together. Here they also learned that they had something else in common: their shyness had driven them to spend most of their time reading and studying, and both were outstanding students. Naturally, therefore, they spent a great deal of time in the library, at first studying alone, then together, and finally at each other's home.

So it was that a friendship, which began timidly from afar, blossomed into a deep and firm relationship that would last a lifetime. Neither had ever dated another person and never would. They not only became best friends, but also really had no other close friends. With each being an only child, their hopes and dreams centered entirely on each other.

High school came and went. There was never a formal proposal, just a mutual understanding that one day they would become man and wife. But a war was raging in Europe, and increasing numbers of young Americans were putting their futures on hold to serve in the Great War that was to end all wars. It was the time of our parents' childhood, and Sharon and I would learn decades later from our families how lives were changed in those days by the exigencies of wartime. George was caught up in the patriotic fervor of the times and enlisted in the Army, but spent most of the war behind a desk, never to go overseas. I don't know if it was his frail constitution that kept him from a more physically challenging, if not dangerous, duty, although I suspect it had more to do with his intelligence and mature demeanor that led to an assignment with considerable responsibility at a munitions depot in upstate New York. Every day he pored through piles of paperwork that were critical to the flow of weapons from factories across the country to our troops on the other side of the Atlantic. It was work for which he was well suited by both talent and temperament, but it was awfully far from his Margaret back in North Carolina. Life in their small hometown, not far from Durham, was typical of every American town during those war years, with everyone trying to pitch in for the common cause. Margaret volunteered for local programs to support the troops, which she balanced with courses at a community college in library science. Their work kept them occupied and eased the pain of separation, but they still longed every day for the time when they would finally be together forever.

After the war, George returned home to his Margaret. He opted against college, because he was anxious to move on with their dreams, and wanted to be able to provide for a family before taking her as his wife. He secured a desk job in their municipal utility company, applying the skills that he had acquired in the army. He was immediately recognized as a valuable employee, but the job provided little opportunity for advancement, and he was content to work at a desk for his entire career. Margaret, upon graduation from the community college, took a job in their hometown library, where the two met every night after work.

From his first day on the job, George began saving every penny toward the purchase of a home. One day he read an ad in the realty section of their local paper, listing a home in a modest but respectable neighborhood on the outskirts of town. It was described as a fixer-upper, but the price was right. He went to check it out the very next day after work. It was a cold, gray day in late winter, and his first impression of the house did little to warm his spirits. Very small and pitifully plain, it needed paint and had only a door and two windows in front, with no yard to speak of except for a single scrawny bare tree at one corner of the house. But George had the gift of a healthy imagination, and where others might see only a dilapidated, anxious house, he saw a quaint little bungalow with a fresh coat of white paint, black shutters beside the windows, bright flowers in the garden, and a profusion of red roses cascading over a white picket fence. The little tree would soon blossom out with the coming of spring and would grow over the years, as would the love inside the home. He bought the house, single-handedly converted it to the home of his dreams, and brought his new bride to their "blue heaven." In their collective dreams, they saw one more addition to the house—an extra room for the one who would make three.

George soon began working on the new room and had nearly finished its loving details when Margaret bashfully announced that she was with child. This caused him to speed up the work, and he did so with a giddy joy that he had never known before. Soon the room would be finished and ready for its precious little occupant. Then came the phone call while he was at work. Something was wrong. The doctor said there would be no baby, and that she would never be able to conceive again. George doesn't recall what he said at that moment, only that he gently hung up the phone and sat in stunned silence at his desk. He was not a man given to emotion, and no tears came. He was, however, a man of deep faith and believed that God had a purpose for everything. But at that moment, all he could think about was being with Margaret and holding her hand. He left his office early and walked the several miles to the hospital, where she was to be kept overnight. The walk gave him time to think and to prepare himself to be brave as he consoled his wife. They sat together quietly; tears moistened Margaret's red eyes; George sat stoically, gently holding her hand until it was time for visitors to leave. When he got home that evening, he slowly closed the door to the room of their dreams. Then he sat in silence and finally allowed himself to cry.

The door remained closed and the little room remained empty for nearly two years. But, with the passage of time, their pain gradually diminished, and their love for each other became ever stronger. They filled their days, when not at work, puttering together in their garden, strolling around the neighborhood hand in hand, and sitting side by side in the evenings, reading their books and listening to classical music on their Victrola. Then one day, as they were walking downtown, they saw a puppy in the pet store window—a cocker spaniel. They looked at each other and smiled. As in the days of their youth, each could tell what the other was thinking just by the look in his or her eyes. They brought the little ball of auburn fur home, and it soon became part of the family, filling a void in their lives. With an unspoken agreement, they opened the door to the little room and created a place for the new member of their family. George could later laugh that no dog ever had a finer doghouse.

The decades flew by for George and Margaret. They weathered a depression and another world war, oblivious to the passage of time, which only seemed to bring deeper love. Even with their combined incomes, they were forced to live frugally, but never seemed to want for anything. Vacations were not important to them, and the few they took, usually with church groups, were most often to the mountains in the western part of the state or the coastline to the east. Their church remained the center of their life outside the home. They continued to attend the same church in which they had met during their youth, with faithful attendance on Sunday mornings and Wednesday evenings. One of George's greatest joys was sitting beside Margaret in church, holding her hand.

Aside from work and church, the rest of their time was spent together in and around their home. They always had breakfast together, would pack each other's lunch before going off to work, and then enjoyed cooking supper and washing the dishes together each evening. The day finally came when they both retired from their jobs and were overjoyed to have even more time together. The hours seemed to fly by, working together in their yard or puttering around the house. Their happiness was only marred on a few occasions when age took one of their pets, but then there was the joy of a new puppy. The little room, always home to their beloved cocker spaniels, had also become Margaret's sewing room. While she worked on her sewing projects, usually something for their church's mission work, George would be nearby, building something in a little woodwork shop or making repairs in the house. They worked hard to maintain a pristine home and yard, and their house became the pride of the neighborhood, their own defined world, which they shared with a peaceful and visible happiness: the hours in the garden, the strolls around the neighborhood, the tranquil evenings side by side. They considered their life together to be God's greatest blessing. And then it happened.

With rare exceptions, George and Margaret had enjoyed remarkably good health throughout the years. Even now, as they approached their ninth decade of life, there was only the stiffness of arthritis and the occasional upper respiratory infections. But one day, as George entered the small room, he found Margaret sitting silently and motionless, with their dog looking up at her in curious concern. Her eyes were closed, and at first he thought she was sleeping, but a foreboding sense told him he should try to waken her. There was no response. Then he did something he had never done before: he raised his voice at her. Still nothing. He shouted and shook her and began to look around the room for help. She was breathing and her color was good. He left her, ran to the phone, and dialed 911. When he returned to the little room, her eyes were open and she gave him a thin smile. Tears of relief burst from his eyes, but then panic returned when he realized that Margaret could not speak to him. At that moment, he heard the siren.

The doctor told George that his wife had suffered a stroke, but that the early indications were encouraging and her chances of complete recovery were excellent. Fortunately, the doctor's prediction was accurate. George brought Margaret home after a couple of days in the hospital, and her recovery filled them both with overwhelming thankfulness. There was a little slurred speech and weakness on one side for the first few weeks, and then it was like nothing had ever happened. They now seemed to enjoy life together more than ever, as though this incident reminded them of their blessings. Their joy lasted for almost a year before it all happened again—the panic, the ambulance, the hospital—but this time the doctor's assessment was more subdued. Margaret came home, but her speech remained impaired and she required help with walking. George was by her side day and night. He was there when, three months later, she had her third and most serious stroke. This time she remained in the hospital and was unable to communicate with George, except through her eyes. He never left her side and was there when her eyes closed for the last time.

The only blessing was that she did not suffer long. George thanked God for that. After the funeral, a church friend brought him home. He sat in the silent house, where Margaret had so recently sat by his side. Their little dog snuggled closer than usual to his leg. He seemed to understand. As George looked around their home, he was flooded with memories of their life together, so much of it in this one little house. The home seemed to provide an element of comfort in this his moment of greatest anguish.

Later that evening, his minister called on him. After praying together, they sat in silence for a long time. Then the minister spoke.

"So, George, where will you be going?"

George didn't seem to understand the question. It had never crossed his mind to leave this house. It had been their home and their world; now it had to become his consoling world. He had to take care of their garden and keep the house, as she would want it. Where else could he be close to his Margaret?

"I'm not going anywhere," he finally said.

"But, George, you can't stay here."

"Why not?" There was a sense of pleading in his anguished question.

"Because you don't drive, and you're too far from everything you will need." The minister was gentle and sympathetic, and George knew he was right.

George and Margaret had only owned one car, and it was more convenient for her to drive him to work before going to the library. Over the years, it became a matter of habit for Margaret to do all the driving, even after they retired. She drove them to church and to the stores, all of which were several miles from their home. George eventually let his driver's license lapse and had not driven in at least twenty years.

"Well, I'll start driving again," he finally responded. "The old car still works fine, and it shouldn't take me long to learn to catch up. Will you help me?"

"Of course, George."

And so, for the next several weeks, George and his minister could be seen almost every day driving around town in the car that he and Margaret had shared for so many years. He also got a driver's manual and literally memorized it in preparation for his exam, and he was confident that he would pass. And he would have passed, except for one problem.

He made a perfect score on the written exam and was feeling very confident until the examination officer instructed him to sit down in front of a machine. The officer told him to look into it and read the road signs. Although George's reading vision was still adequate, he had been noting blurring of vision at distances. Now, try as he might, he simply could not make out the signs in the machine. The officer casually checked off "failed" on his exam sheet. When George saw it, his heart began to race. With an overwhelming sense of panic he tried to explain how critical it was that he get his license. The officer handed him a form and suggested that he take it to an eye doctor, who might be able to help him. And so it was that George Johnston and I crossed paths.

———

Looking back on it now, I am ashamed to admit that my mood that day could not have been farther from that of Mr. Johnston's. Frankly, I was bored. This was not what I had spent over twenty years of formal education to do. My reasons for going into academic medicine had been not only interests in teaching, research, and scientific writing, but also a desire to be at the cutting edge of clinical care. Up to this point, my career goals had pretty much been on track.

It was largely a matter of being in the right place at the right time. I was fortunate that a position in the ophthalmology residency program at Duke University was available at about the same time that I was to be discharged from the Navy. It was the Navy, however, that almost derailed my career plans. When I was accepted into the Duke program, I didn't realize that I had an extra six months of payback for the time in submarine medical officer training. Although I know they weren't happy about it, the Duke folks were kind enough to put someone else in my original spot and give me a subsequent starting time. Years later, I happened to be in a conversation when our chairman groused about an "SOB" who messed up their residency schedule a few years back. Fortunately for me, the chairman had difficulty remembering our names and had forgotten that I was that SOB.

Good fortune struck again when the Duke faculty was being expanded at the very time that I was starting to look for a job. Our chairman not only offered me a faculty position, but also helped me obtain fellowship training before settling down as a member of the faculty. Despite the small size of the eye, it is amazingly complex and subject to virtually every disease process: infections, tumors, trauma and the like, as well as conditions unique to the eye such as cataracts, retinal detachment, and glaucoma. As a result, ophthalmology has been divided into a number of subspecialties: cornea, retina, glaucoma, plastic surgery, pediatric ophthalmology, and several others. As a final stage of formal training, young doctors who wish to subspecialize in one of these areas take additional fellowship training. At the time that I was finishing my residency, the subspecialty positions that Duke needed to fill were in glaucoma and pediatrics. While I enjoyed both, the former seemed a bit more compatible with my temperament, and the chairman pulled some strings to get a glaucoma fellowship for me at Harvard.

Glaucoma represents a group of disorders with the common denominator being atrophy (or death) of the optic nerve (which connects the eye to the brain), that can lead to blindness. The many forms of glaucoma collectively account for the greatest number of people with total, permanent blindness in the world. Pressure in the eye is a major cause of the optic atrophy, although many additional causes have now been identified, and glaucoma has become a discipline of medicine that is associated with nearly every aspect of the eye, as well as with many general diseases of the body. Only cataract, an opacity of the lens of the eye, is more common worldwide, but surgery can restore vision in people with cataracts. For the person who is blind from glaucoma, there is no hope of recovering sight, and only through early detection and preventative measures can their vision be preserved.

In the early 1970s, as Sharon and our infant daughter, Sarah, and I were driving north to Boston, Harvard was one of a small number of programs in the world that were recognized as leaders in glaucoma. I will never forget my sense of awe as I walked into the Massachusetts Eye and Ear Infirmary,

Harvard's teaching hospital, for the first time and passed portraits of the famous doctors who had worked within those hallowed halls. Adding to my awe was Mass General Hospital next door, Harvard's main general teaching hospital, where renowned physicians from all fields of medicine, past and present, worked. The time that I was fortunate to be there was undoubtedly during the golden age of glaucoma at Harvard. Our mentors were Drs. Paul Chandler and Morton Grant, and the young doctors who trained with them at that time went on to become leaders in the field and to train successive generations of glaucoma specialists. Chandler and Grant taught us not only how to care for patients with glaucoma, but also how to perform scientific investigation to discover better ways of helping our patients. What may have been their most important lesson, however, was to do all of this—treating patients and conducting research—with the highest ethical standards of our profession. For me, it was the highlight of my formal education, as well as an opportunity to forge friendships with leaders in our profession, who remain close friends to this day.

And so I returned to the Duke faculty with stars in my eyes. I was finally a "real doctor." I had rubbed shoulders with the giants of my profession, and with naïve ambition, I was ready to become one of them. At least I had all the accoutrements of a real doctor. I had my first office—small, with no window, but mine. Sharon helped me give it a homey feel. We bought some dried flowers, which I had better luck with than the live ones, and hung a few pictures on the walls. There were a couple of oak shelves above my desk, where I kept pictures of Sharon and the children. As a final touch, we hung a calligraphy that I had made while in Boston; a saying attributed to the sixteenth-century French military surgeon, Ambroise Paré: "Je le pansai, Dieu le guérit" (I treat, God heals).

I was also assigned a secretary and a nurse, and in that respect, no one could have been more fortunate. My first two secretaries didn't work out so well and only lasted a few weeks. So, when I met Robin, I was a bit wary. She was only eighteen and she looked it: a sweet, oval face, auburn bangs covering most of her forehead, and a demeanor that gave an initial impression of shyness. Our first meeting was in the administrator's office, where I had been told to come for yet another interview with a secretarial candidate. The administrator had stepped out when I arrived, so I took a seat and noticed there was one other person in the room. We glanced at each other in silence, and I dismissed the possibility that she could be the candidate; she looked so young. But, moments later, the administrator came in and introduced me to the young lady—Robin Goodwin. I must admit that my first impression was not very encouraging. In addition to her youthful appearance and seemingly shy personality, she couldn't spell much better than I could. However, it was not long before I realized that shyness was not one of Robin's traits; she had a wonderfully open, caring, and fun-loving personality, and any spelling deficiency was more than compensated for in every other way. Not only did she become a first-class secretary, but we also became best friends and are to this day.

For my nurse, I was assigned two women to interview. They were both well qualified, and, while one had slightly better credentials, there was something about the other that told me she was the one. Her name was Sharon Clark, and she was to become the other Sharon in my life. (Ironically, her maiden name was Sharon Shields, but she didn't tell me that until years later, not wanting to take unfair advantage during the interview). Sharon was closer to my age (although she would never admit it), tall, slender, and attractive, with dark hair and a marvelous sense of humor. She was originally from the Northeast, but had acquired a subtle southern accent, and you would have sworn she was a native North Carolinian. Sharon was the consummate nurse; she had mastered the art of taking care of patients and their doctors.

As a team, Robin and Sharon had their hands full, keeping me out of trouble. I seemed to have a hard time remembering where I was supposed to be, and Robin was constantly reminding me that I was late for a meeting. On one of those occasions, I walked into a meeting, late as usual, where everyone else was already seated. As I took my seat, I wondered why the room was so quiet and why all eyes were on me; then it dawned on me that I was the one who had called the meeting, and I couldn't for the life of me remember why. Robin, sensing my desperation, bailed me out by starting the discussion, until I could get my wits about me. As for Sharon, she had the task of keeping me from getting too far behind in our clinics. If I was spending too much time with a patient, usually talking more than I should have, she had a gentle way of ushering the patient out and sending me on to the next room. But, more than that, she had a deep compassion for every patient and a sixth sense about their individual needs and always made sure that I was aware when there was a problem in their life that deserved special attention.

So there I was, on the faculty of one of the finest universities in the world, with my own office, a secretary, and a nurse, and billed as a glaucoma expert. I naturally assumed that all the ophthalmologists in the region would immediately begin sending their difficult glaucoma cases to me. Surely they knew that I had been to Harvard and was bringing such knowledge and skill back to North Carolina (or so I thought). But it didn't happen. No one seemed to be very impressed, and the referrals were a trickle at best. So I had to supplement those early months with routine patients and fitting glasses.

I don't mean to belittle the importance of fitting glasses, or refraction, as the process is called. All of us who wear them know how critical a pair of properly prescribed glasses is to our lives. But it really isn't that complicated. It essentially consists of offering the patient a series of lenses until the right one is found. In earlier times, the lenses were taken from a tray and placed in a spectacle frame worn by the patient. Today, however, it is more common to use an instrument called a phoropter, which allows the doctor to dial in the desired combination of lenses until the patient has achieved the best vision, making the process faster and easier for both doctor and patient. With either technique, after some preliminary screening steps, the lenses are presented two at a time, and the patient is asked to choose which provides the clearest image of a letter on the chart: "One or two?"

To reduce the boredom of the refraction process, I developed a little game in which I tried to analyze the personality of my patients according to their responses to my queries. Most fell into one of four categories: the precise, the self-confident, the ingratiating, and the anxious.

The person with the precise personality was not content to simply say which of the two choices was best. All I really wanted to know was which view of the letter on the chart was clearer, one or two. But they had to define the appearance of both images. "Well, one is sharper, but two is darker." This made for a prolonged examination that was frustrating for both the patient and the examiner. I would get frustrated and admonish them to simply say which was best, and they would get frustrated with me, because it simply wasn't that black and white to them. But eventually we would reach compromises, and, with an exhausted patient and an exhausted doctor, I would give them a prescription to take to their optician, praying that it was correct.

The self-confident personality was the person who found it difficult to admit that they might have made a mistake. Having decided that one was better than two on the first query, they became convinced that they had given the correct answer and would stay with that number, no matter in what order I presented the options subsequently. Even when I reversed the order of the same two lenses, the answer was always predictable: "Yes, one is still best." Only with the greatest of effort could I finally convince them that they could give more than one answer and still be correct. I had a feeling, though, as they left the exam room with their prescription in hand, that they were still convinced that "one" was best.

The ingratiating personality was the individual who wanted more than anything else to please the doctor. These were typically the little old ladies, for whom multiple visits to their various doctors had become an important part of their lives. Sweet and gentle, often bringing gifts, they could not abide the thought of upsetting their doctor. If they said one was better, it might imply that they didn't like two, which their doctor had gone to the trouble of showing them, and it might hurt his feelings. The dialogue that followed was predictable. "Which is best now, Mrs. Jones, one or two?" "Well, one is real nice." "Does that mean it is better than two?" "Well, two is just fine also." Those were usually the longest exams.

Then there was the anxious personality. These were the people who feared that, if they gave the wrong answer, they would get the wrong glasses, and then they wouldn't be able to see, and then life as they knew it would never be the same. We have all encountered such people, and the truth is that each of us possesses a bit of this trait; the fear of how our actions, or inactions, may influence how we are perceived by others and how it will influence our lives. But there are some in whom this fear seems to be so strong that it may render them incapable of action and threaten an otherwise peaceful existence. The harder they try to make the right decision, the more anxious they become, and the more difficult it is for them to decide anything. When I would try to fit glasses for these patients, their typical responses included long periods of tense silence, broken by periodic sighs and, finally, a request to view the options again. Mr. Johnston, at least on the day of our first meeting, belonged in this category.

———

I presented the question to him again: "Mr. Johnston, which is better now, one or two?"

After another long pause and a sigh, he timidly ventured a response, almost as a question. "Two?"

I also sighed, which I hoped he didn't hear, as I pulled the phoropter away from his face. His responses had been sufficiently consistent that I was able to get a decent refraction and prescribe a pair of glasses that I was confident would help him. After completing his examination, I wrote the essential prescription for him.

"So, Mr. Johnston, you seem to have early cataracts. They can actually improve your reading vision in the early stages, but blur your distant vision. Fortunately, your cataracts are in an early stage, and your vision can easily be corrected with glasses."

"Does that mean I can drive?" he asked in a plaintive voice.

"Sure," I replied, without looking up from the note I was writing in his chart.

When I did look up, I was surprised to see tears streaming down his face. I assumed he must not have understood that I had just told him everything was okay. But Sharon, with her sixth sense about these things, immediately recognized the situation. While I was trying to think what to say, she stepped over and put her arm around him, whereupon he broke down into uncontrollable sobbing. Sharon stayed beside him, casting a rather disgusted look at my clueless face.

The three of us sat in silence until Mr. Johnston regained his composure and dried his eyes with the tissue that Sharon had given him. It may have been one of the first times that he had allowed himself to break down since losing Margaret, and he seemed to want to talk about it. In fact, encouraged by Sharon, he proceeded to tell us much of his story: Margaret, their life together, their home, and why he needed to drive. I began to worry that we were getting behind in our schedule, but the expression on Sharon's face spoke to me clearly: this was more important. Eventually, she helped him out of the room, with his prescription and an appointment to return in six months. And I was left alone to ponder what had just happened. Should I have picked up on Mr. Johnston's need sooner? Did I miss something in discussing his history? Why had Sharon seen it before I did? Was I letting my thoughts wonder selfishly, when I should have been giving him my full attention? Was I beginning to learn something that had not been taught (or at least I had not learned) in medical school?

I had to admit that I felt good about being able to help Mr. Johnston, even though his medical problem was not that challenging. I was also vaguely aware of something he had done for me that afternoon; something of greater value than the promotion of mere good feeling. It didn't exactly hit me over the head at the time, but he had planted the seed of something that would return to my mind in the years to come with increasing frequency.

George returned to our clinic several times over the ensuing years. We changed his glasses a few more times and finally operated on his cataracts to restore his vision. On each visit, he enjoyed telling us more about his life with Margaret, and we enjoyed listening. He was able to remain in their home until he was well into his eighties. I was told that he died peacefully with a smile on his face, as though anticipating what lay ahead.

———

It has been many years now since George Johnston was reunited with his Margaret, but he remains very much with me. I think of him when I am tempted to trivialize the cares and anxieties of another person without understanding the circumstances in their life that drive their feelings. I see him when I find myself being critical of a person's behavior when that behavior seems inappropriate or out of proportion to the situation. He reminds me that we never really know what is in the mind of another person, nor how it is affecting their life. He reminds me that what may seem commonplace and routine to me could well be a matter of life and death to another person. He reminds me that I should give everyone the benefit of the doubt, just as I would want others to do for me. I have continued to learn from him and am grateful for his gift.

But I was young—still in my early thirties—that afternoon when Mr. Johnston and I met for the first time, and lessons of life are learned slowly. I was still consumed with the desire to do great things in my profession. And I was about to learn another, well-known lesson that I could not ignore: be careful what you wish for—you may get it.

2.

Benjamin's Father

Mr. Johnston and the events of the afternoon lingered in my mind as I returned to my office that evening to wrap up the day's work. On my desk, Robin had left a neat stack of the day's mail, most of which was advertisements, along with a few letters that required my signature. I also had some telephone callback slips. This was before the days of email or even fax, with most correspondence still transacted by phone or regular mail, and I would soon come to dread the long row of callback slips that greeted me each evening. But that night they were few, and one immediately caught my eye. It was marked URGENT!

The call came from an ophthalmologist in the eastern part of the state. Although the hour was late, I took a chance that he might still be in his office, and indeed, he picked up the phone himself. He explained that he had a very challenging case and would like my help.

"Thank you" was all I could think to say.

"Well, I'm not so sure you're going to thank me," he replied. "This is a tough one. I've got a little two-year-old fellow with congenital glaucoma. My partners and I have done a bunch of operations on him. He doesn't have any vision left in his right eye. We had to remove a cataract that developed after glaucoma surgery in his left eye. But the pressure in that eye is still way up, and we're going to lose it all, if something more isn't done soon."

I thanked him again and said that I would be glad to see the child as soon as his family could get him here. He said he would call them right then and felt sure they would come the next day.

As I hung up the phone and reflected on the brief conversation, I knew the doctor was not exaggerating about the difficulty of caring for the patient whom I was about to inherit. Glaucoma can strike at any age. While it is most common in older people, it can also afflict children, even at the time of birth. In some cases, the glaucoma is the only problem the child has, with good health in all other respects, and this is typically called congenital glaucoma. In other children, the glaucoma may be associated with a wide range of additional problems, such as hearing loss, mental deficiency, tumors, and so on.

Taken together, children with glaucoma represent a small minority of all patients who are afflicted with this group of disorders. Consequently, children constitute only a small percentage of a typical glaucoma practice, and yet they are among the most special, challenging, and memorable patients for whom we physicians are privileged to care. Even today, I enjoy keeping in touch with some whom I first met as newborns and who are now married with children of their own.

One of the difficulties about caring for children, as pediatricians often point out, is that children are not little adults. That is to say their diseases and the way they respond to treatment are not always the same as in adults. They are unique. This is especially true of children with glaucoma. They do not respond the same as adults to either the medications or the operations that are used to lower the eye pressure in glaucoma. Although today we have somewhat better drugs and surgery for glaucoma, at the time when I was beginning my practice, we were quite limited in both. For medicine, we had only a couple of eye drops and one type of pill, and these had to be given up to four times each day with a whole host of unpleasant side effects. It was hard enough to convince adults to use their medicines regularly, much less to get young parents to faithfully give them to their child, and even when they did, the medicines usually did not lower the eye pressure sufficiently. Consequently, most children with glaucoma, even today, require surgery, which again is more problematic than in adults. The basic operation for glaucoma involves the creation of a channel inside the eye to allow the fluid that is trapped and causing the high pressure to have a new way to drain out. But the little eyes are extremely delicate and subject to many problems during or just after the surgery. In addition, children have a greater propensity for healing than adults, so even if the operation is initially successful, there is always a risk that the healing process will eventually scar the drainage channel closed, resulting in failure of the surgery.

Added to these technical challenges of caring for children with glaucoma are the emotional burdens. The stakes are never higher, since failure of treatment can mean a lifetime of blindness for the little patient. And the surgeon must also deal with the child's young parents, whose dreams of a healthy baby have just been shattered by those dreaded words "Something is wrong," and who are now gripped with the fear that their child will be blind. I have always had the utmost respect for the pediatricians and other physicians who devote their careers to caring for children. It seems to require a very special temperament. They obviously care greatly for their little patients, and yet they must have a certain emotional detachment so that their feelings do not cloud their judgment in recommending and doing what is best for the child. This is not easy, and I was never very good at it. I could never fully separate my feelings for the child from the need to be pragmatic about their care. But I recognized and accepted the challenge as part of the privilege of caring for my young patients.

These were some of the thoughts going through my mind as I sat at my desk considering the challenge that had just been placed before me. The more mature side of me reflected on the seriousness of the case, and the awesome responsibility that I was about to assume. But the more youthful, exuberant side of me—predominant in those days—rejoiced in the anticipation that I would soon get the opportunity to apply what I had spent so many years preparing to do. The delicate structure and the amazing function of our eyes, and the priceless gift of sight that they provide, were major considerations in my choosing this field of medicine. And what more compelling example of this gift could there be than in the little child, who looks out with wonder on a world of delights through sparkling and hopeful eyes? All the promises of a long, happy, successful life depend so heavily on the ability of those eyes to open up the world of opportunities that lie ahead. It was an exhilarating feeling to realize that I was being given the privilege of enhancing a child's chance of a fulfilling life by helping to preserve their precious sight.

Pulling myself back to the reality of the day, I completed the rest of the work on my desk, jotted down a summary of the phone conversation with the ophthalmologist, left it where Sharon would see it in the morning, turned out the lights, and headed home.

———

When I returned early the following morning, only a few vehicles stood as yet in the visitor parking lot, and one immediately caught my eye—an old red pickup. My mind is never terribly sharp at that time of the morning, but there was something about the truck that registered with me, almost subconsciously. It was obviously old, with only a hint of the dull red paint that had long since lost its shine. The metal sides and the bumpers had numerous scratches and dents, and the bed had been reinforced and elevated with weathered wooden planks. The truck had clearly seen extensive use, but it also seemed to be unusually well cared for, as though it was quite important to its owner. It was one of those fleeting moments in our lives—a quick glance, a momentary thought soon dismissed as I pulled into my parking place behind the eye center. How often we have these transient experiences, most to be quickly forgotten unless some subsequent event calls it back to our consciousness. Such was the case with this early morning encounter, as I would later learn that the truck was where my new patient and his family had slept for a few hours—after driving most of the night.

Sharon found them waiting patiently in the front lobby and brought them back to our clinic area, where I first met them. Six hours they had traveled, from their small tobacco farm near the Carolina coast, to be sure that they would arrive on time for their son to be seen by the doctor. Their name was McFee, and they typified the sturdy Scotch-Irish country folk who came from that part of the state—poor, but dignified and proud. Despite the pressures of their journey and their night in the truck, they appeared impressively clean and neat.

Mr. McFee was a young man, probably in his early forties, but his serious demeanor conveyed the impression of a man whose demanding life had imparted a maturity well beyond his years. He had a full red beard that covered his open collar, and the red hair on his head had been given a close trim, but apparently by someone with limited barbering experience. What skin of his face could be seen amid all the red hair was brown and weathered from a life in the sun, except for the white brow just below his hairline, which was protected from the sun each day by the straw hat that he now held in his hands. He wore a white dress shirt, which was slick from the innumerable washings and ironings that it had undoubtedly received over the years that he had worn it on special occasions. Over the shirt he had pulled the straps of what must have been his best overalls—faded but clean, with holes in the knees that had obviously been mended repeatedly with meticulous care, probably by the same woman who cut his hair. He was a big man and stood tall and proud, with broad shoulders and a barrel chest. As I shook his large, strong hand, the roughness and calluses told me of a life of hard labor, and I felt a bit intimidated by this serious giant of a man. But my fears were largely assuaged as I looked into his eyes and saw gentleness and peace.

His wife stood proudly by his side, with a stature in striking contrast to that of her husband. Mrs. McFee was diminutive and extremely thin, and her faded cotton print dress hung loosely from her narrow shoulders. Her light brown hair was carefully combed back and pinned in a neat bun. Like her husband, it was clear that she was no stranger to hard work. Her weatherworn face expressed strength and courage, but her eyes could not hide the concern and fear that she felt that morning.

On the other side of Mr. McFee stood a small boy, clutching his father's pant leg. With a stature more like that of his mother, he was a frail child, dressed in an oversized T-shirt and a pair of overalls like those of his father. His light brown, nearly blond hair hung over his ears, obviously having been cut by the same family barber who cared for his father's hair. In contrast to his parents, the little boy's face was smooth and pale, and it looked up through eyes that wandered in a way that I knew all too well. They were the searching eyes of a person whose fading world is about to go dark forever. That morning, his eyes seemed to be searching for help—or hope.

That was the scene that greeted me as I stepped into the examination room and introduced myself. There were no smiles. They were here for business. For several moments of awkward silence, they seemed to be examining me in a respectful but concerned way. Were they wondering if I was too young, or whether I was the one who should be responsible for the most important matter in their lives? Finally, Mr. McFee broke the silence.

"This here's Benjamin," he said, softly but firmly, looking down at his son.

From the streaks of gray in the hair of both parents, I guessed that Benjamin had arrived later in their life. I soon learned that he was their only child, and it was clear that he was their life.

For a two-year-old boy, Benjamin was an exceptionally cooperative little patient. I figured this was due to his parental influence, as well as a lifetime in doctor's offices. In any case, I was able to obtain an adequate examination and then sat down with the family to explain the situation.

"Let me first tell you a little bit about glaucoma," I said, beginning with my usual introduction, which I hoped would help them make more sense of what they would hear next. The McFees were obviously hanging on to every word. "Glaucoma is a large group of eye diseases that have three common features. First, there is a pressure in the eye that is too high. Over time, the pressure kills the nerve that connects the eye to the brain. In young children, this can happen pretty fast. The nerve damage leads to the third problem, which is progressive loss of sight. The sad truth about glaucoma is that, once the eye is blind, there is nothing we can do to bring back the sight. I am sorry to tell you that this has already happened in Benjamin's right eye."

Although the McFees were listening respectfully and seriously, I could tell that they had a burning question to ask. So I paused to let Mr. McFee speak.

"Doc, how about if you could give Benjamin one of my eyes?"

I grimaced inwardly at the question, which I had heard many times before. It was an understandable and logical question, frequently asked in final desperation and hope by a blind patient or their loved ones. Most people have heard of "eye transplants," so it is reasonable to assume that eyes can be transplanted. Unfortunately, however, this is not the case. A more appropriate term is corneal transplant, since it is only the front clear window of the eye, the cornea, that can be transplanted. If cloudiness of the cornea is causing a patient's blindness, their vision can be restored by replacing the diseased tissue with a clear cornea from an eye donor. But if the damage is in the back of the eye, as in the case of glaucoma, transplantation is not an option, since this part of the eye is actually an extension of the brain. And yet it is a common misconception that I have had to explain to many patients and their families over the years. It is heartbreaking when they come with such hope that surely their sight or that of a loved one can be restored by this seemingly logical operation. It was especially poignant that morning, as I faced Benjamin and his parents.

"That's a good question, Mr. McFee, but sadly it doesn't work," I continued. "The eye is actually a part of the brain, and the nerve extends into the brain. So a new eye would have no way to connect with the brain, because the nerve is dead. The best we can do in glaucoma is to save what sight is left. Benjamin has already lost a lot of his nerve in the left eye, but we can try to save what he has left by getting the pressure down to a safe level. And that is what we must do for Benjamin."

"How do you do that?" Mrs. McFee spoke for the first time.

"The reason for the high pressure, Mrs. McFee, is that we have a fluid in our eyes that is constantly being pumped in and is constantly draining out. If something blocks the drain, the fluid backs up in the eye and causes the pressure to build up. In young children with glaucoma, the drain is blocked because it never developed properly. So, in the operation, we create a new drainage channel to let the fluid drain out. It is a delicate operation, especially in a young child who has already had previous surgery in the eye, but we can do it in Benjamin's left eye, and it gives us the best chance of saving his sight."

"When can you do it, Doc?" Mr. McFee asked in a firm way that seemed to say, "Let's get on with it."

"Well, tomorrow is my surgery day, and I'm sure we can work Benjamin into the schedule."

I told only a half-truth. Wednesdays were indeed the days set aside for my cases in the operating room—but the full truth was that I didn't have any other patients scheduled for surgery that week, so "working Benjamin into the schedule" was obviously not a problem. I'm not sure if my half-truth was more to reassure the McFees about the experience of Benjamin's surgeon or simply to promote my own ego—probably a bit of both. In any case, I proceeded to explain what we needed to do that day in preparation for the next day's surgery.

"The first thing we need to do is admit Benjamin to our hospital, which is just upstairs, and let you folks get settled into your room. There is an adult bed and reclining chair in each room, and we will bring in a child's bed for Benjamin, so you can all three stay together. Later today, one of our resident physicians will stop by to do a physical examination on Benjamin, and our technician will come in to get blood and urine samples for some laboratory tests. All this is routine, just to make sure that everything is in order for Benjamin's surgery tomorrow."

The McFees listened intently and seemed to acknowledge their under- standing of what I was saying, but neither parent spoke. It was as though they had asked all their questions and were ready to move on. Mrs. McFee seemed to be somewhere in a world of her own, struggling to control her anxiety, while clinging tightly to the hand of her little son. Mr. McFee was looking me straight in the eyes. His gaze never faltered, and his only acknowledgment of my remarks was the slightest nod of his head.

He signed the consent form, giving me permission to operate on the only good eye of his only child, and Sharon took the family to the business office to start the admission process. I went to the next examination room, where the first patient on the day's schedule waited to be seen, rather im- patiently, in striking contrast to the family I had just left: another patient needing reading glasses. Despite their demanding attitude, I approached the day with a heightened level of enthusiasm. Maybe the previous day's lesson from Mr. Johnston had begun to sink in. Or maybe it was because I was about to have the privilege of making a major contribution to the life of a child—and to that of his parents.

Before heading home that evening, I stopped by Benjamin's room to make sure that everything was in order for the next morning. I found Benjamin asleep on the adult bed with his mother lying beside him. Her eyes were open, but a bit red and puffy, and I wondered if it was from lack of sleep or from crying. Mr. McFee was sitting rigidly in a straight chair beside the window, as though he was standing guard over his family. He did not speak, but rose slowly with his eyes locked on mine, and with a slight nod of his head acknowledged my presence.

I whispered that the physical examination and lab tests were all in order and that everything was ready for surgery in the morning. I wanted to say something more. I wanted to tell them not to worry. I wanted to tell them that everything would be okay. But I was afraid that anything more would only ring hollow at that moment.

How could they not worry? I looked down at Benjamin, sleeping peacefully, and at his mother, cradling her son in her arms. She looked up for only a moment and did her best to force a faint smile, as though to say that she was doing her best to cope. Mr. McFee looked over at his wife and child for a long, poignant moment. Then his eyes returned to mine, and, with another nod of his head, he seemed to say, "You can go now."

———

My favorite part of every day was coming home in the evening to my little family. And with the experience of the McFees so full and recent in my mind, this night seemed more special than ever. As I kissed Sharon and picked up Sarah and John for our evening ritual of hugs and kisses, it occurred to me how close in age our children were to Benjamin—we had recently celebrated Sarah's second birthday—and I felt almost overwhelmed by a sense of good fortune.

Sharon and I have been blessed with two beautiful, healthy children. Both came to us through adoption. I never knew why the Johnstons had elected not to adopt, but I am sure they had their reasons. Sharon and I never had a question about it. We both felt that, by whatever means, children amount to God's greatest gift. But we could certainly empathize with the Johnstons. While we were living in San Diego during our Navy years, we thought Sharon was pregnant. But one afternoon, the call came from Sharon while I was at work, much as it had come to Mr. Johnston, that this one was not to be. For us, however, there was still hope, and what followed were years of visits to doctors' offices and waiting and hoping. Finally, after nine years of marriage and shortly after arriving at Duke, a doctor told us we should consider adoption. It was then that we met a wonderfully caring social worker who would help us change our lives forever.

Sharon and I had gone to Oklahoma for Christmas, and driving back to Durham in early January, the cold, gray weather reflected our mood of loneliness and uncertainty about the future. Little could we have known then that a precious five-month-old child was waiting for us in North Carolina. The call came shortly after we returned home, and we went in to high gear, converting our guest room into a nursery. We could only afford used baby furniture, but some fresh paint made it look like new, and Sharon finished off the room with bright curtains and needlepoint pillows. No expectant father could have been more nervous than I was that day as we walked into the building where we would meet our daughter for the first time. But her trusting smile, her bright eyes, and her little hands reaching out to us immediately assuaged all my apprehension. From the moment we laid eyes on her, she became the joy and focus of our lives.

We named her Sarah Elizabeth, and those early months with her were among the happiest of our lives. But it was my final year of residency, and in six months we had to leave for my fellowship in Boston, where our baby grew into a girl. She had always been petite and beautiful and, from day one, all girl. She learned to sit up at an early age, but never seemed to think highly of crawling; we figured that she just didn't want to get her hands dirty. So, within a month of learning to crawl, she rose to her feet and began to walk. All too soon, those precious little legs would carry her out the door and into her own life—but she would always be our little girl, and for the moment she was warm and cuddly in my arms.

We would have been content and grateful with one beautiful child, but we kept our name on the social worker's list for Sarah's sibling. The call came much sooner than we had anticipated, and our son, John Robert, joined us the following year, instantly joining Sarah as the focus of our life. But poor little John, who is just one year younger than Sarah, had a much different homecoming than his sister. We had just bought a new home in Duke Forest, a residential area adjacent to the Duke campus, and were scheduled to move the very day after John's arrival. So he only had one night in the old house, and his new room, unlike his sister's pristine nursery, was filled with moving boxes. He must have thought life in his new family was going to be quite hectic. But Sharon soon had his room in the new house decorated in a cheerful boy's décor, and that house is where Sarah and John grew up. No two children could ever be loved more than ours, with the possible exception of our grandchildren, who would come along many years later.

If anyone ever doubted the cultural difference between the sexes, they needed only to look at Sarah and John. As completely as she was feminine, he was all boy, through and through. At an early age he learned to crawl like a little tank, and that seemed a perfectly acceptable mode of travel for him; a little dirt on the hands only added to the adventure. In keeping with their gender differences, Sarah excelled in quieter endeavors, especially playing the piano and composing her own music. Some of my most nervous moments were at piano recitals, just before she was to play, but she was always calm and confident and performed flawlessly—or so it seemed to Sharon and me. In contrast, John loved the outdoors: camping, fishing, and playing sports. Competing for my most nervous moments were his soccer games. But, like his sister, he was both composed and accomplished, and among our proudest possessions is a large trophy which he was awarded for being the most valuable player on his school team. From day one, John was a cheerful little fellow with ready laughter, and before long he would develop a marvelous sense of humor that keeps us in stitches to this day. But that evening, when I had just left Benjamin's room, John could only express himself with his laughter, which rolled out freely as we tumbled together on the floor.

Not surprisingly, I suppose, what impressed me most about Sarah and John on that evening, with Benjamin still on my mind, was the sparkle in their eyes—so clear and bright and seeming to offer such rich, hopeful futures. It was in striking contrast to what I had seen in little Benjamin's eyes, reminding me once again of our good fortune in having two healthy children. Those of us who spend our lives caring for the health of others and witnessing the suffering of the sick cannot help but be constantly reminded of how fortunate we are to enjoy good health in ourselves and our loved ones. I felt especially blessed that evening, not only for a loving and healthy family, but also because I was, I hoped, about to be able to give back a little of my good fortune by helping Benjamin McFee and his family have a better life.

Sharon and I put the children to bed that evening, and I reminded them, as I did each night at bedtime, "You are both equal."

———

I don't know that I slept too well that night. Benjamin and the details of his surgery undoubtedly weighed on my mind. I was reminded of nights before athletic events in my school days. Never much of an athlete, I nevertheless had a passion for sports, especially football and track, and the night before a game or race always found me apprehensive. But when morning came, apprehension was quickly replaced by exhilaration. I had worked hard to prepare for the sporting event and was ready to show what I could do. Now, on the morning of that surgery, I had a similar feeling. I had spent years preparing to be an eye surgeon, and apprehension gave way to exhilaration—I felt qualified and ready.

It was a beautiful early spring morning with a cool breeze and a warm sun. The daffodils were in full bloom, and white blossoms were beginning to open on the dogwood trees. A clear blue sky provided the perfect backdrop behind the tall pines, and the singing of birds added a fitting soundtrack to the whole scene. I could not have been granted a more perfect setting for the uplifted and exhilarated mood I was in as I drove to work that morning.

Benjamin had already been taken to the operating room when I arrived, and his parents were standing in the hall by the door to the surgical suite. We exchanged brief greetings and I promised that I would come for them in Benjamin's room as soon as the surgery was over. Then I changed into scrubs and went into the operating room, where the anesthesiologist was preparing to put Benjamin to sleep.

He looked so small, lying there on that big operating room table. For a moment, I felt a troubling sense of uncertainty as I considered the awesome responsibility that was mine. But there were preparations to be made, and as I got into the familiar routine, my confidence began to return. Our surgical equipment added to my confidence. We were just entering the age of what is called microscopic surgery. This means that the surgical field is viewed through an operating microscope, which made Benjamin's eye look more the size of an orange than that of a grape. We were also working with very delicate instruments and suture material that was much thinner than a human hair. All this made it easier to operate in such a small area, only a few millimeters wide.

The surgery went smoothly. I had anticipated that we would encounter scar tissue and bleeding because of his previous operations, but this could be controlled. One of the senior residents was my surgical assistant, and he flushed away the blood with a stream of irrigating fluid so I could see where to stop the bleeding sites with a delicate cautery instrument. He sat to my left, looking through one of the viewing ports in the operating microscope. To my right was the scrub nurse, who viewed the surgical field through a third port and kept the instruments coming at our request. Despite its small size, the eye has several layers of tissue, and I worked my way down through one delicate layer after another until reaching the innermost layer of Benjamin's eye, where the new drainage channel was created. With delicate scissors, I cut out a window of tissue where the normal flow of fluid, or aqueous humor, was blocked. After that, it was just of matter of reconstructing the layers of tissue over the internal drainage site with the fine sutures. The fluid, which had been trapped in Benjamin's eye, causing the high pressure, now had a new way to flow out of the eye. After passing through the deep window that I had created, it would filter across the thin outer layers of the eye and finally wash away in the tear film. When the surgery was completed, I felt good. Everything had gone as I had hoped it would, and I was pleased with the appearance of Benjamin's eye. I taped a patch over his eye, and the nurses took him to the recovery room.

I drew a gown over my scrubs and went out to tell the good news to the McFees. They were waiting in Benjamin's room. Mr. McFee stood up as I entered. Neither parent spoke, but their anxious expressions said everything. I smiled and told them that the surgery had gone well and that I was very optimistic. After a brief, reverent moment, Mr. McFee reached out for my hand. I felt a faint tremor in his big, powerful hands as they engulfed mine.

"God bless you, Doc," was all he said.

Mrs. McFee said even less—the look in her eyes spoke for her. I knew that she wanted to be with Benjamin, and I took them both to be with him in the recovery room.

For the rest of that day I rode on the top of the world. Before heading home, I stopped by Benjamin's room. He was sleeping comfortably in his bed, his mother in a chair beside him. Mr. McFee was in his usual place, beside the window, standing guard. I reassured them of my confidence in their son's future. I would see them first thing in the morning, and we would take the patch off of Benjamin's eye then.

Because I got home a little earlier than usual than evening, I decided to go for a short run. We lived near the Duke golf course, which had an excellent jogging path around the perimeter. The good weather had held up, and the daylight was lingering longer into the evening. In my heightened mood, the run seemed effortless. I enjoyed the scent of the pine trees and the softness of the pine needles that covered the trail. Most of all, I enjoyed returning home for another peaceful evening with my little family.

Gray clouds had come in overnight, but they did not dampen my mood as I drove to work the following morning. In fact, I enjoyed the drive more than ever. It was good to be alive. It was good to be a part of this beautiful world. It was good to be able to make a meaningful contribution to my world and to be able to bring happiness to others. And I have to confess that I was looking forward to receiving some recognition for what I had just contributed.

I found the McFees much as I had left them the night before, and it was difficult to tell if any of them had slept much. The nurse informed me that Benjamin had awakened with pain in his eye during the middle of the night, but he seemed comfortable now. There was little said, but it was obvious that all of us were thinking only about what lay behind Benjamin's patch. I took him by the hand and led him to the examination room while his parents waited behind.

Throughout my surgical career, I never overcame the anxiety that I felt when the patch is removed from the eye on the first day after surgery. I learned early that the most successful operation is no guarantee of what the future may hold. But on that morning with Benjamin, my confidence had yet to be tempered by the trials of experience. His surgery had gone well, and I fully expected to find an excellent result behind his patch. What I did find nearly made my heart stop.

I remember a Saturday morning during medical school. Our lecturer was a prominent surgeon—tall and handsome and seeming to exude self-confidence. But he said something that morning that never left me—he warned us that days would come when we, as surgeons, would wish that we could curl up in our mothers' laps and hide our faces from the world. At that moment, looking at Benjamin's eye, I was hit by the full impact of his meaning.

The most feared early complication of glaucoma surgery is major bleeding inside the eye. In patients with glaucoma, the blood vessels inside the eye gradually adjust to the high eye pressure that surrounds the wall of each vessel. When the eye pressure is suddenly lowered by the surgery, the relatively higher pressure in the blood vessels may cause one of the vessels to rupture. The eye quickly fills with blood until the pressure in the eye rises to a level that causes the bleeding to stop. It often happens while the patient is sleeping, causing him or her to awake with severe pain. This is what had happened to Benjamin.

His eye was filled with blood, and the pressure was even higher than before the surgery—but the worst realization of all was that Benjamin could see nothing. Was it because the blood was blocking his sight, or had the sudden rise of pressure destroyed what little was left of the optic nerve connecting his eye to his brain? I dared not even consider the latter possibility, because it would mean a lifetime of blindness for the child.

He was obviously frightened, and I did all I could to hide my own fear and to sound as calm and reassuring as I could. I told him that his eye needed more time to get well and that we would have to cover it with a patch for a little longer. The patch wasn't really necessary, but I hoped it might allay the fears of his parents, whose son now had no vision. I wrote orders for the nurses to resume maximum medical therapy in the hope of bringing Benjamin's eye pressure back down. Then, with a sinking heart, I took him back to his parents.

Still trying to appear calm and to hide my own anxiety, I explained that there had been a temporary setback with the bleeding last night. I tried to reassure them that I was still confident that their son would do well, but they obviously saw through my thinly veiled apprehension. Mrs. McFee knelt down by her son and held him in a tight embrace. She began to cry, and that made Benjamin begin to cry with her. I truly wished that I could cry with them. Benjamin's father looked down at his wife and child for a long moment and then turned his gaze away. He never looked at me, but only nodded his head slowly and then turned toward the window. I whispered that I would check back later and quietly closed the door.

That day I had a full slate of patients in the clinic, and I wondered how I would make it through to the evening. I did my best to stay focused on each patient's problem, all the while wanting to cry or scream or just run away. I used my brief lunch break to check on Benjamin—at that moment, eating was the furthest thing from my mind.

The room was dark and quiet. Benjamin lay curled up and asleep on the adult bed. His mother sat beside him, rubbing his back. Mr. McFee stood at the foot of the bed and we exchanged solemn greetings. Had Benjamin had any more pain? A brief shake of his head gave me some comfort. As I loosened his patch, Benjamin whimpered quietly and shifted positions, but continued sleeping. I could feel that his eye was softer, which also gave me some encouragement. But I knew that the blood was still in his eye, and the question of his vision still loomed like a black cloud over the room. I tried to put the best front on a discouraging situation as I reapplied the patch and told his parents that I would be back in the evening.

The afternoon clinic seemed to go even more slowly and painfully than the morning's. But the last patient was finally seen, and I retreated to my office for some essential solitude. I went through the motions of answering phone calls, sorting through the day's mail, and dictating the necessary letters. Then it was time to face Benjamin and his parents again. My emotions were confused; I dreaded going back to their room, and yet nothing else seemed important.

In a room even darker than at noon, mother and child lay asleep together. Benjamin's father sat at his post in the straight chair beside the window. I wondered if he had slept at all since their arrival. He gently awakened his wife, who brushed a tear from one red eye as she sat up. I told her that I wanted to take a look at Benjamin's eye, and we waited as she allowed time for him to wake up. He cried as I removed the patch, but just a little. His eye was still soft, but as I separated his lids and asked if he could see the light that I was holding in front of his eye, there was no response.

"When will Benjamin's vision come back, Doc?" Mrs. McFee asked the question that I dreaded to hear.

All I could do was shake my head and say, "I don't know."

I tried to follow that lame remark with something to the effect that there is always hope. But Mrs. McFee could no longer hold back the tears, and they came freely, but quietly. Benjamin resumed his curled up position on the bed. His father looked away and then down at the floor, as if deep in thought. I promised him that I would come back and check on Benjamin first thing in the morning and that we would know more then. The nod of his head was barely perceptible, and I slipped quietly out of the room.

Our minds play strange tricks on us in times of overwhelming distress. Driving home that night in a light rain, I had the feeling, with every car that passed, that people were looking at me as though I had just committed a heinous crime. Did they know that I had been given an awesome responsibility and had failed? Did they know that I had destroyed a child's chance to ever see again? A police car passed, and for a moment I truly expected him to pull me over and arrest me for blinding a child.

How could this have happened? I had spent my life preparing for this time when I could do wonderful things to help others—to bring happiness into people's lives. But all I had done was bring pain and misery. I had been so confident—and now I felt nothing but futility. A small child would never see another tree, would never watch another sunset over his parents' farmland, would never again see the warmth of his mother's smile—and all because of me. For a moment, I was so overcome with emotion that I screamed at the top of my lungs, "Why?!" Then I quickly looked around, relieved that no one could hear me.

Sharon has always had a way of reading my moods and knowing how to react to them. My silence told her that something was wrong and that this was not the time to ask about it. Rather than coming over for our evening kiss, she simply smiled and pretended to be in the middle of cooking a meal that demanded her full attention. I appreciated her charade.

Sarah and John must have also sensed that something wasn't quite right. They probably wondered why their daddy hugged them longer and harder that evening, and why there was a tear in his eye. Looking at our beautiful children, with their bright, sparking eyes, made my sense of guilt almost unbearable. Why should I be so blessed, when the McFees were sitting in a dark hospital room with their blind child? And all because of me.

I went upstairs and changed into my running clothes. That night I felt the need to run, not for pleasure or fitness, but for penitence. I slipped quietly out of the house and had run for several blocks before I realized that it was still raining. That seemed only fitting as the rain on my face mingled with my tears. I ran twice my usual route around the golf course that evening. By the time I returned home, it was getting dark. Sharon had eaten with the children and put them to bed. She looked a bit put out with my soaked, chilled condition and suggested that I take a hot shower while she warmed up my supper.

That night, I couldn't sleep. I lay awake for hours, struggling with emotions that went from guilt to confusion, anger, and even self-pity, which brought me back to guilt. Sometime in the early morning hours I must have fallen into a fitful sleep. When the alarm rang, I was relieved that the night was over, but I was afraid to get up and face what the new day would bring. Throughout the night, I had prayed that Benjamin's condition might improve, but my faith was weak, and I knew there was very little hope. Still, maybe—just maybe—a little bit of his vision would return. So I got up and prepared to go to work.

The clouds had blown away overnight, and the morning air was again crisp and clear. Warm sunlight filtered down through the trees that lined the road. Even in my despairing mood, I could not help but appreciate the beauty of the day. Naturally, that only made me think more of Benjamin. Would he ever again be able to enjoy the beauty of a spring morning? My mind was a dark cloud of fear and anxiety by the time I drove into my parking place. I went straight to his room.

A nurse had already taken Benjamin to the examination room. He looked smaller than ever that morning as he sat patiently on the nurse's lap. My examination revealed that the pressure in his eye was normal and that there had been no further bleeding. But he was unable to see even the brightest light in front of his eye. The remaining blood in his eye was not my concern. It would either go away on its own or could be removed later, if necessary. Even with an eye full of blood, however, he should be able to see a glimmer of the intense light. So I knew that the temporary pressure rise in his eye after the surgery had destroyed what was left of his optic nerve, and that Benjamin would never see again. It was time to tell his parents the truth.

It may have been the longest walk of my life as Benjamin and I returned, hand in hand, to his room. How would his parents react? I feared the worst. Would Mrs. McFee become hysterical? And what about Benjamin's father? Would he no longer be able to maintain his gentle demeanor? Would he scream and curse at me? Would he become physical? He certainly had the strength to knock me across the room. And in my current frame of mind, I would almost have welcomed such abuse.

I tried to sound as professional and compassionate as I could as I explained in detail to the McFees what had happened and what the future held for Benjamin. It was probably only a formality, because I think they already knew. Mrs. McFee took Benjamin on her lap and hugged him. There were no more tears. Now she had a peaceful, confident look in her eyes. It was as though she realized what her future responsibility with Benjamin would be, and she was ready to accept the challenge.

Benjamin's father stood still and quiet. He kept his gaze down, away from his wife and child. I swallowed hard, wondering what he was thinking and what he would do next. Was he in denial? Was he about to explode?

Was he planning how to attack me? Slowly he looked up and locked his eyes on mine. He took a step toward me. I braced myself.

"Doc," he said in a firm, gentle voice, "we want to thank you for what you done."

It was the last thing I had expected to hear. He was thanking me? Thanking me for what? For blinding his son? For a moment, I thought he might be trying to ridicule me. But he was not that type of person, and the look in his eyes quickly assuaged any thought of sarcasm. It spoke of nothing but sincerity. He must have seen that I was puzzled and lost for words. So, after several long seconds of awkward silence, he continued.

"We know you done the best you could. That's all anyone can ask, and we're grateful to you for that."

The best I could do? Was this my best? And was it enough to have done my best? It certainly wasn't enough to save Benjamin's sight. But in the eyes of this good man, it was all he could ask. And now those eyes were becoming moist with tears, and I felt the same happening to mine. For a long moment, we stood facing each other—not as a farmer and a doctor, but as two fathers who shared an inexpressible love for their children. We grasped hands and struggled to keep from letting our emotions embarrass us. Neither of us could speak. There was really nothing left to say. We nodded, and I quickly left the room.

I can't say that I felt much better. In a way, my sense of guilt was only made worse by the magnanimity of Benjamin's father. But his kind, simple logic did help me to see the recent events in a broader perspective, which I had been incapable of during my last twenty-four hours of self-flagellation. And I was reminded of an old Scottish verse that the minister of our church was fond of quoting: "Do ye best, with what ye got; trusting in the Lord, and be no afraid."

In the decades that followed, there were many more times when I failed to help my patients. And it never really got any easier. Nor would I have wanted it to. To see another person suffer because of my failure may be the hardest burden of all to bear. And it would be unbearable if I did not feel that I had at least tried to do my best. I have often contemplated what it means to do your best, especially when our best is not enough. It clearly is not an excuse for failure. But, by the same token, we can't let failure so overwhelm us that we become incapacitated. Tomorrow, there will be someone else who deserves our best, whether it be a patient, a loved one, a friend, or even a stranger. The best we can do is to learn from our failures so that maybe our best tomorrow will be better than it was today.

And I am also reminded repeatedly that, alone, my best is never sufficient. But as the old Scottish verse implies, we are never alone. So I have come to believe that if we do our best each day, with a good measure of faith, we can come to the end of our day with a sense of satisfaction that may allow us to close our eyes in peace.

———

Three days after Benjamin's surgery, we walked out of the hospital together. He let me hold his hand as we walked to their truck. It was another beautiful morning, and I hoped that Benjamin could feel the warmth of the sun, hear the singing of the birds, and feel the love that surrounded him. Our parting was brief. I promised to keep in touch through Benjamin's family ophthalmologist. And then they were gone, little Benjamin snuggled in between his parents. As I watched the old pickup fade into traffic, I felt that I was losing a little piece of my life, but I also felt that I had gained something of great value.

I never saw Benjamin again. He is now a grown man, and I sometimes wonder what he has done with his life. Whatever it is, I am sure that he has made the most of it. My confidence, of course, comes from the fact that he and I had the same teacher. In my mind, I can see Mr. McFee putting his big, gentle hand on Benjamin's shoulder. And I can almost hear him say, "Son, just do your best."

3.

Alice Fleming

It was a peaceful, seven-minute drive from our home in Duke Forest to the West Campus of Duke University. Beginning on a quiet, tree-lined street with well-kept yards and middle-class brick homes, the journey took me onto a road that wound through a densely wooded area, then between gothic stone pillars and onto the campus, past the business school, the law school, the chemistry department, and the physics department, and finally to the medical school.

West Campus is the larger of the two main campuses of Duke University, but East Campus has the distinction of being where it all began. Originally known as Trinity College, it was moved from the small community of Trinity, North Carolina, in the 1890s to the outskirts of downtown Durham, largely through the benevolence of the Duke family. The patriarch, Washington Duke, had enlisted in the Confederate army and was confined in a Union prison camp when peace started its return to our nation. Back near his hometown of Durham, one of history's turns of fate was playing out on a farm owned by a Mr. Bennett. While the commanders of the Confederate and Union armies in North Carolina were considering terms of peace at the farm house—prematurely, as it turned out—soldiers on both sides relaxed and helped themselves to the highly regarded local tobacco, known as brightleaf. When peace was formally declared a few weeks later, the soldiers took some of the tobacco back to their homes, and orders were soon coming in from both the North and South for more of the prized leaf. On his return home, Washington Duke found that most of his tobacco stores had been confiscated, but he scraped together enough to sell for a small profit, allowing him to plant a new crop. From that humble beginning, he and his three sons amassed a fortune in tobacco and other enterprises that, by the dawn of the twentieth century, positioned them as one of the country's great family dynasties.

Fortunately, the Dukes were also a very generous family, with a special interest in education. Having helped bring Trinity College to Durham, they continued to support its growth and worked closely with the school leaders toward the dream of expansion to a university that would include a major medical school. In 1924, Washington's son, James B. Duke, established the Duke Endowment, which led to the creation of Duke University.

One of the first steps in developing the new university was the purchase of eight thousand acres of rolling forestland northwest of the original Trinity College. On this vast expanse of densely wooded countryside was carved out the new West Campus, which would become the main campus of the university. It began as a quadrangle surrounded by stately stone buildings in Tudor Gothic style with the magnificent, towering Duke Chapel as the centerpiece and the heart and soul of the university (although there are some who contend that this distinction belongs to Cameron Indoor Stadium, home of the Duke basketball program). A gothic arch at one end of the quadrangle leads to the basketball and other sports facilities. At the opposite end is the original home of the medical school. Although the school, including Duke Eye Center, has long since expanded far beyond its origins, I was fortunate to arrive when the ophthalmology department was still in the stately old gothic structure. In fact, our conference room and library looked out through leaded glass windows onto a pastoral view of the grassy, tree-lined quadrangle. During our first year at Duke, when I was on call every third night, Sharon often brought dinner, which we enjoyed together in the conference room or out on the lawn when the weather permitted. With the benefit of a beeper, which notified me when I was needed in the hospital or emergency room, we were able to take walks on evenings and weekends around the campus and especially in the beautiful Sarah P. Duke Gardens, which we had first visited on our honeymoon.

Although West Campus has undergone remarkable expansion during its first century, most of the vast forestland has remained protected, virgin woodland, known as Duke Forest. It is used by the School of Forestry for research and education, but also by anyone who wishes to enjoy the many scenic paths that venture deep into the woods. When Sarah and John were young, one of our favorite family pastimes was taking long walks on those trails. They took us past towering pine trees and hardwoods and over wooden bridges, from which John loved to throw rocks into the flowing stream beneath us. Sharon would occasionally pack a picnic lunch so we could sit and enjoy the natural beauty that had become our home.

The residential area, which is also referred to as Duke Forest, is adjacent to the protected forestland and is home to many members of the Duke faculty. It is where we lived for most of our years at Duke. Coming from Oklahoma, where a grouping of three or more trees qualifies as a forest, we were not only captivated by the beauty of the trees in North Carolina, but by their sheer quantity. Some friends, who were also from Oklahoma, shared our joy and pride in the number of trees that we each had in our yards—at least until their parents visited them one day from the Sooner State. Having learned to appreciate the wide-open spaces, their only comment upon seeing the trees in their children's backyard was, "It's going to cost you a fortune to cut down these trees." Oh well, to each his own.

The road through Duke Forest, which links the residential area to West Campus, runs beside the Duke golf course and its trails, with a few homes on the opposite side of the road that are set well back in the woods. The trees lining the drive on both sides are so dense that one has the feeling of being deep in the forest, and it was through this natural beauty that I had the good fortune of driving to work each day.

The trees along the drive are a lovely mixture of coniferous and deciduous varieties. The stately loblolly pines, with their tall, straight trunks, rise high into the forest before spreading their boughs over the road and deep into the woods, providing a touch of green in every season. They are joined by a profusion of elm, oak, sweet gum, sycamore and tulip trees, whose leaves and flowers provide the changes for each season. Together, the large trees rise high into the sky and then bow in toward each other, creating a natural gothic arch over the road and providing a fitting approach to the gothic architecture of Duke's West Campus.

Down below the gothic arches, the larger trees allow tantalizing views deeper into the woods, where they are joined by their smaller cousins: the cedars, dogwoods, redbuds, and beech trees. Around their feet rise the green leaves of rhododendron, mountain laurel, and a wide variety of ferns and other flora. A thick layer of pine needles and dried leaves complete nature's masterpiece with a rich, fragrant, and protective blanket. And the crowning beauty of these woods is their ever-changing loveliness and moods—the image and the emotion, the eye and the soul—that come with each new season.

Spring comes early to the Carolinas, bringing with it a renewed sense of excitement, energy, promise, and hope, and that urge to be out-of-doors, digging in the earth and being a part of the cycle of renewal. In late February, the tender shoots of daffodils begin to break through winter's brown carpet, and by March the woods are awash with their brilliant yellow blossoms. As the yellow colors fade, they are replaced by the deep-pinkish-purple blossoms of the redbuds and the lavender clusters of wisteria, which hang down from the trees beside the road and impart a delicious fragrance to the spring air. Soon they are joined by the white petals of dogwoods, making the forest appear as though it is filled with giant snowflakes.

Amid this cacophony of color and fragrances, there are other more subtle signs that winter is transitioning into spring. At first, it is hard to tell if it is only the eye playing tricks on us, as the entire forest seems to take on a new, pale-green hue, but soon it becomes clear that tiny buds are beginning to swell on every branch. With the unfolding of the leaves and their ever-deepening shades of green, the character of the forest completes its annual spring transformation. Deep views into the woods are now partially obscured by the heavy foliage, allowing only occasional glimpses of pink and purple blossoms on the rhododendron and mountain laurel.

As the flowers of spring disappear and the leaves mature on the trees, the forest settles into the long, lazy days of summer. The air is still and the leaves of the dense woods seem listless as though they are trying to conserve energy against the heat. Carolina summers can be oppressively hot and humid, but the warmth also provides lovely summer fragrances in the woods, rising as sweet and pungent aromas of the dried pine needles and leaves on the forest floor. As the summer days grow longer, the mood of the forest and its inhabitants seems to become increasingly slower and more relaxed, if not lazy. All those things we promised ourselves to take care of "next summer" seem less important or are forgotten altogether. Such moods probably have their purpose in our lives, however, as they force us to slow down and enjoy the beauty around us: the flowers, the green grass, the blue sky and white clouds, the songs of the birds, and the occasional coolness of the woods.

It was the sense of coolness, evoked by the dark woods, that I remember most about those summer days in North Carolina. Driving home on hot evenings, the road would turn gradually from the campus into the forest, and I would suddenly enter the gothic arches of the massive shade trees, engulfing me in their cool, serene beauty, encouraging me to leave my cares behind, and welcoming me home.

The dogwoods are typically the first to announce that fall is approaching, as their leaves take on red, yellow, and purple hues. The other trees gradually follow suit, and by October the forest is again awash in color, but this time with the broad strokes of burnished gold, russets, and deep purples, blending among the dark greens of the conifers. In especially good fall foliage years, the brilliant yellows, oranges, and reds seem to be ablaze when touched by the shafts of sparking sunlight that filter down through the trees. The colors and the coolness of fall seem to beckon an awakening from the slow, tranquil pace of summer. But unlike the excitement and energy of spring, the deeper, warmer, somehow wiser colors of fall seem to evoke a mellower, more peaceful mood—a time to put away the garden tools and begin to contemplate the warm glow of festive occasions that lie ahead with family and friends. It is a feeling that often comes to me at the closing of the day, regardless of the season, when the day's labor is over and the fading sunlight casts long shadows and illuminates the world with a final golden hue. I suppose it is also a metaphor for the days of our lives, as we transition from the summer of our midlife and begin to settle into the quieter, more contemplative phase of our existence.

And then winter invariably comes. The last colorful leaf finally falls and fades to brown. The forest becomes quiet like our changing mood as we hunker down beside a crackling fire on the hearth, curl up with a good book, or find our own way to pass the long nights of winter solitude. But outside, the woods are cloaked in a new and special beauty. The fallen leaves provide a fresh, new carpet, and the denuded tree limbs now display the delicate, intricate patterns of their branches. An occasional dusting of snow accentuates the beauty of the bare trees and provides them with a temporary carpet of white. Once again we can look deep into the woods, where the pines and cedars still offer a touch of green, and the small beech trees show off their lovely beige colored leaves, which they retain throughout the season. And even when the woods may begin to seem bare and lonely and life starts to feel tedious and even a bit depressing, there is always the promise that daffodils will soon be breaking through winter's blanket and the cycle of life will begin anew.

This was the constantly changing beauty that I was privileged to enjoy every day during our years at Duke. And on that particular early spring morning, while driving to work, I was being treated to one of the forest's finest days. The sky was clear blue. The air was cool and dry, with the gentlest of breezes. The sunlight was warm and sparkled as it filtered down through the trees, reflecting off the new crop of tender green leaves and the yellow and white blossoms down below. All the birds were singing at the top of their lungs, announcing how special this day was. But for all the beauty surrounding me as I drove along that morning, I felt none of it.

———

I would like to say my mood was unusual on that day. But it wasn't. In fact, that was the problem. It was a day like so many others had become for some time now. You might call it ennui—that sense of weariness and dissatisfaction for which there is no ready explanation. Or maybe you would just call it daydreaming. My mind was often so far away from the present that I could be oblivious to the sights and even the voices around me. And yet, if pressed to do so, I could rarely recall where my thoughts had just been. If there was a theme to my reverie, I guess it would have been worry, if not fear—worry and fear for our children, our marriage, and my patients. In truth, a fear for which I rarely had an explanation, but which had become too much a part of my psyche.

Four years had passed since Benjamin and his parents had driven out of my life. Sarah and John were no longer babies, and the whole family was beginning to experience the stress of transitioning from the leisurely days of *Sesame Street* to the challenges of formal education. Sarah was in the first grade and seemed to be struggling more than most of her peers with reading. Both children would eventually be diagnosed with a learning disability, but in those early days Sharon and I were perplexed because they otherwise seemed to be so bright. We didn't recognize it at first (at least I didn't), but a tension was growing in our family. Sarah was frustrated with her struggle in school, and Sharon, whose top priority from day one has been our children, was also frustrated and seemed increasingly preoccupied. I was trying to balance the stress of an academic medical practice with the problems at home and was not doing a very good job of it. There never seemed to be a time when I was not agonizing over one or more patients who were not doing well, and it seemed increasingly inappropriate to bring my professional problems home, so I kept most of them bottled up inside. I was also beginning to work on my textbook, which occupied most evenings and large portions of weekends, robbing time from the family and adding guilt to my feelings of frustration and worry. Sharon was always patient with the time that work kept me from the family, but I vaguely sensed that something was fading from our relationship, which compounded my feelings of melancholy.

But, if truth be told, what we were experiencing were the growing pains of most young families, to one degree or another. In reality, I had everything to be thankful for—a beautiful and loving family, dear friends, an enviable position in one the world's finest universities, and a promising future that seemed to be well on track. In fact, sometimes I wondered if my sense of anxiety did not derive from the fact that life was so good that I feared it could not last. Whatever the explanation, I seemed to be constantly preoccupied with concerns that I could never fully explain to myself, much less to anyone else.

And so it was on that morning in early spring as I drove to work. My eyes were fixed on the road ahead, oblivious to the beauty around me. I have no idea where my mind was—probably mired in some vague, dark feeling for which I had no logical explanation. In fact, I am quite certain that I would have no recollection of that morning whatsoever, were it not for the fact that one of my patients that day was to be Alice Fleming.

———

My spirits lifted a little when I glanced at the list of patients for the morning and saw her name near the top. Since most forms of glaucoma are chronic conditions, the majority of my patients returned for visits on a regular schedule, and we came to know each other rather well. For me, this was a very positive aspect of my practice, since the relationships with most of my patients were wonderfully rewarding. I will have to admit, however, that there were some patients whose appearance on the day's list did not always conjure up a positive emotion, but were more likely to evoke a sigh and a "Why today?" It was usually not the patient's fault—only rarely did differences in personality challenge civil communication—but rather, it was my own ego. We physicians are a peculiar lot. It takes a strong ego, I suppose, to devote a third of one's life in preparation for your chosen profession and to then spend most of the rest of it in long, demanding hours, with the life and health of others always in the balance. But one aspect of the physician's ego is that we don't like to lose. When a patient is not doing well, whether it is after an operation that we performed or a medical regimen that we prescribed, there is a sense of failure, and the responsibility we feel for our patient can be a great burden. And there were some patients whom I could always count on to remind me that their vision had never been as good since I operated on their eyes, and all I could do was agree.

But then there were other patients—and these made up the vast majority—who always conjured up a positive emotion when I saw their name on the day's schedule. In some cases, the good feeling came from the memory that their surgery had been successful or that they were respond- ing well to medical therapy, and that I would most likely be able to give them another good report on this day. And then there were those patients whose name on the list never failed to bring a warm and positive feeling, irrespective of how they were doing medically. These were the people who always appeared to be doing well, no matter what their circumstances might be; they possessed a perpetual cheerfulness that seemed to rub off on those around them. Alice Fleming was such a person.

She was in her ninety-first year that spring morning and had now been a widow for many of those years. Her husband had been a professor of theology at Duke and one of the most beloved members of the University faculty. Both husband and wife were legends at Duke, and most of what I know about them comes from stories told by admiring faculty members, including some of my colleagues in the eye center. Dr. Fleming often preached at the Duke Chapel on Sunday mornings. His slight stature and thin, white hair seemed to be in striking contrast to the large, ornate oak lectern before him, but his strong, lilting voice wafted like music through the huge gothic sanctuary, captivating the congregation. The affection and admiration for Dr. Fleming extended far beyond the Duke campus to all corners of the world, where he was known and respected for his lifelong study of the New Testament.

As a result of his international reputation, I am told that he was in constant demand as a visiting professor, and he traveled extensively around the country and abroad, where he taught, lectured, and preached. And wherever he went, Alice went with him. They seemed to be inseparable. Of all the accomplishments and good fortune in his life, Dr. Fleming was said to take no greater pride than in the woman by his side. She was always known to have a twinkle in her eyes and a smile on her lips—a quiet person, but one who spoke with a mature blend of modesty and intelligence. Those who knew the Flemings loved and respected her as much as they did her famous husband.

It was obvious to even the casual observer that Dr. and Mrs. Fleming were deeply in love. They did not show this in any overt public display of affection, but in the quiet way their eyes would meet; in the way they listened to each other; in the way they were not afraid to disagree with the other, but always respectful of the other's opinion; and in the genuine delight they took in each other's subtle sense of humor.

They had one child, a girl, who was said to have shared her mother's sparkle and warmth. But in the summer of 1948, the great fear that gripped every parent in the country fell upon the Fleming's home. Their little daughter acquired polio and died, after spending the last months of her life in an iron lung. It was a loss from which the Flemings never fully recovered, but they were able to fill their great void with faith and their love for each other. From that time on, I am told, they were rarely separated. They apparently did all their shopping together and especially enjoyed helping each other on the rare occasions that they had to decide on a new item of clothing. They attended concerts and theater productions and even ball games together. On many evenings, they could be seen walking hand in hand around their neighborhood at twilight, and then they would settle down in their modest home to read, work, or talk, as she would tell me years later, about the day's events or about their deepest thoughts, dreams, and hopes.

One of the things they seemed to enjoy most was travel, which they always did together. Because of his international reputation, Dr. Fleming was able to choose from numerous invitations to speak and preach around the world. He and Alice would sometimes visit a new, exciting place, while on other occasions they would return to one of their old favorite spots that were full of memories and where they had established lasting friendships. Wherever they went, they enjoyed studying the culture and history of the area, which was the topic of many happy conversations in the years that followed, and which I enjoyed hearing about from her distant memory when she came for her medical appointments.

They were obviously no strangers to airports, but I suspect that they rarely experienced the same emotions as so many people in these byways of our lives. Having also spent many hours in airports and observed the people around me, I was constantly impressed at how the full range of human emotion often plays out in front of our eyes. Within a single span of our vision, we may take in the highest expressions of human joy, right beside the lowest depths of grief and despair. Little children running toward the outstretched arms of joyful grandparents, while nearby a young couple quietly embrace—him in a uniform, her with tears in her eyes, and neither wanting to let go, not knowing when or if they will embrace again. Another young man in a uniform walks up to an older man, who bears resemblance to him—a tentative moment of eye contact and an awkward handshake before they too embrace, struggling to control their emotions. A young woman—a girl, really—with a small duffle bag that bears the motif of a college stands beside her parents; excitement, fear, sadness all mingle in her eyes—off to her first semester? And the parents, with pride and hope and the same sadness in their eyes—are they returning home alone to an empty nest? Young parents holding a small bundle excitedly run up to an older couple, presenting the miracle in the bundle—grandparents for the first time? Nearby, an elderly woman sits in a wheelchair, surrounded by her family, young and old, and they all look sad—is she returning home to the old country? For the last time? Who can say? A family leaves on a vacation—excited children; preoccupied parents. A traveling businessman is on yet another trip, traveling alone, bored—maybe traveling life alone? Others just wanting to get somewhere—frustrated with a delay, or just frustrated with their life? And so the emotions of human life play out, often within the single scan of the eye, at any airport in the world, just as they once did in train stations for earlier generations.

I am sure that the Flemings were not insensitive to these emotions all around them in the airports; in fact, I rather suspect that they were more sensitive to them than most of us and likely talked about people they had observed during their long flights. But I doubt if they often experienced any of these emotions themselves. Airports for them were simply a necessary part of their travel, and they were just as happy when they were leaving on a trip as when they were returning home together. The reason, of course, was that they always had each other. In fact, not since the loss of their daughter had Alice Fleming known the pain of separation from the person with whom she had been closest for all her adult life. But then the day came when she was left alone.

By the time I came to Duke and assumed the privilege of caring for Alice Fleming, her husband had been dead for many years. On one of our first visits, I mentioned that I had heard much about him and of their relationship. For what seemed like a long time, she was quiet, and her eyes suggested distant thought, and I feared that I had said too much. But then she smiled, and with no show of self-pity or suggestion of impropriety on my part, she simply said, "We had a wonderful life." Those words brought back to my mind what a senior colleague, who was caring for both of the Flemings at the time, had once told me. One day, he saw in the newspaper that Dr. Fleming had died quietly in his sleep. His first thought was of Alice. She was scheduled to return soon for her routine visit. Under the circumstances, he expected that she would reschedule her appointment for a later date, and rather hoped that she would. But he greatly underestimated this remarkable woman.

She not only kept her appointment, but was right on time, as always. He had wondered how she would appear so shortly after losing her soul mate and dearest life companion. Would she be dressed in black? Would she have difficulty maintaining her composure? Would all the sparkle be gone from her eyes? No, my colleague told me, there was none of that. She was the same Alice Fleming he had always known. After the usual pleasantries, he felt compelled to express his condolences. And even then, at what must have been the time of her greatest despair, her gentle, serene response was just the same as it had been for me many years later.

Alice Fleming remained a vibrant part of the community, actively working in her church and helping in community projects. It may be that she did this partly to fill the great void in her life, but she gave no outward signs to suggest it. There was always the same sparkle in her eyes, the same kind words for everyone, and the same positive attitude, and never a hint of feeling sorry for herself. As the years went by, however, time began to exact its toll; her mind remained as alert as ever, but her body was showing signs of gradual failure, and she eventually elected to move to a nursing home. It was shortly after that that I had the privilege of assuming her eye care.

From day one, she insisted that I call her Alice, and those brief times in the office with her were among the most enjoyable that I ever spent with a patient. I invariably got behind in my clinic schedule on the days she came in, because I could not resist talking with her. I loved to hear stories about her famous husband and all the adventures they had together. More times than not, however, we just talked about simple things: the weather, what was happening at Duke, and even the success of Duke's basketball team. But what I remember the most is that after every appointment, no matter how short our time together had been, I always seemed to feel better for the rest of that day. And so it was that I looked forward to yet another visit with her on that spring morning.

She was helped into the examination room by a young man from the nursing home. My colleague had performed cataract surgery on both of her eyes several years earlier, and had then referred her to me because of her glaucoma, for which I was seeing her every four months. She also had macular degeneration, a disorder of the central retina. Both conditions are common among elderly persons and often occur in the same individual with serious consequences, since glaucoma first effects peripheral vision, while macular degeneration reduces central sight. With each visit, not only were her eyes getting weaker, but it was also obvious that her general health was steadily failing. The young man helped her into the examination chair and, after making sure she was comfortable, returned to the waiting room, leaving Alice and me alone.

After briefly reviewing her medical record, I asked her how she was feeling—one of those formalities with which most doctors feel compelled to begin each visit. With that same old sparkle in her eyes and the serene smile, she simply replied, "How could I not feel fine on such a lovely day as this?"

Having failed to notice anything lovely about the day, I didn't quite know how to respond, and I guess my silence was telling. In her typically insightful way, she seemed to correctly interpret the meaning in my reticence, and so she continued to speak.

"Driving over here in the van this morning was such a joy," she exclaimed. "The nice young man drove slowly for me and let me roll down the window. That marvelous, warm sunshine filtering down through the trees mingled so beautifully with the cool morning breeze. And the birds! My, there were so many of them this morning, singing so lovely at the top of their lungs. And don't you just love the sweet fragrance of those flowers hanging down from the trees beside the road?"

The truth is that I had felt neither the warmth of the sun nor the coolness of the morning breeze. I had not heard the birds singing, nor smelled the flowers along the way.

And then it occurred to me: Alice had come down the very same road that morning that I take to work each day. We had passed all the same things in the forest. She had seen the beauty, its coolness and its warmth, its songbirds, and its fragrant flowers. She had seen it all, and I had seen nothing. And what made it all the more remarkable—Alice Fleming was blind.

In my profession, we measure sight by the ability to see letters on a chart, pictures in a book, or trees in a forest. And while the ability to see with our eyes is truly one of our greatest gifts, I have learned from Alice Fleming and many patients like her that there is a light within us that no darkness can put out as long as we allow it to shine. As I have had the privilege of observing many remarkable patients over the years, I have been increasingly impressed by how much more this gift of the spirit can do for a person than my efforts to preserve or restore their physical sight.

The miracle of sight is truly a blessing. Our eyes can take millions of light rays that appear as a chaotic blur and focus them into meaningful images that allow us not only to see clearly where we are going, but also to enjoy the beauty along the way. And yet, the light within us can bring into focus even greater chaos in our lives. It can take a life that is mired in dark despair, in which there seems to be no hope or reasons to carry on, and it can show us the beauty around us—the love of family and friends, opportunities, hope for a better tomorrow—which brings everything back into focus.

As I have thought about Alice Fleming over the years, I have wondered what special gift she had that allowed her to see beauty around her against physical odds. She seemed to be happy and grateful no matter the circumstances of her life. Maybe it was because she was not so concerned about what others could do for her, but what she could do to bring happiness to others. Or maybe it was simply that the beauty she saw all around her provided a hope and assurance that there is surely someone who cares for us all.

Alice has been gone for many years now. Sometimes at night when I look up into the sky at the countless twinkling stars, I can't help but wonder what new world she and Dr. Fleming may be visiting. I'll bet they're having a grand old time. One thing I know for sure, however, is that her spirit lives on in the hearts of those of us who knew her and that were fortunate to learn from her.

There are still many times when the cares and burdens of the day blind me from the beauty around me. But those are the times that I try to remember Alice and the thousands like her: people who may be blind, deaf, crippled, or alone and yet radiate a joy for living, because they have learned to see the beauty in life no matter what their physical circumstances may be.

I was certainly thinking of Alice as I drove home that spring evening after our visit in the clinic. As I rounded the curve that took me into the wooded drive, beneath the gothic arch of the trees, I rolled down the window and smelled the flowers and marveled at the beauty of the forest that I had so recently ignored. And I felt a renewed sense of excitement to be going home to a loving wife and two precious children. And, for that moment at least, I felt that I was seeing my life through new eyes. And I thanked Alice Fleming for her gift of sight.

Ω

4.

Barry and Craig

Wednesday mornings at Duke Eye Center had somewhat of a theatrical atmosphere back in the early 1970s. All the doctors, from the chairman down to the most junior resident, would congregate in a large, dimly lit room, where we stood about in small groups amid hushed voices. Everyone's attention was directed toward the center of the room, where a small child lay on a large stretcher—asleep.

While the mood may have seemed somewhat dramatic on the surface, the purpose of those Wednesday mornings was anything but frivolous. It was to perform examinations under anesthesia, or EUAs, on children who were too young to cooperate for an adequate exam in the doctor's office. Since the process required a nursing staff, an anesthesia team, and often several ophthalmologists with differing subspecialties, it was felt in those days that it was most efficient to set aside one morning for all the EUAs that were scheduled for that week. An added benefit was the excellent learning opportunity it afforded those of us in training. I was a lowly first-year resident at the time, and I look back on those Wednesday mornings as the moments when I first began to appreciate the many trials of caring for children with impaired vision.

There are many layers of complexity in managing the child with a sight-threatening disease as I would one day learn with Benjamin and his parents. First is the unique nature of their small eyes, which not only creates technical problems with surgery, but also increases the risk of postoperative complications, such as bleeding and excessive scarring, all too often leading to unhappy results. I remember standing back with the other residents in the EUA room, watching the senior doctors shake their heads and confer softly over a child whose eye was filled with blood or whose eye pressure was too high. But it would not be until I had the primary responsibility for Benjamin and many like him that I would fully understand the feeling of helplessness that caring for these difficult little patients can often engender.

The next layer of complexity, adding to the challenge of caring for the child with a serious eye disease, is that they come with young parents. So often, it seems, this is their first child, and they are full of the wonder and excitement that comes with embarking on a life of parenthood. For months their dreams have been filled with the hopes and aspirations of watching their child grow up strong and healthy and enjoying all the good things in life. Then the awful news comes. Their baby's eyes have not developed properly, and their precious child could be faced with a lifetime of blindness. Their emotions of denial, sorrow, and anger gradually turn to desperate hope as they reason that modern medical technology can surely save their child's sight. And so they look to their ophthalmologist to work the miracle. Sometimes their prayers are answered, but other times their hope gives way to despair as one operation after another fails to reverse the blinding disease.

Those EUA mornings were a microcosm of all the parental emotions associated with having a sick child. The young parents would sit together with their children in a waiting area adjacent to the EUA room. Some were there for the first time, and they were the anxious but hopeful ones. Others had returned many times, and their body language spoke of a different emotion—no less anxious, but more resigned to what they might hear. They usually sat closer together, often holding hands, trying to console each other, and always giving their full attention to their little child. Eventually, a doctor or nurse would come out and take their child into the EUA room. Some of the children cried, while others seemed oblivious to the events. After long, anxious minutes, the doctor would return with the sleeping child. Sometimes he would discuss the findings in front of all the parents. Other times he would suggest that the family step into a room for a private discussion—and all the parents understood.

And then there is the third layer of complexity—the emotions of the child. As with any sick child, there is the fear associated with the doctor's office. But for the child with visual impairment, there is the added terror of the dimly lit unknown—not knowing for certain where they are or what may be coming at them—and so they cling to the security of their parents. Yet for all this, there is something remarkable that happens to these children over time. I will never cease to marvel at the resilience of children and how they can adapt to their circumstances. In them there seems to be an unwillingness to let their handicap rob them of life's joys. The same physical limitation that in an adult might create a complete invalid is often only a minor detour in a child's life as they explore new pathways to happiness. Sometimes these explorations can lead to adventures of danger, humor, fear, anger, or abiding companionship. In the story of Barry and Craig, it was all the above.

—

The two boys had attended so many EUAs that all the residents could recite their medical histories by heart. We could also tell you a great deal about their young mothers. Back in the early 1970s, all the residents at Duke Eye Center, I am embarrassed to admit, were men, and we did not lack our gender's propensity for appreciating members of the opposite sex. On the Wednesday mornings, when little Barry and Craig were brought in by their mothers, there was a decided air of interest among the young doctors as we shared furtive glances and sly smiles. Most of us had completed military service before our residency, so we were close in age to the two women. And the fact that neither was ever accompanied by a man only added to the intrigue. But they were both devoted mothers whose focus was always fully on the needs of their struggling baby boys. And yet, as much as they had in common, no two women could have been more opposite.

The differences between the two mothers began to appear as soon as they drove into the eye center parking lot. Barry would arrive with his mother in a late-model, dark blue BMW sedan. Rumor had it that she was also seen on occasions driving a Mercedes sports convertible. In any case, it was obvious that this was a lady of means, and the way she carried herself suggested the comportment that comes from a lifetime of privileged living. Her clothing was conservative and yet complemented her feminine attributes—typically a cashmere sweater with a simple string of pearls and a plaid woolen skirt that came to just below her knees. Her soft, light brown hair touched her shoulders and was held back by sunglasses that she wore above her forehead. She seemed to require little or no makeup, and her skin had a light tan that suggested several hours each week on the tennis court or golf course. Her demeanor was quiet, but friendly; she did not talk much, but always had a smile for everyone and an appropriate, pleasant response in a cultured southern accent whenever spoken to. We were told that she lived in one of those huge, stone houses on a spacious, perfectly manicured yard that backed up to the golf course of the city's most exclusive country club. It was also rumored that her husband was a very successful businessman, whose long workdays and frequent travels kept him away from Barry and his mother a great deal of the time. If this were true, Barry's mother seemed to compensate by devoting herself to the many demands of her baby boy.

And then there was Craig's mother. She would arrive with her little son at the eye center parking lot driving a shiny pink Chevy pickup. If that was not enough to get the attention of every male eye within range, the appearance of the driver surely was. Tall and full-bodied, she never wore anything that approached her knees - usually shorts or a mini skirt, accompanied by either a tight sweater or an open blouse. Her peroxided hair was piled high on her head in the ratted style of the time, with what must have been a full can of hairspray keeping it in place. She had a pretty face with a full mouth that was accented by bright-red lipstick, sparkling eyes with dark eyeliner, and a generous application of rouge. Her personality was as bright and colorful as her truck and dress; she wore a constant smile and spoke freely and often, with a rather loud voice and an accent that dripped of the Deep South. It was impossible not to like her, even when trying to suppress laughter at her audacious demeanor.

Need I say that Barry and Craig were not neighbors? Word had it that Craig and his mother lived on the outskirts of town in a small, wood-frame house with a couple of rusty cars on cinder blocks in the front yard. The house also served as the place of business for Craig's mother, who was a hairdresser, and apparently a very good and successful one. It was rumored that there was no man in the house, although many young men were frequently seen coming and going. But, like Barry's mother, the most important person in the life of Craig's mother was her baby boy, who was struggling to hold on to a thread of vision.

When Craig was born, his family and friends remarked on what big, beautiful eyes he had. An astute pediatrician, however, sensed that something was not right. She realized that the eyes were too large and that the corneas—the front, clear windows—had a faint, telltale haze. During his final months of development, before Craig's birth, his eyes should have been forming a series of fine drainage channels through which the fluid, called aqueous humor, could flow out of the eyes at the same rate at which it was being produced. In Craig's case, this did not happen. Instead, a thin film of impermeable tissue remained, obstructing the drainage channels and trapping the aqueous humor inside the eyes. As the volume of fluid increased, the pressure in the eyes also rose, leading to several changes. Because the cornea and the sclera—the thick, white part of the eye—are not fully developed during the first years of life, they respond to the elevated eye pressure by stretching, causing the eyes to be abnormally large. The stretching also alters the structure of the corneas, causing them to become cloudy. The most devastating change, however, occurs in the back of the eye, where the high pressure gradually destroys the optic nerve—the vital connection between the eye and the brain. Failure to control the elevated pressure not only leads in short order to irreversible blindness, but can also result in a deformed, painful eye. Craig's pediatrician correctly recognized his condition as congenital glaucoma—the same disorder with which Benjamin would be born later that decade—and referred him to an ophthalmologist at Duke.

Craig was not yet one month old when he was first seen at the eye center, but already the cloudiness of his corneas had progressed to the point that even his mother could tell something was seriously wrong. The initial treatment for congenital glaucoma is to surgically incise the layer of impermeable tissue, so the aqueous humor has egress from the eye and the normal pressure can be restored. This was performed immediately on both of Craig's eyes, and for a while, it seemed to be working. His corneas cleared and healthy color returned to his optic nerves. But, like a cruel joke, it did not last. Before he reached four months of age, Craig's pressures began to go back up in both of his eyes, with all the associated problems—the progressive enlargement of the eyes, the cloudiness of the corneas, and the continued destruction of the optic nerves. The operations were repeated, but this time the right eye filled with blood after the surgery, and the pressure went even higher. He was taken back to the operating room to remove the blood, only to find that he had now developed a cataract in that eye from all the surgery. The cataract was removed and a different glaucoma operation was attempted, this time to bypass the obstruction to aqueous flow, but by then the optic nerve was totally destroyed and his right eye showed no response to light. Craig was not yet six months old and already he had undergone seven operations, was totally blind in his right eye, and had very limited vision in the left eye. The final operation for the right eye was to remove it because of pain when he was three years old and replace it with a plastic artificial eye. And so Craig faced the rest of his life hanging on to a thread of vision in his only eye.

Barry's eyes also failed to develop properly before birth, but in a different way from Craig's. His was a rare condition called sclerocornea, in which the cornea does not develop the normal clarity, but is white and opaque like the sclera. Unless the cloudy corneas are surgically replaced with clear corneas—called corneal transplant—the child is faced with a lifetime of severe visual impairment. The timing of the surgery is critical, since the outcome with regard to a clear cornea is usually better when the child is older, but early restoration of vision is needed to avoid amblyopia, or lazy eye, in which the vision fails to develop for lack of normal visual stimulus. When he was approaching his first year of life, a corneal transplant was attempted on Barry's left eye. As too often happens in young children, however, graft rejection began to occur. Blood vessels grew into the periphery of the transplanted tissue, and the clarity of the new cornea was gradually replaced by a dense, white opacity, forcing the little child back into a world of dimness and fuzzy, meaningless forms. To make matters worse, scarring from the surgery obstructed the delicate channels for aqueous drainage, creating a form of glaucoma with a high pressure that threatened to destroy his optic nerve and rob Barry of what little vision he had left in his eye. Thus he was taken back to the operating room, now in hopes of correcting the glaucoma.

The first glaucoma operations attempted on Barry's left eye were similar to the later procedure that had been tried on Craig's right eye—an effort to bypass the obstructed drainage channels. But the strong propensity for healing, so typical of young children, led to repeated failures, as the channels would close with new scar tissue. The next surgical approach was to lower the pressure in the eye by destroying some of the tissue that produces the aqueous humor. In those days, this was most often accomplished by placing a freezing probe on the eye over the tissue to be treated. A major problem with the freezing operation was that, if too much of the fluid was destroyed, the eye lacked the aqueous humor needed to survive and it became shriveled and blind. Sadly, this is what happened to Barry. And so, after months of repeated surgery, frustration and heartache, he was left with a deformed eye that would never again see the light of day. Because of this disastrous course of his left eye, the surgeons at Duke, my mentors, wisely decided not to attempt the same surgical course in the child's only remaining right eye, which provided him with limited vision to move about.

And so it was that two little boys, with only one eye each, eyes that provided only the dimmest of sight, embarked on their long and uncertain journey through life. And two young mothers—so different in almost every way, and yet so alike in the one thing that mattered most— set out with determination to insure good lives for their sons. And as the years passed, a most remarkable thing happened that neither they nor any of us during those Wednesday morning EUAs could have ever foreseen.

———

I didn't recognize him when he entered my office that first day. He walked with the cautious movements that are typical of a person with limited vision. But he also had the carefree demeanor of youth. He carried his head high, as though looking up at the lights on the ceiling, and his eye moved about in a constant, searching manner. He had a cute, round face with a full mouth that seemed to be fixed in a perpetual smile. He felt the examination chair before sitting down, as though he had done it many times before, and his mother took a chair close to him. After a brief greeting, I opened his medical record and noted that his name was Craig.

It had been nearly a decade since the Wednesday morning EUAs, and I was now a junior member of the Duke faculty. The chairman had long since decided that the concept of tying up the whole department every Wednesday morning wasn't really that efficient, and the collective EUAs had been replaced by individual exams in the operating room. As a result, I had not seen Craig or his mother in many years, and a flood of memories began to wash over me. I looked up at Craig, trying to reconcile this young man in front of me—now in his tenth year—with the image of a child from long ago, but what I saw was more reminiscent of a young mother I had known back then. I looked over at her, again trying to reconcile the person before me with the one from the past. She must have perceived my perplexity and simply smiled, as though to say, "Yes, it's me."

Craig's mother was still attractive, but the years had brought change. Her hair was still blond—and it was obvious that she was continuing to help support the hair spray industry—but the beehive was gone, replaced by a softer style that reached to her shoulders and was pulled back on the sides with barrettes. Her face was accented with the same basic cosmetics as before, although significantly less of it, and her manner of dress was decidedly more modest. Although the colors were still bright, she now wore slacks, albeit formfitting, and a cardigan over a cotton blouse with a high collar. The most striking change, however, was her demeanor. She was still friendly and spoke freely, but now with several decibels less volume and with a touch of reserve and maturity that I had not seen before.

She explained that the ophthalmologist who had been following Craig was becoming worried about his one eye and felt that he should come back to Duke for his continued care. She handed me a note from the doctor, which indicated that the glaucoma in Craig's only eye was indeed becoming more difficult to control and might eventually require further surgery. During this time, he had been sitting quietly, but attentively and with the perpetual smile on his face. He was tall for his age, but of slight build, with closely cropped dark brown hair, a bit of residual baby fat in his face, and the beginning of the teenager's complexion problems. As we began to talk, it was quickly apparent that Craig had the same open and delightful personality as his mother—and this despite his serious handicap. He had only a small island of peripheral vision in his one eye, which allowed him to see large forms as shadows, and with this he was able to move about with surprising facility. He was especially conscious of lights and particularly enjoyed those with vivid color.

"Look, Ma, it's a blue light!" he exclaimed, as I brought an instrument toward his eye to measure the pressure. His mother smiled, as though she had heard it before.

"That's Duke blue, Craig," I jokingly told him.

"It's Duke blue, Ma. Duke blue!" he repeated excitedly, bringing a big smile to his mother's face.

My examination confirmed the other doctor's report. The optic nerve was badly damaged, accounting for the limited vision, and it would be necessary to keep the pressure very low in the eye to prevent further damage and complete blindness. But I was hopeful that we could do this by adjusting his medications and avoid further surgery.

After discussing the changes in his medications and giving the prescriptions to Craig's mother, I arranged for them to return in a month and said good-bye.

As they were beginning to leave, Craig asked me, "Have you seen Barry?"

"You know Barry?" I asked. With the passage of so many years, I assumed that the two boys had long since gone their separate ways.

"Sure, he's my best friend!"

His mother again interpreted my perplexed expression and, shaking her head and laughing, explained that the two boys were in school together at the Governor Morehead School for the Blind in Raleigh. She smiled from ear to ear, as did Craig, when she described how much fun the boys had with each other. The students at Governor Morehead lived in dormitories during the week, but those with families nearby could go home on weekends. Barry and Craig spent every weekend together, alternating between their two homes. They enjoyed listening to music and the radio and building things with their Legos and just laughing and telling stories and tussling, like any two young boys. But they could also be a handful and tended to be in and out of trouble both at school and at home. His mother's countenance changed to a rare moment of seriousness as she recalled a particularly frightening experience a few years back.

It started on the Fourth of July, when the two mothers had taken their sons to a fireworks display. The boys had never seen anything like it, and they were spellbound. It is hard to imagine what it must be like to live in a world of darkness and have it suddenly explode with brilliantly colored lights to the accompaniment of loud booms. It was an experience like no other for the two boys, and they wanted more. That weekend they were at Barry's home, and he had learned—or so he thought—of a fireworks stand not too far from his neighborhood. And so the boys began to plot their great adventure. Barry had some money in his pocket and had calculated the route to the fireworks stand, not realizing it was probably closed for the season. The boys agreed that, if they stayed close to the curbs, and kept a careful count of each intersection, they could find the stand, make their purchase and return before anyone would know. So, hand in hand, they headed out. Of course, they got hopelessly lost, but fortunately it was in Barry's relatively safe neighborhood. As the hours passed and the boys began to recognize their plight, however, they started to panic, as did their mothers. Barry's mother, unable to find the boys in her house or yard, called Craig's mother, and the two women began driving around the neighborhood in search of their wayward sons. They finally found them sitting on a curb, crying their hearts out, and they were so thankful to find them that they couldn't bring themselves to severely reprimand the boys. In fact, they later had a good laugh about it.

Craig's mother was now laughing as she finished the story, although Craig seemed a little miffed that his Mom would tell such stories on him. But what struck me the most, as I listened to the story, was the implication that, not only were Barry and Craig best friends, but apparently the mothers had also become friendly. That seemed so implausible, remembering how different they were, that I found it even more amusing than the escapades of their sons.

"So you and Barry's mother are also friends?" I asked, trying not to sound incredulous.

"Ain't that a kick!" She laughed. "Yeah, you might say that our two boys have made us all best friends."

I couldn't help but laugh, and then we all three laughed. I finally answered Craig's question by saying that, no, I had not seen Barry since he was a young child, but that I would surely like to see him again someday. With that we said good-bye until Craig's next appointment.

About two weeks later, another young man walked into my office. He was approximately the same age as Craig and moved in much the same manner—cautious, head erect, with aimlessly wandering eyes and sensitive hands feeling carefully as he made his way forward. I knew that Barry had been scheduled for an appointment that day, and I was looking forward to seeing him and his mother again after so many years. He was shorter and stockier than Craig, and his light brown hair was longer and carefully combed. His skin was clear, and his demeanor was pleasant but somewhat serious. Again, as I tried to reconcile the little boy from the past with the young man who now stood before me, what struck me most was the similarity to his young mother I had once known. She had not really changed that much. The style of her hair was about the same, although the sunglasses were gone. Her face and figure were a bit fuller, and her hemline was even farther below her knees than before. But she still carried herself with the elegance of the privileged, and her demeanor had remained quiet and reserved, but pleasant. As I glanced at Barry's medical record, I noticed that he no longer had a father living at home.

I told Barry and his mother how pleased I was to see them, but something in my voice must have revealed my curiosity as to why they had made the appointment at this particular time, just weeks after Craig's visit. In any case, Barry's mother felt obliged to explain.

"As you recently learned," she began in her soft southern accent, "Barry and Craig have become best friends through their attendance at the Governor Morehead School. Craig apparently told Barry that you have a Duke blue light, and he had to see it." She laughed openly at her explanation, as did I.

Barry nodded his head in confirmation of his mother's explanation and in eager anticipation to get on with the examination and the Duke blue light. His serious expression had now given way to a big grin, and I was struck by how much he made me think of Craig. And so we began the examination.

No further surgery had been attempted on Barry's eyes since the frustrating series of failures on the left eye during his first years of life. That eye was now shrunken and totally blind. Although the cornea of the right eye was still white, like his sclera, he was able to see light and even large, formed objects, much as Craig saw with his left eye. Of added concern, however, was that the pressure in Barry's right eye was now elevated, which is not uncommon in children with developmental abnormalities such as his. Since I could not see his optic nerve through the opaque cornea, it was hard to know what pressure he needed to prevent further loss of vision from glaucoma. But to be on the safe side, I suggested to his mother that we start him on a glaucoma eye drop. She agreed and asked if I would continue to see Barry. I told her that I would be pleased to follow him along with his family ophthalmologist, to whom I would send a report.

As they were leaving, I asked Barry about his friendship with Craig.

"Yes, sir," he politely but enthusiastically replied, "old Craig and I are best buddies. And our mamas are also best friends."

I looked over at Barry's mother for confirmation of the latter statement, still finding it hard to believe.

She laughed and said, "It's true." And then, after a moment of serious thought, she explained, "The boys are so close, and Craig's mother and I gradually came to realize that we also enjoy each other's company. It's interesting how differences that once seemed important can become so trivial in comparison to the one thing in life that is most important, and Craig's mother and I have found what that is for us."

I looked over at Barry and thought about what a lucky young man he was. I asked him and his mother if they would like to start coming on the same day that Craig and his mother came to Duke, to which they both enthusiastically agreed. And so began a rare experience for all of us—certainly for me—the ending to which none of us could have ever guessed.

———

I cherished those visits with Barry and Craig, and even now look back on them with the fondest memories. It was good to see the playful interaction and the mutual affection that the boys shared, and also the warm friendship of their mothers. There were always new adventures to relate—some told by the mothers that the boys, who were still a handful, would have just as soon forgotten—but most related enthusiastically by the boys. On one occasion, they told me about their new entertainment center, which, with the help of their mothers, they had set up in Barry's room. It consisted of wall-to-wall speakers for their music, a lighting system that coordinated with the music, and a thick shag rug, where they could lie and listen to the music and talk about whatever young boys talk about.

"So, what types of music do you guys like?" I asked.

"Country," Craig replied with a big smile.

"And rap," Barry added.

Both mothers just smiled and rolled their eyes.

"And who is your favorite country singer?" I asked.

"Ronnie Milsap!" Craig answered, to which Barry nodded enthusiastically.

That brought a decided smile to my face, but I saved the story for another day.

"And we got lots of lights in old Barry's room!" Craig exclaimed. "All colors."

"Got a Duke blue one?" I asked.

"Sure do," he responded with pride. "You still got yours?"

"I do indeed. Would you like to see it?"

"Yeah!"

And so we proceeded with the boy's examinations. Much to my relief, they were both still doing as well as could be hoped for, which I related to them and their mothers and prepared to say good-bye until our next visit. But Barry's mother surprised me with a remark that came with a smile and a twinkle in her eye.

"Barry, do you want to tell Dr. Shields what else you and Craig like to do?"

"You mean the impersonations?" he asked rather hesitantly.

"Yes," she replied with a smile toward Craig's mother.

"Craig and I do impersonations," he informed me.

"Oh, really. Who do you impersonate?" I asked.

"Mostly rap singers."

"Don't you want to tell Dr. Shields who else you boys have started impersonating?" Barry's mother prompted.

"You mean Dr. Shields?" he asked with a touch of embarrassment.

His mother nodded, which Barry seemed to sense.

"Well, old Craig does it best," Barry hastily responded, obviously becoming increasingly self-conscious. "Craig, you want to do it?"

Craig, who was decidedly less inhibited than Barry, immediately launched into his routine. He affected his most serious look, pursed his lips, stroked his chin and proceeded in his lowest, slowest droll voice.

"Wall, tha inner oclear pressure is a little too high in tha eye. Looks like we're gonna hafta use some moha eye drops."

It was the best laugh I had had in ages, and the mothers joined in with me. I hated to admit it, but Craig's impersonation was pretty accurate. The two boys slowly joined in with us, and before long we were all laughing so loud that I am sure the patients in the waiting room wondered what was going on.

———

The years flew by, and the boys became teenagers. Although they were bigger in stature, their youthful enthusiasm seemed unabated, and they simply found more sophisticated ways to get in trouble. Some of these drove their mothers to distraction, but most were innocent and often humorous, and some even proved to have a silver lining. There was one in particular that they all look back on with considerable amusement and satisfaction. It happened at Craig's home.

By all accounts, Craig's mother was never married, but she still had a steady stream of suitors—some of whom she tried desperately to get rid of. One of these was at the top of Barry and Craig's list of most-hated people. They always knew when he arrived by the sound of his motorcycle. He would walk in to the house without knocking, as though he owned the place, take one of whatever beer he could find in the refrigerator, sprawl out on the living room couch, and fill the air with his smoke and foul language. When Craig's mother asked him to leave, he said things to her that the boys did not fully understand, but were pretty sure weren't nice. He was especially mean to the boys, humiliating them and threatening to beat them up if they didn't do whatever he demanded. So they kept their distance, staying in Craig's room.

Over time, they hatched a plan. One night, when Suitor had had a few too many beers, the boys began shouting from Craig's room at the top of their lungs. As Suitor staggered to his feet to check it out, the door flew open, and the boys tumbled out, nearly knocking Suitor over. It was obvious that they were extremely angry at each other and about to get into a major fight. Suitor wasn't sure what to think, but was always ready to watch a good fight. So, with a sinister grin, he fell back onto the couch.

"You sumbeech," Craig yelled at Barry, with a beet red face and veins pulsating in his temples, "I'm gonna rip your dang tongue out for what you said about my ma."

"Oh yeah!" Barry retorted. "Well, I'm gonna tear your eye out for looking at my mama in the bathroom."

"Yeah, you and what army?" Craig responded.

The boys tumbled on the floor in front of Suitor, kicking and gouging at each other. Suitor thought things were getting good and settled back in the couch, amused that the little punks could scrap so hard and make such outlandish claims. But as he watched through inebriated eyes, he thought he was seeing something that couldn't be. Barry had his fingers in Craig's eye, and the next thing Suitor knew, Barry stood up with the eye in his hand!

"My God, you done tore out my eye!" Craig cried out in anguish. "I'm blind! I'm blind!"

Barry now stood over the ashen Suitor, with Craig's eye in his hand. With his hair going in all directions, sweat pouring from his red, tense face, and his wandering eyes giving him a wild, insane look, Barry stared right into Suitor's eyes and yelled.

"You're next!"

Over the years, the boys would often debate as to exactly how many seconds it took Suitor to get out the front door. But one thing was beyond debate—none of them ever heard from him again. After Suitor was gone that evening, Barry helped Craig clean his artificial eye and put it back in place. Then they stayed up all night, laughing and reliving their moment of triumph.

Unfortunately, most of their antics did not have such favorable outcomes, and it was beginning to show in the appearance of their mothers. Over the years, the two women had become very close to each other. It was amazing how the physical differences between them had progressively blurred, giving way to an inner strength that now shone through in both of them. It was obvious that each would continue to de-emphasize her personal needs and focus on those of her son for as long as he needed her and as long as her life and health permitted. But it was becoming increasingly difficult to handle the boys. While their peers were playing sports, going places by themselves, and learning to drive cars, Barry and Craig were essentially limited to the same things they had been doing for the past decade. They began to rebel and attempted increasingly dangerous adventures, like the time they tried to drive the pink pickup and wound up in a ditch across the road from Craig's house. As boys are wont to do, each blamed the other for their mishaps. This often led to lapses in their friendship, although they were typically short-lived—that is, until everything went terribly wrong.

One day, Barry and his mother showed up alone for the boy's regularly scheduled visit. While this in and of itself was quite out of the ordinary, what was even more puzzling was something different I sensed in both son and mother. Neither were in their usual pleasant mood, and they seemed to be going mechanically through the steps of just another doctor's visit. When I tried to lighten the atmosphere by asking about Craig, it had just the opposite effect. Barry looked down with the closest thing to anger I had ever seen in his face.

"Craig's not my friend," he finally said in a low, solemn voice.

This unexpected turn of events left me unsure of what to say next, and a moment of awkward silence ensued.

"He's a jerk," was the only additional comment that Barry cared to offer on the subject.

I looked over at Barry's mother, who shook her head slowly with a sad, despairing smile. She later told me the story.

It seems that some of their friends at Governor Morehead had told the boys about smoking and how "cool" it was. Suddenly, this seemed like the thing that every teenage boy must do to experience the pleasures of growing up. And the boys vowed to experience it. Craig had heard about a cigarette vending machine in the employee lounge. Barry was against the idea at first (or so he claimed), but Craig convinced him that the merits of the plan far outweighed the risks. So, late one night, the boys felt their way along the dark halls of the school. The darkness was no problem for them, since they got around mostly by feel anyway and had memorized nearly every nook and corner in the school. Although the employee lounge was off-limits to the students and the boys had never been in it before, they found it without difficulty and began groping around in the dark room until they felt something that resembled the description they had heard of the cigarette machine. They felt over it several times until they both agreed on the location of the coin slot. Barry had some coins in his pocket, which he dropped into the slot, and Craig began pulling all the levers he could find. When they heard something drop with a dull thud near the bottom of the machine, it was all they could do to keep from shouting with joy.

The boys wisely reasoned that it would not be in their best interest to smoke at school, since that could lead to their expulsion. Furthermore, they didn't have any matches there, and Barry knew where some were in his mother's kitchen. So the boys began to make plans for an unforgettable weekend.

They weren't entirely sure what smoking involved, but they knew it included fire from the matches, and that alone offered great fascination for them. Making sure the door to their entertainment center was closed, and sitting on the shag rug, they embarked on their new adventure. After a few abortive attempts, Craig was finally able to light one of the matches. The sudden burst of light thrilled them both and Craig held it until it burnt his fingers and he dropped the spent match on the rug. Barry was next to try and he too was eventually successful in lighting a match. However, he did not hold onto it, but let it fall to the shag rug, which soon began to smolder and then blaze.

The boys were so intent on trying to light another match that they weren't immediately aware of what was going on next to them. Within minutes, however, the different smell and the heavy smoke alerted them that something was wrong, and when the saw the large light coming from the floor, they knew they were in big trouble.

Barry's mother heard the screams and came running, finding the boy's room filled with smoke and flames coming from the shag rug. With quick thinking, she pulled the spread from Barry's bed and threw it over the flames, which were soon extinguished. By this time, the boys were nearly hysterical, and Barry's mother was not much better off. She called Craig's mother, who drove over as quickly as she could.

When Craig's mother arrived, the whole house smelled of smoke, and the two boys were sitting in silence on the living room sofa. After conferring between themselves, the mothers came in and began to explain to the boys the seriousness of what they had just done.

"Well, it wasn't my fault," Barry suddenly blurted out, trying to hold back the tears.

"What do you mean?" Craig responded angrily.

"It was your idea to get the cigarettes."

"Yeah, but you got the matches."

"But you were the one that started lighting them."

"But it was yours that started the fire."

By now they were starting to shove each other, and just before the first blow could be thrown, the mothers stepped in between them. They knew that, as serious as the fire incident was, the loss of the boys' friendship would have even graver consequences, since their relationship offered the greatest hope for the boys' present and future happiness. The mothers reasoned, therefore, that it would be best to temporarily separate Barry and Craig, and they told them that their punishment would be to not spend the weekends with each other for one month. Unfortunately, the result was just the opposite of what they had planned.

The fine line between love and hatred shifted to the dark side as each boy smoldered in his isolation and plotted revenge against the other. Craig was the first to make his move. His impersonation routines had, in recent times, risen to a nearly professional level, and he decided it was time to put it to good use. The one telephone number he knew, besides his own, was Barry's home. One afternoon, after classes, he slipped off to a pay phone, called Barry's mother, and gave his best impersonation of their principal.

"I'm afraid we're having problems with your son, Barry."

"Oh my, what has he done?" she implored.

"Well, we found a box of cigarettes in his pocket, and we think he's been smoking at school."

"I can't believe he would do that," she responded with a mixture of shock and puzzlement. "I'll talk with him at once, and I promise it will never happen again."

"Yes, I think you should do that," the voice came over the line, and then there was a click and silence.

Barry's mother felt that something wasn't right. She started to call the principal back, but knew her son would be home the next day for the weekend and decided to first discuss it with him. As she expected, he denied everything, and she knew him well enough to know that he was telling the truth. She next called Craig's mother and explained the situation to her.

Among their many good traits, Barry and Craig were both basically honest young men. Therefore, when his mother confronted him with this latest prank, Craig confessed in full. But it made him even more angry with Barry, who he felt had ratted on him. To make matters worse, Barry spread it around the school when the returned on Monday, and everyone began teasing Craig for a botched prank that wound up getting him in trouble.

Things went from bad to worse, and what had once been the warmest of friendships was now turning into a cold war. The boys no longer spoke to each other at school, but each took every opportunity to berate his old buddy whenever talking with classmates. Each disparaging remark eventually worked its way back to the other boy, and they soon seemed to be trying to see who could outdo the other in saying the nastiest things about their once best friend.

What they could not see at the time was that each ugly remark only made them increasingly miserable and unhappy with themselves. Something was being lost in their lives, but if they were able to recognize it, they didn't seem to know how to change it. Then the most remarkable thing of all happened.

When it appeared that matters could not possibly get any worse between the boys, Craig's glaucoma suddenly went out of control. The pressure in his only eye rose to a level that threatened to destroy what little nerve tissue he had left. If that happened, he would spend the rest of his life in total darkness. I had tried every medicine that was available at the time, and it was obvious that further surgery was now the only hope.

The procedure I selected for Craig was the same type that had been tried on his right eye as an infant, in which a small drainage channel is created in the eye to allow the aqueous humor to escape, thereby lowering the pressure. Since Craig was older now, the chances of a successful outcome were better, but the risks were still high. The operation worked well at first, but as so often happens, especially in young people, the body's natural tendency to heal worked too well in Craig's eye, causing the drainage channel to eventually scar closed and the pressure to rise again.

Our situation with Craig was now desperate. I felt that our best chance, at this point, of saving the small amount of vision he had left was one of the operations that reduced the amount of aqueous coming into the eye by destroying some of the tissue that produces the fluid. Fortunately, in the years since Barry and Craig were infants, we had acquired a new way to do this with a laser, which was better than the old freezing technique. However, there were still risks, and it was possible that the operation itself could rob Craig of his remaining sight. I explained this to his mother.

Although the two boys had not talked to each other for several months now, their mothers had remained in close communication. Barry's mother had apparently told her son about Craig's critical situation and his impending surgery. Barry didn't say anything then, but told his mother later in the day that his eye was hurting and he needed to see me right away.

When they came in to my office the following morning, Barry asked his mother if she would wait outside for a few minutes while he and I talked. I was afraid that he was going to tell me something bad about Craig, but what followed was one of those unexpected moments that I will never forget.

Once we were alone, there was a long silence as I waited for Barry to tell me what was on his mind. He seemed unsure as to how to begin, so I finally decided that I had better open the conversation.

"Is your eye still hurting, Barry?"

"No, sir. It never was"

"Oh?"

"I just told Mama that because I needed to talk to you."

"Oh? What is it?"

"Is Craig's eye pretty bad?" he asked.

"I'm afraid it is, Barry."

"Is he going to have to have more surgery?"

"Yes, he is," I replied.

"Well, I've been thinking," he proceeded slowly and thoughtfully. "I'm better at braille than Craig, and I get around real good in the dark."

"Yes?" I was beginning to suspect where this was going, but I thought, 'Surely not.'

"Well, I don't need my eye all that much," he proceeded. "So if Craig's operation doesn't work, I want you to take my eye and give it to him."

The last thing I wanted to tell Barry just then was that his unbelievable offer was not medically possible. As I had told Benjamin's father, when he made the same offer for his son, it is not possible to successfully transplant the whole eye. But that was not what really mattered at the moment. What Barry had just done represented a far greater miracle—he had let love conquer all.

"Craig's your best friend, isn't he, Barry?" I said quietly, struggling to choke back my emotions.

"Sure is!" he exclaimed, with that big smile that I had missed for so long.

I spoke briefly with Barry's mother as tears welled up in her eyes, and then I said good-bye to both of them.

Craig's surgery was a few days later. After the operation, I walked out of the operating room and down the hall to the room where his mother was waiting. As I approached her, I noticed that two other people were standing with her—Barry and his mother. Just then, Craig was wheeled into the room on a stretcher. After speaking briefly with him and his mother, and assuring them that all was going well so far, I told Craig that he had visitors. His mother looked at me with a smile and winked. I stood back with the two mothers as Barry felt his way up to Craig's bed.

"Hey, Craig."

"Hey, Barry."

"How ya doing?"

"I'm okay."

A long silence followed, and then Craig continued.

"My ma told me what you told Dr. Shields," he said quietly.

"Well heck, what are friends for?" Barry shrugged.

"You're my best friend, Barry."

"You're my best friend too, Craig."

Their hands slowly reached out until they found each other's, and then they gripped their hands tightly together and began to laugh with that joyful laugh of released, uninhibited emotions.

Both mothers had tears in their eyes, and I noticed that they too were holding hands. And I decided it was time for me to make a graceful exit before I revealed emotions unbecoming a physician. But as I walked back to the operating room, I blotted my eyes and could not suppress a big smile.

Barry and Craig are now grown men. They each retained the small amount of vision that they had in their one eye. More importantly, they retained their friendship. And what is most important of all, they and their mothers demonstrated once again the unconquerable power of love—a love that can overcome cultural differences to unite two young mothers, and a love that can trump any issue that two people may have, as long as it is given a chance to work its magic.

5.

Ronnie

The Smoky Mountains were like a second home to our family when Sarah and John were young. We made the four-hour trek from Durham several times each year, courtesy of Duke Eye Center. As part of our residency training program, the senior residents spent three months at the veterans' hospital in Asheville, North Carolina, on the eastern slope of the Smokies. They stayed in comfortable residential quarters on the hospital grounds and ran the eye clinic for a sizable population of regional veterans. Several excellent ophthalmologists in the area provided backup support and assisted the residents with surgery. On Fridays, a faculty member from Duke would come to work with the resident in the operating room and clinic. I volunteered for this duty more than most of my colleagues, because our family enjoyed making a weekend vacation of it.

We would leave on Thursday afternoon as soon as I had seen my last patient. Sharon always had the station wagon packed and ready to go, including the most indispensable items—diversions for the children. Although Sharon and I felt that the drive to Asheville added to the enjoyment of our weekend vacation, Sarah and John did not exactly share this view—four hours must have seemed like an eternity to them. So Sharon would always prepare two sacks with some after-school snacks, small toys and games to occupy the children for at least the first part of the drive. We were all creatures of habit, and there were certain traditions along the way from which we seldom deviated, such as our stop at Mayberry's in

Winston-Salem for a late afternoon ice cream snack. That was about the halfway point, and Sharon's diversion sacks had usually run their course by then, so we would begin the family games, like seeing which side of the car could be first to find all consecutive letters of the alphabet on the road signs, as most families have probably done on long trips. But the last game was the most anticipated and exciting: who would be first to spot the mountains?

At first it was hard to tell if clouds or mountains were on the distant horizon—they were simply gray, formless structures rising into the sky. But as the miles rolled by, the mountains gradually declared themselves as distinct blue-gray silhouettes, often with lighter gray clouds overhead—and, of course, Sarah and John would both insist that they saw them first. We would first pass small mountains in the foothills of the Smokies, which gradually changed from gray to blue to green and then revealed their individual trees and the homes scattered among them. But the first evidence that we were approaching the real mountains was an especially long, steep stretch of highway. The truck drivers must have hated it. Going up, they would grind along in lowest gear, often making barely ten miles an hour. Going down was even worse for them. To keep from going too fast, they had to use their brakes, and sometimes the brakes gave out. So there were deep, sand-filled turnoffs at several points along the decline where runaway trucks could make a violent but merciful stop. At the top of this stretch was the Eastern Continental Divide, which always intrigued Sarah and John, since water could flow either east or west from that point. After cresting the divide, we would begin the more gradual drive down into the valley and Asheville. And beyond the valley lay the Great Smoky Mountains.

The Smokies differ from the Rocky Mountains of Colorado, whose relatively bare, rocky, cathedral-like elevations rise to heights of more than fourteen thousand feet. In contrast, the Smoky Mountains are older and more worn down by the eons, with maximum heights of just over six thousand feet and much denser foliage. This gives them their more peaceful, habitable, and welcoming appearance. Driving down the western slope of the Continental Divide, the Smokies stretched out before us in ridge after ridge of gently rolling peaks with gradually diminishing colors from blue-green to blue to gray and finally becoming nearly indistinguishable from the sky above. It was usually early evening by the time we neared Asheville, and in the warmer seasons we would often be treated to spectacular sunsets. On some occasions, I would pull off on the siding, jump out, and try to capture an especially beautiful sunset with my camera, but I could never come close to the grandeur of the real thing. In the winter months, the sun had usually set by the time we crested the divide, and there might be just a residual rim of orange glow separating the dark, blue-gray mountains from the lighter blue sky above. The glow would eventually disappear, leaving only darkness and a thousand twinkling lights from homes up in the mountains that now surrounded us. Behind each light, a family was probably sitting down to supper, and it was comforting to think that our little family would soon be settled into a motel, enjoying dinner and a peaceful night together.

Early Friday morning, I would drive to the Veterans Hospital to work with the resident, leaving Sharon and the children still asleep. They would enjoy a late breakfast and then swim in the pool or play around the motel. My work at the hospital was usually finished by early afternoon, and I would have a growing sense of exhilaration, thinking about the pleasant weekend in the mountains that lay ahead for our family. There were many attractions that families could enjoy together. Sarah and John especially enjoyed little theme parks, like Santa Land and the Cherokee Village, where many members of the Eastern Band of the Cherokee Nation still live in their ancient homeland, keeping their heritage alive. There was also a resort motel on the very peak of a ridge, which offered rustic but comfortable lodging, excellent home-cooked meals, hiking trails, and spectacular views. We came back there often. But the attraction that I believe the whole family agreed was number one on our list was the Blue Ridge Parkway.

The Blue Ridge Parkway is a noncommercial motor route that extends for 469 miles along mountain crests through the Appalachian Mountains from the Shenandoah National Park in Virginia to the Great Smoky Mountains National Park in North Carolina. In was built during the Great Depression and today is administered by our National Park Service. For my money, it is the most beautiful roadway in the world. The eastern stretch in Virginia passes through rolling farmland, dotted with split-rail fences, an occasional log cabin, and rustic lodging that features wonderful home-cooked cuisine by the women of the area. One of these lodges near the North Carolina border was our favorite. Sharon and I loved the walking paths, their wide variety of flora, including Scottish thistle, and the many butterflies they attracted. Sarah and John especially liked taking a short trail down from the lodge to an old, abandoned whiskey still—a reminder of what life in these mountains was like in the past, and maybe even today in places.

As the parkway continues west into the Smokies, the elevation gradually rises, and the scenes become increasingly majestic, culminating in the rugged peaks above the timberline at six thousand feet. Along the way, the scenery changes with the seasons. In the winter, there is an austere beauty. The deciduous trees are bare, but often covered with snow or a thin layer of ice, giving an entire mountainside the appearance of one giant snowflake. Huge icicles, glistening in the winter sunlight, hang down from sheer stone cliffs beside the road. By late spring, hardy shoots of rhododendron and mountain laurel bloom forth from crevices in these same stone cliffs, while larger bushes fill the mountainsides with their pink and purple blossoms. Rounding a bend in the Parkway, one may suddenly behold a stand of stately pine trees, with their tall, straight, parallel trunks and their green boughs high above. The next bend may offer a growth of deciduous trees whose leaves are just beginning to appear. By summer, the leaves are full and deep green, and the ground beneath them is covered with flowers, ferns, and a variety of other flora. And then, in the fall, the Smokies achieve their crowning glory with the arrival of the fall colors. On weekends during the peak fall foliage season, the traffic may be bumper-to-bumper on the parkway, as thousands come to enjoy this perennial spectacle, when the mountains are ablaze with rich oranges, yellows, and reds. And then the leaves fall, and the mountains prepare for another winter.

Throughout the seasons, one consistent feature of these mountains is the smoky appearance imparted by the clouds, from whence the Smoky Mountains derive their name. On clear days, the clouds would often appear white and wispy as they drifted lazily across the mountain peaks and through the valleys and gaps. At other times, they would completely fill the valleys with a dense, ocean-like carpet of white. Looking down from higher vantage points, we could see mountains rising through the clouds, like islands in the ocean or ships at sea. But as we descended into a bank of these white, fluffy clouds along the parkway, they would take on a darker, more ominous gray appearance, and suddenly we would be engulfed within the cloudy fog. At times, the fog was so dense that we could barely see the side of the road or the taillights of a car just ahead of us. To be on a winding mountain road under such conditions is frightening. But then, with a gust of wind or a rise in the road, the fog would vanish as quickly as it had come, and the full beauty of the mountains would again fill our view and lift our spirits. Such moments as these gave me a renewed sense of wonder and gratitude for the gift of clear vision, but were also a sobering reminder of those for whom the fog never lifts.

———

Somewhere up in those Smoky Mountains, high on a steep slope, there once was a four-room cabin built of undressed lumber. It had neither electricity nor plumbing and was at the end of a dirt path, a half mile from the nearest road. A boy grew up in that home. In his eyes was the fog—the type that never lifts. Like Benjamin and Craig, he was born with congenital glaucoma. But his family was poor, and he did not receive early medical care. The most he can remember seeing as a young child was a little light with his left eye when he looked directly into sunlight. His mother could not abide the thought of having a blind child and abandoned him when he was one year old. He went to live with his paternal grandparents and an uncle in the four-room cabin. Later, his parents divorced, and his father joined them in the cabin.

And so the boy grew up in the mountains without sight and without even the knowledge of modern conveniences. But his early childhood was happy. He was lovingly raised by his grandparents. Although their home was humble, his grandmother kept it clean and orderly, and her family was well fed. His grandfather, to whom he was especially close, took him hunting and fishing. Life was good—until, that is, he reached the age of six.

The four-hundred-mile drive to Raleigh, North Carolina, was an exciting adventure for the young boy. Even when they toured the North Carolina State School for the Blind (which was renamed the Governor Morehead School for the Blind by the time Barry and Craig attended), the boy was enraptured by the rolling lawns and massive buildings of the school. But then his life suddenly came crashing down around him when his grandfather told him that he would not be returning with the family. North Carolina offers an excellent educational opportunity for the visually handicapped at Governor Morehead School, and the boy's family knew this was his best hope for a brighter future. But that was hard to understand for a child at the tender age of six, who had already been abandoned by his mother and now felt that he was being abandoned by everyone he loved. He cried hysterically for hours.

With time, he made a few friends and gradually began to adjust to the foreign way of life. The school was a residential facility, although some students who lived nearby got to go home on weekends. But for the young boy, who was four hundred miles from home, there were only two homecomings each year—Christmas and summer—and those trips proved to be among the most frightening experiences of his life. It was a two-day bus trip. He was with fellow students for part of the way, but they all got off before him, and then he was alone. He counted the stops to make sure he would get off in Asheville, where he had an overnight layover. And this was the worst part of all—a little boy alone all night in a large, smelly, and scary bus station. He dared not go to sleep for fear he would miss the morning call for the next bus home, or that he would be robbed of his few possessions. All night he sat in his dark, lonely world, with strangers prowling around him, praying that he would soon be home.

Poor. Blind. Abandoned. Alone in a dark and frightening world. What would happen to a young boy, who seemed to have so little hope for the future? What happened is that he grew up to become one of the most successful and beloved country singers of all time—Ronnie Milsap.

To thousands of adoring fans for more than four decades, Ronnie Milsap has not only brought joy through his music, but has been an inspiration in the way he lives his life with a relentless work ethic, an indomitable will against all odds, sincere warmth and good humor, love for his family and friends, and an unquenchable desire to share his good fortune with others. His is truly one of the most inspirational stories in which I was privileged to play a small role.

—

"I'm afraid I'll flunk your light test."

Those were the first words I ever heard him say. They were spoken without irritation or self-pity, but with an open, good-humored laugh. My nurse, Sharon, had gone in first to take his medical history and document his vision, as she did for all our patients. She was getting a little frustrated when he didn't respond to any of the standard measures for visual acuity, even moving her hand in front of his face. It was only when she tried shining a bright light in either eye that he let her know he had no vision. I was next door with another patient, but could hear the conversation, especially his rich, clear voice. I suspect that Ronnie may have been teasing Sharon a bit—I would soon learn that he was a great one for little jokes.

It created quite a stir in our clinic when we first learned that Ronnie Milsap would be coming to us as a patient. All the staff, especially the women, positioned themselves strategically to get a look at the star when he came in. He was in Durham to help with a benefit for our state chapter of the National Society to Prevent Blindness, an organization dedicated to the preservation of sight. But Ronnie was also having some problems with one eye and asked if he might be seen by the glaucoma person at Duke, which is how I came into the picture.

His warmth was apparent the moment I walked into the room, where he sat in the examination chair. Although he had no vision in either eye, he "looked" straight at me when he spoke, belying any evidence of a person without sight. His easy-going nature and good humor immediately made me feel comfortable around him. After a brief chat about Duke basketball and his participation in the benefit the night before, we got down to the matter of his medical condition.

Ronnie's left eye had been removed many years earlier. Now he was having severe, throbbing pain in his right eye. He had gone to a doctor who gave him a strong painkiller with codeine, which only partially relieved the pain and caused nausea and vomiting. It was interfering with his work and his life, and something more had to be done. He jokingly asked me if medical science had come up with a "bionic eye," like in the popular television show of the time, the *Six Million Dollar Man*. If so, he was willing to be a guinea pig for it. In a much more serious vein, he asked if removing his only remaining eye would close the door to any future chance of regaining sight.

His latter question was one that many people, including scientific investigators, have asked. The problem with glaucoma is that the optic nerve is destroyed all the way from the eye to the brain. The only hope of restoring vision in such circumstances is to achieve regeneration of the nerve. That was not a possibility when Ronnie and I first met, and I doubted that it would be developed in our lifetime (and over thirty years later, it is still only a distant hope). And so, after much serious discussion, we agreed to proceed with the removal of his only remaining eye. Ronnie would later say it was one of the hardest decisions he ever made.

It was early December 1980, and Ronnie's surgery was scheduled for the sixteenth of the month, while his concert tour crew was home for the holidays. Since they were coming to Durham a few days early, Sharon and I invited the Milsaps to dinner at our home the night before Ronnie was to be admitted to the hospital. They kindly accepted, and that evening a large, unmarked bus pulled up in front of our house with Ronnie, his wife, Joyce, and their son, Todd, who was just a few years older than Sarah and John. Todd delighted the children with a tour of the bus, which was outfitted as the Milsaps' home away from home. That was the beginning of a warm friendship between our two families, and during dinner that evening, we learned more about the inspiring life of Ronnie and his family.

He had persevered at Governor Morehead, where he experienced some of his best times—and some of his worst. One of the greatest tragedies in his life occurred during those years, when he was struck by a school employee in his left eye, which could still perceive light. The eye filled with blood, became totally blind and painful, and was finally removed. Before that, he could at least distinguish day from night, but now he was in total darkness. It was a bitter pill for a young boy to swallow, but true to his character, Ronnie did not let it derail his life goals. He would later praise many of his teachers at Governor Morehead, who helped him become proficient at braille, type 120 words per minute, and acquire many other skills. But his greatest accomplishment and his first love was music—in all forms. He could play a dozen instruments, including the violin, cello, guitar, and his favorite, the piano. When he graduated with distinction at age nineteen, who could have known he would one day return as his school's most famous alumnus? The dormitory where he had wept bitterly as a six-year-old and spent his first three years away from home is now called the Ronnie Milsap Dormitory.

With his strong academic performance, Ronnie had scholarship opportunities at many large colleges, but he elected to attend a junior college in Georgia that was close to relatives. He studied pre-law and was on track for law school at Emory University in Atlanta. However, two things happened along the way that would shape the rest of his life: his musical career began to show promise, with bands, performances, and even a recording—and he met the most important person in his life, Joyce Reeves.

Ronnie graduated from junior college in 1964 and married Joyce the following year. The decade that followed was a rough one for the young couple, with an uncertain career singing in honky-tonk nightclubs in Memphis and Nashville. But Ronnie continued to persevere, and Joyce stood by her man, and as they say, the rest is history. By 1976, Ronnie was in the headlines, touring the world's concert halls, and the following year one of his hit records was named "Album of the Year" and he was voted "Entertainer and Male Vocalist of the Year."

That December evening, as we all sat together for the first time in our home, I'm sure my family recognized how privileged we were to have such special and wonderful new friends as Ronnie, Joyce, and Todd. If Ronnie was concerned about his upcoming surgery, he did not show it. But I, for one, was apprehensive.

Following our decision to operate, matters had become increasingly complicated. Ronnie not only had the problem with his eye, but he also had a blockage in his nose that was diagnosed as a deviated septum by an ear, nose, and throat colleague, who recommended surgery. Because of his tight performance schedule, Ronnie asked if both operations might be done at the same time. We knew this would be an awful lot of surgery at one time, but he was strong and healthy, so we agreed. To add to my concern, our anesthesiologist refused to give general anesthesia, which would involve putting a tube down Ronnie's throat. He was understandably concerned about the risk of injuring those valuable vocal chords. That left us with local anesthesia, which meant multiple needle injections around the eye and nose.

The next day I checked Ronnie in to the Duke Eye Center hospital for the necessary preoperative physical exam and laboratory studies. Joyce was visibly distraught about the upcoming surgery, and even though he didn't show it, I suspect Ronnie shared her feelings. The surgical removal of an eye, called enucleation, is difficult for the patient from both physical and emotional standpoints, especially when it is their only remaining eye. It is not an operation that surgeons particularly like to perform, because it represents failure to achieve our primary goal of preserving a healthy, seeing eye. But there are times that it is in the patient's best interest, and I reminded myself that this was clearly the case with Ronnie.

As I drove to the eye center early the next morning, the pale light of day was just beginning to filter down through the bare trees that arched over the road. The sky was gray, and it was cold and a bit misty. I was listening to the local news on the radio, and just as I drove in to the parking lot, the reporter announced that Ronnie Milsap was scheduled to undergo eye surgery at Duke that morning. Stepping from my car, I felt a cold chill go through me and somehow felt that it was not because of the weather.

I visited Ronnie and his family in the hospital room before going with him to surgery. Joyce had obviously been crying, and her eyes were still red and moist. Ronnie, in his characteristic way, was trying to cheer her up with his light-heartedness and good humor. But that only seemed to make her more distraught. I left them alone for a few minutes, and then we walked together down the hall to the operating room beside Ronnie, who was being wheeled on a stretcher. As the doors to the surgical suite swung open, Joyce reluctantly released her husband's hand. Ronnie tried to cheer her up with one last joke, but that just brought more tears. As we left them there, Todd stood by his mother's side, trying to be brave like his father.

I performed the enucleation as the first of the two procedures. It is technically not a difficult operation, and I was satisfied that everything went according to plan. After completing the surgery, I applied a large, tight dressing over the surgical site and then turned Ronnie over to my ENT colleague. Ronnie would later laugh about that experience, as he had listened to the surgeon cutting away on his nose while talking about slaughtering pigs on his farm over the weekend.

When all the surgery was complete and Ronnie was back in his room with a wife whose spirits were noticeably improved, I left them to see my patients in the clinic. Local anesthesia lasts for several hours, and Ronnie was comfortable when I left him. A few hours later, however, I got a call from the ward that he was having severe pain and that the pain medicine I had prescribed for him was not touching it. As I walked up the stairs to check on him, I was convinced that the pain must be coming primarily from the nose, which is typically the more painful of the two procedures. When I entered the room, however, I was chagrined to discover that the pain was coming almost exclusively from the eye surgery.

In those days, it was standard practice to apply a large, bulky head-roll bandage after an enucleation and to leave it in place for five full days. It was taught that, if the pressure of the dressing was relieved prematurely, it might allow severe bleeding or tissue swelling, resulting in an undesirable cosmetic result. I first checked to make sure there was no bleeding through the dressing, which there was not. My next thought was that the dressing might be too tight, so I loosened it as much as I dared. But the pain persisted, and all I could do was increase the strength of the pain medication. Nothing seemed to work until I finally resorted to an injection of morphine, and this only brought partial relief. As I trudged home that evening, I was dismayed by this unexpected turn of events, but I was confident that he would surely be feeling better by the next day.

Early the next morning, I went straight to Ronnie's room and was again disheartened to learn that he had had a terrible night. The morphine, which he was requiring as frequently as allowed, was providing only partial, temporary relief. Joyce had spent the night with him and told me that he would cry out at times that he couldn't take it. Ronnie is not only a big, strong man, but also one who is stoic and not given to unwarranted outbursts of emotion. I knew his pain was real. I wondered if something had torn loose or otherwise gone wrong beneath the dressing, but I was afraid to remove it before the prescribed five days had passed. I tried to put on an outward air of confidence, assuring everyone that things would get better very soon, but I doubt that I convinced anyone.

Those were among the longest five days of my life, and I am sure they were even longer for Ronnie and Joyce. The pain did not let up appreciably, and the only encouragement was that he was gradually able to lengthen the time between morphine injections. When the fifth day finally came, I removed the dressing with a degree of fear and trepidation as to what might be found beneath the bandages. But much to my relief, everything appeared to be in order. The stitches were all holding, and the tissues appeared healthy with good early healing. I was thankful to finally be able to give the Milsaps some encouraging news and to assure them that the pain would soon disappear now that the pressure of the dressing had been relieved. Once again, however, I would be proven wrong.

Although the pain was a bit less, it still could not be controlled with anything less than continued injections of morphine. This now posed a problem, because it was just a few days before Christmas, and the Milsaps did not relish the idea of celebrating it in the Duke Eye Center. They desperately wanted to go home. So we agreed on a plan in which a close family friend, who is a registered nurse, would fly to Durham and drive back to Nashville with the Milsaps, so she could administer the morphine as needed. I gave her several vials of the morphine with suggestions for its use and instructions on care of his eye and nose, and we finally prepared for Ronnie to go home.

On December 23, the bus was ready at the crack of dawn. Ronnie put on a heavy bathrobe over his clothes, slipped on his dark sunglasses beneath a large cowboy hat, and went sauntering down the hall of the hospital, wishing everyone Merry Christmas, as though he had just been on a relaxing vacation.

It was another gray, cold, misty morning, and many of our faculty and staff had already gone home for the holidays. I stood alone in front of the eye center as the bus pulled out and disappeared down the road. I was concerned, of course, as to how Ronnie would get along. But I could also not help wondering what they must be thinking, at that moment, about a doctor who had just put them through a bit of hell.

—

During his hospitalization, between morphine injections, Ronnie was working on the final stages of his latest album. He would later say that this album was one of his personal favorites. It is certainly the most special to me of all his albums, not only because of the time during which it was produced and the music it contains, but most of all because of what it says about Ronnie as a man.

The album is dedicated to "Gentleman" Jim Reeves, another beloved country singer of a slightly earlier era. In one of the songs, written expressly for the album, Ronnie tells of a teenage boy who listened to Gentleman Jim on his radio. Because of Reeves' untimely death, Ronnie never got to meet him, but still considered him to be one of his closest friends and certainly a role model. This is quite appropriate, because Ronnie is also one of the true gentlemen of his profession. He has remained faithful not only to his wife and son, and now their grandchildren, but also to his many friends, including a doctor who once caused him great pain.

A few years later, when I came to Nashville to lecture at Vanderbilt University, the Milsaps insisted that I stay with them. They have two very comfortable guesthouses on either side of the swimming pool behind their lovely southern home, which sits on a palatial, wooded estate. It was my first exposure to how the "rich and famous" live, and I was pleased to find that—for Ronnie and Joyce, at least—they live pretty much like the rest of us. Ronnie gave me a tour of their home, always being careful to turn on the lights when we entered a room for the sole benefit of his guest, although sometimes joking, "My, it's dark in here." He showed me his braille typewriter and his large braille books, which he loved to read. Most impressive was his amateur ham radio room, where he built his own electronic equipment, soldering together the wire circuitry by feel. We had a very relaxing, comfortable evening together, and I think we all sensed a strengthening of our friendship.

On another occasion, when our family was driving to Oklahoma, we stopped in Nashville at the invitation of the Milsaps to spend a few days with them. It was during an annual event in Nashville called Fan Fair in which the country recording industry promotes their latest recordings and the fans get a chance to meet their favorite recording artists. It was a huge affair, held at the county fairgrounds, and made me realize what a broad-based and loyal following this industry has, with fans coming from all parts of the country. But of all the performers, at least that year, there was no doubt that Ronnie was the most popular. I stood back and marveled at how he captivated the throngs of adoring admirers who crowded around him.

Later that afternoon, we went back to the Milsaps' home and had a pleasant, quiet visit beside their pool while the three children played on Todd's skateboard ramp. As evening approached, a sleek, gray limousine pulled up in the driveway, and Ronnie announced that it was time to go to dinner. Sarah sat in the back seat on Ronnie's lap and loved it when he said to the chauffer in his deep voice, "To the Casbah, James." We dined at one of the finest restaurants in Nashville, and it was obvious that the Milsaps were well known to all the staff there by the special attention we received. I suppose the privilege of having Ronnie Milsap's patronage was sufficient reason for their attentiveness, but when I saw the generous tips he gave everyone, I realized there was added incentive.

As we drove on toward Oklahoma the next day, Sarah and John still had stars in their eyes. And I think all four of us felt privileged to have such special friends.

—

One of the problems with having prominent and wealthy patients is that the hospital administrators expect you to pressure them for charitable donations. It is true that academic medical centers could not provide their vital programs without the generosity of private donors. It is very expensive to educate medical students, interns, residents, and fellows, and even more expensive to conduct the medical research that allows each new generation of doctors to give their patients the best possible care.

At Duke Eye Center, we were fortunate to have a skillful and caring fundraiser by the name of Sandy Scarlett. She was very effective in helping people give away their money and in making them feel good about doing it. But she depended on the doctors to help her by identifying potential donors among our patients and making the first ask. Sandy and I had talked about Ronnie, who was obviously a prime candidate for a major gift, but I simply did not know how to go about it. For me, one of the hardest things in the world is to ask people for money. Then one day, it just seemed to fall into my lap.

The call came from a lawyer in Detroit, which seemed like a long way from Nashville. He explained that he represented Ronnie Milsap, who was establishing the Ronnie Milsap Foundation to provide financial assistance for the education of young people with visual handicaps and to fund research in university medical centers for the prevention of blindness. The lawyer said that Ronnie wanted me to serve on the board of trustees for his foundation, and he hinted that it could prove beneficial for Duke. Talk about divine intervention! I was appropriately thankful.

My elation was somewhat tempered, however, as I began to learn more about the entertainment industry. Lesson one was that the stars do not enjoy complete independence, but must adhere to certain rules and demands of the companies for which they work. Lesson two was that a performer's schedule can be very unpredictable and inflexible, and that certain events must be squeezed in when time allows, often at a moment's notice. Thus it was that the lawyer informed me that the first meeting of the board of trustees was to be held in Nashville—that weekend. It gave me a moment's pause, but I fortunately did not have any conflicts for the weekend (and would have cancelled virtually anything, anyway). So I gratefully accepted and immediately called an airline for reservations.

The meeting was held at one of the nicest hotels in Nashville. The board was composed of about twenty individuals from all parts of the country and from all walks of life. There were recording artists, executive directors of organizations for the visually handicapped, and captains of industry. They were all prominent in their particular fields and not only had the potential to help organize effective fundraising programs, but many could also dig deeply into their own pockets—or so the foundation hoped. The only other physician on the board was the chairman of Kresge Eye Institute in Detroit—I was beginning to learn that Detroit and Nashville have rather close ties through the country music industry. He was a little older than me, but we quickly bonded since we both felt a bit out of place among the powerful board members. He and I were appointed as a subcommittee of two to recommend which medical centers in the country should be first to receive the foundation's funding for research. It probably came as no surprise to anyone when we proposed that Duke and Kresge should be the first recipients. The board accepted our recommendation with minimal discussion, probably because Ronnie was in agreement with it. And so we seemed to be well on our way toward significant funding for research in our institutions.

When I returned to Durham, I was anxious to tell Sandy and our chairman and everyone else in the eye center of my accomplishment. They shared my enthusiasm, and we began to consider options as to how the money might best be used. But weeks passed, and then months, and there was no check in the mail. I finally called the lawyer in Detroit to inquire as to the status of the funds. He assured me that Ronnie was still committed to making a major donation to Duke but that the fundraising was progressing a bit slower than had been anticipated. So we waited.

It was nearly a year later when a memo on my desk informed me of a call from Detroit that I was asked to return. 'This is it,' I thought. But it turned out that the call was to request my attendance at the next meeting of the board of trustees, which was to be held at the Detroit Athletic Club. It came as no surprise when I learned that the meeting would be in less than two weeks. So, with somewhat less enthusiasm than the first time, I again scurried to make my flight reservation.

The Detroit Athletic Club is one of those venerable, exclusive, and somewhat stodgy institutions of vintage brick and stone with dark, hardwood halls adorned with old paintings of someone's relatives. I arrived a bit early and decided to spend some time in the reading room (at least that seemed to be the appropriate name for it). It was a large, darkly paneled room, with shelves of dusty, ancient books, dull brass chandeliers, thick Persian rugs, deep leather wingback chairs, and the stale aroma of cigars. I sank into one of the chairs and tried to concentrate on a book, but could not resist studying the others in the room, who I assumed were members of the club. They moved about slowly with an air of privilege, speaking in hushed voices and carrying their *Wall Street Journal*s, which seemed to be primarily for sleeping under. They were, for the most part, octogenarians, and while they may well have once been athletes, that title now seemed to be among the laurels on which they rested.

The scene in the reading room was in striking contrast to the bright and boisterous reception in the club's ballroom later that evening, which marked the opening of the board meeting for the Ronnie Milsap Foundation. In addition to the board members, there was a large gathering of Detroit's celebrities and leading citizens, who sparkled in their evening gowns and tuxedos. But one person was notably absent. Ronnie had every intention of being there, but at the last minute his recording company needed him elsewhere. This was yet another example for me of how demanding and confining is the life of a top entertainer. While the rest of us were sleeping that night, he would be out somewhere on the road in his bus—in fact, he might even be running down the highway. To keep in shape, he and a coworker would often get off the bus in the middle of the night and run for a mile or so to where the bus would be waiting for them. It must have been a strange sight for nocturnal travelers as they drove past the early morning joggers. On one occasion, they were stopped by a highway patrol car and had to do a bit of explaining as to what they were up to. But that was Ronnie.

The next morning, the board members convened around a large oak table to begin our business. The mood was not quite as upbeat as it had been at the first meeting in Nashville. The initial year of fundraising had not been as productive as had been anticipated. It was at a time of financial uncertainty in the country, and most charitable organizations were feeling the effect. But there was some money, thanks primarily to Ronnie's personal contributions, and it was agreed that this should be used first to provide scholarships for visually handicapped young people. The names of the recipients were announced, which was clearly the high point of the board meeting. It was then reported that there were as yet no funds available to support research at the medical centers, but that Ronnie remained committed to this pledge. I could not disagree with the board's priorities, but I did feel a bit disheartened as I returned home with only promises.

Another year passed, and another call came to inform me that the next board meeting would again be at the Detroit Athletic Club—where I was starting to feel at home—but this time I had nearly a month to make my arrangements. Ronnie and Joyce were there, which was fortunate, since Ronnie was scheduled to give a benefit concert in conjunction with the meeting. It was a black-tie affair, which began with a gala reception in the Athletic Club that was even better attended than the year before. In addition to a host of Detroit's leading citizens, there were both local and national celebrities.

The theater where the concert was to be held was just a few blocks from the club, and most of us walked. There was standing room only, and the audience was particularly impressive in their glittering evening gowns and tuxedos. It was obvious that a considerable amount of wealth and prestige was represented collectively in the theater that evening. But everything else paled when the curtains rose and Ronnie began his performance.

It was the first time I had seem him give a full, live concert, and to say it exceeded my expectations would be quite an understatement. He truly has a gift for captivating his audience. He seems to put everything he has into each performance, as though it is the most important one he has ever done or ever will do. And what made it doubly amazing to me that evening was that no one who did not know him could have guessed that he was doing it all without sight. The way he moved about the stage, even standing on his piano bench, and the way he "looked" directly at his audience, often coming toward them within inches of the edge of the stage, were not the typical moves of a person who is blind. I suspect that most people in the theater that evening, who were only vaguely aware that Ronnie was visually handicapped, must have assumed that he had some useful vision. What they didn't realize was that every move was carefully orchestrated, even down to the toe cues—ridges at the edge of the stage—to maintain his orientation. There had been those rare occasions, however, when even the best laid plans went awry—like the time he missed the toe cue and fell into the orchestra pit. True to form, he just laughed it off, got back onstage and finished the concert with a broken finger. But that evening in Detroit, his performance was flawless, and everyone must have realized that they had just witnessed one of the music industry's most gifted performers, if not its most dedicated.

As I moved with the flow of the crowd from the theater, listening to the enthusiastic comments about the performance, it suddenly struck me like a bolt of lightning. This was the way to raise money for our department! If Ronnie would agree to give a charity concert in Durham to benefit the Duke Eye Center, it was bound to be a success. I raised the possibility with Ronnie the following morning, and he was immediately enthusiastic about it and told me to consider it done. And so I again returned to Durham, but this time with more hope than ever.

But the months again passed, and then a year, with no word about the concert. Ronnie had warned me that he could not promise how soon it would be and that he might have to work it into one of his tours when the occasion arose. But as the time passed, I began to wonder if we would ever see our Ronnie Milsap concert at Duke. Then one day the lawyer from Detroit called. My spirits fell slightly when he explained that he was calling to ask if we might have the next board meeting in Durham. I told him I was sure we could arrange for that. And then he hit me with the long awaited news—while he was there, Ronnie would give the charity concert for Duke Eye Center!

To say that I was overjoyed would be the grossest of understatements, but I quickly came back down to earth when the lawyer gave me the timetable. Based on past experience, I don't know why I should have been surprised. Actually, this was the most time I had been given yet—six whole weeks. I asked the lawyer if this was enough time to organize a concert, and he assured me that it was. So I thanked him, hung up the phone, and sat there for some time trying to collect my thoughts.

The next thing I did was call Sandy, who would be responsible for organizing both the board meeting and the concert. She was, of course, as elated as I had been initially, until I gave her the date. There was a long silence at her end, as I am sure she was counting the number of weeks until that date. "Can we do it that fast?" she asked. I told her the lawyer said we could, but I doubt if the tone of my voice was very convincing. There was now an even longer silence, as she was undoubtedly trying to think of all that would have to be done between now and then. I don't think she was quite as convinced as the lawyer that it was possible, maybe because it would be her and not him that would have to do it. But she assured me that she would give it her best shot, and I am quite sure that she went to work on it at that very moment.

It is probably not stretching the truth to say that it was our development office's finest hour. Sandy had two capable people working with her in the office, and the work those three folks did over the next six weeks would qualify for the fundraiser's hall of fame if there was such a thing.

The first thing we needed was a place to hold the concert. The good news was that the date was in late June, when most of the Duke students had gone home for the summer, and we were able to get Cameron Indoor Stadium. The bad news was that Cameron is not air-conditioned and can get pretty toasty that time of year, especially when packed with several thousand warm bodies. But we were thankful to get anything at this late date and gladly signed the contract. Obviously, we didn't have a clue as to how the building should be prepared for a concert. But the Cameron staff assured us that they knew the basic requirements and would get in touch with the Milsap people regarding details, so that everything would be ready for them to set up their equipment on the afternoon before the evening concert.

The next step was to find a venue for the board meeting. For this we were able to procure the President's House, which is a rather palatial home in Duke Forest that was built for the president of the university, but which the presidents apparently didn't like, and which, therefore, was converted to a housing and meeting facility for university-related functions. So far, so good.

We then turned to the more difficult issue of selling tickets. Sandy found a printing company to make the tickets and a few vending locations around the city for ticket sales. Our concert seemed to be well on the way, but the hardest part still lay before us: getting the word out to the community. Late June is probably not the best time of year for a concert, with graduations, weddings and vacations competing for the time. And advertising for a major concert in the proper way required significant funds, which we simply didn't have. So, with a little more than a month to go, we printed our own posters and began hand delivering them to every establishment in town that would let us put them up. We were also able to get a few local radio stations to promote the charity concert as a public service announcement. Our head football coach at the time, Steve Sloan, was a fan of Ronnie and was kind enough to do a television spot for us on a noontime program.

While all this was going on, I was in the process of finalizing the second edition of my glaucoma textbook. Because of my friendship with Ronnie and my admiration for him, I decided to dedicate the book to him. But I wanted him to at least be able to read the dedication, which meant doing it in braille in the copy I would present to him. After a little checking around, I discovered a gentleman who was blind and worked as a masseur in his home. We spoke on the phone, I explained the situation, and he said he would be glad to help. So one afternoon, I drove to his house, which was modest but tidy and filled with the aroma of rubbing liniment, a mark of his trade. He led me back to his office, feeling the wall as he went, and we sat down at his desk. I had seen Ronnie's typewriter, which prints in braille, but this gentleman had only a metal stylus and template, with which he punched out the characters on a thick paper with amazing agility and speed. Within seconds, Ronnie's dedication was complete, and I was so grateful, but my new friend refused to accept any money. So I returned to my office, feeling that we were now ready for Ronnie's arrival. But my optimism would soon prove to be premature.

Our fears regarding the impact of a late start, limited advertisement resources, and the time of year were starting to be realized. Ticket sales indicated that we would have a good attendance, but not a packed house. As the board members began arriving at the President's House, this was a point of concern. The lawyer, who had assured me that we had enough time, now seemed to imply that we should not have agreed to the concert if we didn't think we could do it in the allotted time. He pointed out the negative impact this could have on Ronnie's reputation, which we had certainly appreciated. But then Ronnie arrived, and everything suddenly seemed to be okay.

He was late because of mechanical problems while crossing the mountains, and with the concert scheduled for that evening, we were all starting to worry. But the bus finally pulled up to the President's House in the early afternoon, and Ronnie stepped out with his usual flare of enthusiasm and good humor. He did not seem concerned about the ticket sales, but just laughed and said, "We'll have a good time." And we did from that point on. The board meeting broke up by late afternoon, and we all went off to freshen up for the evening.

Sandy had arranged a lovely reception for Ronnie in a building on the Duke campus not far from the concert site. On our way there, Sharon and the children and I stopped by the President's House, where the board members were staying, to see if anyone needed a ride. Sarah and John were thrilled when our rider turned out to be Richard Sturben, bass singer for the very popular Oak Ridge Boys. The reception was a festive affair, with dignitaries from across the university and community. Everyone wanted to have their picture taken with Ronnie. We had a brief ceremony, during which I thanked Ronnie for all that he had done for Duke and for so many people. I then presented him with the book that I had dedicated to him, whereupon he gave me a bear hug that nearly took my breath away.

It was a warm, clear summer evening as we walked over to Cameron Indoor Stadium. I was encouraged to see that the parking lot was nearly full and that a large crowd was moving in our same direction. We did not fill the stadium that evening, but it was a very good size audience, and if Ronnie was disappointed by less than a sellout, he certainly never showed it. He came on the stage to a roaring ovation and proceeded to give us a performance that again seemed like it was the most important one he had ever done. The less-than-full house was more than made up for by the enthusiasm of those in attendance, all of whom obviously loved Ronnie. They shouted, clapped to the music, sang along, and even danced in the aisles. When it was over, I think we were all drained, but we unanimously agreed that we had just experienced a truly special moment in our lives.

After the concert, I tried to get backstage to thank Ronnie, but was delayed by well-wishers. When I finally did get outside where his bus had been waiting for him it was gone. One of his crew members told me that he said to say good-bye and to apologize for rushing off, but he had to drive all night to get ready for his next concert, which was the following evening. I was sorry to have missed him, but was thankful that the frenetic events of the past six weeks had come to a successful conclusion. There was a cool breeze outside, and I enjoyed a moment of quiet solitude as I thought about Ronnie and his people heading back to Nashville.

The bus would be crossing over the Smoky Mountains in the middle of the night. It would be dark and quiet in those mountains, as though they were protecting their stories for another day—stories of Indians trying to preserve their heritage; of pioneers who built log cabins and whiskey stills; of workers during the Great Depression, who gave us the Blue Ridge Parkway; and of mountain women, who toiled over hot stoves to provide nutritious meals for their families and even now for weary travelers. Sometime during the night, the bus would pass within a few miles of a steep mountain slope, where a four-room cabin once stood and a boy spent his first six years. There too is a story that the mountains preserve. It is a story of courage, a story of perseverance, a story of hard work and making the most of one's gifts, a story of an open and loving heart, and a story of faith in God. It is also a story of good fortune. But even if Ronnie Milsap had not risen from his humble beginnings to become an internationally renowned celebrity, I believe his story would be no less inspiring.

For those who truly know him, I believe Ronnie's legacy will be the gift of seeing life through a giving and forgiving heart. He has certainly given of himself, not only in bringing joy to millions through his music, but also in helping visually handicapped children receive hope through education, in supporting medical research to preserve sight, and in so many other ways that continue even today. Ronnie could be excused for being bitter about the hand that was dealt to him: a mother who abandoned him, a school employee who robbed him of his last vestige of vision, and even a doctor who caused him undue pain. But he was able to look beyond the bitterness and the hurts and to see, through a forgiving heart, the beauty of new possibilities for happiness that open to those who are not blinded by their misfortune, but who can see the opportunities that are waiting just around the corner.

6.

Rei-Ying and Raimonda

A small commuter plane sat all alone at the end of a runway in the still darkness, just before dawn. Somewhere beyond the tarmac, a thin ribbon of reddish-orange glow was beginning to split the darkness into earth and sky. The stillness too was suddenly split by the piercing whine of twin turboprop engines, straining to propel the little plane, which seemed unwilling to move. Inside the plane, a small band of sleepy passengers was brusquely aroused to full alertness by the deafening roar of the engines and the violent shaking of the entire plane, which was still making no forward progress. The pilot had warned us that this would happen. It was standard operating procedure to check out the plane before the first flight of each day by revving up the engines with the brakes locked. We all had window seats, because there was only one row of seats on either side of the aisle, but there was nothing to see outside in the darkness, and I suspect all of us were more focused on hoping the plane would pass the test. Moments later, the brakes were released and we lurched forward down the runway. Soon we were skimming over the tops of pine trees, leaving Raleigh-Durham International Airport behind and heading into a gray morning sky.

As we gained altitude, I began to relax and enjoy the view down below, where another day was starting, with lights coming on in homes and cars beginning to traverse the roads. I was also able now to muse on the irony of how inauspicious was the start to the longest trip of my life. My destination was the heart of mainland China, where I would be working with an organization called Orbis. Fortunately, this first leg of my trip was just a short flight to Washington, D.C., where I would transfer to a larger plane. I comforted myself in thinking that the remainder of the trip—although two days and ten thousand miles—would be more relaxing and less adventuresome than the outset had been; but it was just as well that I did not know what lay ahead.

Orbis is one of many fine organizations that are dedicated to improving health care around the world. The need for such care is great—actually overwhelming—but the specific needs vary considerably in different parts of the world. In some areas, the basic infrastructure for adequate health care is nonexistent, and individuals and groups have gone into many of these areas to build clinics and hospitals and to provide clean water and proper sanitation. In other areas, the problem is insufficient numbers of health care providers to serve the overwhelming masses in need. Here, medical missionary teams may provide full-time care in underserved communities or come in on a short-term basis to provide medical and surgical treatment for large numbers of patients. In still other parts of the world, the need is not so much for more doctors and other health care providers, but for better medical education. It is easy for those of us who are privileged to live in more prosperous nations to take for granted the excellent education that our doctors and nurses receive both in school and in continuing education throughout their careers. But doctors in many parts of the world, who want to give their patients the best possible care, lack proper training and yearn for better education. One approach to this problem is for teams of medical educators to work with local physicians in clinics, operating rooms, and lecture halls on a short-term basis to upgrade their skills and improve the quality of medical care they can provide their communities. This latter approach is the mission of Orbis.

Orbis was launched in the early 1980s, based on the dream of a prominent Texas ophthalmologist. In his world travels, he observed that eye doctors and nurses in many countries could not afford to attend medical meetings to keep up with the continuous advances in their field. He proposed bringing the education to them in the form of a flying eye hospital. He and a small group of supporters were able to procure a vintage DC-8, which was donated to the nonprofit organization after a long life as a commercial airliner. They also obtained private donations, which they used to convert the plane into a flight-worthy operating unit for eye surgery that traveled around the world providing the facilities for educators to update local physicians and nurses on the latest in medical and surgical eye care.

The headquarters for the organization is in New York City, where a full-time staff confronts the logistic and diplomatic challenges of maintaining a busy, worldwide schedule of outreach programs. Every mission project has to be arranged years in advance as the staff works with local and national governments and medical communities. Many countries are sensitive about the adequacy of the health care they provide their people, and a front team from Orbis meets with the political and medical leaders to assure them of their goodwill and of the benefits they have to offer their community. Permission is usually granted, and arrangements are then made for a visit by the flying eye hospital and its team of medical educators.

A commercial pilot volunteers his time to fly the plane from one location to the next, where operations are set up at the local airport. Regional doctors and nurses are invited well in advance to attend the several-week program, and the event is usually well attended not only by health care professionals, but also by politicians and the media. Orbis has a full-time staff of physicians, nurses, and technicians who travel with the plane to oversee the daily operations and provide continuity for the programs. In addition, surgeons are invited to volunteer their time for short tours to demonstrate and lecture on the latest advances in special aspects of eye surgery. It was for the latter purpose that I was embarking on my trip to China.

The sun was well into the sky as our little plane touched down at Washington International. Although my journey had barely begun, I felt a sense of relief to have this leg of it behind me. It was turning into a beautiful day, and I looked forward to the next leg of the flight, which would be across the country to San Francisco. This has always been one of my favorite flights because of the panoramic view it affords of our country's vast and diverse geographic beauty. Almost immediately after leaving our nation's capital, the verdant Appalachian Mountains can be seen, stretching northeast and southwest as far as the eye can see. Gradually, the mountains recede and eventually give way to America's heartland, where thousands of farms provide of mosaic of varied colors and geometric patterns. This goes on for a couple of hours before the next mountain range comes into view—the majestic, snow-covered Rocky Mountains. The magnitude of these mountains gives a sense that the plane is flying at a lower altitude. But soon they are left behind and the seemly barren desert land of the Great Basin comes into view. This segment of the flight is the most fascinating to me, because of the vast stretches in which no sign of life can be seen, other than lonely roads that seem to be going nowhere. Then a final range of relatively low mountains, the Sierra Nevada, takes the stage, as the plane begins its descent across the lush valleys of California and into San Francisco.

Because we had gained three hours in time zones, it was only noon when we arrived on the west coast. One final leg of the first day's journey lay ahead: an eleven-hour flight across the Pacific Ocean to Hong Kong, where I was scheduled to spend the night at an airport hotel. I was intrigued by the thought that this would be the longest time I had ever sat in an airplane. As it turned out, however, it would be even longer than advertised. We had stiff head winds for much of our flight, which slowed the plane and consumed additional fuel, leaving us without enough to make it to Hong Kong—the next adventure on my journey. The captain announced our situation and explained that we would be making an unscheduled stop in Okinawa for refueling. As it turned out, this was not unusual, and the captain assured us that it was part of a contingency plan and standard operating procedure, much as our commuter pilot had tried to assuage our fears that morning—which now seemed like an awfully long time ago.

My memory of Okinawa is only a nondescript tarmac at nighttime as seen through the small window of our 747. We did not get off the plane and were no doubt collectively relieved when, within about thirty minutes, we were again airborne and soon making our approach into Hong Kong. But the day held one final adventure. We were heading straight toward a large hillside that sat perpendicular to the runway. At what seemed like the last minute, our jumbo jet made an abrupt and sharp right-angle turn and dropped down onto the Hong Kong landing strip. Once again, however, it was simply SOP. The hilly terrain around the old Hong Kong Airport, which has since been replaced, did not allow a direct approach to the runway, at least not for the large, international carriers. It was necessary, therefore, to head straight toward the hillside and make the last minute turn before the final approach to the tarmac. Of course, we couldn't see our apparent peril in the dark, but the sudden, sharp turn caught everyone's attention, and we gave a collective sigh as the wheels touched down. The following morning, while waiting for my next flight, I was fascinated as I watched this remarkable landing by one huge airliner after another, as they came in from all parts of the world.

The airport hotel was comfortable and more than welcome. Although it was only 9 p.m. local time on the first day of my journey, I had crossed twelve time zones and had been traveling for over twenty-four hours. Fortunately, my next flight was not until around noon, so I was able to sleep in and enjoy a leisurely breakfast. It was another beautiful morning, and as I sipped a second cup of coffee, I began thinking about where I would be by the end of the day. My destination was the city of Chengdu in the Sichuan Province of southwest China. Sadly, because of the tragic earthquake in 2008, the city is now known around the world. But on that morning in March of 1989, it was only one of thousands of unfamiliar cities in a vast country, and yet one that would soon become forever an important part of my life.

Up to this point, I had been flying on United States carriers, but the remainder of the trip would be on Chinese planes under the auspices of the Civil Aviation Administration of China, or CAAC. As I boarded the plane, it seemed that I was the only Westerner on the flight, which should not have surprised me, since our destination was far from the standard tourist locations. We were scheduled to make one stop in Guangzhou, which is only about one hundred miles from Hong Kong, before a final eight-hundred-mile flight to Chengdu. I was hoping it would be a direct flight so I would not have to change planes. But such was not to be the case, and for a while that afternoon, I thought I might be spending the rest of my life in Guangzhou.

After landing at Guangzhou, everyone got off the plane, and I figured that I had better do the same. As we made our way down a rather ancient-looking, portable stairway, I saw that our plane was in the middle of the tarmac, quite some distance from the terminal, toward which my fellow passengers were heading on foot. It was a scene that I had never before witnessed: planes in a seemingly haphazard distribution all over the tarmac, hundreds of passengers walking to and fro among them, and airport employees whizzing around on their bicycles. Inside the terminal, I suddenly found myself in a crush of people, all of whom seemed to know where they were going, except for me—I didn't have a clue.

At first I thought it might be wise to follow some of my fellow passengers from the first flight, but it soon became obvious that they were heading into the city. So I returned to the terminal, as a sense of concern began to approach panic. As far as I could tell, I was the only Westerner in the terminal. No one seemed to speak English, and I didn't even know enough Chinese to say "Help".

I found Chengdu on the departure board, beside the equivalent in Chinese characters, which I attempted to commit to memory. The board also provided what appeared to be the departure gate, but I couldn't figure out the system of getting from the exit door to the appropriate plane. I noticed that large groups of passengers would congregate at a departure gate and then hurry off across the tarmac in various directions to one of several different planes. My problem, of course, was knowing which plane was mine. So I began glancing down at tickets that other passengers were holding, hoping to find someone with a Chengdu ticket, whom I would then follow to our plane. The only problem was that it was nearly two hours before our flight, and I would have to wait until my fellow passengers began congregating at our departure gate if I was to have any hope of finding the right ticket holder.

The Guangzhou terminal was large, but didn't seem to have a single chair. Most people were sitting on their suitcases or on the floor. I only had a small, cloth bag, which didn't make a suitable seat, and the floor did not seem to be a good option either. It, like nearly everything else in the terminal, was covered by a considerable layer of dust. This was my first realization that mainland China did not seem to adhere to the same standards of hygiene of other Asian cultures that I had visited. And so I stood and waited.

As departure time approached, I joined the crowd gathering at my gate and began looking over shoulders for someone whose ticket matched the Chinese characters on the departure board. Much to my relief, I found someone who seemed to have a match and stuck with that person like glue as we scurried across the tarmac. As we entered the plane, I still wasn't sure if I was on the right one, but the flight attendant looked at my ticket and gave me a reassuring nod. With a great sense of relief—and not a little self-congratulation—I found my seat, sat down, leaned back to relax, and promptly collapsed on the passenger behind me.

I tried to figure out how to lock the back of my seat in the upright position, but it kept collapsing into the lap of the poor passenger behind me. No one, flight attendants included, seemed concerned with my plight or offered any assistance, so I leaned forward for the entirety of the flight. I was just so thankful to have found the right plane and to be on the final leg of my journey that I didn't really mind the inconvenience. Even the supper that we were provided—a box of rice with a half dozen peas on top—tasted great.

It was dark by the time we finally landed in Chengdu. As I stepped off the plane and looked about, the first thing I saw was rather thrilling. The dim light from the terminal was just enough to illuminate the sleek silhouette of a DC-8 with the Orbis logo on the tail. What thrilled me even more at that moment, however, was a tall, blond woman who stood nearly a head above all the others in a crowd that was waiting outside to greet the passengers. She waved, and after I was able to make my way to her, she introduced herself as one of the nurses on the Orbis crew.

We drove through the dark night and into a dimly lit city to the hotel that would be my home for the next week. We then went directly to a briefing session that was already in progress. There I met the rest of the Orbis team, which included an old and dear friend, Dr. Jim Martone, who had worked with me at Duke and was now medical director for Orbis. It was a good feeling to have finally reached my destination and to be with this dedicated group of people, and I was looking forward to what lay ahead.

I awoke on my first morning in Chengdu anxious to see what the city looked like in the light of day. Although it might be considered a medium-size town in China, the city has a population of four million. With our hotel situated in the middle of town and it being the start of a workday, I expected considerable noise and activity. As I opened the window of my hotel room, the first impression to touch my senses was the strong odor of burning coal, the fuel used for most heating and cooking. The next sense to be affected was my hearing—more precisely, I was stuck by the lack of any auditory stimulus. There was an eerie silence that seemed inappropriate for a city of four million at the height of rush hour. But as I looked down from my fourth-story window, through the early morning haze, I saw that the street below me was, in fact, clogged with people, all moving silently and in unison on their bicycles.

After a breakfast of oranges and tea in my room, I went downstairs to join the crew and board a van that would take us to our first day on the job. As was the custom for Orbis, this first day would be spent in a local hospital, screening several hundred patients to select those who would undergo surgery in our flying eye hospital throughout the remainder of the week. And so we headed off, our Chinese driver honking and weaving through a maze of bicycle riders, who seemed to pay us no mind.

As we drove toward the hospital, I was disappointed with the views out the window. I was hoping to see the Chinese architecture of the travel books—the pagoda-style structures with their gracefully upturned roofs and red walls, gilded with ornate gold. Instead I saw plain, uninspiring buildings of gray concrete or red brick, which I soon learned is typical of the communist era. When we arrived at the hospital grounds, however, it was obvious that we were back in an earlier era. Although they were old and dirty, the buildings were of the more traditional, ancient Chinese architecture. We were told that this was the West China University of Medical Sciences.

We were let out of our van at one of the ornate gateway entrances to the medical campus and walked for several blocks along dirt paths between decaying but fascinating examples of Oriental architecture. At one point, we passed a long pool, transected by two arched bridges and lined by several ornate buildings. At the far end of the pool stood the largest and most beautiful of the buildings. It was about five stories in height, with each level diminishing in size from the one beneath it and separated by pagoda-style roofs, with a steep, graceful, Oriental roof topping it off. In my mind, I could only imagine how it once looked—lily pads on placid, reflecting water in the pool, surrounded by a profusion of green, manicured bushes setting off the stately red and gold buildings. But now there was only mud in the pool, most of the bushes were dead, and the buildings were faded from age and dirt.

On the other side of the road, a small structure caught my eye. It was set back from the road and apart from the other buildings. It was one of the most ornate structures that I saw that morning, and yet it was in the worst condition of them all. An old wooden cart, half-filled with straw, sat on the packed earth in front of the building. Most of the windows were boarded up, but through one I could see that it was being used to store bales of straw and a few garden utensils. It was hard to make out any details of the dirty, ill-kept structure, but above the front entrance I thought I could discern the faint outline of a cross.

It was a long and very busy day. Instead of hundreds, it seemed like there were thousands of patients lined up outside the hospital doors, patiently waiting to be seen by the Western doctors. We also had several Chinese doctors and nurses from the university hospital, who were there to help us and to observe. Most of them, especially the doctors, spoke reasonably good English. In my travels around the world, I have always been impressed by how the professional people have mastered English as a second language. It has become, at least in the medical profession, an international language. I am always embarrassed and apologetic that they speak my language and I have not taken the time to learn at least a little of theirs. But on that busy day, I was grateful that they could expedite our work by translating our communication with the patients.

I was impressed not only with the Chinese doctors' ability to speak English, but also with their knowledge and skill, and especially with their dedication to helping their patients. They did not have the equipment or access to continuing medical education that we enjoy in the United States, but they made up for much of that through devotion to their work and compassion for their patients. With so many people to care for, they have to put in long hours, with meager compensation, but they do it without complaining. I quickly gained great respect for them. The chairman of the ophthalmology department, who went by Jimmy among his Western colleagues, was an especially capable, dedicated, and affable gentleman. We became good friends and have kept in touch over the decades.

The room in which we examined the patients was large, with chairs around the periphery where many of the patients waited to be seen. Since the patients did not speak English, the doctors were able to talk among themselves about a patient's status without concern of being overheard by the other patients. At one point during the morning, I asked Jimmy about the small, boarded-up building I had seen on the way in. For a moment, I felt a tension in the room as the other doctors exchanged glances. But Jimmy smiled and replied in a relaxed, friendly manner that it was just a shed that the gardeners used for straw and tools and was of no significance. I was content to drop the subject, but noticed that one of the patients, an elderly woman, suddenly become rather agitated, if not angered, by the comment. It seemed that she was about to say something, but then she sat back with an expression of disgust. However, since our conversation had been in English, I assumed that her apparent response was just my imagination.

The next day we drove out to the airport for our first day of surgery on the plane. Except for the brief glance on the night of my arrival, I had never seen the Orbis plane and was fascinated to discover what they had done with it. The original DC-8 has since been replaced by a more spacious, wide-body DC-10, but the older plane had great character, and every inch of available space was utilized.

In the tail section, the bathrooms also served as dressing rooms, where the doctors and nurses donned their surgical scrubs. Adjacent to this was the sterile processing room, which was used for cleaning and sterilizing the surgical instruments and washing and storing the linens. If one proceeded forward through a door, the next section was the operating suite, which had state-of-the-art equipment for microscopic eye surgery. However, it was a small room with limited access, and since the principal mission of Orbis is to update surgeons and nurses by demonstrating new surgical techniques, the room was equipped with television cameras to allow remote viewing of the surgery.

One of the remote viewing sites was just forward of the operating suite, where some of the original passenger seats had been left as a small classroom. However, this did not begin to accommodate the more than one hundred eye doctors who had come from all parts of the region to take advantage of this learning opportunity. My regard for the dedication of the Chinese doctors was further heightened when I learned that these doctors were staying in modest hotels near the airport, where several shared a single bed. Most of them never even had a chance observe on the plane, but spent each day in an airport building that had been converted into a classroom with remote television viewing. In both classrooms, attendees could observe live surgery, as well as lectures that were given in the onboard classroom, with the television monitors serving as the screens for slides that accompanied the lectures. A small section of the plane, adjacent to the classroom, had been converted into a communications center, where a technician controlled all these video interactions.

The final section of the plane, forward of the classroom and communications center and just aft of the cockpit, was the laser room. This was equipped with two modern lasers, which also had video cameras for remote viewing. Even the space in the cockpit was not wasted—this was where the patients waited before and after their laser surgery.

The days spent on the plane were long and intense. When one of us was not operating, we would be in the classroom lecturing. We got back to the hotel late each night, with only enough energy left for supper and brief conversation, and then we were off to bed and another early morning start. But it was immensely rewarding to see the gratitude of both the doctors and the patients and to feel that we were making a significant contribution. I am afraid, however, that the whole experience would have eventually become one indistinguishable blur in my memory, had it not been for the showstopper on the third day of surgery.

Her name was Rei-Ying, and she was scheduled for the second operation of the morning. In general, her appearance was much like that of all the other patients—poor and dressed in peasants' clothing. But of all the patients I had seen during the past four days, there was something distinguishing about her. I couldn't quite recall why she seemed to stand out in my mind. Maybe it was the way she carried herself with an air of dignity. Maybe it was the look of intelligence in her eyes. Although she was in her mid-eighties, she was alert and seemed to take in everything around her with keen interest. But her ability to see was failing. Glaucoma had already robbed her of vision in one eye and was threatening to take what was left in her only seeing eye. A successful operation was her only hope.

She lay on the surgical table in the operating suite of the plane. The other members of our surgery team were back in the sterile processing room, getting the instruments ready for the next case, and I was alone with Rei-Ying. I was preparing to give her an injection of anesthesia beside her eye when she reached up and took my hand. She did not do this in a threatening or apprehensive way, but with a gentleness that seemed to say she wanted a moment of my time before we proceeded. She looked up into my eyes with a serious but serene expression, and then dumbfounded me.

"Are you Christian?" she asked in a soft, firm voice.

I am not sure if I was more amazed by the question or by the fact that she spoke English. But at that moment I remembered why she stood out in my mind—she was the lady who had seemed to want to say something during the first day of screening in the hospital. Now I realized that she could speak English and must have understood everything we were saying that day. But what was it that had caused her such agitation? There was much about this person that I wanted to know. But at that moment, it was important to get on with her surgery, so I just nodded and from behind my surgical mask said "Yes."

With my reply, she closed her eyes, smiled, and gave my hand a gentle squeeze. Then, after a few moments, she opened her eyes and released my hand, as though to say, "You may proceed now." Her surgery went well, and when it was over I put a patch on her eye and told her that everything had gone fine. She again reached up for my hand, smiled in her serene, gentle way and simply said, "Of course."

That afternoon, we did not have any patients or lectures scheduled, so Jim Martone and I went with one of our Chinese hosts to see a major attraction of the area—the Giant Buddha of Leshan. This is an enormous stone statue, carved from the side of a mountain, beginning in the eighth century. It stands seventy-one meters high. It is so huge that Jim and I could both stand on the toenail of the Buddha's big toe and still have room for several others to join us. There was a series of steps carved into the mountain on which visitors could climb from the feet to head of the statue. Along the way, there were many recesses in the stone that we were told had once contained smaller statues of Buddha and other religious images and sayings. But these had all been purposefully destroyed during the Cultural Revolution. At least the government had not blown up the Giant Buddha as the Taliban would do in Afghanistan many years later. Maybe the Chinese were just more practical about the tourist revenue that the statue generated. In any case, their destruction of the smaller religious symbols was a sad reminder of how some governments try to expunge a culture of religions other than their own—or of any religion.

The next day, Friday, was our last day in Chengdu, and we had another full schedule of surgery and lectures. Toward the end of the day, I received a message that one of our surgical patients from earlier in the week was having problems and asked if I might stop by the hospital to see her. It was Rei-Ying.

The driver of the van let me out at the gate to the hospital, and I told the crew I would catch up with them at the hotel later in the evening for our final dinner together. The sun was just setting as I walked past the reflecting pool and the boarded-up building with its cryptic image over the door. The patients were being served dinner in the hospital, but Rei-Ying was happy to leave hers and go with me to the examination room. She seemed to be doing fine. Her vision was only slightly reduced, which is common during the first few days after surgery. She was not having any discomfort. The eye had an excellent pressure and appeared to be healing well. I told her that I could find nothing wrong and thought she was doing very well.

"I know," she responded with a somewhat sheepish smile.

I gave her a quizzical look, and she apologized for bringing me back under false pretenses, but explained that there was something she thought I would want to hear. And this is the story she told me.

"You ask about building that stands alone," she began in her slow, broken English that had just a touch of a British accent. "This campus once called West China Union University. It built with help of Christian missionary group at turn of century. My parents both doctors, and I go to university and become biochemist. Become professor at university. My family loyal to Nationalist Party of Sun Yat-sen. But after civil war in 1940s, after Mao Zedong's Communist Party defeat Nationalist army of Chiang Kai-shek, many our friends move to Taiwan with Chiang. My family choose to stay and try adapt to new ways. But during Cultural Revolution in 1960s, government strip me of professional title and force me into menial labor. Now I live out last days on meager pension."

Her eyes were beginning to mist over, and she had to pause to regain her composure before proceeding with the most difficult part of her story.

"The building you ask about was church of university. That where my parents and I become Christians. I baptized there. My happiest memories are attending services there with my family and friends when I was little girl. After People's Government come into power, they take over university. With Cultural Revolution, we forbidden to worship in church. Christian missionaries forced to leave. Our church closed, and you see what it like today. They try to destroy cross above door, but not possible—just like not possible to destroy flame of faith in heart.

"You take this message please home with you," she concluded. "Tell your people there is flame that still flickers constantly inside us—that cannot be taken away. And someday, when this oppression lifted, flame will burn bright again. And maybe I yet return to worship in my church."

It was dark as I walked back along the dirt path, leading away from the hospital. I was filled with the emotion of having just said good-bye to Rei-Ying. I promised her that I would never forget her story, that I would share it with others, and that we would try to keep in touch. As I passed the church, it was only a silhouette against the night sky. All the ugliness was lost in the darkness, and in my imagination I could see it as it must have once appeared. I could imagine lights in the windows, and music, and Rei-Ying sitting inside with her family and friends.

The following morning, Jim and I flew to Beijing, where he had to make final arrangements for the next Orbis stop in that city, and where we would then spend a couple of days sightseeing before I flew home. We walked for a short distance atop the Great Wall of China, visited the Forbidden City, and stood in Tiananmen Square. Wherever we went, there was a sense of optimism in the air. There was evidence that the government was beginning to relax many of its economic restrictions. Foreign investors were being allowed to enter the country and share ownership with Chinese entrepreneurs. Local citizens were being allowed to set up small shops and keep part of their profits. It gave me hope that, if such freedoms continued to expand, maybe Rei-Ying would yet realize her dream. But as we stood in Tiananmen Square that day, watching locals and tourists mingling casually and peacefully, I could not have guessed what would begin to transpire on this very spot within the next few weeks.

I had only been home for a few days when I was surprised to see Tiananmen Square on the evening news—right where I had stood less than a week before! The television news was reporting that students had occupied the square. At first, it was peaceful, and some of the Orbis crewmembers even joined the crowds. My initial thought was that this was good and that it heralded the acceleration of freedom in China. As the weeks passed, there were many speeches, and the crowds grew larger. Then the tanks came, and on June 4, 1989, the killing began. I watched in horror as this drama played out before the eyes of the world. The optimism for China that I had felt on my return home was now being dashed by the harsh reality of the moment. It was becoming painfully clear that freedom would not come soon to China, at least not likely in the lifetime of Rei-Ying.

———

At the same time that things were going from bad to worse in China, another, more encouraging drama was playing itself out in Eastern Europe. The grip of communism in those countries was inexorably slipping away. In the Soviet Union, Mikhail Gorbachev had been introducing reforms that were giving the people a taste of freedom. As hope spread to neighboring countries, and as Soviet support was gradually withdrawn, one communist regime after another began to fall. Some transitions to democracy were peaceful, as in what was then Czechoslovakia, while others, such as that in the former Yugoslavia, were bloody. But the most symbolic event of 1989, the same year as the Tiananmen Square massacre, was the fall of the Berlin Wall, ultimately leading to the reuniting of Germany.

I am privileged to have a reminder of that historic event on a table in my study. From time to time, medical students from other countries come to study for brief periods of time in US medical schools. One of those students with whom I worked at Duke in the early 1990s was from the old West Germany. On the day she was to return home, she gave me a small piece of concrete with graffiti on one side. She had personally obtained it from the Berlin Wall as it was being torn down. Of all the gifts I have received from students over the years, none is more significant than this one. I put it in a small glass box, where it remains today as a valuable reminder of that important moment in history.

The series of dramatic events kept up into the early 1990s as communism continued to collapse in Eastern Europe. Then, in 1991, the final act played out as communism was abolished in Russia that summer, and before the year ended, the Soviet Union was no more.

It was in this setting of rapidly changing world events that I embarked on my second Orbis mission. My destination this time was Lithuania, one of the three Baltic states that had been forced to join the Soviet Union in 1940 and had only in the past few years regained their independence. I would be traveling with another close friend, Dr. David Campbell, who was a professor of ophthalmology at Dartmouth University. He and I had studied together at Harvard in the early 1970s and had remained friends over the ensuing twenty years, during which time he had become an internationally respected expert in the field of glaucoma.

It was the summer of 1992. I had an overnight flight from New York to Zurich, Switzerland, where I met up with David at the airport early on a Sunday morning. From there, we flew together to Vilnius, the capital of Lithuania. Our final destination, however, was Kaunas, which was a one-hour drive west of Vilnius and the site of Lithuania's major medical complex.

We were met at the Vilnius airport by the chairman of the department of ophthalmology at Kaunas, who would drive us in his car to Kaunas. He was a soft-spoken, warm, courteous young man. Before the collapse of the Soviet Union, he had been a member of the Communist Party, and his father had apparently been a high-ranking official in the party. David and I immediately liked our new friend, who greatly softened my image of the prototypical Soviet communist. However, we would later be reminded that some parts of the past die hard.

As we drove out of Vilnius, I noticed a large tower on the horizon and asked our host about it. Much as Jimmy had done when I asked about the boarded-up building in Chengdu, our Lithuanian host seemed a bit evasive and said it was just a television tower and of no significance. He said it in a way that discouraged any further discussion on the subject. Before we left Lithuania a week later, however, we would learn the rest of the story.

When we arrived at our hotel in Kaunas, we were greeted with the first of several reminders that the influence of the old communist government was still being felt in the former Soviet Union. We were informed that there were no rooms available for us, because there was no water. It seems that water is heated in central locations around the city and piped to surrounding homes and buildings. Every so often, these facilities are closed for cleaning, during which time the people have no water. As bad timing would have it, this was one of those times for our hotel, which was apparently the only hotel in town.

At this point, our host resorted to the authoritarian manner that he must have wielded as a member of the Communist Party. A long and heated discussion ensued between him and the hotel manager, which culminated in our being grudgingly permitted to have our rooms. However, we were told that they could only provide cold water, and we soon learned that they were not kidding about that. Although it was late June, it was still cool in Kaunas, and the water was frigid. At least we were wide-awake when we went to work each morning after our cold showers.

After settling in, David and I went for a run through a nearby park and residential area. Running—or jogging, to be more precise—was something that we had enjoyed doing together over the past twenty years when we would meet at medical meetings, although our pace was now becoming noticeably slower. We returned a bit hot and sweaty, but especially hungry. That was when we had our next experience with the old Soviet culture—there was no restaurant in the hotel. In fact, the only place open for dining on Sunday evening was a fruit store in town.

We finally located the fruit store, only to find a sizeable number of people, mostly youths, forming a line that extended out onto the sidewalk. It seems that fresh fruit was at a premium during the communist years, and it was now a rather popular treat. So we took our place in line and watched as young men purchased a banana or orange for their date. The new Lithuanian government had printed paper currency, which rampant inflation had already rendered nearly worthless. To buy a single banana, one man counted out a stack of bills that must have measured at least an inch high. I began to fear that the price of our dinner might be exorbitant, but was surprised to find that the same banana in US currency was less than a dollar.

Early the next morning, we were driven to the hospital for our first day on the job. The format of our week in Lithuania would be different from what I had experienced in China. While most of the Orbis projects involve the plane, they also have a program called an off-plane project, in which all the work is done in a local hospital. This had the advantage of exposing us to the conditions under which the local doctors must work, which was truly an eye-opener. Another legacy of the communist era was a nearly bankrupt medical system. For the treatment of glaucoma, they could not afford medicine, and the few lasers they had were broken, and they couldn't afford to have them repaired. So the only available treatment was conventional surgery, which we performed each day with the local surgeons.

Our daily schedule was otherwise much as I had experienced in Chengdu—long days of surgery interspersed with lectures, which David and I gave to a large audience of doctors in the hospital auditorium. The patients we examined and treated were also much like those I had met in China—although somewhat better dressed, they were people who struggled in the lower economic strata of their society. There was one notable exception among these patients, however. Her name was Raimonda. She worked in the hospital as a technician, a position that she had apparently procured because her parents had been members of the Communist Party. And this connection still carried some weight, in that she was able to arrange a private examination by one of the visiting doctors, who turned out to be me.

Raimonda was in her early thirties. She was a tall, blond, poised woman, who seemed to take pride in her excellent English, explaining to me that she had once visited Chicago. Despite the fact that she was quite intelligent, charming, and attractive, she was single and still lived with her parents in a two-bedroom flat. Although her parents had been communists, she never fully accepted their beliefs, which had put her in an awkward position between communists and non-communists in her community. She was obviously an independent-minded young woman, and I surmised that all of these factors had contributed to her current marital status.

Her reason for requesting the appointment was that her eye pressures were a bit high, and she had been told that she might be developing glaucoma. My examination confirmed the elevated pressures but revealed no evidence of glaucoma. I explained that she was at risk of someday developing glaucoma and should continue to be followed closely but that nothing more needed to be done at this time. Thus ended her examination, but not our relationship.

As a way of thanking me, Raimonda invited David, two members of the Orbis team, and me to her parents' home for dinner that evening. After checking with the others, I told her that we would be delighted. We made plans to meet after work at the hospital entrance, where she would arrange for a car to pick us up.

When we convened at the scheduled time, Raimonda told us that there was a problem with the car and it would be an hour or two late. We all decided to take advantage of the time to do some final shopping for souvenirs, as we would be leaving Kaunas the next day. I had seen an icon in a basement antique shop earlier in the week and wanted to go back and take another look at it. The others wanted to check out some stores in a different direction, so Raimonda said she would go with me.

As we walked down the narrow, cobblestone streets of Kaunas, I asked Raimonda what the one thing was that had changed the most in her life during the past year since communism was no longer present in Lithuania.

Without hesitation, she replied, "One year ago, you and I would not be having this conversation."

She went ahead to explain that no one could be fully trusted under the communist regime, and that conversations had to be guarded, especially with relative strangers. But then she became quiet and thoughtful for a moment before announcing with a teasing smile and a twinkle in her eyes, "But there is something else even more important."

She paused to let that statement have its full impact, and I responded with a quizzical smile.

"Would you like to see it?" she finally asked.

I replied that I would like that very much. So Raimonda took me by the arm and led me down an even narrower side street until we suddenly came into a large courtyard. Before us stood a beautiful cathedral with spires reaching into the blue afternoon sky. She gave me a radiant smile, grabbed my hand, and led me as we ran across the courtyard like two school children. Our pace slowed as we approached the church and entered it with a sense of reverence.

For a weekday afternoon, I was surprised to find so many people in the church—Kaunas was not a tourist attraction in those days. There were people of all ages. Some were lighting candles. Some were praying. Some were just standing quietly, holding hands.

"A year ago, this was an art gallery," she whispered. "As you can see, many of the paintings are still on the walls, and they may stay there as a reminder. But on the day of our freedom, the bells rang, and doors were again opened to worshipers. Since then, the church has seen weddings and funerals and a full house for worship every Sunday morning."

We walked over to a booth, behind which sat a young man with a long, dark beard and a simple woolen robe. Raimonda handed him one of the new Lithuanian bills, which I judged to be worth a few cents, and the young man gave her in return two small, tapered beeswax candles. She gave one to me, and we walked over to where others were lighting candles. Following her lead, I lit mine from another candle and placed it in one of the small, brass holders. We stood there for a moment, watching the candles burn, then she bowed her head and closed her eyes. I followed suit, but only for a few seconds, lest I miss what was happening around me. When she looked up, her eyes were moist and there was a serious but serene expression on her face. Then she broke into a smile and whispered, "Come on. There's more."

The bright afternoon sun dazzled us as we stepped out of the church into the courtyard. She led me to the center of the court and asked me to look up again at the church spires. I had not paid it much attention the first time, but now noticed that the upper part of the building was encased in scaffolding.

"You have probably noticed," Raimonda said, "that although we now have our freedom, we are still very poor. There is simply no money to repair our decaying buildings, much less to build new ones. But the people have given their own money, what little they have, to repair the churches, and that should tell you what is most important to us."

Now that she had called it to my attention, it was apparent that what little reconstruction was going on in the city was primarily on the churches. As we walked down other streets and passed more churches, it was the same everywhere. Windows that had been boarded up for decades were being opened, and stained glass was being repaired. Scaffolding surrounded many of the structures for repair and refurbishing. Inside, churches that had been converted to museums, theaters, and factories by the communists were being returned to their original conditions. And to every church the worshippers were returning.

Our tour finally ended at the basement antique shop, where I was pleased to find that my icon had not been sold. It had a hammered brass design that surrounded a delicate, miniature painting of Christ's face, which was typical of the pre-communist era icon paintings. The paint was now cracked from a hundred years of exposure, but it otherwise seemed to be in good condition. Raimonda examined it critically and finally announced that it was good, but the price was too high. She haggled with the shopkeeper, and after I finally made my purchase, we headed back toward the hospital.

The car had still not arrived, nor had our colleagues yet returned, and we were grateful for the chance to sit on a bench and rest our tired feet. I was glad to have this extra time with Raimonda, because a question had been building in my mind. It was a delicate issue, and I wasn't sure how or if I should approach it with her, but my curiosity prevailed.

"Raimonda, there is something I must ask you."

She smiled but gave no response, as though she had anticipated what I was about to say.

"Your generation grew up in a communist society that discouraged formal religion. I presume that you had little, if any, exposure to religious education or role models for spiritual inspiration in your schools or workplaces. Even in your home, I wonder if faith was discussed."

She sat quietly, looking down at the grass, with eyes that gave no hint of what she might be thinking. I feared that I was delving too deeply into her personal life, but since I had already gone out on the limb, I continued.

"And yet today, less than a year since these constraints were lifted, you have shown me something remarkable. Suddenly, it is as though these religious privations never existed, with so many people returning to their churches. But what amazes me most is the young people, like yourself, who appear to have embraced a faith to which you were never formally exposed."

Still looking down, she nodded her head with a serious expression that seemed to say this was a fair question.

"What you say is true," she began, slowly. "But what you fail to understand is that a government can only take so much from its people. It can close down churches and convert them to museums and factories. It can prohibit inspirational messages in the media and reward those who publicly profess their lack of faith. But it can't keep you from looking into the sky at night and marveling at the order of the universe. It can't keep you from looking in a physics book with wonder at the order of the atom. And it can't keep you from believing that there are things larger than the heavens and smaller than subatomic particles that our mind can't even begin to grasp.

"I suppose what makes the human race different from all the other animals on this planet," she continued, "is something within that causes us to stand in awe of these wonders; to reflect on their meaning; to question the notion that it could all just be random chance. And I suppose it was that innate characteristic of the human soul that kept us going during all the years of communist oppression, whether we had formal religious training or not. It was something that burned within us."

'Something that burned within us.' Her last words lingered in my mind and brought back memories of Rei-Ying. She too had spoken of a "flame" that flickers within and will again one day burn brightly when oppression is lifted. But Raimonda had more to say.

"This human tendency, to ascribe the wonders about us to a higher source, has been used by some in our society as evidence that God does not exist. They say that, since we have this innate need to believe in God, we have simply created him in our minds. But I ask them, 'What is the source of that innate need?' Is it simply by chance that virtually every civilization throughout recorded history has felt the need to incorporate some form of religion into their culture? Or is it part of a master plan that people are endowed with a conscience that causes them to marvel at the wonders of creation and to attribute it to a creator?"

Wow! It is probably a good thing that her beautifully articulated reasoning left me speechless, since nothing I could have said at that moment would have been a worthy response. What amazed me most was that these thoughts were coming from a person who had never had the opportunity to study religion in a formal way. But I guess that was the very point she was making. In any case, I was spared the need for a response by the arrival of our colleagues, returning with bags filled from a successful shopping spree.

The car showed up a few minutes later, and we all piled in and headed off to Raimonda's flat, where we had a lovely evening. Her parent's apartment was small, but being crowded together just made it more fun. They had an upright piano, which Raimonda's mother played, and we sang along. Most of the songs were popular tunes from our Western culture, and I never knew if they were songs that our hosts also liked, or if they just chose them in deference to their guests. At any rate, it was a fitting ending to a memorable day.

The following morning, we prepared to leave Kaunas. After a picture-taking session with all the doctors and staff on the lawn in front of the hospital, David and I shook hands with our new friends, wished them well, and headed toward a waiting car. I was about to get in the car when I saw Raimonda hurrying toward us. She handed me a small, brown envelope with the inscription "For Dr. Shields," which she explained was a gift, but was not to be opened until I got home. Then she reached up and kissed me on the cheek, and we parted for the last time.

Before heading back to the States, David and I were scheduled for a day of sightseeing in Vilnius and then a brief visit to Saint Petersburg, Russia, which is just a short flight from Lithuania. While we were in Vilnius, our host was a prominent ophthalmologist, who had not been a member of the Communist Party. She took us to the large tower that I had noticed a week earlier when we had first arrived in the city—when we had been told that it was "only a television tower" and "of no significance." In truth, it turned out to be quite significant. This was the site of the television station that Lithuanian young people had surrounded to defend it from invading Soviet tanks during their country's bid for independence. Many of the youth had been killed that day, and flowers around the tower and station were still fresh, as were the memories of that tragic moment of recent history. And, as with my experience in China, the communists had attempted to minimize the significance of the event.

Saint Petersburg, the city built by Peter the Great and renamed Leningrad during the communist era, still had much of its old world charm. David and I walked down Nevsky Prospekt, the main street of Saint Petersburg, which held reminders of poignant history around every turn. We toured the Hermitage, with its world-famous collection of art, and visited the Peter and Paul Fortress, where the city had its beginning. But what impressed me most was the same thing that Raimonda had pointed out in Kaunas, and which we had also seen in Vilnius.

The buildings in Saint Petersburg were a mixture of ornate pre-communist architecture and the uninspired, gray structures of the Soviet era. But they were all a bit dirty and in disrepair. With the recent collapse of the Soviet Union, the economy was such that there was no evidence of either new construction or renovation of existing buildings—with one exception. Wherever we looked, cathedrals and churches were encased in scaffolding and undergoing refurbishing both outside and within. And, as in Lithuania, the people were returning in large numbers to their former places of worship.

David and I had separate flights home and said good-bye at the Saint Petersburg airport. As I sat looking out the plane window at the Atlantic Ocean far below, my mind was awash with the experiences of the past week. Of course, my time with Raimonda was the most vivid. It was then that I remembered the gift she had given me, which I had put in my briefcase. Since I was almost home, I didn't think she would mind if I opened it now.

Inside the brown envelope was a note that had been carefully wrapped around a small object. I unfolded the note to find a tapered, beeswax candle, just like the ones we had lit in the church in Kaunas. The note read:

> Dear Dr. Shields,
>   I hope you will keep this candle as a token of our time together. May it always remind you of the flame that burns within each of us, which no oppressor can put out.

Thank you for coming to our country to help our doctors and our people. Until we meet again, I will light a candle for you and hope that you will remember me.
Your friend,
Raimonda

As I looked back down at the Atlantic, the distance that separates America from Europe and Asia didn't seem nearly as great as it had when I had set off for China three years ago. It wasn't so much the physical distance that seemed different—I now sensed a common bond that I had come to realize has no boundaries.

Two women had changed my perspective of the world and of the people who live in it—one in the twilight of her life and the other in the bloom of womanhood, but each with a flame that burns within her. I had seen it in the eyes of Rei-Ying, who once stood beside her parents in their church in Chengdu, and who had kept the flame alive for decades in her heart. And I had seen it in the intelligent and inquisitive eyes of Raimonda, who marveled at the wonders around her and could not accept the notion that it is all by chance. And it occurred to me that this flame, burning in the hearts of these two remarkable women and in millions of people like them, may well be the strongest evidence we have for the existence of God.

7.

Pearl and Bud

For most surgeons, the operating room is a sanctuary. It is an escape from the frenetic demands of a busy office practice: a waiting room filled with patients, who are becoming increasingly disgruntled as the minutes since their appointment time continue to tick away; dashes between exam rooms and attempts to be efficient while still giving each patient the time and attention they need and deserve; telephone calls from patients with concerns or other doctors who want to discuss a problem case; emergencies coming in unscheduled; and patients with postoperative complications, all of which set the day's schedule further and further behind. And amid the demands that seem to come from all directions at once, the doctor must remain calm and focused, remembering that any error in judgment could spell harm for a patient.

But then the surgeon enters the operating room, as though passing through a hallowed portal and into an atmosphere of tranquility. The cacophony of the busy office is suddenly replaced with a symphony. It is not so much that the tempo slows, but that everything now flows in unison with only one focus—the patient on the operating table. And each person in the room, rather than pulling the doctor in every direction at once, is helping to achieve a single goal—the best outcome for the patient. On most days, it is truly a well-orchestrated symphony and a source of great satisfaction for the surgeon and all the operating room staff. But when something goes wrong, really wrong, there is no greater crisis or agony that a doctor can face. For me, one of those moments came the day I was scheduled to perform surgery on Pearl Overbee.

I had only known her for a short time prior to the surgery. She had a long history of glaucoma that had been well controlled with medication, but progressive cataracts had now severely impaired her vision. Because of the combined cataracts and glaucoma, her family ophthalmologist had elected to send her to Duke for her surgery. Mrs. Overbee was an attractive, white-haired octogenarian with a charmingly sweet and serene demeanor. She was brought to the office by her daughter, who was about my age. The two women were obviously very close, and the daughter took pride in telling stories about her family, especially her mother and father. She must have sensed my genuine interest in the stories, because she not only continued to tell me more on subsequent visits, but also brought in copies of old newspaper articles from over the years. By the time of the surgery, I felt that I had come to know the family quite well. As it turned out, I had come to know them too well.

Mrs. Overbee's surgery went smoothly, and I felt good when we sent her back to the hospital room, where all her family was waiting for her. I sent word by the nurse that I would come to their room as soon as I finished the last case. That case was just getting started when a nurse rushed in to the operating room in obvious distress. A hush suddenly fell over the room amid whispers and gasps. Something was very wrong, and I could tell they were debating whether to disturb me with it during the surgery. I paused for a moment and looked up from the operating microscope at the nurse, who came over and whispered in my ear. My blood ran cold and my whole body trembled as I digested the news. I wanted desperately to leave the operating room, but that wasn't possible. My only responsibility at that moment was the patient in front of me, and we were far enough into the surgery that I had to complete it. I momentarily closed my eyes, took a slow, deep breath, forced myself to relax, and then began to move robotically through each step of the operation. But I could not keep my mind from being flooded with the stories I had heard during the past few weeks—stories that spanned more than half a century.

———

It was the summer of 1940. The night was young and the air was warm and still. Up above, the sky was clear, the stars twinkled, and a full moon shone down on a small North Carolina town.

There were not many lights on in the town that evening. But far off to one edge of town, the lights glowed so brightly that they literally lit up the sky in their small speck of the world. It came from the city's minor league ballpark, and nearly everyone in town was there. Spectators filled every seat in the wooden bleachers and crowded together on the grassy slopes that surrounded the outfield. They had come to see their hometown hero, who was leading the league in batting that year. But tonight they had come to see him for another reason. This was to be his wedding night.

Bud Overbee had grown up in the little town. Most of the adults had known him since his youth, when he was active in Boy Scouts, his church, and all his school's athletic teams. He seemed to be a natural athlete. He was the starting fullback on the high school football team, a forward and leading scorer on the basketball team, and catcher on their state championship baseball team. But for all his talents and opportunities, it was clear that baseball was his passion, and no one was surprised when he turned down prestigious scholarships in other sports and opted for a more modest one in baseball at a local college.

He was the starting catcher on his college team all fours years and led his conference in batting average. By his sophomore year, he was attracting the attention of major league scouts, and in his senior year he received several tempting offers. He could have entered the minors at one of the higher levels, which might have shortened his time to the major league, but when he got an offer to play for his hometown team, which was in the lowest class of the minors, he couldn't resist. It was not so much the thought of returning home that prompted his decision as it was the person who waited for him there.

Pearl and Bud had been high school sweethearts. She was a petite, auburn-haired beauty with a warm, ready smile and soft, sensitive eyes that told you her beauty was more than skin deep. It was obvious to everyone, especially to the two young people, that they were meant for each other. Bud was two years older than Pearl, which had undoubtedly influenced his decision to select a college that was not too far away. But even with frequent trips home, the separation was hard for both of them. After high school, Pearl spent one year in her community junior college and then took a job as a waitress in town to help support her family. When she learned that Bud would be coming home to play in their city's minor league club, she wept with joy.

They had agreed not to marry until Bud could support a family. That first summer was not easy for them. His team's frequent road trips kept Bud away from home even more than when he was in college. Pearl continued to work, but attended every home game that she could, since they had few other opportunities to be close to each other. When fall came and the season ended, Bud took a job as assistant foreman in a meat packing plant in town. Now they had more time to be together, and their courtship entered its final stage. But it was not a lavish courtship, since both of them were saving every penny they could toward their common goal.

By early spring, they agreed that their savings were sufficient to justify starting a family. In addition, Bud's first year in the minors had been successful, and he had received word that one more such year would ensure his advancement to a significantly higher level within his club's farm system, with its associated salary increase. And so, on a warm spring Sunday after church, they went to their local lake for a picnic, and there Bud proposed to Pearl.

The proposal did not come as a surprise to Pearl, who nevertheless was unable to hold back her tears of joy as she readily accepted. What came next, however, did surprise her. Bud told her that he wanted them to be married at the ballpark. For years, Pearl had dreamed of a church wedding, with flowers and soft music and men in tuxedos and women in flowing pastel dresses. Suddenly, all that vanished, but to her surprise it didn't really seem to matter. She knew how much baseball meant to Bud and how much a part of their life it would always be. And the only thing that really seemed to matter at that moment was becoming Mrs. Bud Overbee. And so she smiled and told him that would be wonderful.

The old ballpark organ squawked out a slow, stately rendition of "Take Me Out to the Ball Game." From the home team dugout, Bud's teammates marched with dignity onto the field and formed two lines between first base and home plate. Their uniforms were spanking clean, which was no mean feat in those days, when most players were lucky to have their uniform cleaned more than once during the season. Their heads were bare, and each player had slicked back his hair with uncharacteristic care. They each carried a bat, which they raised on cue high in the air, forming an arch between the two lines.

Then, from the dugout, Bud appeared. He too wore his best, clean uniform and was bareheaded. However, he had also removed his baseball shoes and replaced them with black patent leather loafers, because he didn't think it would be proper to wed in an old pair of baseball cleats. He walked slowly beneath the arch of bats and took his place at home plate, where the minister was waiting for him.

Bud cut a striking figure standing there on home plate. He was a large man with broad shoulders and a barrel chest, although he had a boyish face with a shy but ready smile and a thick tassel of wavy dark brown hair that, except for tonight, was rarely in place. His most striking feature, however, was his dark, penetrating eyes that looked right at you when he spoke. Tonight, those eyes were only for one person.

The opposite dugout was festooned with flowers. As Bud turned to face it, the organ music paused and then, probably for the first time ever, began a respectable version of "Wedding March." The old wooden bleachers creaked as everyone stood in unison, and those on the grassy slopes moved forward to surround the infield. All eyes joined Bud's as Pearl stepped forth from beneath the flowers. She wore a traditional but simple white wedding dress that tapered down to her slender waist and then flowed out gently before ending just above her ankles. For reasons of practicality, she had chosen not to wear a train.

Pearl's father was waiting for her just outside the dugout, and together, hand in arm, they began the slow walk toward home plate. Their path was lined by Pearl's four closest girlfriends, who wore soft chiffon dresses, each in a different pastel color. As she approached Bud's side, Pearl looked up, her soft brown eyes gazing deeply into his, and at that moment neither young person was aware of the existence of anyone else in the world.

If time could stand still, that would have been the moment for Pearl and Bud. But the ceremony proceeded, the vows were repeated, the 'I dos' were whispered, and the kiss was short but tender. Then someone yelled, "Play ball!"

The flowers were moved to an area in the bleachers just behind home plate, where Pearl sat with her family and the wedding party to watch her husband play ball for the first time. That evening, Bud had two runs and a homer. Later he would say that he hit two home runs that night, and there was no question on that magic evening that Pearl was a home run in anybody's book.

Bud's batting average fell off a bit that season. Any man who can remember his first year of married life will understand. He gained a little more weight than he should have from Pearl's excellent cooking, and he found it hard to maintain the necessary concentration at all times on his ball playing. This was especially true during road games, when his mind kept drifting back to his wife, who had to stay home to work. By the end of the season, he still had the best batting average on the team, but it was not up to his personal standards, and his parent club suggested another season with his present team before being considered for a move to a higher level in the minors.

This disappointment was quickly assuaged by the joy he found in being able to spend each day, for the first time, with his young wife. He returned to his job at the meat packing plant, and she continued to work as a waitress. The days passed quickly, because their spirits were constantly buoyed by the thoughts of another blissful evening together. It was the most beautiful autumn of their lives, and before they knew it, winter had come, and it was Christmas. That holiday season, they shared the joy that can only come from giving happiness to the one you love. With winter howling outside, they were warm and secure in their little home. There was no way they could have known at that moment that, before the next Christmas came, their lives would have forever changed.

A war was raging in Europe. Across the Atlantic, people in America followed the daily events with keen interest and apprehension. But for the average person, life went on pretty much as usual. With the first sign of spring, Bud began a rigorous training program, running long distances each day and practicing batting and throwing with a few of his teammates who were spending the off-season in town. By the time formal spring training began, Bud had never been in better shape.

That summer was also his best season ever. Bud led his league in batting. During the late summer playoffs, he was approached by representatives of his parent club and told the he was to be advanced the following season to their farm team, which was in the highest class of the minors. With a couple of good years on that team, his chances of advancing to the major league was excellent.

Pearl received the news with mixed emotions. The advancement would, of course, mean moving to a new town, at least during the summer. She had never lived anywhere else, and the thought of leaving her family and friends frightened her. But she knew what this meant for Bud's career, and it thrilled her to see him so excited. Besides, she knew she could be happy anyplace as long as she was with Bud.

They spent another blissful autumn together. But as the last leaves settled to the ground, Pearl sensed that something about her was changing, and by December she was certain. And so it was that, on a Sunday in early

December, Pearl told Bud she wanted to go to the lake after church—the same lake where he had proposed to her less than two years earlier. This was an unusual time of year to be going to the lake, but Bud never denied Pearl anything she wanted. So they went, and as they sat in their car beside the otherwise deserted lake, eating a picnic lunch, Pearl told Bud that by early summer he would be a father.

It was their greatest moment of joy since they had stood together at home plate on their wedding night. They couldn't wait to drive back to town and tell their parents. But as they drove down Main Street, they sensed that something was wrong. The town was unusually quiet. The few people who were out were standing in small groups, talking and looking very somber. It was a cold, windy day, and despite the warmth in the car, the young couple felt a chill go through their bodies that they could not explain. Bud didn't have a radio in his car, so it was not until they got to his parents' home that they learned of the bombing of Pearl Harbor.

The next morning, Bud went to the recruiting station and volunteered to enlist in the Army. For a hometown hero, no one would have expected anything less. Pearl tried to be brave. She told him how handsome he was going to look in his military uniform and how proud she was of him. But when she was alone, she wept bitterly.

Christmas that year was far more somber than the year before. Bud had already received his orders and was to report for basic training in January. Again they were separated. Pearl stayed home and worked, volunteered for every local war effort, planned the nursery, and wrote letters to her husband every day. He was only able to come home once that spring, and it was then that he told her his division was scheduled to embark for Europe in one month, before the birth of their child.

This was the hardest time that either young person had ever known. They relished every moment of their brief time together, and when the troops boarded their ship, Pearl and her parents drove to the coast to say good-bye for one last time. They kissed as tears streamed down their faces. As they were finally forced to part, Pearl put a small locket in Bud's hand. It contained her picture, and she said it was to remind him that she would be praying for him constantly and living only for the day when he would return.

The days passed painfully slowly for both of them. Pearl wrote every day, but mail reached Bud late and sometimes never. His Division was somewhere in France and was moving slowly to where they were told a fierce battle was raging. At nights, he slept in a foxhole. In the dim light, he would hold the locket close to his eyes and look at Pearl's picture. And when he slept, he dreamed of her and of their baby. He didn't know if it was a girl or a boy, but he knew it was time for the arrival. The last letter he had received from Pearl was more than a month old, so he didn't know when he would receive the word that he was a father.

One night, his dreams of home where shattered by deafening roars and anxious voices. He opened his eyes to see the smoky darkness lit by bursts of fire on the horizon. His commanding officer was shouting at them to assemble and prepare to advance. For Bud and his fellow soldiers, the moment of their fate had arrived.

As dawn came through the smoky sky, his platoon crouched behind a stone wall just outside a small village. They were told it was occupied by the Germans and that they had orders to take it. On command, they rose to begin their advance on the town. But as they did so, a barrage of thunder and smoke came from all the windows in the nearby houses. Bud heard a sickening scream and turned to see his companion beside him fall over the wall, blood coming from his neck. He reached down to help him, but then saw to his horror that his face had been blown away and that he was dead.

Bud looked up to see that his other companions were crawling through the wet grass toward the houses, and he rushed forward to join them. But before he could take cover, he felt a burning pain tear through his lower body, and he fell to the ground. He tried to move, but realized he had no control of his legs. The pain was moving up through his body. He felt weak and all about him was becoming dark. At that moment, he had only one thought. With his last ounce of strength, he struggled to reach into his shirt pocket until he felt the locket and pulled it out. He held it close to his eyes, and the last thing he saw, before his world went dark, was Pearl. When they found him, he was still clutching the locket close to his heart, and someone noted that there was a smile on his ashen face.

———

When the letter arrived, Pearl was afraid to open it. It had been well over a month since she had received a letter from Bud, and she had heard stories of what these official letters from the US government might contain. She knew that she had to be brave, but also knew that she could not handle it alone. So she went to the nursery, where their three-week-old daughter was asleep. With tears running down her cheeks, she bundled up the little baby, put her in a bassinette, and drove to her parents' home. Bud's parents had been asked to come over, and they all sat together in the living room in fearful silence and braced themselves as Pearl's father opened the letter and began to read.

Bud had been seriously injured and had been rushed to a hospital in England. He was expected to live, but was too weak to travel and would have to stay in the British hospital for several months. Her father led the family in a brief prayer of thanksgiving. Then Pearl could be brave no longer and gave way to uncontrollable sobbing of relief and pain. Her prayers had been answered and her greatest fear had not been realized, but her husband was hurt and alone and she wanted desperately to be by his side, but knew that was not possible.

The days that followed were the longest the two young people had ever known. They moved especially slowly for Bud, who was confined to a bed for most of his hospital stay. The highlight of each day was reading and rereading the letters from Pearl, which she sent on a daily basis, but which usually arrived in clusters of several at a time. Many of the letters contained pictures of his daughter, whom he had yet to see in person. In one picture, Pearl was holding their daughter in front of their little home, and his longing to be there with them was so great that Bud thought his heart would break.

It was fall when they got word that Bud was coming home. Pearl's parents drove them to New York to meet his ship. Her heart pounded and her legs became weak as she stood on the dock and watched the young men file down from the ship. Some had lost a leg or an arm and others wore a patch over a missing eye. Then she spotted Bud. He was thin and looked so much older than when he had left. He supported himself on crutches and, as he drew closer, Pearl could see that he dragged one leg as though he had no control of it. But when he saw Pearl, he literally ran on his crutches and one leg. She too ran, and they fell into each other's arms. Everything else in the world vanished at that moment, and time stood still.

Pearl's parents waited patiently at a distance. Her mother was holding their baby. As Pearl rested her head on Bud's chest, he looked up and saw the child, and for the second time in as many minutes, he was overcome with emotion. Pearl went over to her mother, gathered the five-month-old baby in her arms, and proudly presented the beautiful little girl to her father. At first Bud was afraid to hold such a delicate little thing, but she smiled at him and held out her arms and all his fears vanished. He held his daughter for the first time and gently kissed her as tears of joy streamed down his face. As the little family, finally united, stood together on the dock with their arms around each other, even the night on home plate and the Sunday afternoons at the lake paled in comparison to the beauty of that moment.

As for so many young couples trying to resume their life after the experiences of war, the times were not easy for Pearl and Bud. He had to spend more time in an army hospital in North Carolina. She temporarily quit her job and found a small apartment near the hospital so that she and the baby could be with Bud as much as possible. By Christmas, he was able to come home. Their third Christmas together was bittersweet. Pearl went back to work at the restaurant, and Bud learned how to take care of their daughter when the two of them were home alone. For Bud, the future was uncertain. His general health was now excellent, but his injured leg remained stiff and weak, and he was finally forced to accept the grim reality that he would never again be able to play baseball.

That spring, he spent a great deal of his time at the ballpark, watching his old team practice. But nothing was the same. The war continued to rage across both oceans, and most of his old teammates were still over there fighting. Some, he learned, had been killed. The team was largely made up of young boys, many of whom were still in high school, and a few older men who were exempt from military service. Bud knew hardly any of them, and they didn't seem to know him.

Bud drifted into a bit of melancholy that summer, and Pearl began to worry about him. One night, after their daughter was asleep, they sat down to talk about their future. They agreed that they did not want to leave their hometown, and it was an unsaid given that, whatever they did, they wanted to do it together. As they considered their options, the possibility of opening a restaurant rose to the top of the list. They lived in an area where good pork was readily available and barbeque was a passion. With his knowledge of meat and hers of running a restaurant, it seemed to be a natural choice. Furthermore, one of the deficiencies in their town was a quality barbeque restaurant. And so it was, on that summer evening, that their combined hopes and dreams for their future gave rise to Bud's Barbeque.

With his GI stipend and a generous loan from the local bank, they were able to open their new restaurant by the fall of that year. And it was an instant success. It gradually became an institution in the town. People drove from miles around just to dine on the famous barbeque at Bud's. The two of them did it together. He selected the meat, oversaw the kitchen, and handled the finances, while Pearl supervised the tables and waitresses. As much as anything else, the success of their establishment came from the warmth and friendliness of Pearl and Bud. They were almost always there together, and they knew most of their clientele by name, and everybody knew and loved them. And this happy scene was to last for more than half a century.

The winds of time continued to sweep over the little North Carolina town. The war finally came to an end, and the world began to rebuild. Pearl and Bud had two more children: a boy and another girl. They were a happy family. The intense love that the children saw in their parents gave them a strong sense of security, self-worth, and confidence. Everything they did, they did as a family: reading and homework, movies and ball games, Sunday school and church, and many picnics at the lake.

But as the winds blew, the leaves fell, new ones budded out, and one season followed another, the passage of time became a blur in their minds. Before they knew it, the picnics at the lake had grown from a family of five to an ever-increasing number as weddings came and grandchildren began to fill the air with the joy of their laughter. Pearl and Bud never noticed the world turning cold, because they lived each day in the warmth of their love.

But the years began to inevitably take their toll. Bud developed diabetes. At first he could control it with diet and pills, but eventually he had to resort to daily insulin injections, which Pearl carefully measured out and gave him. Pearl was also having her own medical problems. She developed glaucoma, for which she had to take eye drops, and her vision was gradually declining, which she was told was coming from cataracts. They met these new challenges just as they had met all the others in their life when they were young, and it brought them even closer together and only continued to strengthen their love.

In the summer of 1990, the old ballpark was once again the focal point of the little town. It was no longer used by their minor league team. A new brick ballpark had been built several years earlier for that purpose. The old park was only used occasionally for local school games, and all those were during the daytime, since the lights had long ago been taken down. The old wooden bleachers were in disrepair, but they had recently been patched up and painted and now bore some resemblance to their appearance in the old days. The reason for all the preparation was that the town people were returning to the old ballpark to once again pay their respects to their local sweethearts. For Pearl and Bud were about to celebrate their fiftieth wedding anniversary.

The bleachers were once again filled to capacity, and the overflow surrounded the infield. To one side of home plate stood seven of Bud's old teammates and three of the women who had been Pearl's bridesmaids. To the other side stood Pearl and Bud's three children with their spouses and all the grandchildren and even two great-grandchildren. Then, as a recording of "Take Me Out to the Ball Game" was piped over a portable sound system, the two daughters walked over to the dugout and escorted their parents to home plate. Pearl, dressed in a dignified suit, walked beside Bud, who was pushed in a wheelchair by their son.

At home plate, the daughters stood to one side, while the son helped his father, who stood up with difficulty. Then a young minister from their church came forward and led them in repeating their marriage vows. The couple now both had pure white hair. Pearl had put on a bit a weight over the years, but Bud never thought of her as fat. "She's just right," he would say, and mean it. He was now very frail and stoop-shouldered. But if everything else in the world had changed, one thing had not. As they gazed into each other's eyes, they saw the same eyes filled with the same love that they had known every day since they first stood together on that very spot fifty years ago.

Bud's health continued to fail. The diabetes eventually affected his kidneys, and he had to go on dialysis. He also had to increase his insulin injections to twice daily, which Pearl continued to administer faithfully. One day she found Bud in their den, collapsed in his chair and unconscious with an ashen face. She dialed 911, and he was rushed to the emergency room, where it was determined that he had had a heart attack. He was admitted to intensive care and remained in the hospital for nearly a month. During this time, Pearl rarely left his side, day or night, going home only occasionally to clean up and change clothes. Because of his fragile health, heart surgery was not advised. He was put on additional medications and finally discharged to their home, where Pearl continued to care for him.

During all this time, Pearl's only concern was the welfare of her husband. Bud too had only one concern. He was worried about Pearl. He had noticed that her vision was becoming very poor, even though she would not admit it. She had been told that she needed cataract surgery, and Bud had begged her to go ahead with it. But she had been reluctant, because she did not want to leave Bud or be unable to care for him, even for a brief period of time. Finally, however, she realized that her impaired vision, even with the aide of a magnifying lens, was preventing her from accurately measuring his insulin and reading the labels on his pill bottles. It was only because it would allow her to better care for Bud that she at last agreed to proceed with the surgery. And so it was that I had the privilege of meeting Pearl Overbee and her family.

———

"Dr. Shields, there has been a code in Mrs. Overbee's room."

Those were the words the nurse had whispered in my ear. As most people know, a code is a bad thing. It means that someone is dying: they may have stopped breathing, or their heart may have stopped beating. The code is an urgent alert for all available medical personnel in the area to come to the designated location as quickly as possible to administer life-saving measures. Sometimes a life can be saved—sometimes it cannot.

I wanted desperately to go to her room, but I was assured that several doctors and nurses were already there and doing all that could be done, and my responsibility was the patient on the operating table before me. As I moved methodically through the operation with thoughts of Pearl and her family swirling in my mind, a nurse walked slowly into the operating room, and my hopes darkened as she whispered to the others, who seemed to be wiping back tears. How could this have happened? She had seemed to be doing so well when she left the operating room—she even had a big smile on her face when I last saw her. When I finally completed the case and told the patient that everything had gone fine, I rushed out of the operating room and was met by the head nurse, who was waiting to tell me the whole story. She explained that the problem was not with Pearl. It was Bud.

I had only met Mr. Overbee earlier that morning, when I had stopped by Pearl's room before going to the operating suite. His health had prevented him from coming with his wife for the office visits, but he insisted on being there for her when she came out of surgery. He was a frail man in a wheelchair, although there was still some evidence of the virile person that he had once been. He reminded me a great deal of Pearl in his kindness, good humor, and positive, serene nature. But his most striking feature was his deep love for and devotion to Pearl—a love that was obviously reciprocated.

When Pearl returned to her room after the surgery, her family was overjoyed that the operation had gone well. In addition to Bud and their oldest daughter, their son and younger daughter had also come in for the surgery, along with several grandchildren. They waited outside the hospital room while the nurses helped Pearl into her bed and arranged the pillow and covers for her. Despite the patch over her eye, everyone said she still looked lovely lying there with her neat white hair and ever-present smile.

The son wheeled Mr. Overbee back into the room to a position beside the bed where his wife lay. They said he looked deeply into her uncovered eye, smiled as he took her hand, and spoke softly and lovingly to her.

"Well, honey, as long as you're okay, I'm okay."

And those were the last words that Bud Overbee would ever speak. No sooner had he spoken than his eyes closed with a painful grimace. He slumped forward, and his hand fell from Pearl's. She screamed for help. Within seconds, the nurse rushed into the room, saw what had happened, and sounded the code alarm.

They placed Mr. Overbee on the floor, and Pearl watched in horror as several doctors and nurses administered life-saving measures to restart his heart and breathing. An intravenous line was started, medicines were given, and electric paddles were placed on his chest in a vain effort to stimulate his heart to beat. It went on for nearly a half hour as Pearl watched, crying uncontrollably. The room was too small to get her out over all the activity on the floor, and all her daughters could do was sit on the bed beside her, holding her hands and crying with her.

I'm not sure what I was expecting as I hurried out onto the ward, but I was not prepared for what I encountered. Everyone in the hall was crying, even the nurses and the families of other patients who hadn't even known the Overbees. As I approached the room, Pearl was being wheeled in Bud's chair into an adjacent room, where Bud lay on a stretcher beneath a white sheet. I stood in the hall, looking through the cracked door, as a nurse pulled the sheet back from his face, and Pearl put her arms around him and softly kissed her Bud for the last time.

We closed the door and allowed Pearl to be alone with Bud for as long as she wished. I have never handled emotional situations very well and had to step quickly into an empty room to regain my composure. I knew that what I had to do next would not be easy, but that I had to do it with as professional a demeanor as I could muster.

I was waiting for her in the hall with her family when Pearl came out of the room. I don't know what I had planned to say, but it didn't really matter, because at that moment, despite my firm resolve, I was incapable of speech. All I could do was kneel down beside her and hug her for a long time while she continued to cry and I struggled to hide the fact that I was on the verge of doing the same.

After we got Pearl back in bed, I stood with the family in the hall talking about our next steps. Of course, we would help arrange to have Bud's body taken back to their hometown. But I suggested that Pearl stay in the hospital overnight so that I could check on her in the morning, after which they could all go home and make arrangements for the funeral. Then I left them to grieve together and went down to the clinic, where patients were waiting.

The next morning, Pearl was neatly dressed, but she looked very tired. I doubt that she had slept much. It was the first night that she had been separated from Bud since he had come home from the war over fifty years ago. Fortunately, her eye was continuing to do well, and I told her that it would not be necessary for her to come back until the following week. The funeral was a few days later, and as much as I wanted to attend, my heavy clinic schedule would not permit it. But we did send flowers on behalf of the eye center.

When they returned the following week, they brought a large newspaper clipping from their local paper. It actually spanned several pages. On the front page was a large picture of Pearl, standing in their den with a patch protecting her recently operated-on eye, looking up with her other eye at all the athletic trophies that Bud had won when he was a young man and the hometown hero. The accompanying article summarized the life of Pearl and Bud. On the last page were two more pictures: a young man in his baseball uniform and a slender, auburn-haired beauty in a simple cotton dress. It was just as they were in the summer of 1940.

I sat at my desk that evening after the rest of the office staff had gone home. The events of the past week had touched us all deeply. As I reread the newspaper account and gazed at the pictures of the two young people, I felt a sense of overwhelming sadness. But my sorrow was not for Pearl or Bud. It was, rather, for the countless thousands who will pass through this life and never experience the joy that those two people had found in each other.

For over fifty-five years, they woke up each morning knowing that they were loved. And they lived each day wrapped in the security of that love. When one was sad or troubled, there was the assurance that the other would be there to understand, give comfort, and cry with them. And when they were filled with happiness and wanted to shout for joy, they knew there was someone who would rejoice with them. And wherever they went, whatever wonders they beheld, and whatever emotions they felt as their life unfolded, they knew there would always be someone by their side to share each new experience with them. When they marveled at the beauty of a sunset or the majesty of a snow-covered mountain or the simple splendor of a newly opened flower, they did not do so with the sense of incompleteness that often comes from experiencing life's treasures alone, but with the warmth and satisfaction that comes from sharing every new adventure with someone you love. They shared the joy of each newborn child, grandchild, and great-grandchild. They stood together with thankful hearts as they watched the children learn to stand, walk, talk, love, and finally go out into the world to seek their own happiness. They shared each other's dreams, hopes, fears, and faith. And when they bowed their heads with their hands gently intertwined, they prayed as one.

And, what may be most important of all, when the seasons of life had nearly run their course, and changes began to warn of the coming of winter; when the children were gone, and the old house no longer rang with the joy of their laughter; when ambitions had been realized or abandoned, and there didn't seem to be any more mountains to climb; when the future was uncertain, and the chill of doubt crept deep into their bones, and when they were afraid; it was then that their love reached to its highest level yet, bringing warmth and security and promise. And maybe the strength that they derived from their shared love was knowing its source.

I have thought often about Pearl over the years. I know that she never stopped missing Bud, but I rather suspect that she had ample memories and love to sustain her until the day their love was reunited forever. And I have also thought often about all the lonely people who have struggled through life never knowing the gift of true love. But I am thankful for people like Pearl and Bud, who remind us that the gift is there for each of us, if we will only open our eyes to see it.

Ω

8.

Emily

It was the perfect vacation. A pristine, picturesque log cabin was nestled among stately pine trees on the gentle slope of a Virginia mountainside. A profusion of bright flowers and soft, dark-green grass surrounded the cabin and flowed down to a crystal clear stream that was aptly named Crystal Creek. The winding stream meandered peacefully around the cabin site, and the bubbling sound of water flowing over smooth rocks mingled with the hushed flutter of soft breezes in the trees overhead.

This was the bucolic setting in which our family would enjoy some of our happiest days together. We would wake to the sounds of the birds beginning their new day and to the warmth of the morning sunlight filtering down through the trees and into our open cabin windows. Our days would begin with a hearty breakfast in the nearby communal dining hall, followed by a seemingly endless choice of exciting and relaxing activities to fill the day. For the children, there would be games, crafts, hiking, swimming, horseback riding, and drifting on inflated tubes down Crystal Creek. For Sharon and me, there would be quieter pleasures to enjoy. In the mornings, we would take long, slow walks along the many woodland paths with their spongy, fragrant beds of pine needles, admiring the colorful flowers and toadstools, the delicate ferns, the soft mosses on rocky outcroppings, and all the natural beauty that carpeted the mountain floor. We would delight in the butterflies as they fluttered around their favorite Scottish thistle; look up into the trees, trying to identify the birds that were serenading us with their songs; or peer deeply into the woods with silent awe at a mother deer and her fawn. In the afternoons, we would sit in rockers on the front porch of our log cabin, reading our books and watching the children drift by with their floats on the lovely Crystal Creek

In the evenings, after dinner, we would join the others around a campfire, visiting, singing, and enjoying inspirational talks about the beauty of nature and how fortunate we were to be enjoying it. And then, tired but content from a day well spent, we would all go back to our lodgings and peacefully settle into our soft beds, pulling the comforters over us against the chilly mountain air. Sleep would come quickly and sweetly with promises of another glorious day that lay before us.

And to top it all off, the whole thing was entirely free.

Such were my thoughts as our family happily sped down the highway in our Oldsmobile station wagon, crossing the North Carolina border into Virginia. Our destination was Camp Crystal, and each of us had been looking forward to this moment for months. It all began with a colleague at Duke, who had attended the camp since his youth. Although it was actually a summer camp for girls, he had worked there as a camp counselor during his teenage years. And he had come to love it so much that, after returning to North Carolina as a physician on the Duke Medical School faculty, he continued to spend part of each summer at Camp Crystal as the camp doctor. They had a very generous arrangement, whereby one or more daughters could attend the camp for as long as they wished in return for one week of service by their physician parent as the camp doctor. In fact, the whole family could come and stay in the doctor's special quarters (our pristine log cabin in the mountains).

Although my colleague's children were now beyond the age of the camp attendees, he continued to enjoy going every summer as a camp doctor, just for the beauty of the place and the friendliness of the people. For years, he had been regaling me with descriptions of Camp Crystal and insisting that I take advantage of the opportunity once Sarah was old enough to attend. My only reservation was that I had not practiced general medicine since my navy days, and I feared that I would not be qualified. But he assured me that there were never any significant medical problems, and besides, there was an excellent nurse who took care of most of the children's minor cuts and scratches.

So, when Sarah became old enough to attend the camp, I asked the family early that spring if they would like to spend part of our summer vacation at this most marvelous place. Sarah, who had a way of making new friends easily, warmed quickly to the idea. But John wasn't so sure. "A girl's camp?" he asked incredulously. It would be many years yet before John reached the age at which being around a lot of girls was considered a positive thing. Now, it was quite the contrary. I could appreciate his reluctance, and it took a bit of convincing, but the promise of our hiking, fishing, and swimming soon won him over. Sharon, of course, was only concerned about the happiness of her family, and this seemed like a good idea to her. And now, as we sped down the highway toward Camp Crystal, she was performing her usual function on our family trips: keeping the children apart in the back seat and patiently answering them as they alternately asked, "Are we there yet?"

———

As we neared the exit to turn off the interstate, I half expected to see a large, impressive sign indicating that one was approaching Camp Crystal. But there was none. That didn't really bother me, especially when I remembered that Virginia doesn't allow billboards on their interstates. After a few miles on a state highway, however, we came to our next turn, and here I was rather sure that there would be a nice sign. But again, nothing. We pulled over to check our directions and make sure we were on the right road. We were. By now, it was starting to get rather quiet in the car, but I assured everyone that, when you are as exclusive as Camp Crystal, you don't need to advertise with flashy signs; people just know. We were now on a country dirt road, and our final turn put us on an even narrower road that was more grass than dirt. I stopped to take another look at the directions. Just then, John noticed a small board, nailed to a fence post, on which someone had roughly painted "Camp Crystal."

"Must really be exclusive," he offered. John was a bit young to appreciate the finer points of sarcasm, although I couldn't help but wonder as I checked his expression in the rear view mirror.

Soon our narrow road turned into what seemed like an open field, and I began to worry that we had mistakenly wandered onto someone's farm. The silence in the car now was palpable, and I knew what they were thinking: 'Dad's done it again.' My most common failure on our trips was not looking at the map. But this time there was no map, only my friend's directions, and they seemed to indicate that we had arrived. And yet there was no sign of a camp. In fact, the road we were on, such as it was, had come to an end, and all I could see was a rusty pickup. I was just about to turn around, convinced that we were lost, when a young fellow came around from behind the pickup. From his appearance, I assumed he must be from the nearby farm. I got out to ask him for directions and was about to open my mouth when he stuck out his hand and said with a big grin, "Welcome to Camp Crystal!"

I looked around and still couldn't see anything that resembled a camp. He obviously recognized my perplexed state and indicated that it was "just across the creek." That's when I became conscious of a sound that I had been hearing. A roaring sound.

"You have to come around the bend to see it," he explained.

We walked around the bend and there it was—a wide, muddy, wildly flowing river.

"What is it?" I finally asked.

He gave me a look like I was from another planet. "Crystal Creek," he said proudly.

I could only stare in disbelief as I tried to reconcile my thoughts of that gentle, bubbling, crystal-clear creek in my dreams with this wild, muddy river. He again perceived my thoughts and explained, "We've had a lot of rain lately, and she's a little higher and faster than usual." I nodded my understanding and resignation.

"So we have to cross it to get to the camp?" I asked.

He gave me another look like "Where is this guy from?"

"Yeah, that's right," he said with strained but cheerful patience.

The problem was, as I looked up and down the "creek," I couldn't see how we were going to get across. There was no bridge in sight. I finally concluded that it must be around another bend, and that was why he came for us in his pickup—since there wasn't any more road.

"I'll help you put your bags in the truck, and we'll take them across and then come back for your family," he explained.

We walked back to our car and I told the family that everything was fine, that we were there, and that I would come back for them as soon as we took the bags across. The silence in the car was now reaching crisis level, and I thought maybe I should break it by introducing our escort, which reminded me that I had yet to learn his name.

"I'm Bruce," I said as I turned around and offered him my hand.

"Billy," he responded, taking it.

"This is Billy," I announced to the family. Sharon smiled and nodded. Sarah just gave him a doubtful look. John was gazing off at the countryside, probably beginning to think of the possibilities that lay ahead for our week at Camp Crystal.

Billy was a strapping young man in his mid-teens who had the casual demeanor of a farm boy with the intensity of an ambitious future in his eyes. His red, tousled hair and freckles accentuated the deep blue of his sparkling eyes, which accompanied his perpetual ear-to-ear grin. His jeans and sneakers were well worn, and an old T-shirt announced "Camp Crystal" across the front. I would soon learn that Billy was the head junior counselor for the camp.

So Billy and I proceeded to load our bags in the back of his pickup, and then I took a seat beside him in the cab. What happened next is largely a blur in my memory, except for a few moments that are exquisitely vivid even today, much like a disturbing dream in which parts seem so real and yet nothing makes sense. As we took off in Billy's pickup, I fully expected that we would be driving along beside the river until we rounded a bend and came to the bridge. But instead we headed straight down the embankment directly toward the river. And we were gaining speed as we approached a metal pier along the near bank. We hit the pier and kept going out on it. In fact, we were continuing to go faster. Within a few more yards, we would be hurtling off the end of the pier. Something was terribly wrong. Had the brakes failed? Was Billy insane? Images from *Deliverance* flashed across my mind. Whatever the problem was, we were in serious trouble.

They say that, at times like this, your whole life passes before you. I don't think so. At least that wasn't happening to me. My mind was totally focused on determining the best time to escape from Billy's pickup. If I jumped then, I would probably break every bone in my body on the metal pier. A better option might be to open the door and leap out as we hurtled into the river. Maybe, if I was lucky, the truck wouldn't land on me. A third option was to brace myself for the impact with the water and then get out through the window before the truck sank into the muddy Crystal Creek.

I was glad that I had chosen option three when Billy suddenly slammed on the brakes and the pickup came to a screeching halt within a few feet from the end of the pier. And that's when I realized we weren't on a pier. It was actually a barge, and we were now floating quietly and slowly across the river. Billy glanced over at me with a sly grin, as if to say "gotcha." He explained that this is how one crosses over to Camp Crystal. He pointed out an overhead cable that guided the barge. Since the barge lacked its own means of propulsion, it required the momentum of the truck to make the crossing. 'You got me, all right,' I thought as I began breathing again and pried my frozen hand from the door handle. My heart was racing overtime, but I did my best impersonation of composure, nodded thoughtfully, and whispered, "Interesting."

After we unloaded our bags on the far bank, we repeated the process of crossing the river to pick up the family. They had been watching the whole thing from the bank, and as I got out of Billy's pickup, it was obvious that the situation was now beyond the silence level. Sharon and Sarah, the blood drained from their faces, stood in disbelief. "You have got to be kidding," read the unmistakable message in their body language as I cheerfully announced that it was their turn. John, on the other hand, who was always ready for new adventure, seemed to be warming more and more to the situation.

I tried to assure each of them that there was really nothing to it and, crossing my fingers behind my back, that it was actually rather exhilarating. So Sharon and Sarah squeezed into the cab with Billy and John and I sat in the back as the pickup again sped down the embankment. I'm sure that both girls kept their eyes closed the whole time, and I doubt if Sharon breathed until the crossing was completed. But we made it, and the four of us walked in heavy silence onto the bank of Camp Crystal. At least we were finally there, and I am sure that all of us were more than ready to get settled into that beautiful log cabin home that awaited us on the wooded mountain slope.

Billy and two of his fellow camp counselors helped us with our luggage and escorted us to the doctor's quarters, which was to be my next image of Camp Crystal that would go the way of most dreams. To my dismay, our quarters turned out to be a small, cinder block structure without the slightest suggestion of charm or character. It was situated on a flat, open space that was more dirt than grass, without a flower or tree in sight. The single room was barely large enough for the two beds that constituted its sole furnishings, and the concrete floor looked like it had not been swept since last winter. A communal bathroom and shower in the back were connected to additional dwellings of similarly uninspired architecture that were occupied by other members of the camp staff.

Things began to pick up, however, when we met some of the staff members who would be our neighbors for the coming week. They were very nice and started to make us feel at home. I was especially impressed with the camp nurse, whose name was Martha. For her, this was an all-summer job, and she gave me a sense of comfort with her friendly, calm, and professional demeanor. She gave me a tour of the infirmary, which was a small wooden building with a single room that contained two beds and little medicine cabinet. It also had a front porch with a bench, which served as the waiting room. She reiterated my Duke friend's assurance that serious medical problems were extremely rare.

Martha had a son, Joey, who spent the summer at the camp with her. He was just a little younger than John, and both boys seemed pleased with the prospect of having a playmate for the coming week. Sarah also soon made new friends when three of the young campers came to our quarters to greet her and take her to where she would be spending the week with the other girls. So, with both children now happily occupied and Sharon busily trying to make our little dwelling take on some semblance of a home, I went for a walk around the camp. Looking up at the surrounding mountains for the first time, I realized that this really was quite a beautiful place. Although very little of my anticipation for Camp Crystal had thus far been realized, I was beginning to think that it might well be a pleasant week after all.

That evening, Sharon and I met the camp director and had dinner with him, his wife, and the other members of the adult staff. We were in a large, rustic communal dining room with all the campers and junior counselors. We could see Sarah, who seemed to be enjoying herself with her new friends. John and Joey were off in a corner at the counselors' table, undoubtedly making plans for their adventures in the week ahead. Yes, this was going to be a delightful week for us all.

As it was Sunday, an evening vesper service was held immediately after dinner. The site was an outdoor meeting area up a mountain slope that was reached via a narrow walking trail. A few logs provided the seating, but the most notable feature was the magnificent view of the mountains that were now bathed in the warm, reddish colors of the setting sun. The service was short and consisted mostly of old, familiar songs, but it seemed to impart a sense of peace in all of us as we quietly retraced our steps back down the mountain path. I for one felt an especially serene sense of peacefulness at that moment. Our family was together and happy, and the shadows of twilight were softening the appearance of the camp down below so that it almost fulfilled the beauty that I had once imagined. Yes,

I assured myself, we truly were in for a lovely week. And that is when I met Emily.

———

The evening's peaceful stillness was suddenly split by a blood-curdling scream from somewhere in the camp. It was, in fact, a series of rhythmic screams followed by moments of eerie silence, only to be broken again by another series of screams. The mood of all of us on the path suddenly changed to one of horror as the sequence of alternating screams and silence continued unabated. But I suspect that my horror was the greatest when I suddenly realized that all eyes were on me and seemed to be saying in unison, "Well, you're the doctor; do something." So I took their cue, broke ranks, and began running toward the sound.

Martha was there when I arrived, and a small girl was lying on the ground beside her. Martha quickly briefed me. The child's name was Emily. She was six years old, and she had just arrived at camp earlier that day. Her medical record was unremarkable except for a history of asthma. But this did not appear to be an asthma attack. She was breathing freely, but was totally unresponsive. I knelt beside her and attempted to talk with her, but it was as though she was in a coma. I must have jumped when she suddenly opened her eyes widely, stared straight ahead with no apparent recognition of her surroundings and let loose with another series of screams. To say that I had no idea what was wrong with Emily would have been the understatement of the day. I felt her pulse, and it was fast but strong. Her color was good, and her breathing remained free. Nevertheless, we tried giving her a puff of her asthma inhaler, which not surprisingly had no effect on her condition. It seemed that Emily was having some sort of a seizure, but not like any one I had ever seen or heard of.

We tried to call Emily's parents, but no one was home, and this was before the days of answering machines and long before cell phones. By now, it had been nearly thirty minutes since Emily's attack had begun, and the alternating sequence of screams and silence had continued with remarkable regularity. It was quite obvious by now that Emily needed far better medical care than I was able to offer. Martha explained that the nearest hospital with an emergency room was in a small town about forty-five minutes away. To further complicate matters, Billy told me that the river had continued to rise and that it was no longer possible to cross it on the barge. We would have to use a rowboat. And so, with Emily in my arms and Billy and another of the strongest camp counselors at the oars, we began our struggle across the rapidly flowing river. Everyone else in the camp stood silently on the bank, with the only sound being Emily's periodic screams echoing down the river and through the valley.

Fortunately, Billy had left his pickup on the other side, so we piled into it, and with Emily still in my arms, Billy gunned his old truck down the dirt road and onto the highway toward the hospital. By now, it had been over an hour since Emily's bizarre behavior had begun, and it had remained amazingly unchanged. But then, as suddenly as it had started, it stopped. In fact, to my added horror, everything stopped. Emily wasn't breathing!

"Stop the truck!" I yelled at Billy.

He slammed on the brakes and screeched to a halt on the grassy siding. I flung the door open and literally threw Emily on the ground and was about to begin CPR, when she started breathing again. I jumped back in the truck, with her in my arms, and yelled, "Floorboard it, Billy!"

With a faint smile on his face, Billy did just as I asked and gave that old truck everything it had. I don't know how fast we were going, although I rather hoped that a patrol car would spot us so that we could be escorted to the hospital. But the road was deserted that Sunday evening, and we sped uninhibited toward the hospital. Since getting back in the truck, Emily's status had changed significantly. The screaming had stopped, but she remained in an apparent coma, totally unresponsive to my attempts to talk to her.

When we reached the hospital, Billy drove up to the emergency room door, and I jumped out with Emily still in my arms. And then, just as I was charging through the entrance, to the surprised expressions of the small emergency room staff, Emily woke up. She looked into my eyes for a moment, with a quizzical but detached expression. Then she looked around with a slight sense of disorientation, but without crying or showing any of the fear or distress that I would have expected. In fact, Emily seemed surprisingly calm and curiously normal.

There was a young doctor on call that evening and, to this day, I don't think he believed a word I told him about Emily's condition, especially when I explained that I was an eye doctor. He checked her over carefully and announced that there was absolutely nothing wrong with her. Although Emily had nothing to say about the matter, her body language seemed to agree with the young doctor. If anything, she seemed preoccupied and kept looking around the room as though she was trying to find something.

The doctor suggested that we take Emily back to the camp, but the events of the last couple of hours were still giving me chills, and taking her back right then was the last thing that I was willing to do. What followed was a somewhat unpleasant exchange between the young doctor and me as we argued about the appropriate care for Emily. But he finally gave in, probably just to get me off his back, and agreed to keep her overnight for observation.

So Billy and I drove back to the camp much more slowly and with little said. Martha and the camp director were waiting for us, and I briefed them on Emily's course and management, but still could offer only vague guesses as to the cause of her strange behavior. I told them that I would go back and check on her first thing in the morning.

It was now dark and quiet throughout the camp, and I trusted that Sarah was in one of the tents, asleep with her new friends. John was staying with Sharon and me, and both were sound asleep when I finally got to our quarters. I didn't wake them, but lay awake much of the night thinking about all that had happened on our first day at Camp Crystal—and especially trying to make sense of the strange saga of Emily. I played the scene over and over in my mind, trying to match her behavior with any medical condition that I could recall, but without drawing any reasonable conclusions. I finally drifted off to sleep just as the first rays of morning sun appeared over the mountaintops.

With Sharon and John still sleeping, I dressed and roused Billy to row me back across the river. He had other chores to do that morning, so I took our station wagon and drove alone back to the hospital to check on Emily. When I got to her room, she was sitting up and appeared to be well rested and alert, but showed no interest in talking with me. A nearly empty tray beside her bed suggested that she had just finished her breakfast. The young doctor had gone home, but the duty nurse told me that Emily had an uneventful night, except that she cried quietly off and on throughout the night. Whenever the nurse went to check on her, however, she was asleep, and the crying seemed as though it was coming from bad dreams.

The hospital staff felt that she was healthy, with no explanation for her reported behavior, and cleared her for discharge. So, after the nurse helped her get dressed, Emily let me hold her hand as we left the hospital. She crawled into the back seat of our station wagon, and I was just about to get behind the wheel, thinking that this was surely going to be a better day, when Emily proceeded to throw up her entire breakfast over every inch of our car's back seat. I wiped her face with my handkerchief and held my hand to her forehead until her nausea seemed to pass. I told her not to worry about the mess, which probably wasn't necessary, since that seemed to be of no concern to her. As we drove back to the camp with Emily in the front seat, I attempted to make conversation with her, but she appeared to be on the verge of tears and had her arms wrapped tightly around herself as though she was holding something. And so we road in silence, and I marveled to myself that we had now been at Camp Crystal for less than one day.

—

Martha was at the infirmary conducting the daily sick call when Emily and I arrived back at camp. I was surprised by the number of young girls who were sitting on the front porch waiting to be seen. As Martha had assured me, however, they were all minor medical problems—a cut, a bruise, a sniffle, or just the need for a hug. I was starting to update Martha about Emily when one of the counselors came in to tell me that I had a phone call in the director's office. It was Emily's mother. She didn't seem very concerned as I explained the events of the last two days. "That's just like Emily," she seemed to say. I'm not sure that she believed everything I was telling her. In any case, she explained that there were pressing matters at home and that it would not be possible for anyone to come see Emily until the weekend.

When I told Martha about the conversation, she just rolled her eyes and said she wasn't surprised. She worried that many of the girls got very little attention at home, which probably explained why several of them came to the infirmary each day with minor problems—just for a little TLC (I noticed that Martha gave each a big hug before they left). Sadly, many girls spent their entire summer at the camp, apparently because their busy parents didn't have time for them. It was not uncommon for a child to learn at the end of the summer that their parents had gotten divorced while they were away at camp, and that the life they had left in the spring would never be the same.

I couldn't help but wonder how this sad commentary might explain Emily's behavior. In any case, we checked her vital signs, all of which were normal, and then contacted her counselor to come help her back to her tent for rest and observation. I stayed with Martha in the infirmary until all the other girls were taken care of and then decided I had better go and clean out the backseat of our station wagon.

As I was finishing up the cleaning, Billy happened by and seemed to be amused when I told him the latest in the saga of Emily. We chatted for a while, and I asked him if there were any trails around the camp where I might do some running. What he told me next would prove to offer a highlight of the week at Camp Crystal for me. A railroad had once run through the valley, paralleling the course of the winding Crystal Creek. The bed for the train track had been cut out of the mountainside that sloped down to the river. The tracks had long since been removed, but the smooth granite bed remained, providing miles of perfect running surface with majestic scenery. Billy assured me it would be one of my most memorable running sites, and I was soon to learn how right he was.

It was now approaching noontime, and I went back to check on the family and get a bite to eat with them before exploring Billy's running trail. Sharon had obviously been cleaning our quarters all morning, and it now looked quite livable. She said John and Joey had been out all morning, and about that time the guys returned, covered in dirt from head to toe, but obviously having a grand time. Sharon had seen Sarah earlier in the morning, and she seemed to be content with her new friends. They planned to spend the afternoon in the arts and crafts pavilion, and Sharon was going to help them. So everyone seemed to be happy. We had a light lunch together in the communal dining hall, after which I went back to our quarters and changed into my running clothes.

The old railroad bed and the scenery it offered truly lived up to Billy's rave reviews. It provided some of the most spectacular vistas I have ever enjoyed. On one side of the trail, the mountains rose high above me, with tall pine trees, multicolored flowers, and outcroppings of majestic rock formations. At one point, a small waterfall bubbled down amid the trees and flowers and rocks until it disappeared beneath me on its way to the river far below. Crystal Creek was a considerable distance down on the other side of the old railroad bed, and from my perspective, it was actually quite beautiful as it wound peacefully through the valley. It became progressively wider as it flowed down between the mountains, and soon I could to see occasional small islands in the river with pine trees on the rocky surfaces. It was truly a tranquil setting, with the total silence broken only by the distant sound of the water flowing in the river down below and the singing of the birds overhead. In fact, it was so tranquil and inspiring that all my cares were soon left behind and I ran effortlessly and mindlessly, disregarding time and distance. When fatigue finally brought me back to reality, I realized that I had covered several miles and that it was an equal distance back to camp. Furthermore, my effortless running had been partly due to the gradual decline of the railroad bed, and now I had to face the harder incline all the way back.

There was some advantage to my predicament in that fatigue now forced me to walk for a while, and that, in turn, forced me to listen and to think. The sounds of the river became more distinct, and I could now distinguish many different bird songs, the bubbling of the waterfall, and even the wind in the trees high above me. And listening seemed to clear my mind, and I began to think—especially about Emily. She posed so many unanswered questions: her behavior Sunday evening, of course, but also this morning; the sense that she was looking for something; and the fact that I had never heard her speak. My thoughts took me back a decade to when Sharon and I first met in the hospital room of another child with a seemingly inextricable medical problem. Petey had been admitted with the sudden onset of blindness for which there was no physical explanation. Only after listening to the little patient and his family did it become clear that Petey had most likely suffered a conversion reaction, in which emotions are believed to be transformed into physical manifestations. In his case, the emotional trauma presumably stemmed from an irrational fear that he would go blind if he was a bad boy. I couldn't help but wonder if something had upset Emily in a similar way to provoke her behavior the night before, and, if so, what had it been. I hoped that some answers would be forthcoming in the week that lay ahead.

When I finally made it back to camp, late in the afternoon, I headed toward our quarters, which took me by the infirmary. As I came around the side of the building toward the porch, I heard the sound of a young girl in what seemed like nonstop chatter, although I could only make out bits of her conversation: "...listen to the birdie ... be a good girl ... don't have to swim ... let's pick flowers ... play by yourself ... be a happy girl ... don't complain ... look at the bug ... Mommy is very busy."

It was a voice that I did not recall hearing before, but something told me whose voice it might be. Sure enough, when I rounded the corner, there was Emily sitting on the porch of the infirmary all by herself. Actually, she was not entirely alone. She was sitting much as she had been in our station wagon earlier that morning, with her arms wrapped tightly about her.

But this time there was something in her arms—a doll. She was talking earnestly and nonstop to her doll. But when she saw me, she once again fell silent. I walked over and sat down a respectable distance from her on the bench.

"What's your doll's name?" I asked.

She gave me a rather annoyed glance, as though to register her irritation that I had violated her private space. Or maybe I had insulted her companion by calling it a doll. In any case, she pulled it closer to her and maintained her silence. From what I could see of the doll, it was not what you would expect for a child of her privileged socioeconomic background. It seemed quite old and worn. The hair was made of brown yarn, and the face appeared to have been painted on a skin-colored muslin that was stretched over the original face. The arms and legs were the hard, molded type of an earlier era and hung loosely from the stuffed body. The dress, which obviously was also quite old, had a flowered print with lace around the neck and sleeves. Whatever story there was behind the doll—and I was sure there must be one—it was clear that she meant the world to Emily.

"You have a sweet baby," I offered, trying to smooth over my opening blunder.

But it was to no avail. She had already withdrawn back into her silent world and looked down at the floor without showing any further outward sign of interest in my presence. I tried a few more times to make small talk about how she was feeling and how she liked the camp, but it was obvious that Emily and I were not going to have a conversation. So I wished her and her companion a pleasant evening and left her sitting on the infirmary porch

After breakfast the next morning, John and Joey were off on their latest adventure, and Sharon and I went for a walk along one of the mountain paths. It was a lovely morning, and we enjoyed the softness of the pine needles under our feet and the variety of beautiful flora. We were especially taken by the colorful toadstools. It seemed that the forest floor in the mountains was always moist and provided an ideal nurture for the toadstools, which grew large with bright red-orange tops over white stalks. At one point, we came to an opening in the woods with a stand of Scottish thistle that attracted a variety of butterflies (at least some of my dreams about Camp Crystal were being realized). It was fortunate that Sharon and I shared the same appreciation for the beauty of nature, and it made for a delightful walk.

On our way back to the camp, Sharon asked about Emily. I told her of my theory about the cause of the Sunday night incident, and we reminisced for a moment about Petey and those early days. But there were so many unanswered questions. What had provoked her reaction? Why was she reluctant to talk? What was so special about her doll? And why would she only talk to the doll?

Sharon thought about the last question for a minute and then offered, "Maybe it's because the doll listens."

———

Later that morning, I went to the infirmary to help Martha with the sick call, although I was more of an observer than a helper. There was the usual number of girls with the usual number of minor problems, and Martha handled each skillfully, giving every girl a hug before sending them back to the day's activities. Emily was not among them, but when I went out on the porch, there she was, sitting on the bench with her doll. Sharon's suggestion had been burning in my mind ever since our walk, and I had decided on a plan to test it. I walked over to Emily and sat down beside her—a little closer than the day before—but did not say a word. I think the two of us (or should I say three) sat there for about fifteen minutes. For me, it was a very long and difficult fifteen minutes, but I was determined to keep my mouth shut. Eventually, I got up and left, without a word.

After lunch, I went for another run on the old railroad bed. It was just as pleasant as the day before, but I was more anxious to get back to the camp this time. As I walked past the infirmary, I was pleased to see that Emily was there, just as she had been that morning and the day before. I stepped up on the porch and took a seat beside her, although leaving a bit more room between us this time so as not to offend her with my perspiration. I was tired from the run, and it felt good to sit quietly as the minutes ticked by.

"Clementine."

Her voice was barely audible, and I wasn't sure if she had actually spoken or if it was just the wind or my imagination. I looked over at her, and our eyes caught for a brief moment.

"Her name is Clementine." She was answering my question of the previous day.

I didn't know if I should speak or not, but after a moment of silence I said, "That's a nice name," to which she nodded in agreement with a very serious face—it was then I realized that I had never seen Emily smile.

That was the extent of our conversation for the day. But as I got up to leave, I thought I saw a fleeting moment of wistfulness in her eyes.

"See you tomorrow?" I asked from the bottom of the porch stairs. She nodded, and I thought I saw just the hint of a smile.

That evening, Sarah came over to spend some time with us, and it was good to have all the family together again. But I couldn't get Emily off my mind, and I asked Sarah what she had learned about her. The girls considered her to be shy and a bit aloof, although she was obviously bright and generally well liked by all. The one thing that was peculiar, however, was her attachment to her doll. When she had arrived on Sunday afternoon, the doll was apparently misplaced during the transfer of belongings across the river. This seemed to cause Emily an inordinate amount of distress, and no one was able to console her. The pieces of the puzzle were beginning to fit into place.

———

Over the next three days, Emily and I continued our twice-daily visits—in the mornings after sick call and in the afternoons following my railroad run. We always met on the porch of the infirmary, where Emily and her doll would be sitting patiently on the wooden bench. For me, those were truly memorable moments. It was slow at first, with long periods of silence, but it seemed that Emily wanted to talk, and I was thrilled when she actually began to do so. With each progressive visit, I witnessed an amazing transformation in Emily; she became animated, with a sparkle in her eyes and even a smile. Before long, she was talking nonstop, and all I had to do was listen. But it wasn't just Emily and me—it was the three of us, as she always included Clementine in her discourse. By the end of the week, I felt that I knew them both rather well, from what she told me and my attempts to fill in the gaps. In any case, Emily's story answered a lot of questions.

She was the only child of a well-to-do family in northern Virginia. Both parents worked and apparently had important and demanding jobs, which left little time for family life. Emily had several nannies during her early childhood and never grew attached to any of them. Her closest relationship seemed to be with her father, who tried to be there when she was sick or had a bad dream or a boo-boo. Emily gave me the impression that father and daughter were quite close. Then one day, when she had just turned four, he was gone. Her mother explained that they "could not live together," but that Emily would continue to see her father. Within months, however, he moved to the West Coast. There were frequent phone calls, but they were brief and no substitute for his presence. He promised her that, when she was older, she could fly to be with him during the summer, but to a four-year-old child that seemed like another lifetime.

Emily loved and respected her mother. In fact, she would defend her to me by observing that "she is very important" and "very busy." I wasn't really sure if she was saying this for my benefit or Clementine's—or maybe for her own. One of the things that Emily especially enjoyed was visiting her paternal grandmother, who lived close by. Grandma lived in the old house where Emily's father had grown up, and she loved rummaging through the attic, finding things that had belonged to her father. One day, she found an old doll in rather bad shape. She took it downstairs to ask Grandma about it and was told that it had belonged to her father when he was a very little boy. While it was not fashionable for boys to have dolls, this one seemed to be an important companion for the little boy, and they were rarely separated. But as he grew older, his interests gave way to trucks and baseballs and other boys' things, and the little doll was put away and soon forgotten.

Emily must have pondered this story for some time. She inquired as to the doll's name. "Your father called her Clementine." Emily wasn't terribly impressed with the name, nor with the disheveled appearance of the old doll, but something seemed to be drawing them together. She asked her Grandma if she might take it home with her. "Of course."

It wasn't that Emily lacked dolls or other toys. By her own admission, she had a plethora of material possessions. She had a large bedroom and playroom that were lavishly decorated. One entire wall was lined with shelves that held the complete collection of Madame Alexander dolls. Emily enjoyed playing with the dolls, but they were only toys, while Clementine soon became her companion. They were as inseparable as her father and the doll had been in a previous era. Like so many children with imaginary playmates, Clementine became for Emily the "person" who was always there and who would always listen.

In medical school, although I don't recall it being a part of any curriculum, we were taught the importance of listening to our patients. I remember standing with other students in a hospital room as one of our professors would listen thoughtfully to the complaints of a patient. In the days before all the modern diagnostic tests, a careful medical history was often the best way that a doctor had of arriving at the correct diagnosis. And even today, with all the sophisticated diagnostic tools at our disposal, there is still no substitute for listening carefully to what our patients can tell us.

Of course, making a proper diagnosis is only one of the many merits of thoughtful listening. For the patient, it also imparts a sense of comfort and even self-worth that the doctor cares enough to listen to what they have to say. And this is obviously true in every walk of life. It is easy to underestimate the impact that simply listening carefully and thoughtfully to what another person has to say can have on that individual. For a child, it tells them that they are important and builds their self-esteem. And for all of us, it simply says that we care. Over the years, I have been reminded of this important lesson many times by medical colleagues, friends, and patients. But I don't believe that anyone ever drove the point home for me more convincingly and indelibly than Emily.

I suppose she is married now, with children of her own. And somewhere in their home, a well-worn doll most likely enjoys a place of honor. I doubt that Clementine could survive another generation of youthful love, but I rather suspect that her spirit of listening and caring lives on in that home and in all the lives that have been touched by Emily.

———

We left Crystal Creek on Saturday morning, one week after our fateful arrival, and I have to admit that we were all ready to go. The week had not turned out exactly as any of us had anticipated. Sarah had been a trooper, as always, but for such a prim and proper young lady, sleeping in a tent that leaked over her bed and using bathroom facilities that would have passed no hygiene inspection, one week was quite enough, thank you. John probably enjoyed the week more than anyone, romping through the woods with Joey. The only problem was that those woods, unbeknownst to us, were full of poison ivy, and the poor little guy was covered in a rash from head to toe and was more than ready to say good-bye to the source of his misery. And Sharon had patiently endured the week with her usual good humor, but I knew that she could not wait to get her family back to the cleanliness and order of our home.

For me, there were mixed emotions. I had gone over to the infirmary to say good-bye to Martha, hoping I might also see Emily one last time. But she wasn't there. Martha told me she had stopped by earlier, but wanted to go off with her girl friends to the horse stable for riding lessons. She had asked Martha to tell me good-bye, if I stopped by before leaving. I must confess that it gave me a twinge of sadness that we could not say good-bye in person, but it was far more important that she was now interacting with the other girls. As I stepped off the porch of the infirmary, Martha came to the door, having just remembered one more thing that Emily had said. "She wanted you to know that Clementine also said good-bye."

Billy was waiting for us on the riverbank with his row boat, which seemed like a much more civilized way to depart than our initial mode of crossing Crystal Creek. The level of the river had gone down some, the flow was much gentler, and the water almost seemed clear. It was still a far cry from the images that I had once entertained before our arrival, but as I sat beside my little family in the boat and looked back at Camp Crystal for a final time, I couldn't help but think that—for me at least—maybe this had been the perfect vacation after all.

$$\Omega$$

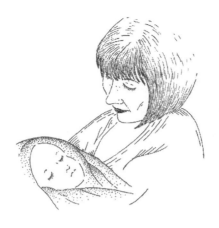

9.

April's Mother

I was in a foul mood as I came down the stairs to breakfast. And I was willing to admit it. But then I had good cause—or so I reasoned.

The problem was that Duke had lost the night before. For those who have not spent at least one basketball season in the Atlantic Coast Conference, this may be hard to understand. Indeed, when Sharon and I first came to Durham in the early 1970s, we had little interest in basketball and wondered why a game should preempt a television program that we wanted to watch. Having come from Oklahoma, where football was the all-consuming passion, basketball season—at least in those days—was largely a time to talk about the prospects for next year's football team. But we had not been at Duke long before we sensed an entirely different atmosphere.

At first, I simply found it amusing that people seemed to live and die by their basketball team from one frenetic game to the next. And it didn't seem to be limited to any particular segment of the community—women and men, children and grandparents, farmers and bankers were all caught up in the fever. Kids would come into the office proudly wearing T-shirts that proclaimed allegiance to their chosen team, and little white-haired ladies would have to discuss the most recent game or the next one on the schedule before settling in for their examination. And what amazed me most was that, within less than a year at Duke, Sharon and I were also hooked and found ourselves among the most rabid, incurable fans of the Duke basketball program.

One of the things that fanned the flames of our passion for basketball was the success of nearly all the teams in the ACC, especially the four in North Carolina. The two main ones, of course, are Duke and the University of North Carolina at Chapel Hill, the campuses of which are less than ten miles apart. Over the years, rarely has a season gone by without at least one of the two teams—and often both—being in contention for the national championship, and frequently winning it. And the other two ACC teams in the state—Wake Forest and North Carolina State—which are both just down the road from Durham and Chapel Hill, have also enjoyed their share of national success. As a result, within any workplace throughout the state, it is usually possible to find staunch supporters for at least two or more of the schools, especially Duke and UNC, which leads to intense rivalry. And the Duke Eye Center was no exception. Nurse Sharon and I faithfully upheld the honor of Duke, while Robin was a die-hard UNC fan and had plenty of company, even though we worked under a Duke roof.

When the time approaches for Duke and UNC to face off on the hard court, the passion of the season reaches its zenith. Students literally stand in line for days—weeks, actually—camping out in tents, to ensure their chance of getting into the game. A common high school graduation gift for young people who are headed to Duke is a tent for just that purpose. In our office, jokes and verbal jabs were tossed back and forth with abandon as we prophesied the outcome of the big game. A few bets exchanged hands, but no amount of money, won or lost, could compare to the sheer ecstasy of defeating our archrival, or the unthinkable agony of having to face our conquerors in the office the next day.

I must confess that I sometimes envied my colleagues who simply had no interest in sports and were amazingly able to stay above it all, not even realizing that there had been a game. For them, the next morning was just another day, irrespective of who had won or lost the night before. On the occasions when we won, I felt a bit sorry for them to be missing the thrill of victory. But when we lost and I slogged through the mire of depression while they continued on their merry way, I was truly envious and even a bit irritated by their lack of feeling, although inwardly I wished that I could be like them—at least for that moment.

Last night had been the big game. Duke had played well, but UNC had played better. When the final buzzer sounded, we had three fewer points showing on the scoreboard. And so it was that I was in a foul mood as I joined the family for breakfast.

I guess I wasn't hiding my feelings very well. John, who was only five years old, apparently picked up on it first.

"What's wrong with you, Dad?" he asked casually as he glanced up momentarily from studying the back of his cereal box.

His nonchalant attitude only added to my lousy mood. Even though he was only five, I felt that he should be aware of and appropriately distraught by an event of such magnitude. Being the "good father," therefore, I decided to give him a little education that morning on appreciating things of profound importance. I began by patiently stating the basic facts.

"Duke lost to Carolina last night," I gravely announced and then waited for his response of alarm.

"That's not important," he replied, without even looking up from his cereal box.

Now I sensed that we had a real problem, and could feel my ire rising. Was he trying to be smart with me, or was he really that out of touch with the importance of something like a Duke-UNC basketball game? I vowed to be calm and reasonable and to give him a fatherly lecture to help straighten him out. But first I decided—rather cleverly, I thought—to put a little heat on him by asking him a question.

"Well then, what is important?"

He read a few more words on his box, and then looked up at me. Our eyes locked for just a moment as he gave me his answer.

"Love," he replied and then went back to his reading.

Well, so much for fatherly advice. It was not the first time in the life of our family, that the tables were turned, and I found myself learning from our children. Basketball has never seemed quite so important since that morning (although I still have my moments), but I continue to be increasingly struck by the truth of John's statement—without love, there really isn't much in life that is important. It is a lesson that I have had to learn and relearn throughout my life, but it was our five-year-old son who reminded me of it that morning.

There seem to be many different levels and expressions of love, and I have been privileged to witness most of them in my years of caring for patients. I have seen the love of parents who would sacrifice anything for the health of their child. I have seen love in the face of an exhausted old man as he selflessly cares for his invalid wife. I have seen love in a boy who offers to give his eye so that his friend might see. But of all the inspiring examples of love that I have been privileged to witness, none has ever touched me more deeply than that shown in the life and story of April's mother.

———

In high school, Jean had been the type of person whom you can't quite recall when you return for a class reunion. She had been unremarkable in nearly every respect. She was of average height and less than average weight. Her thin nose and sunken cheeks were framed by straight, brown hair. Her pale skin was accented only by a few freckles under her eyes and had rarely known the blush from summer's sun or the benefit of cosmetics.

She was of average intelligence, but more than average shyness. Her teachers apparently recognized both qualities in her and rarely called on her to speak in class. As a result, she occupied a seat in a schoolroom day after day, year after year, and few of her classmates were ever consciously aware that she even existed. But there must have been something about her. Maybe it was the look in her eyes that promised a special quality waiting to be released. In any case, it was noticed by one young man.

Jimmy Honeycutt was also painfully bashful, but he hid it behind the typical bravado of male youth. He derived most of his sense of self-worth from automobiles. Ever since he was a young boy, he loved to tinker with engines, and by high school he was a skilled mechanic. He was never happier than when he was alone with a car, locating a problem, changing a part, or tuning her up. His hands were so constantly in greasy machinery that his fingernails had not known a clean day in years, and no amount of scrubbing would probably ever remedy that. To him it was a source of pride—a sign of his skill. But what he wanted most of all was to prove his skill in auto racing.

Jean and Jimmy had been in classes together for years and yet had never spoken a word to each other. The fact was that he had never spoken to any girl in any of his classes, and it may have been their mutual shyness that caused Jimmy to notice Jean and to develop a vague and carefully masked feeling for her. It seemed destined to go no further when the last day of their senior year arrived, and the class received instructions for their graduation exercises.

It was a typical high school graduation: hot and boring. Each student, in cap and gown, had to walk alone across the entire stage to receive his or her diploma before the next student followed, in what seemed like an ordeal that would never end. When Jean made her trek across the stage, few besides her parents took notice. Only one other set of eyes followed her from one side of the stage to the other.

The senior dance was a welcome relief for most of the new graduates, but for Jean it was just one more ordeal to endure. She had never danced and would have been terrified if anyone had asked her to do so. She positioned herself in a dark corner of the room, near the punch bowl, and wished for the night to end. When someone gently bumped into her, she first felt irritation and then embarrassment. She looked down and away, hoping the person would move on, but that didn't happen. There was a voice apologizing to her, and there was something about the voice that made her turn and look. It was Jimmy.

He too had been hiding in the corner, nursing a glass of punch, and had not been aware of Jean's presence—or so he claimed—until he "accidentally" bumped into her. For what seemed like an eternity to both of them, they stood facing each other with their eyes directed toward the floor. Then Jimmy finally summoned the courage to speak.

"Want some punch?" he asked, offering her his half-emptied glass.

She looked down at the glass in his hand and said the first thing that came to her mind. "You should've washed your hands before comin' to a party like this."

"Well, I did, but I'm a mechanic, and there ain't nothin' can get this dirt out."

Jean's face flushed with embarrassment as she wondered how she could have said such a stupid thing, but what surprised her even more was that Jimmy didn't seem to mind.

"Your name's Jimmy, ain't it?"

"Yeah."

"Mine's Jean."

"I know."

Another long, embarrassing silence followed. This time it was Jean who summoned the courage to speak.

"What kind of mechanic are you?"

"I fix racing cars," he replied in a somewhat less-than-half-truth.

For Jean that was the end of the conversation. Nothing was of less interest to her than the noise, dirt, and violence of auto racing.

"Wanna come see me race?" Jimmy asked, showing a trace of enthusiasm for the first time since their meeting.

"Maybe."

"Well, if you do, I'll be racin' at the fairgrounds next Friday night."

For the first time, their eyes met, and they remained locked for only a second. But for two young people whose emotions were imprisoned within and yearning to be released, that second offered an epiphany of what the future might hold, and their lives changed in that instant.

"I gotta go," Jean said hurriedly, and she awkwardly rushed away, leaving Jimmy to wonder what he had done wrong or if he would ever see her again.

It was true that Jimmy was scheduled to be in a race at the fairgrounds the following week. What he had failed to tell Jean was that it would be the first race in which he had ever competed. Furthermore, he had neither the credentials nor the car to be competing in professional racing, but a friend of a friend, and a little money under the table, had allowed him to get tacked on as the last car in the last race of the evening. None of this bothered Jimmy, however. He was young and still believed in miracles. And on top of that, he told himself that "his girl" would be there.

His eyes scoured the grandstand as he stood beside his car inside the racetrack, waiting for his event. He couldn't see her, and he lost a bit of his courage as he allowed reality to edge in to his dream. But then the loudspeaker announced his race, and his courage returned with a rush of adrenaline as he prepared for what he was sure would be his big moment.

The other drivers were older than Jimmy, and their cars were shinier and had logos representing numerous sponsors, of which his car was bare. None of the drivers had spoken to Jimmy, and even those who bothered to glance his way did so with a look of disdain, as though to ask why he was degrading the dignity of their profession. Things went bad from the very beginning of the race. His car was positioned at the back of the pack, and he soon realized that he was not able to maintain the speed of the other cars as they left him farther and farther behind. Again he felt his courage ebbing. As he passed in front of the grandstand, he glanced up at the crowd, this time hoping that Jean was not there watching him. Unfortunately, he looked a second too long, and when his eyes returned to the track, he discovered that he was heading straight toward the retaining wall in the curve.

There was a loud crash of scraping metal and a shower of sparks as his car hit the wall and then spun around several times on the track.

Fortunately, he was so far behind the other cars that there was no risk of tangling up with them, but they had to take the caution flag and slow their pace while Jimmy's car was towed off the track. He was not hurt, but his car was disabled and was left in the infield as the other drivers completed the race.

After the race, the crowd left and the floodlights were turned off. Jimmy sat alone on the grass beside his car in the semidarkness, wondering how he was going to get home. It was some time before he realized that he was not entirely alone. He looked up to see the thin silhouette of a girl against the pale nightlights from the stands.

"You sure was the most exciting driver tonight." Her voice came over the grassy field and echoed around the empty track.

Jimmy couldn't help but smile to himself. He stared at her as she continued to stand there, some fifty feet away. Then he jumped up and walked to her.

"Yeah, well, it's too bad that wall got in the way, cause I was just startin' to gain on 'em."

"How you gonna get home?" Jean asked.

Jimmy looked back at his helpless car. "Don't know."

"I got my folks' car tonight. Want a ride?" she offered.

Jean and Jimmy drove home in the moonlight that evening. But they didn't go straight home. They discovered something in each other that night, and it was the beginning of a long and beautiful summer.

———

By late summer, Jean began to realize that something about her was changing. Her monthly cycles had always been a bit irregular, so she was not too concerned when her period was two weeks late. But by September, when she was six weeks late, Jean knew that she was pregnant.

Having had time to anticipate what was happening, she did not panic, but carefully considered her options. Abortion was not one of them, as far as she was concerned. Besides, she had come to believe that she loved Jimmy and was sure that he loved her. Therefore, she would go to Jimmy first, and then they would go to their parents.

He was under a car when Jean walked into the garage where Jimmy worked. He seemed happy to see her and wiped his hands before coming over and giving her a hug and a kiss. They shared small talk for a few minutes before Jean made her announcement.

"Jimmy, looks like I'm gonna have your baby."

Silence followed as Jimmy's pupils dilated and his heart quickened.

"What you aim to do about it?" he was finally able to ask her.

"Well, I reckon we oughta get married, so we can make a home for our baby."

More silence.

"Shoot, Jean, I'm only nineteen years old. I ain't ready to be no father."

Now it was Jean who could find no words. She was crushed and buried her face in her hands as she broke out in uncontrollable sobbing. Crying was a tactic for which Jimmy had no defense. He did care for Jean and was finally persuaded to her point of view.

They went to her parents, whose principles were of another generation but whose love for their daughter was stronger than any social mores. They took Jean to a doctor, who confirmed the pregnancy, and then arranged for a quiet wedding by a justice of the peace. And so it was, as September drew to its close, that Jean became Mrs. Jimmy Honeycutt.

The marriage did not go well from the start. Jimmy had been living in a room over the garage where he worked and was unable to provide more for Jean. Her parents insisted that they move in with them. Jimmy reluctantly agreed, but he was never comfortable there. He spent longer and longer hours at the garage and often spent the night there in his old room. This worried Jean, but she was confident that things would be different when the baby arrived and they would have a common bond to draw them together.

One day in mid-October, some relatives came to visit at Jean's home. It was her cousin and his wife with their six-year-old son, Jason. The boy had not been feeling too well, and Jean noticed a fine rash on his face. His mother said it had come on only the day before and was probably just one of those childhood things. Later they learned that Jason had rubella, also known as German measles.

Rubella is a common communicable disease of childhood. The symptoms are typically mild, and Jason was feeling and looking better by the third day. During that time, however, he was releasing virus particles into the air and on the things he touched. The adults, including Jean, were immune to the disease through prior exposure, but the baby inside Jean was not. The virus entered her body, crossed the placenta, and went to the developing child, who was still in the first trimester of the pregnancy. The rubella virus consists primarily of RNA, which provides genetic instructions as to how the cells in our body are developed and maintained.

This can have devastating effects on the developing baby during the first trimester, causing a condition known as congenital rubella syndrome. It is associated with birth defects that can involve any part of the body, but most commonly the heart, brain, eyes, and ears. The most severe cases are stillborn, but those children who survive may not only be deaf and blind, but may also have heart defects, severe mental disability, small stature, and paralytic or spastic arms and legs.

All of these things and more were happening to Jean's baby. But she was unaware of any of it and was becoming happier and more optimistic by the day as the due date in April approached. She and Jimmy had agreed that, if it was a boy, they would name him Jimmy Jr. If it was a girl, they would call her April, after the anticipated month of her birth. The delivery occurred a little earlier than expected but did make it into April. It was a girl. And so it was that April Honeycutt entered the world.

It was a difficult delivery, and Jean was heavily sedated as she lay in her hospital room. But she was aware of people talking in hushed voices some distance from her bed. She heard her mother cry. Then, through blurry eyes, she saw Jimmy talking to the doctors. At first he seemed to be confused, and then he became angry. He shook his head and shouted something. Then he turned and bolted from the room. It was the last time any of them ever saw Jimmy.

—

Over the years that I was privileged to care for my patients, I was repeatedly struck by how God seems to provide inner strength or coping abilities commensurate with the challenges that people must face in their lives. April's mother was going to need that strength in spades. Within less than a day, her world had gone from dreams of a home with a husband and a healthy baby to being a single mom with a child who might never even know who she was. In addition to her defective development of mind and body, April was destined to be deaf and blind. But in the years that followed, this small, frail, shy mother would demonstrate strength far greater than any army of strong men could muster.

April was nearly a year old the first time she was brought into my office in her mother's arms with her grandmother—Jean's mother—beside her. This was to be the way that I would see the three of them for the next thirteen years. During those years, I would hear most of their story. But on that first day, I only knew that April carried the diagnosis of congenital rubella syndrome. As an infant, she did not appear, on the surface, to be significantly different from other children. She was small for her age, and her head was even smaller in proportion to her body. But she had a pretty face and delicate, pale skin, like that of her mother. She kept her eyes closed most of the time, and when she did open them there was the cloudy, wandering appearance of blindness. Congenital rubella syndrome can cause blindness in several ways, including glaucoma, cataracts, inflammation, and retinal disease. My initial examination disclosed several of these developmental abnormalities in April's eyes, but the main problem was congenital glaucoma, which had already destroyed most of her optic nerve in both eyes. Considering her general health, I hoped to avoid surgery and was pleased to find that the glaucoma could be controlled with eye drops. However, neither this nor any other treatment could bring back her sight.

April's mother and grandmother faithfully administered her glaucoma drops twice each day and brought her in for regular appointments like clockwork, several times each year. The scene was always the same: April in her mother's arms with her grandmother by her side. Our routine was also the same with each visit, beginning with comments on how pretty April looked. And in those early years, this was true—she really was quite a pretty little thing—and I could see the pride and joy in the eyes of her mother and grandmother and sense their anticipation and hope that things would yet turn out well for their baby.

But as time passed, it was increasingly obvious that April's condition was only continuing to deteriorate. She was getting bigger, but was steadily falling behind the average weight and size for her age range. She was becoming extremely frail, owing in part to the fact that she had a weak heart and could only be fed liquids through a tube that was passed through her nose and down her throat. Her body was developing a rigid spasticity, in which her neck and back were bowed backwards, and her arms and legs were drawn in toward her body. What few, poorly developed teeth she had were constantly grinding against each other. She was apparently deaf, although her severely limited mental status prevented her from communicating in any way to confirm this or to show any signs of emotion. Her cloudy eyes continued to wander, and if she had any vision, she had no way of telling us.

Despite the continuing change in April, the one thing that never changed over the years was the way the three of them came into the office, with April in her mother's arms and grandmother by her side. This became increasingly remarkable as April grew older and larger. I doubt that her weight ever exceeded fifty pounds, but her rigidity and spastic movements made her ever more difficult to hold. On top of this, Jean appeared increasingly tired and frail with each visit, and I suspect that her weight was never much more than a hundred pounds. And the visits were becoming more somber. Long gone were the days when we commented on April's beauty, but I would routinely inquire as to her condition since their last visit, and the answer was always the same: "She's doing fine." Of course, she wasn't fine, and we all knew it, but Jean's eyes continued to express a mother's love and hope. And I continued to marvel at the strength and resolve that came from within this frail young woman.

There came a time—indeed, it had long passed—when I could really do nothing to help April, other than simply check her eyes and tell her family that nothing had changed since the last visit. It was also quite apparent that these trips to my office were becoming increasingly hard for all three of them, and I finally suggested to Jean and her mother that they might want to come less frequently. But Jean was firm in her insistence that her daughter should have the best care possible, and so I continued to see the family on a regular basis.

One day they missed an appointment. It was the first time this had happened in the nearly thirteen years that I had been seeing April, so I called their home. Her grandmother answered the phone. The tone in her voice told me that something was wrong—very wrong. April had died. It seems that her feeble heart, which had miraculously sustained her all these years, had simply stopped beating.

The news of a death, no matter the circumstances or how remote our knowledge of the deceased may be, rarely fails to give us pause in our life, if only for a moment. Our thoughts and concerns are typically for the bereaved, and I suspect the most common reaction is to rationalize the death. For the elderly, we say, "They had a long life." For those who suffered a long, painful illness, we say, "They are now at peace" or "in a better place." But too often our attempts to rationalize death fall hollow or fail to find any words at all, particularly when it is the death of a child or a young parent in the prime of their life. At such times, we can only confess that there are just things that we have yet to understand. But what do you say about a thirteen-year-old girl, who, for all we know, never even knew that she was alive? My concern, of course, was for her mother.

After the momentary shock of the news passed, I must confess that I felt a strange sense of relief. April had never had any quality of life, and she most likely was now in a "better place." As for her mother, I knew that she would go through a period of mourning, but I couldn't help but feel good that she would eventually have the chance for a new life. There was no question in my mind that Jean had spent every moment of the past thirteen years worrying about and caring for her daughter. I seriously doubted that she had ever left the house except to take April to one of her many doctor's appointments or maybe to give her a little fresh air around the neighborhood or in a park. Had she ever gone to a movie or had dinner out with a friend? I felt that I knew the answer and hoped that she would one day soon be able to devote more time to herself and start a new life with the happiness that she so richly deserved.

After a moment of respectful silence, I asked about Jean and how she was doing. There followed an even longer silence, and I began to sense that the tone I had heard in grandmother's voice had been prompted by something more than just the loss of April.

"Jean had to be placed in a hospital," her mother finally replied.

That didn't surprise me too much at first. Jean had a frail constitution, which had been strained to the limit over the years in caring for her daughter with an almost superhuman will. Often, when we are finally relieved of the demand for a sustained effort, concentration, or worry, the body momentarily gives way and takes a little time to recover. There were times following surgery that I would notice a tremor in my hands after I had been concentrating on keeping them steady during the operation. And that, of course, was nothing compared to what Jean had been going through day after day, year after year. I assumed that this was why she needed some rest in the hospital, but for lack of knowing what else to say, I asked her mother what the problem was.

"At first they thought it was a nervous breakdown," she replied slowly, with palpable fear in her voice. "But now the doctors think it is something worse—something about a psychotic depression from losing April. She can't talk or hardly move and is having to be fed by a tube. The doctors don't know if she will ever come out of it."

Now I was the one responsible for a long, emotional silence. I finally told April's grandmother that she and Jean would be in my prayers and hung up the phone.

I was thankful to be alone in my office with the door shut, because I needed time to compose my emotions and my thoughts. Frankly, I was stunned. For thirteen years, Jean had devoted the full measure of her physical and emotional energy to caring for a child who never spoke a word to her, who could never see or hear or even touch her, and who could never show even the slightest sign of emotion to her mother. And yet she loved that child as much as any parent could ever love the most gifted, beautiful, healthy child. Talk about unconditional love. What but love of such rare quality could cause a person to deny herself year after year and give the full measure of devotion to her beloved? And what but love so pure could cause a person to lose her will to live when the object of her love is taken from her? It was humbling to realize that, as intensely as I have loved, here was love far beyond anything that I have ever felt or given.

Love has many forms. There is the aspiring, fulfilling love, which often has a sensual or sexual quality. In its purest form, it is the consummation of love between husband and wife in which both give and receive something of priceless value. At a higher level, there is love that transcends the physical—the love of an elderly couple who has walked through life together and now find their primary focus and joy in life to be the well-being and happiness of their mate—or the love of parents and grandparents who would make any sacrifice to see that their children have a healthy, successful, and happy life. But even at this level of love, there is a reward, whether expected or not—the reward of seeing happiness and success in the ones we love, and the reward of love returned. There is yet an even higher form of love that expects nothing and receives nothing in return—a love that would give it all, even to the point of death, for the sake of that love. In my lifetime, I have never seen this form of love more beautifully portrayed than in the life of April's mother.

Ω

10.

Mark

"Okay, now, what is the best part of the trip?"

"Right now," Sarah and John would respond in unison, rolling their eyes and settling down into the backseat of our station wagon.

I would nod with satisfaction, put the car in gear and begin to back out of our driveway. This was the tradition with which all of our family trips began—at least since the day we discovered that the children were totally devastated when our vacation was over and we were returning home. Of course, they would enjoy the fun along the way—with the notable exception of long drives in the car—but then they would look back longingly when it was over and wish they could do it all over again. A movie of the time had popularized the phrase "carpe diem" (seize the day), and I had tried to instill in Sarah and John this concept of enjoying each moment of life's experiences, rather than looking back later with regret. Hence our tradition of starting every trip with my "clever" question—in other words, the moment we were leaving was the best part of the trip, because all the fun was in front of us—and I hoped that it would cause them to think about their enjoyment throughout the trip and have fewer regrets when it was over.

But the lessons we try to teach our children are the same ones that we too should put into practice in our own lives and yet so often fall short. It has been wisely said that we should not worry so much that our children may not always listen to us, but remember that they are always watching us. I must confess that, as much as I believe in the concept of carpe diem, I constantly find myself violating it and having to be reminded of its value for a happy life. And of all the times that I have been reminded of this truth, none ever brought it home more powerfully than through my acquaintance with a friend and patient by the name of Mark.

———

My mind was a confused mixture of memories, fears, and uncertainties as I shuffled with deliberate slowness through the moist autumn leaves that covered the sidewalk leading to his home. It was an unusually warm afternoon for late fall. The air was still damp from a recent rain, but the clouds were breaking now, and occasional shafts of sunlight filtered down through the trees and sparkled off the few leaves that still clung to the branches. The truth is that it was a lovely fall afternoon, but I was totally oblivious to any beauty.

I suppose I could have blamed my melancholy on that fact that another Duke football season had just come to an inglorious conclusion. Unlike the basketball program at Duke, most seasons had found the Duke football team in the cellar of the Atlantic Coast Conference. But there was always hope with each new year, and I would faithfully attend the games, yell until I was hoarse, and then go home completely dejected. And yet that wasn't my problem on that particular afternoon, and I chastised myself for even entertaining such mundane thoughts under the circumstances. Still, I couldn't help but smile inwardly to think back on those Saturday afternoons at Wallace Wade Stadium.

Mark and I had gone to many of the games together. We shared an interest in sports and were both faithful Duke supporters, although each with a decidedly different frame of reference. In those early days of our friendship, he had a laid-back attitude about life, at least when it came to sports. He seemed to enjoy the pageantry of the game, but was philosophical when it came to winning or losing, and his good humor had sustained us through many an unsuccessful contest on the gridiron. He would make fun of my despair with each new loss and try to cheer me up with his repeated reminder that "if losing builds character, we must be two fine characters."

Those good times now seemed so long ago, and I yearned to relive them so that I could savor the moment—carpe diem—more than I had done when I had the chance. But those days would never come again, and now I had to face the present and the future.

Mark had been my patient, and I had been his, but along the way we had also become good friends. It all began nearly twenty years back, when we first came to Duke to complete our medical training. We both remained at Duke, first as junior and then as senior members of the faculty. He was a cardiologist, and his compassion for his patients, as well as his teaching and research skills, soon gained for him a distinguished reputation both at Duke and around the country. He was a bit nearsighted and had a family history of glaucoma, which is why I began seeing him at the eye center. Shortly after returning from my fellowship in Boston, I began experiencing some dull chest pain, and Mark diagnosed a minor defect in a heart valve. Thus we continued to serve as each other's doctor, and our professional relationship gradually grew into a warm friendship.

Most of those times when he would come to my office or I went to his, we enjoyed talking about our common interests in medicine, sports, politics, and life. It wasn't so much that we saw things eye to eye; in fact, we were quite different in many ways. In addition to our opposing philosophy when it came to sports, he was quite a liberal, at least from my perspective, and I am sure he saw me as an archconservative.

But we respected each other enough to enjoy lively and good-natured disagreements—debates, as we liked to call them—and usually concluded that our views were, after all, not that far apart. I don't recall that we ever discussed faith, at least not in those early days. He knew that my family went to church, and I knew that his did not, but we both respected this as a private area where we did not go. And so it was that our friendship blossomed.

Those days now seemed like another lifetime as I trudged ever more slowly through the wet leaves on the walkway that led to his home. The events of the last few years weighed heavily on my mind, and I cringed once again to think how many years he had been living with a nightmare that none of us had seen.

It all began rather early in his career, when he was performing a cardiac catheterization, a procedure that he had probably done several hundred times. This involves threading a thin plastic tube (catheter) through the patient's blood vessels until the tip reaches the heart, at which point a great deal of information can be gained about the status of the heart. It is performed in a darkened room, with the attention of the doctor and medical staff focused primarily on a set of monitors that surround the patient. As Mark shared with me later, there was the usual entourage of residents and medical students who followed him wherever he went in the hospital. They stood back in silence, listening intently to

Mark as he concentrated not only on his patient, but also on the education of his students.

Before beginning the procedure, Mark briefed the staff and students about the patient whose heart they were about to invade. He was a young man with a congenital heart defect for which he would probably require surgery to give him a chance at a full life. His social history was also significant in that he was known to be a drug user, and the injudicious sharing of unsterile needles was most likely what had led to the hepatitis of which he also suffered. This created a particular risk for the medical team, since there was a significant chance of transmitting the viral infection if someone accidentally cut themselves and came in contact with the patient's blood. Mark was actually in the process of explaining all this to his students when it happened.

The precise details were never entirely clear. It may be that a medical student attempted to ask a question at an inappropriate time. In any case, the patient apparently moved just as Mark was inserting the catheter needle through his skin. With a reflexive movement, Mark withdrew the needle and, in so doing, pierced his rubber glove and the skin of his finger with the needle that contained the patient's blood.

For a fleeting moment, Mark was filled with panic at what had just happened and what he knew were the potential consequences. But his professional integrity quickly dominated his thinking and actions, and he reasoned that it was in the patient's best interest to complete the procedure. Without a word or any sign of pain or concern, he pressed his fingers together to stop the bleeding and proceeded to perform a flawless catheterization. A nurse who was standing beside him was the only one in the room who saw the event and knew what happened that day.

When the procedure was completed and the patient was properly cared for, Mark removed his gloves and gown and quickly retired to the doctors' lounge, where he washed his hands and inspected the wound in his finger. The bleeding had long since stopped, and the puncture site was so small that he could hardly see it. It seemed so benign, and yet Mark knew all too well of the potential seriousness of its consequences. If he contracted hepatitis, it would, at best, mean a prolonged, acute illness that might force him to stop his practice for up to a year or more. At worst, it could lead to chronic liver damage and possible death.

After changing from his scrubs and donning his white lab coat, Mark went to discuss the situation with a colleague in infectious disease. They agreed that he should immediately take a course of gamma globulin in the hope of increasing his immune resistance to the hepatitis virus. Beyond that, they could only monitor his blood for the presence of hepatitis, wait, and hope.

Those were undoubtedly trying days for Mark as he waited for the answer. And yet he showed no outward signs of anxiety, but went on caring for his patients and teaching his students. He did, however, take appropriate precautions to avoid transmitting possible disease, including cancellation of all invasive procedures, so as not to put his patients or fellow workers at risk until the incubation period for hepatitis had passed. That time came and went, and Mark's blood studies remained normal. It looked like he had escaped. What no one could have known at that time, however, was that the blood of his young patient contained more than just the hepatitis virus.

The bane of existence for most doctors in academic medical centers is attending committee meetings. Of course, the committees serve important purposes, but they take away from the already precious time that the doctors spend in patient care, education, and research, and most of us accepted our committee duties with reluctant resignation. Fortunately, there always seemed to be a few good souls in every medical center who actually enjoyed committees and were willing to chair them and deal with all the tedious and seemingly trivial details that most committee work required. Mark and I were not among these, but were pleased when we were assigned to the same committee. We shared a common lack of enthusiasm for the functions of our committee and agreed that the most challenging aspect of it was staying awake during the one hour that we were required to attend every month. We helped each other in this regard by sharing the occasional raised eyebrow or suppressed smile when discussions droned on over issues the gravity of which we failed to appreciate. The only reason we both agreed to stay on the committee was the fear that we might simply be assigned to another that was worse.

I can't put my finger on the exact moment it began to happen, but there came a time when I started to see a change in Mark. At first I just wrote it off to the idiosyncrasy of a liberal, although I began to get concerned when I noticed that he was starting to take our committee seriously. In fact, the day came when he began to argue with more emotion than anyone on the committee over issues that he and I would have previously only laughed about. Even the chairman of our committee, who normally would have been thrilled for any of us to show interest in his latest issues, became annoyed at the way Mark would simply refuse to let an argument drop. Finally, he began missing the meetings and then resigned from the committee.

I didn't see Mark too often after that, but kept up with him indirectly through his medical students, who also rotated through our department. What I heard was disturbing. He had become short-tempered with his office staff, as well as with the junior doctors and his students. He became very agitated when things did not go smoothly in the clinic. There were days when he would exclaim that he simply couldn't take it any more and would walk out in the middle of the day, leaving the nurses wondering what to do with the patients who were still waiting to be seen. People saw him driving around town in the middle of the workday, and it was rumored that he was seeing a psychiatrist.

All of this was so totally foreign to the Mark I had known, and it was obvious that something very serious had occurred in his life. Not knowing if I should call him or what I would say if I did, I finally elected to send him a brief note, simply saying that I was concerned as a friend and was always available if there was anything I could do to help. After sending it, I worried that I might have overstepped my bounds and feared how he might respond to my questioning his behavior. But his response was more than I had expected. He wrote back immediately to say how much he appreciated my concern and how much our friendship meant to him. This was far more effusive than I had ever known him to be, and it only fueled my concern that something very serious was happening in his life. He went on to say that he hoped we could talk soon so that he could explain some things.

Before we were able to have our talk, a major piece of the puzzle was revealed, unfortunately on the front page of the Durham paper: "Duke Physician Reveals That He Is HIV Positive." The headline, of course, immediately caught my attention. But with over eight hundred doctors at Duke, my first thought was that I probably wouldn't know the person. Then I began to read the article, and when I saw Mark's name, my heart must have stopped. Suddenly the events of the past several years began to fall into place.

At the time that Mark had performed the cardiac catheterization on his young patient, the world was just being to learn about a devastating disease that was spreading at an alarming rate through parts of Africa and the Caribbean and increasingly in North America, especially among gay men. These patients suffered a marked loss of their normal immune system, which made them unusually susceptible to certain infections. Scientists

165

gave it the name "acquired immunodeficiency syndrome," and it soon became known worldwide as AIDS.

Initially the cause of AIDS was unknown, although a viral etiology was suspected. It would be several more years before this was proven and the virus was isolated. Consequently there was no test for AIDS in those early days and only speculation as to how it was transmitted. Furthermore, the prolonged incubation time allowed the patient to harbor the virus (referred to as human immunodeficiency virus, or HIV) for long periods before showing any outward signs of the syndrome.

The newspaper article went on to state that the doctor had known of his HIV status for the past six years and yet had elected to continue treating patients. Naturally, the media went for the sensational angle, speculating as to how many patients he might have exposed to AIDS by treating them while he harbored the deadly virus. A local television station added to the sensationalism by interviewing one of Mark's patients who was known to have AIDS. Any informed physician could have told them that the stages of disease in the two men made it almost impossible that Mark could have given the virus to his patient, who also happened to be gay. Nevertheless, they interviewed the patient in front of the medical center and asked him if he thought he got AIDS from his doctor. Of course, the poor young man could only admit that he had no idea.

A follow-up article in the newspaper announced that Mark had been relieved of all his clinical duties. It went ahead to quote an anonymous source from the hospital administration saying that they weren't sure what other actions would be taken, but that they were very concerned about the number of lawsuits they might be getting. To the best of my knowledge, no malpractice suit was ever filed against the hospital or Mark, which is a testament to the good rapport that he had with his patients and the outstanding reputation he continued to enjoy within his profession, despite his struggles in recent years.

I was sitting in my office at the end of a clinic day, trying to assimilate all I had seen and heard in the past twenty-four hours, when Robin called in to say that I had a visitor. I looked up to see Mark standing in the doorway. Neither of us seemed to know what to say, and for a moment we simply looked intently into each other's eyes. Then I walked over to him and we hugged each other, too choked with emotion for words. Finally, I closed the door, we both sat down, and Mark proceeded to tell me the rest of the story.

The young man on whom Mark had performed cardiac catheterization many years ago eventually underwent open-heart surgery, which had been successful. He did well for quite some time, but eventually began to exhibit unusual symptoms. It was not his hepatitis, but rather he was having recurrent infections, as though his immune system was failing. This was at a time when doctors and scientists were just beginning to recognize and understand AIDS, so there was some delay in diagnosing the condition. Because of the long time between Mark's encounter with the patient and his diagnosis of AIDS, Mark eventually put the incident in the back of his mind and went on with his career and his life. By the time the young man finally became ill with and eventually died of AIDS, however, the virus had been isolated and the HIV test was available. Remembering the needle stick, Mark obtained the test, and that was when his life went into a tailspin.

He had a lovely wife and two beautiful children who were just beginning grade school. Should he tell her? Of course he must, and he did. But what should he tell their children? And what should he do about his practice? Was it safe for his patients for him to continue treating them? How would he otherwise provide for his family? He could no longer sleep for the constant worry, and the lack of sleep and the preoccupation with his overwhelming problems made him increasingly irritable both at home and at the hospital.

He first sought the guidance of a leading expert in the field of AIDS. It was the opinion of this physician that Mark could safely continue to practice, including invasive procedures, as long as he took appropriate precautions. As he told me this, I recalled the students telling me how he had begun to make a fetish of washing his hands before touching each patient and how he would sternly lecture the doctors and students who failed to do so. More pieces of the puzzle from the past years were falling into place.

For a time, Mark's work had allowed him to suppress the worries about his condition. Physically, he still felt fine and exhibited no signs of disease, other than his positive test for HIV. But as the grim reality of AIDS became better understood, the realization that he would eventually become sick and probably die gradually began to take its toll. He began showing signs of depression. He couldn't sleep. Little problems became monumental to him. Life at home became strained. His children knew something was wrong, but did not understand what it was. They started to fear him and tried to avoid being around him. His wife, who was nothing short of a saint, did her best to maintain a stable family, but even she finally confessed to Mark that she did not know how much longer they could live together like this.

As I listened to his story, his behavior over the past several years—in his practice, with his colleagues and students, and in our committee meetings—all became clear. He went on to explain that he did eventually seek psychiatric help and for many years had attended weekly psycho-analytical sessions. He was never sure how much this helped, but the day finally came when he agreed that he must publicly disclose this HIV status.

He had hoped that the hospital would allow him to continue his practice in some way, and he was totally unprepared for the cold, if not hostile, response that he received not only from the public, but also from the hospital administration and even from some of his fellow physicians. In the years to come, he would give lectures around the country on the plight of doctor with AIDS, hoping that our society would eventually adopt a more informed, if not compassionate, attitude toward all those afflicted with the disease. For now, however, he felt it was best that he leave Durham. His parents lived in a small community in the Smoky Mountains, and he planned to spend most of his time with them, while his family remained behind and tried to adjust.

With his story finished, we sat together in silence for a rather long time. Mark had said all that he had come to say, and I was trying to think of what a friend should say in response. Of course, I finally told him how devastated I was for him and his family and that I would always be available to help his family with anything they might need and to support him in any way I could. And then I said something that came very naturally to me. I looked him in the eyes and said that I would pray for him. I wasn't sure how he would feel about that statement, but his response made me even sadder. He laughed.

I guess I should have expected it. Although we had never discussed faith, I had a pretty good idea of his position. Nevertheless, I was hurt that he would take my most serious expression of friendship as a joke. But I knew he meant no ill will, and I felt a bit ashamed at being overly sensitive. I tried to force a laugh in response to his as we shook hands and promised to keep in touch.

Several years passed, during which time I never saw Mark. He made occasional trips back to Durham, but preferred to spend the time only with his family. I also heard that he had been doing a bit of traveling and lecturing. We kept our promise to write, and his were very special letters. He spoke of friendship and family, of life's beauty and frailty, of hopes and dreams and of memories. But between the lines, I sensed that he was struggling with something that was missing in his life. I longed for the right words that might give him some comfort, but was never sure what I could or should say to him. I wanted to share with him my belief in a loving Creator who has promised that this life is not the end of his love. But that last experience in my office left me with doubt that he would be receptive to thoughts of a spiritual nature. So I confined my letters to inquiring about how he was doing and telling him what was happening in Durham. I wished I could do more—and I did continue to pray for him.

Then one day word came that Mark had just been admitted to Duke Hospital. He had been rushed from his parents' home in the mountains because of an alarming turn in his health. I went to see him immediately, but was not prepared for what I would find. As I walked into his room, I was shocked that I barely recognized my old friend. He had lost so much weight that his ashen skin clung to the bones of his face. His eyes were sunken back into their sockets, and his once thick, black hair was now thin and streaked with gray. An intravenous tube was dripping fluids into a vein in his arm, and a feeding tube hung from his nose. To make matters worse, he seemed disoriented, and I was never sure if he recognized me that first day.

AIDS was finally taking its toll on Mark. He was not absorbing his food properly and would probably require continued intravenous therapy and a special liquid diet. He had been started on the AIDS drugs that were available at the time, although these were only likely to prolong life, not save it. Nevertheless, his strength gradually improved, and he was finally discharged to his home in Durham to wait and hope.

I was hesitant to visit him at home right away for fear of invading his privacy. But one day I received a phone call, and the faint, trembling voice was that of Mark, asking if I would come see him. And so it was that I found myself walking slowly up to his house on that warm fall afternoon.

———

The reason for the hesitancy in my steps was the uncertainty of what I would find when we faced each other, but my main concern was what I should say to him. Should I keep it to small talk, avoiding the real issues?

Would he want to rehash the painful details of the recent Duke-UNC football game? Or should I be frank and talk of what was obviously foremost on both of our minds? Should I say "I'm sorry"? That seemed so weak. Or should I remind him of my promise to watch after his family? Should I try to express my belief in eternity? What could I possibly say to him that might, if not give him hope for the future, at least give him happiness now? As I rang the doorbell, I vaguely hoped that no one would answer.

There was a long delay, but eventually the door was opened by his daughter. She didn't speak, but motioned for me to follow her. We walked through the house and out into their backyard, where Mark was sitting on the patio, bathed in the warm sunshine. Despite the warmth of the day, he wore a heavy sweater and had covered his legs with an afghan. But he looked far better than he had in the hospital. He had regained some weight, and the color had returned to his face. What impressed me most, however, was his serene countenance, with almost a twinkle in his eyes. Something told me that our visit was not going to be as difficult as I had feared.

We did share a bit of small talk, and he kidded me once again about taking Duke's latest loss in football too seriously. But I was growing increasingly curious about the source of this new, radiant nature I was seeing in him. It was not like the Mark I had known—not like the old, liberal Mark when he was healthy, and not like the agitated, cynical Mark when he had first learned of his illness. Finally, I could hold back no longer.

"Mark, what is it?" I asked with a quizzical smile.

He looked at me for a moment, pretending not to understand the meaning of my question, but then a shy smile crossed his face and he said something I will never forget.

"Well, I've found the secret to happiness," he finally responded, and then paused to let the impact of that statement sink in. Our eyes locked, and we shared another smile as I waited with eager anticipation for what would come next.

"I lived for nearly forty years," he continued, "and I witnessed a lot of beauty in my life. I saw sunrises and sunsets. I saw rain and snow, and I saw flowers in the spring and colored leaves in the fall. I saw love in the eyes of my wife and fellowship in the eyes of my friends. And most of all I saw our children growing up strong and healthy. But do you know when I appreciated all this the most?"

I shook my head.

"When it was too late," he said with a slight edge of disgust in his voice.

"Sometimes it would be months or years later that I would think back on a special moment in time. And I would think, 'Boy, was that great! I sure wish I could live it again.' But, of course, I couldn't.

"Many mornings in the mountains, when I couldn't sleep, I would get up before dawn and walk out on the deck in the darkness and sit and wait to watch the sunrise. And it was beautiful. And then one morning, sitting there alone, enjoying the moment, I suddenly realized that this was one of those special times that I would someday look back on and wish I could relive. And yet there I was, right at that moment, living it, and enjoying it. And that's when I realized that the secret to true happiness is to enjoy each special moment while it is still there within our grasp. And then, when it is over, we can at least be content in knowing that we didn't waste the moment; we won't look back someday with regret that it was so beautiful, but we didn't enjoy it when we had the chance."

Wow! And I was worried about what I would say to inspire him. I realized then that my role that afternoon was to listen.

"So, Bruce," Mark continued, "don't worry about me. I don't know how much longer I have. And I don't guess any of us do. But I do know that I am far better off than most people. They may live a full lifetime and never truly enjoy a sunrise. But I plan to enjoy every moment that I am allowed to remain on this planet."

We sat in silence for quite a long time, enjoying the moment. Then Mark said he had better go in the house. He saw me to the front door, and we hugged for the last time. I was about half way down the walk when he called out.

"Oh, by the way, thanks for those prayers!"

I turned back to look at him to see if he was making a joke. But his eyes were sincere and at peace. And my eyes, which suddenly became moist, probably registered a bit of pleasant surprise. I could only smile and nod and continue on my way.

So he remembered after all those years. We just never know what impact our words may have on others, and I couldn't help but wonder at what point the promise of my prayers was no longer a joke to him. I would never know the answer. Two months later, I laid a poinsettia beside his grave.

But on that autumn afternoon, it was not my words but Mark's that rang with truth. They were words that I will never forget.

The leaves seemed to have dried some as I walked down the sidewalk from Mark's home. The sky was blue, the sunshine was warm, and I suddenly realized that it was a beautiful day. My steps were brisker now than they had been earlier, when I was heading in the other direction. When I got to the corner of his block, I stopped. And I looked around at the beauty of the day. And maybe for the first time in my life, I truly enjoyed the moment.

11.

Miss Nanny

He stopped halfway across the room. His large, portly frame was motionless, his head was bowed in silence, his shoulders were slumped, and his flaccid arms hung without purpose by his sides. His body language spoke of a person in despair.

He wore old sandals without socks, and his baggy polyester trousers were faded and frayed. A rumpled, short-sleeved cotton shirt was only partially tucked in at the waist and was open at the neck, revealing a few white, curly chest hairs. The thin hair on his head was also pure white and hung unusually long for a man of his generation. It framed a puffy, pasty, white face with slack jowls and large bags beneath his eyes, which at that moment seemed sad and distant.

Sharon had just brought Mr. Jones into our examination room and was still standing beside the door that she was about to close. I was on the other side of the room, beside the examination chair, waiting to help him into it—but still there was no movement. Sharon and I shared quizzical looks, wondering what the problem might be. I began to fear that he could be having a stroke or a seizure and finally asked him if he was all right. He remained silent and motionless for another long moment and then raised his shaggy head and looked up at nothing in particular. He gave a slow, deep sigh and again dropped his head and shoulders.

"I just realized," he said in a slow, barely audible monotone, "I have become old."

At first I thought he might be making a joke, but Mr. Jones was not a man given to humor. To this day I am thankful that I did not laugh, because his intent was anything but levity. It truly seemed that at that moment, as he trudged across the floor of yet another doctor's office, he was suddenly struck by the reality of his finite state and that time was running out. Sharon, with her usual sixth sense for the feelings and needs of our patients, walked over to him and gently took him by the arm. She made a light but warm comment that he looked just fine to her, but even her best efforts seemed to ring hollow in his ears.

She helped him over to the examination chair, and he sat down passively. My examination that day was not unlike the several dozen others I had performed on him for over a decade. As long as I had known Mr. Jones, he had been a gentle, courteous man of few words, who rarely showed any emotion and for whom smiling seemed to be an effort. I had seen other patients like him, and sometimes wondered what, if anything, in their lives brought them happiness. In the early years of our acquaintance, he had seemed to be at peace and content with his lot in life. But, as the years passed, I began to notice a gradual change in his demeanor. The loss of his wife a few years back was undoubtedly a major factor in that change, but it was only recently that I had begun to worry that he might be suffering from true depression.

At the conclusion of the examination, I tried to cheer him up by noting that his cataract surgery was still giving him excellent vision in both eyes, and that his glaucoma was well controlled on the present medication. I told him how pleased I was that he had maintained such good sight for so many years and that the prospect for continued excellent vision looked very promising. But my efforts seemed to provide meager consolation as he looked down and slowly nodded his head. At my urging, he promised to see his family physician for a complete physical examination, and Sharon and I said we would look forward to seeing him on his next visit in four months.

"Perhaps," he murmured as he shuffled toward the door.

That evening, as I sat at my desk going over the stack of papers that Robin had left for me, I couldn't get Mr. Jones out of my mind. Over the course of my career, like most physicians, I have watched the cycles of life in my patients: I have watched children grow to adulthood, I have watched adults grow old, and I have seen people die. And I have been impressed by how differently various people seem to deal with the inevitable progression of their days. I have seen those who accept the passing of time and the finite limits of life with grace and good cheer, while others became bitter and depressed. And I suppose we are all guilty, to a greater or lesser extent, of denying our mortality, simply by refusing to think about it or by using humor as a defense to ease the thought of growing old and dying.

My nurse, Sharon, and I were certainly among those guilty of rationalizing the aging process with humor. She was a few years younger than me, and we took great delight in teasing each other about our age, never missing an opportunity to get in a good age joke. And for us, the enduring symbol of our ribbing was a small potted plant. Neither of us could quite recall who first gave it to the other, but it began as a living plant that one of us gave to the other on a birthday. Not only could we not remember (another age joke) who bought it, neither of us could remember to water the plants in our office, and the little plant soon went the way of our other horticultural endeavors. But one of us put it away and presented the dry, withered plant to the other on their next birthday (I suppose we thought it was symbolic of our aging—or maybe our forgetfulness). In any case, we thought it was a great joke and continued for years to exchange it at every birthday until the poor thing was reduced to a pile of dust.

During our early years at Duke, when aging was still a relative state of mind, Sharon and I were unmerciful in our attempts to one-up the other with birthday jokes. We undoubtedly spent countless hours planning the next celebration and searching for the perfect card to remind each other that we were not getting any younger. And Robin, who was considerably younger than both of us, was a willing accomplice on each occasion.

On my fortieth birthday, which I naively hoped my office staff would forget, Sharon came in while I was examining a patient to say there was an emergency outside for which I was urgently needed. If I am anything, I am gullible—so I went immediately. Our waiting room was just outside the examination room, and it was filled with patients, most of whom had been waiting beyond their scheduled time and were in a less than charitable mode. As I hurried into the waiting room, ready to deal with an emergency, my heart sank when I saw what was standing in the middle of the room—a clown! It was a young woman, dressed to the hilt in a clown outfit, with a huge grin on her face and the strings of a large arrangement of colorful balloons in her hand. My first instinct was to retreat into my office, but I was nudged closer to the clown, who proceeded to belt out a song at the top of her lungs. Some of the patients laughed politely, and others just looked at each other, and I was sure they must have been thinking, 'Well, now we know why they are so slow around here.' And as I stood there in front of all those patients, mortified, I could only think of one thing: I was going to get Sharon for this.

For the next several years, I plotted with Robin's help. We arranged a surprise luncheon for Sharon on her fortieth birthday and decorated the room with every black "over the hill" product that Hallmark had to offer that year. With the room darkly lit by black candles on a black crepe tablecloth, and all attendees solemnly wearing black armbands, Sharon was ushered in to her party. Of course, there was much laughter, and she was good-natured about it, as always. But I had yet to reveal my coup de grace, which was my gift for her. Since I thought of Sharon not only as a highly valued employee but also as a friend, I wanted to give her something nice, but appropriate for the occasion—so I presented her with a rocking chair. I am not sure if it was the cost of the gift (I was never known as a big spender) or the not-too-subtle implications behind it, but she seemed visibly shaken and unable to come up with her usual quick and witty response. And I began to realize that we were all moving into a new phase of our attitudes toward aging.

After that, the age jokes and the birthday reminders became progressively gentler, until we were finally reduced to exchanging gifts that were devoid of age implications and cards that were downright maudlin. I guess we were moving into a more sobering time of life, when our children were beginning to leave home, our lives were settling into the doldrums of middle age, and the sands of time seemed to be moving ever faster toward old age and beyond.

So, as I sat at my desk that evening, thinking about Mr. Jones and the inevitable progression of life, I couldn't help but wonder how I would one day deal with my advanced years (should I be so fortunate to reach them) and the approaching end to my life. Would I be like Mr. Jones and become despondent or even bitter that my youth had run its course—that there was nothing left in life to live for? Would the thought of aging and death so depress and consume my remaining years that I could only trudge through each day until I closed my eyes for the last time? Or would I be like other patients I have known, who never seemed to tire of the beauty of each new day, who continued to find life exciting, with something always around the next corner to be explored and enjoyed, and who loved so intensely that they never felt the cold winds of time? I was blessed to have many such role models of the latter type among my patients, two of whom stand out especially vividly in my mind. One was a man well known to most people around the world, while the other was a petite woman known only to her family and friends. But they had in common a precious gift. Let me first tell you her story.

———

She was well along in years when we first met. Unless you knew her birth date, however, you would have been hard-pressed to come within twenty years of her true age. She was petite and trim and always dressed immaculately. I remember her in suits or tailored dresses of gray, lavender, beige, and especially royal blue, often with white lace at the collar and sleeves. She typically wore white hose with black patent leather shoes, and occasionally carried white linen gloves in her small hands. Her hair was short and meticulously coiffured and had the appearance of pure white silk. But the most striking feature was her face, with slender lips, a delicate nose, sparkling eyes, and skin smooth like velvety chocolate, which belied the harsh life she had known.

Nanny Vereen was born in 1887, just twenty-four years after Abraham Lincoln proclaimed the emancipation of her people. Her grandparents had all been slaves until they were young adults, and both her mother and father were born during the early years of reconstruction in the South. Her father's family had lived on a modest tobacco plantation in North Carolina, and they remained there after the war, working no longer as slaves to any man, but now subject to the burden of poverty. Hard work and a measure of good fortune, however, would gradually improve the lot for future generations of Nanny's family.

The end of the Civil War brought with it new forms of prosperity in the South, and the greatest of these was the tobacco industry. Huge new markets in the North and the eventual mechanization of cigarette manufacturing soon established tobacco as the most lucrative cash crop per acre in the South. A farmer with a small plot of tobacco land could provide adequately for his family, and Nanny's folks eventually became one of many such small acreage tobacco farmers in North Carolina. Her grandfather worked hard for his former owner and was finally able to acquire a small corner of the farm on which he was allowed to sharecrop. This meant that he was provided with the land, equipment, and a home, in return for which he gave a share of his tobacco profits to the landlord. He had three sons, all of whom began working in the field beside their father before they were ten years old.

Her father married when he was in his early twenties, and he and his bride moved into one of the small, three-room houses that had once been quarters for slaves. A year later, Nanny was born in that house. Her two uncles eventually moved to Durham to take jobs in factories, but her father stayed on the farm with his father. In the years that followed, hard work and a good price for tobacco led to relative prosperity for the family. They saved their money and were finally able to buy the land outright. Her parents also prospered in other ways, and their family soon outgrew the small house. Her father built a new home of red brick on the highest point of the farm, from which they could look out across the rich, rolling Piedmont countryside, with blue-green, pine-covered hills on the far horizon. The house would change many times in size and shape as the family continued to grow over the years, but it would remain the homestead where Nanny would live out the remainder of her long, full life.

As the final seconds of the nineteenth century ticked off and the world was ushered into a new century, Nanny found herself a young lady of thirteen and the oldest of seven children. She had a bright, inquisitive mind and a keen desire to learn as much as she could about the exciting new world that was opening up around her. But for a black girl in the South at the turn of the twentieth century, there was limited opportunity for formal education. Her primary responsibility was to care for her younger siblings while the men labored in the fields and her mother struggled with the limitless chores of a farmer's wife. She was only allowed to complete the fourth grade and was fortunate even for that. But for the remainder of her life, she would spend her few spare moments reading and learning all she could about the life she so enjoyed.

When she was approaching twenty years of age, her grandfather became ill and was no longer able to help her father with the farm. As a result, it became necessary to employ additional workers, and one of them was a young man by the name of Albert Vereen. He was strong and handsome. His admirable work ethic won the respect of her family, and his good nature and kind heart won their love. But he especially won the heart of Nanny, who eventually accepted his proposal and became Mrs. Nanny Vereen.

The Vereens continued to live at the homestead. All her siblings grew up, married, and left their home, but she and Albert stayed on, caring for her grandparents until their death and later looking after her parents until they too passed on in their advanced years. During this time, Nanny gave birth to eleven children, ten of whom lived to adulthood and eventually gave her twenty-six grandchildren, thirty-four great-grandchildren, and twelve great-great-grandchildren. And so it was that Nanny Vereen became known as wife, mother, grandmother, and great- and great-great-grandmother. But to all of us who knew and loved her she was simply Miss Nanny.

She was truly the matriarch of the Vereen household. Her word was law, and her children knew better than to disobey her orders. She taught them the virtues of hard work, self-discipline, education, love of family, and fear of the Lord. But although she was stern and demanding, she never required as much from others as she gave of herself, putting in long, hard days from the crack of dawn until long after dusk. Nor did her children ever doubt that she loved each of them more than life itself. It would not have been possible to say that she loved one of her children more than another, but there was one who held a special place in her heart throughout all her days. Zachary was her fourth-born, and she lost him when he was two, during an epidemic of influenza. It nearly broke her heart, and she might not have been able to carry on had it not been for the family who needed her and her firm belief that they would one day be reunited. But from the day of his death, her weary head never touched the pillow at night until she had said a special prayer for little Zach—that the angels would watch over him until she could one day come and again take care of all her children.

Life was not easy for Miss Nanny. Their small tobacco farm was not sufficient to support such a large family, and she had to supplement their income by selling eggs and finding domestic employment in the homes of white families in the city. When the Great Depression came in the 1930s, they nearly lost everything. Most of their children were grown by this time, but were unable to find full-time jobs, so they all continued to live at the homestead along with the first two grandchildren. They all did what they could to provide income for the family with whatever work they could find, and somehow they survived. But in the darkest hours, when it was not certain where they would find their next meal, much less the money to pay the mortgage on the farm, it was the strength and courage of Miss Nanny that caused her family to hold their heads high with dignity, to cling to the power of the family united in love, and to trust in the grace of God.

Miss Nanny sent up her most fervent prayer of thanksgiving when the last of her children and grandchildren returned home safely from World War II. Little could she have known, however, that even harder times lay ahead for her family. During the first half of the twentieth century, most black families in the South tended to accept segregation as the way things were. That is not to say that it was easy to accept, nor that there were many black people during those times who did not have bitter feelings. But if Miss Nanny ever harbored any bitterness, it was said that she never showed it; she was probably too busy taking care of her family and making the most of what life gave her.

As the late 1940s gave way to the '50s and the civil rights movement began to sweep the nation, Miss Nanny became increasingly concerned for the safety of her family. Her children and grandchildren visited her at the homestead with stories of marches, sit-ins, and school integrations. She also heard of churches being burned, black people being arrested, and some even killed under hushed circumstances. When two of her great-grandchildren came to her to announce that they were joining a small group of black youths who were going to seek entrance to an all-white school, she wanted to reach out and beg them not to put themselves at such risk. But she knew that she could no more stop them from this than she could stop herself from praying for them. She could only look them squarely in their eyes and sternly admonish them to keep their heads high with pride and dignity and to remember who they were and in whom they put their trust. This is how Miss Nanny had lived and would continue to live her remarkable life.

——

She was well into her eighties when I first met Miss Nanny in my office. Her husband had been dead for nearly twenty years, and she had outlived two of her sons, who died of natural causes in their sixties. But she had seen her great-grandchildren graduate from some of the finest colleges in the South, and she was looking forward to even greater opportunities for her great-great-grandchildren. She still lived at the homestead with one granddaughter, but the house was rarely empty. Although a few members of the family had moved out of state, most still lived nearby, and some of them were always visiting her to bring her up-to-date with their activities, ask her advice, seek her blessing, or just renew the inner strength that comes from the power of a united family. Miss Nanny was clearly the anchor of that family, and it was their love for her and their need for her strength and wisdom that seemed to give her a purpose for living—and joy in each new day.

It was obvious from our first meeting that this was a special lady. I was surprised, however, when I noted her date of birth—she could have easily passed for a woman ten or maybe even twenty years younger. This was in part due to her outward appearance. But even more, it was her demeanor that belied her age. She walked sprightly and with purpose. She had a keen curiosity and was always well informed about what was going on at home and around the world. Her eyes would sparkle when we spent a few minutes on each visit talking about current events. Her enthusiasm was infectious, and I found myself looking forward to her visits and thoroughly enjoying our chats, especially when I could get her to tell me about her life and her family, which she did over the course of many years.

What I found most enticing about Miss Nanny was that, despite her engaging, charming personality, she was a woman of the strongest conviction who had become accustomed to receiving unswerving respect from all those around her. This was especially true within her very large family—she was clearly the matriarch, and no one could say that she had not earned this respect through the way she had lived her long life. What amused me most was the deference that all her family paid to her every bidding. She usually came with her granddaughter, and whenever she would ask for something, the response was inevitably "Yes, ma'am." There were times when other family members would come with her, often bringing a young child. To me, these children seemed remarkably well behaved, but if she felt they were talking too much, she would quietly say, "Child, you hush now," and there would be an immediate "Yes, ma'am" followed by absolute silence. She would usually decide when it was time to leave my office, and on cue her family would stand and say, "Yes, ma'am."

The years passed, and as Miss Nanny entered her nineties, I began to notice a gradual change in her nature. Her steps were slower, and she was becoming quieter and more withdrawn. Of course, anyone reaching her age would have reason enough to be slowing down, but she was also experiencing progressive loss of vision, and I couldn't help but wonder if this was contributing to her general decline. For most of the years that I had been following her, the main eye problem was glaucoma, but this was still well controlled and did not explain the progressive deterioration of her sight. She was also developing early macular degeneration, a condition of the central retina that is common in advancing age, but this did not seem to explain her declining vision either. What did seem to be the culprit were cataracts in both eyes. These had been coming on for years, and we had talked about the possibility of cataract surgery, but she kept putting it off because there was so much else going on in her life. Now, however, the situation was becoming critical—she was legally blind, and the family recognized how it seemed to be correlated with her general decline. Something needed to be done, but it would not be a simple decision.

She was in her ninety-sixth year when the family brought her in for her regular visit. I had talked with several family members during the past few years about the state of her eyes and the possibility of surgery. On this visit, she was with the largest contingent of family members ever. In fact, they filled the examination room so full that Sharon offered to step out to make more room. It was obvious that there had been family discussions about Miss Nanny, and they were coming today in the hope of deciding what was best for her. She was now confined to a wheelchair and was extremely frail and stooped over, giving the impression that she might not be fully aware of all that was going on. But she was as neat and well dressed as ever, and it was clear from the deference accorded by all her family that she was still the matriarch. They told me that she no longer seemed to recognize most of her family, even up close, and wondered if this was due to her loss of vision or something more ominous.

After a thorough examination, I told her once again that her glaucoma was well controlled, that the macular degeneration seemed to still be in an early stage, and that the cataracts were the main cause of her poor eyesight. She nodded her head, but did not offer any other response, and I stepped over to the other side of the room to discuss the matter with her family. I explained that cataract surgery was the only hope for restoring her vision, but that there were concerns about the surgery in her case. For one thing, I was concerned about her general health and how she would tolerate the ordeal of surgery. It was also unclear just how much vision she would regain after the cataract surgery, because I could not be certain about the influence of the macular degeneration. But the main concern—and this was obviously the main concern of the family as well—was her age. I had to confess that I had never performed cataract surgery on a person of this age. None of us wanted to say it, but I am sure we were all wondering how much longer she would live to enjoy any benefit from the surgery.

During all this discussion with the family, I was violating a very important principle—I was failing to include the patient in the decision-making process. And Miss Nanny was not going to let me get away with it. She straightened up, raised her head, and although she could not see us, conveyed her feelings loud and clear.

"What you takin' 'bout over there? I cain't here a word y'all are sayin'."

I immediately left the family and went over to sit beside Miss Nanny and tell her everything we had been discussing. But before I could finish, she stopped me and spoke in that firm voice as she would to one of her family.

"There ain't nothin' to talk about. I got a grandchild 'bout to be born"—it was actually her third great-great-grandchild—"and I aim to see that child. So just do it!"

Well, that certainly ended the discussion. I looked over at her family, who just smiled at me as though to say that the final word had been spoken. At that moment, I could only think of one appropriate response.

"Yes, ma'am."

Fortunately, her surgery went well, and much to my pleasant surprise, she had nearly full recovery of vision in the operated eye. She saw her newborn great-great-grandchild and lived to see nine more. Her family and I marveled not only at the recovery of her sight, but also at the improvement in her general well-being. But she seemed to take it all in stride, as though it was simply a part of God's plan to allow her to enjoy the beauty of each new day.

A few years after the surgery, she came in one day with her granddaughter for her regular appointment, and Sharon quietly directed my attention to two dates on Miss Nanny's chart. It was her birthday, and she was exactly one hundred years old that day! Sharon, who always knew the right thing to do, slipped out of the room and returned just as I was completing the examination. She had gone to the gift shop and brought back a large, helium-filled balloon, with "Happy Birthday" printed across it in bold, bright letters. Miss Nanny's eyes widened and sparkled, and she smiled bigger than I had ever seen her do before.

"My, what a pretty balloon!" she exclaimed. "Bless you, child." (Sharon loved being called "child.")

Among the pictures that I think will never fade from my memory is that of Miss Nanny being wheeled down the hall on her hundredth birthday, her neat, white hair just visible over the back of the wheelchair and her birthday balloon floating overhead.

Miss Nanny lived to be 103. She retained useful vision until the end, although her health finally failed, and she was no longer able to make her appointments in the final year. I couldn't bear the thought of not seeing her one more time, and so I decided to make a house call, which is something I rarely did. On a sunny, spring afternoon that I happened to have free, I drove out into the countryside to the homestead. It was my first time to see it, but the family had provided good directions, and I arrived just about on time. The homestead was much as I had imagined it over the years—a neat, red brick home, with large shade trees and a well-kept yard. As I stepped out of my car, I looked out over the landscape—the rolling farmland and the pine-covered hills on the horizon. And I thought about the decades that Miss Nanny had looked out on that same scene, where her grandfather and father and husband and their children had worked the land while she labored in the home to provide for all the needs of her family.

It came as no surprise to see how immaculately the interior of the house was maintained. Although Miss Nanny was no longer able to do it, she had taught her family well, and I was sure that even now they would not dare cut any corners while she was watching. A few of the family members had come over for the visit, and they had made a cake and lemonade for the occasion. Miss Nanny was sitting in the living room in her wheelchair, and I was allowed to sit beside her. I had brought a few instruments and did a cursory examination of her eyes, but for most of the visit we just sat and enjoyed the refreshments and stimulating conversation. Even now, her mind was alert, and she took delight in talking about all the exciting new things her family was doing. It was obvious that she was still full of life and looked forward to each new day. Not wanting to overstay my welcome, I finally said that I should leave and reluctantly said good-bye to Miss Nanny for what I was sure would be the last time.

Driving back to Durham and thinking about this remarkable lady, I realized that I had learned many important lessons from her. For one thing, she taught me that we should never think of age as a limitation to any medical treatment, as long as it has a reasonable chance of making the patient's life better, if even for a short time. But most of what I learned from Miss Nanny came from observing the way she lived her life. She died not long after my visit, and her granddaughter told me that she never lost her zest for life and that she died just as she had lived—with thankfulness for each day that she had been given and confidence in what lay around the next bend in the road. There was no doubt that she looked forward, without fear or question, to being with those members of her family who had gone on before her. She knew her day would come in God's good time, and that until then she would make the most of each new day that she was allowed to live. And that, I believe, is the greatest lesson I learned from Miss Nanny.

Ω

12.

Sir Rex

I don't want to give the impression that I was ever a "doctor to the stars." Nothing would be further from the truth. In fact it was the extreme rarity of such visits that caused such a stir when the phone call came in the early fall of 1989.

The caller was an ophthalmologist from New York City with whom I had a professional acquaintance. He was originally from Great Britain, but now had a thriving practice in Manhattan, as well as an academic appointment at one of the local universities and an international reputation as a glaucoma expert. He was calling to ask if I might see a patient of his while he was in Durham for a brief stay. Of course, I said I would be pleased to do so. He thanked me and proceeded to provide the details.

"His name is Rex Harrison," he informed me

"Oh, really? Like the actor?" I asked.

"Yes, well, actually, he is one and the same," he casually replied.

"Oh really?" I repeated, wishing I could have been a bit more original and hoping that I too sounded casual.

He proceeded to inform me that it was actually Sir Rex Harrison, since he had recently been knighted by Queen Elizabeth.

I hoped that my gulp was not audible over the phone, and I was at least thankful that I was able to suppress the impulse to say, "Oh really?" for a third time, although I am sure I said something equally inane. I had never met a world-class actor, much less one who had been knighted by the Queen of England. But I was finally able to repeat my willingness to do whatever I could to help. I figured that being available while a person was in town for a short time couldn't be too challenging. Little did I know what a gross underestimation that would turn out to be.

"The problem is rather dicey, actually," he proceeded to explain. "Sir Rex developed glaucoma several years ago. He had been doing well on medicines until just recently, and now the blasted thing is totally out of control. It couldn't have happened at a more rotten time, since he was just leaving for Durham to open a new play. I told him he shouldn't leave just now, until we could get things under better control, but he's rather headstrong and would have none of it. I'm really sorry to dump him in your lap like this, old boy, but I'm afraid he's yours for now."

"Right," I said and assured him that I would be pleased to see Sir Rex at any time.

"I'm afraid it will be sooner than you think," he replied. "He is in the air as we speak, and I instructed him to come straight to your office from the airport."

"Right," I responded, continuing my pattern of repetitious speech. I finally thanked him for the referral, and we hung up.

I went out to inform my staff that we would have one more patient that afternoon. When I told them who it was, it evoked the expected excitement, and they all seemed to be humming "The Rain in Spain" as I returned to my office. We finished the afternoon clinic a bit earlier than usual that day, and I sat down at my desk to do some paperwork before Sir Rex arrived. But I soon found it hard to concentrate on my work, as my mind drifted into the past—to movies I had seen and the things that were happening in my life at those times.

The first time I could recall seeing Rex Harrison was when he played Caesar in the movie *Cleopatra* in the early 1960s. My father and I had gone to an out-of-town football game and were staying overnight, so we decided to take in the movie that evening. Although neither of us was willing to admit it, I am sure the highlight of the film for both of us was the young, glamorous Elizabeth Taylor. As for Rex Harrison, I must confess that I knew very little about him at the time, which revealed the naïveté of an Oklahoma schoolboy. He had already been a huge star of the screen, and especially the stage, for over a quarter century, and yet the truth is that I thought he might have made his mark in western movies (I guess I was confusing "Rex" with "Tex"). I later learned that he hit on the name Rex when he was ten years old, probably having heard someone calling for his dog, and preferred that over his given name, Reginald.

His most memorable screen role, of course, came a few years later when he starred in *My Fair Lady* as Professor Henry Higgins, a role that he had essentially created on the stage a decade earlier. That movie holds special memories for Sharon and me—both good and bad. The happy memory is that we went to see it two nights before we were to be married. The less pleasant memory began as I was driving Sharon home after the movie and asked her where she had put our marriage license. To my dismay, she informed me that I had it, which I was sure I did not, having distinctly remembered giving it to her. That was a tense drive to her apartment, where she searched everywhere, while I did the same in my apartment—both yielding nothing. So the following day we went back to the marriage bureau to obtain our second marriage license. After the wedding and honeymoon, when we arrived at our new apartment in Philadelphia, we found the first marriage license—packed in my boxes. Sharon thought we should put both licenses in our honeymoon scrapbook, an idea that seemed pointless to me. But there they both reside to this day, the first of many reminders that I am well advised not to disagree with my wife.

In the next and last movie in which we saw Rex Harrison, he was talking with the animals as Doctor Dolittle. This was, of course, a light and playful film, but for us it will always have bittersweet memories. By now we were living in Connecticut, where I was stationed at the naval submarine base. The following day, after seeing *Doctor Dolittle* together, I was to deploy for Scotland and my first submarine patrol. On a pitch-black, drizzly morning, Sharon drove me to the sub base, where our crew was to board a bus that would take us to the airport. We would be apart for three months, and at that point in our young, tender marriage, three months seemed like an eternity. I can never think of *Doctor Dolittle* without reliving the emotions of that melancholy time in our life.

My reverie was suddenly broken when nurse Sharon came in to announce that Mr. Harrison and his party were in the next room. As I walked toward the door, I wondered what I was going to see. Caesar? Professor Higgins? Doctor Dolittle? But I had failed to take one thing into account—it had been over twenty years since we had seen *Doctor Dolittle*. What I found as I entered the room was an elderly gentleman in his eighty-first year of life. He was not unlike my many other octogenarian patients, and I was momentarily disappointed. But then, with a twinkle in his eye, he spoke in his marvelous, rich voice with a beautiful British accent, and I truly felt that I was in the presence of Professor Henry Higgins—Sir Rex Harrison.

He was with his wife and two assistants. After we exchanged a few brief pleasantries, I could think of no further small talk and felt that it was best to get down to business, which is obviously what he preferred. I soon discovered that my New York colleague's assessment of "dicey" was all too accurate for his patient's situation. The left eye had been essentially blind since a bout of measles in early childhood. He had made it through his long and distinguished career on the stage and screen with only one good eye, and now that eye was threatened with blindness. He had undergone successful cataract surgery of the right eye several years earlier, but advanced glaucoma had now significantly and irreversibly reduced his vision and would continue to do so if his eye pressure was not brought under better control. Furthermore, in the course of my examination, I found that he had been bleeding in the back of his eye, which further reduced his vision and raised the concern of a retinal detachment.

I had two treatment options to control his glaucoma, which would otherwise rob him of his remaining sight. The first was to operate, which could be done—initially, at least—with laser surgery. The procedure had a good chance of success, but there was always the possibility of complications. If something should go wrong, it could lead to the need for more surgery, this time with the scalpel, which had an even greater potential for complications and could lead to further loss of vision. I certainly did not cotton to the idea of making my name as the doctor who blinded Sir Rex Harrison.

The second option was to try adjusting his medications in the hope of getting his glaucoma under reasonable control. This was not likely to be a long-term solution, but it might at least get us through the next few weeks, and there was no way of knowing how long the medical control might last. In any case, I discussed the two options with Sir Rex and his wife, explaining why I favored the less risky medical option, to which they both readily agreed.

Although there had been some question about his compliance with recommended medical therapy in the past—a problem that is all too common among glaucoma patients—he promised to do his best to be faithful to our treatment plan. His wife also assured me that she would hold him to his promise, which gave me more confidence that our plan might work. I discussed with both of them the changes that we would make in his medications and explained the side effects that he might experience. I also called in one of my retina colleagues, who felt that the blood in the back of the eye was not of recent origin and that there was no evidence of retinal detachment. So we all shook hands, and they agreed to return in two days to see how the new treatment was working.

On the return visit, they began by informing me that his vision was significantly worse than before. Whereas he had previously at least been able to read large print, he was now even having difficulty walking around in unfamiliar settings. This was especially disconcerting, since it was now less than a week before his play was scheduled to open. To make matters worse, I also found that the pressure in his eye had actually increased, rather than coming down as my treatment was supposed to have accomplished. At this point, I suspect that the Harrisons were beginning to have doubts about the qualifications of their new, southern doctor. As I proceeded with my examination, I discovered that there had been additional bleeding in the back of the eye since the first visit, which probably explained the further reduction in vision. This was especially troublesome, since the eye drop that I had added to his regimen—an old medication called pilocarpine—can cause retinal detachment and associated bleeding. But once again, my retina colleague found no evidence of a retinal tear or detachment and felt that it was safe to continue the pilocarpine. I asked Sir Rex to give his current medical treatment a little more time to work and markedly restrict his activities in the hope that it would accelerate the clearing of the blood and improve his vision.

When he returned two days later, the vision in his right eye had improved significantly, with a corresponding reduction in the hemorrhage. To my dismay, however, his pressure had only continued to rise and was now nearly three times higher than was safe for his eye. As I tried to figure out what was going on, I wondered if Sir Rex was failing to take his pilocarpine as prescribed. This would not be surprising, since it is not a pleasant medication to use. It had been a popular glaucoma treatment for over one hundred years, having been introduced in the late nineteenth century, but had fallen out of favor in recent years as newer drugs came along. Among its many distractions are induced headaches and dimness of vision, especially during the first few days of use, and the fact that the drops must be instilled into the eye four times each day. But, for most patients, it is still a very effective method of lowering the eye pressure. In any case, I instilled a drop of his pilocarpine in the office and asked if I might stop by their hotel suite in a couple of hours to check his pressure on my way home.

The Harrisons were staying at the Washington Duke Inn, named after the patriarch of the Duke family. It is a castle-like hotel nestled among a forest of stately pine trees on the university campus and adjacent to the Duke golf course. I passed by it each day on my way to and from the office. As I entered their suite, the first thing that struck me was the heat and humidity in the rooms, which Sir Rex apparently found necessary for his health. There was also the strong medicinal scent of liniment in the air, and I had the feeling of walking into a hospital room.

Mrs. Harrison met me at the door and ushered me to their bedroom. By my count, she was actually his sixth wife, but I was impressed by how devoted she seemed to be to her husband, as though they had been married forever. Not only was she willing to contend with what struck me as rather stifling living conditions—the heat and humidity—but she was totally attentive to his every need, with a genuine sense of concern, good humor, and loving warmth.

As we entered their bedroom, the next thing that struck me was the large number of poster boards scattered across his bed and about the room. Each board contained a few sentences, written with a broad marking pen in letters that were about five inches in height. At first I thought they might be cue cards, but Mrs. Harrison explained that this was how Sir Rex memorized his lines. The large letters were necessary since his vision had become so poor in recent months. For the past several days, he had been sitting in the bedroom of his hotel suite, memorizing the lines for his play, which was now scheduled to open in two nights.

Sir Rex was sitting in a wingback chair, wearing a smoking jacket with an open-collar white shirt, slacks, and house slippers. He gave me a cordial greeting and apologized for the mess in his room. But my only thought at that moment was the pressure in his right eye, which I checked with a portable instrument and was delighted to find was now entirely normal. The Harrisons also seemed to be delighted, and I was hopeful that this would reinforce the importance of using his medicines. We again discussed the options of medical treatment versus laser surgery, and they reiterated their preference for the former, vowing that they would try harder to follow the prescribed medical schedule.

Before leaving, I asked the Harrisons if I might bring a colleague by their suite a week from the coming Saturday. That was the day of our annual Duke Glaucoma Symposium, a continuing medical education course for practicing ophthalmologists in our region. By coincidence, one of the guest speakers that year was a long-time friend and noted glaucoma expert from Baltimore, Dr. Irvin Pollack. When the play ended its two-week run in Durham, it was scheduled to move to Baltimore, where it had already been arranged that Irv would take over the care of Sir Rex. I thought it might be nice for the Harrisons to become acquainted with Dr. Pollack while he was in Durham, and they seemed to be very receptive to and pleased with the idea.

As I drove on home that evening, something greatly puzzled me. Here was a man who seemed to have accomplished everything that his profession had to offer. Not only had he been knighted by the Queen of England, but he had also received innumerable other honors, including an Oscar for his role in *My Fair Lady* and an honorary doctorate from Boston University. He had appeared in forty-three films and an even larger number of stage plays. He had rubbed shoulders with royalty and with all the great names of stage and screen for over half a century. He had once earned fifty thousand dollars a week for his performance on stage, and he owned a lovely villa on the Italian coast. At this very moment, he could be relaxing on his yacht in the Mediterranean, sipping his scotch and basking in the glow of his life's success. And yet, he was sitting in a small, strange bedroom in a hotel in Durham North, Carolina, in his eighty-first year, struggling against formidable medical odds to memorize his lines for yet another play. I could not help but wonder why. It was clearly not for the money or the fame. In time, I believe I came to understand the answer.

The play opened on schedule and received courteous, if not enthusiastic, reviews from the local critics. The name of the play was *The Circle*, a romantic comedy written by Somerset Maugham in the 1920s. Sir Rex had long admired the play, but this was his first appearance in it, which seemed all the more remarkable, as he was taking on something entirely new at this time in his life. It was also a grueling schedule, with matinees and evening performances nearly every day. He continued to come to my office every few days between the afternoon and evening shows, and I was thankful each time to find that his eye condition was holding stable.

On the Saturday of the glaucoma symposium, Irv Pollack and I broke away from the meeting during the luncheon and walked over to the Washington Duke. The Harrisons greeted us cordially in their suite, and I introduced them to Dr. Pollack. We had brought a few instruments with us, and I asked Irv to take a look at Sir Rex's eyes to make sure that I was not missing something. He agreed with the diagnosis and current therapy and indicated to the Harrisons that he would look forward to taking over the care of Sir Rex when they arrived in Baltimore. Little did he know at that moment what he would be getting in to.

My last week with Sir Rex was by far the most pleasant of his three in Durham—the play was doing well, his eye was staying under control, and I had the privilege of learning a little more about this remarkable man. He was first and foremost of true professional of his craft. He had made the decision to be an actor when he was a young schoolboy, and he had never wavered from nor apparently regretted the choice. Furthermore, he took his work very seriously, always giving his full attention and energy to each role he played. His philosophy of the acting profession seems to be summed up in his autobiography, entitled *Rex*, in which he states, "The actor, who is on earth to entertain all those people who do things great and small, cannot measure himself until he realizes that that is the full aim of his job: not to dictate or to preach, not to be too damn clever for his own ends, or think he has anything more important to do than, simply, to entertain." I felt that I was beginning to understand what drove this dedicated man.

Sir Rex was also a very human individual. While his demeanor was most often that of a courteous, considerate, somewhat serious-minded gentleman, he also possessed the full range of emotions, from a marvelous sense of humor to sudden outbursts of anger. During my brief time with him, I felt that I had observed all but the latter characteristic, and was actually hoping that I might be privileged to witness some of those irascible qualities that he had used so effectively and that had so endeared him in his role as Henry Higgins. On one occasion, during that last week, my wish was granted.

Before he left, I wanted to introduce Sir Rex to our department chairman, Dr. Robert Machemer, who was internationally renowned for his major contributions to retinal surgery. As it turned out, there were several others from the medical school who wanted to meet our famous guest, so the room was rather full that afternoon. After introductions had been made all around, Dr. Machemer briefly examined Sir Rex's retina, and then the group of us huddled to discuss his situation. But we made the same mistake that I had made with Miss Nanny—we were talking in hushed tones with our backs to the most important person in the room. And, like Miss Nanny, Sir Rex would have none of it. With a clear edge of irritation in his voice, he thundered out in his finest Higgins-esque manner.

"I say, I cahn't understand a word that chap is saying!"

Like a school of fish that darts this way and that in perfect synchrony, our little group immediately turned as one person to hover around Sir Rex. He sat there with a faint smile of satisfaction on his face, as though he had just returned from the Embassy Ball. Although momentarily embarrassed for all of us, I must confess that I was delighted.

Another event that made his last week with us so special was a message I received from the Harrisons, inviting my family to be their guests at the final performance in Durham and then to join Sir Rex afterward in his dressing room. Needless to say, we were all very excited. Sarah and John were now in their mid-teens and had watched our video of *My Fair Lady* at least three times since learning that the star was their father's patient.

The play was on the Duke campus in the Bryan Center, a place that holds special memories for our family, because of my patient, Mr. Joseph Bryan, but that is for another story. The Bryan Center is essentially the student union, which includes the bookstore, restaurants, study areas, and the theater. We had been to several performances there, but we had never had such good seats as on this special evening. The theater was full, which surprised me a bit after twice-daily performances for two weeks in a relatively small community. It was clear that the audience had come primarily to see Sir Rex Harrison. They gave him a thunderous ovation when he made his first appearance late in the first act, and he nearly brought the house down with one of his outbursts of feigned irritation, which everyone had obviously been anticipating, just as I had in my office.

I must confess that I remember very little about the play itself. It may have been that I was focusing too much on Sir Rex and hoping that his poor vision would not result in any mishaps during his performance. Even back when his right eye was still good, his blind left eye had occasionally gotten him in trouble on the stage, like the time he poured wine into glasses that were upside down. But like the true veteran he was, he made it successfully through the entire evening and received a standing ovation at the curtain call.

By the time we got to his dressing room, Sir Rex had already changed into his smoking jacket and was waiting for us. Considering the celebrities who had come to his dressing room after shows of years gone by—Marilyn Monroe, Spencer Tracy, and Louis Armstrong, to mention a few—I wondered if he would see our visit as a boring obligation to be dispensed with as promptly as propriety allowed. But if he had harbored any such feelings that evening, he definitely did not reveal them. He greeted us with a warmth that made us all feel truly welcome and proceeded to chat with us for quite some time. He delighted the children with amusing stories of his past, including how he was selected for the movie version of *My Fair Lady*, while his costar in the stage version, whom he referred to as "that girl," was passed over. (That girl, of course, was Julie Andrews.) We ended the visit with a picture-taking session of Sarah and John with Sir Rex, which remains one of our family treasures to this day.

The Harrisons were leaving Durham the next morning, and when we said good-bye to them that evening, I wished them well for their time in Baltimore. The next day, a lovely gift appeared on my desk, with a touching note from Mrs. Harrison. She thanked me for "all your kindness in helping Rex." She went ahead to explain their gift of appreciation, which was a handsome porcelain box: "During the Cultural Revolution in Asia the 'mob' broke a great many antique porcelain objects. But they kept the pieces of these glorious works of art and now are using them in lots of ways, for example this box. I hope you like it as much as we do." She ended by asking us to let them know whenever we were in New York. Talk about a family treasure.

I never saw either of them again, but I tried to keep up with Sir Rex through medical reports and the media. The first of those reports actually came sooner than I had expected. It was from Irv Pollack. It seems that Sir Rex no sooner arrived in Baltimore than he developed a severe toothache, and Irv scrambled to arrange an emergency dental appointment. Next, his glaucoma medication apparently quit working, forcing Irv to proceed with the laser surgery that I had tried to avoid. Fortunately, the procedure was successful, and the show opened on time. But the third and most ominous development occurred during a performance, when Sir Rex became disoriented on the stage, requiring cancellation of the remainder of that show. Again, Irv had to scramble, this time to obtain the emergency services of a neurologist, who apparently found no definite explanation for the episode. Despite this rash of medical setbacks, Sir Rex stayed with the show, which completed its run in Baltimore and then moved on for the final round of pre-Broadway performances in Boston.

The trial runs in the three venues were apparently successful enough to justify taking the show to Broadway, where it finally opened with its star, Sir Rex Harrison. The play also did well in New York and was said to be vying for "best revival" honors in that year's Tony Awards. I felt a bit of satisfaction in all of this, as though I had played a small role in their success. But most of all I was just happy for Sir Rex and his faithful and loving wife.

Life moved on for our family, and thoughts of Sir Rex gradually moved into the recesses of my mind. Until, that is, one morning at breakfast, as I was sipping coffee and reading the paper. I suspect my heart stopped momentarily when I saw the headline: "Actor Rex Harrison Dies at 82."

He died of pancreatic cancer at his home in Manhattan and had worked up until three weeks before his death. He must have struggled greatly during those last months on the stage, and I marveled again at the courage of this true professional. I received a very sweet letter from Mrs. Harrison. In it she said, "Well, if dying can be called beautiful, Rex had a beautiful death—so peaceful and painless."

Somehow those words did not surprise me. I felt that I was beginning to understand why a man like Rex Harrison continues to push himself long after most people have sat back to reap the rewards of their labor. He did it for the same reason that Miss Nanny never stopped working for her family. They both had a purpose in their life, a zest for living, and an excitement for the challenge that each new day may bring. And, when the last day came for both of them, there were no regrets.

The lives of Sir Rex and Miss Nanny were a world apart—his stage was the world, and hers was a small farm in North Carolina. But they shared a common gift. Though their combined ages totaled 185 years, neither ever truly grew old, because they never stopped living. Each new day for them offered a new challenge and a new reward. He had his adoring public to entertain, and she had her equally adoring family to serve. Both simply lacked the time to worry about growing old.

Of course, Miss Nanny had an added gift. For her, the last day of this life was just a steppingstone to the next, where she never doubted that she would be reunited with her little Zach and all her family. I never got to know Sir Rex well enough to ascertain where he came down on that score. But I would like to think, with a bit of whimsical conjecture, that they have become quite good friends up there, and I can just imagine their conversations.

"Now, Rex," I can hear her say, "how many times I got to tell you? You pronounces it 'cain't,' not 'cahn't.'"

And with a twinkle in his eye, he replies like the rest of us.

"Yes, ma'am."

Ω

13.

The Peanut Man

I simply couldn't seem to get into the Christmas spirit. It had never been a problem in my youth—just one of those things that happened without really trying. Like most children, I was captivated by the joy and the wonder of the season—mysterious boxes hidden in closets, the secretive smiles of our parents, shoppers bustling about in the frosty winter air, fragrant trees, sparkling lights, brightly wrapped presents, carols, delicious treats, school pageants (when such things were still allowed), a long vacation, anticipation of the big day, and the wonder of a child's birth. How could you help but feel the spirit of Christmas when you were a child? But as the years passed and I entered adulthood and life became more complex and demanding, it seemed like that treasured feeling of years gone by was becoming more and more elusive.

This year it seemed especially hard to get into the spirit. And that in and of itself made it all the more difficult, because it gave me a sense of guilt—I felt that I was not properly observing the holiness of the season if I did not feel the spirit of Christmas that I had as a child. I wanted it for myself, but even more, I wanted it for our children—I so wanted them to feel the same joys and wonders of Christmas that I had experienced at their age, and to understand the real reason for our celebration. But it was one of those things in which the harder we try, the more distant the goal seems to become. And I really didn't know why it was so hard—especially that year.

It might have been the weather. Little wonder that we tend to equate Christmas with cold temperatures and blankets of new fallen snow, especially those of us who live in the northern hemisphere. I suppose we could blame it on Currier and Ives or maybe Bing Crosby. In any case, I was like pretty much everyone else. Although I had only known a few truly white Christmases in my life, I lived in hope. At least I hoped for cold weather, so people would still go bustling about as they shopped for their treasures. But, with only two days to go before Christmas, the weather in Durham was downright balmy. How could you get into the spirit of Christmas when people were sauntering around in short-sleeved shirts?

The eye center was scheduled to be closed on Christmas Eve. Earlier in the day, Robin, nurse Sharon, a few others in our little glaucoma group, and I had enjoyed our annual Christmas party. We shared punch and homemade cookies, exchanged gifts, and wished each other well, and then they left early to prepare for special times with family and friends. I decided to take advantage of the quiet time and clear some of the work off my desk. And that may have been when I recognized another possible reason for my seasonal melancholy. As I went through the medical records, I was reminded of how many of my patients were suffering. It appeared to be more than at any other time of year, or maybe it just seemed that way because of the time of year—all our problems seem to be magnified at Christmas, when we should be happy and carefree. But illness is no respecter of seasons, and people do get sick at Christmastime. And it seems harder to bear than usual—for the patients, for their families, and for their doctors.

The building was nearly empty when I finally closed my office door and headed down the hall and into the eye center lobby. And there I encountered yet another reason for my meager sense of holiday cheer—the Christmas tree. Why would anyone want a tree made of gold aluminum foil with purple satin bows? Why did things have to change? What was wrong with the old fashion Christmas trees—the real trees, with their wonderful fragrance and their sparkling lights? I stood in the quiet lobby for a few moments, puzzling over those questions and beginning to feel like the true Christmas curmudgeon. As I carried my sack of newly acquired presents out into the balmy night air, I just hoped that my temperament would improve before I got home.

I decided to take the long way home through the campus that evening.

With the students gone, there was hardly any traffic. Above the pine trees, I could see the tower of Duke Chapel, flooded in lights. Were there people inside preparing for the Christmas Eve service? Or was it dark and empty? As I drove past the school of engineering, and the physics building and chemistry building, and the law school, I could see a few lights on in windows here and there—probably the janitorial crew cleaning up for the semester break, or maybe graduate students completing their experiments and papers before heading home for the holidays. In a few windows I could make out a wreath or a candle, and I wondered if the people in those buildings had also celebrated with colleagues earlier in the day. Were they now anxiously anticipating the completion of their work and the joy of soon being home with their families? And that thought—of leaving school and traveling home for the holidays—suddenly stirred something inside me and brought back a rush of old, sweet memories.

It was my first semester of medical school, and I had just finished our last exam. There was nothing left to do but pack up and head home, and for the first time, I could relax and relish that anticipated joy. I tossed my clothes, most of which were dirty, and other belongings into the backseat of the car and then carefully nestled a few presents among the piles of clothes. I hadn't had much time (not to mention ideas or money) for shopping during the weeks of final exams and looked forward to completing that when I got home. My old car, a light blue '54 Ford, which I had driven since high school, had worn tires, but the engine was still reliable. Unfortunately, however, the heater was not as reliable, and I draped a small blanket over my knees as I headed out beneath a full moon across the flat, frozen Oklahoma farmland. Through the static from my car radio, the old Christmas music never sounded sweeter, and I felt my spirits rising with each mile as I reflected on Christmases past and the prospects of yet another one with my family.

My parents did a wonderful job of instilling the Christmas spirit in us, and it was truly a time of joy and wonder for me. To this day, no matter where I am or what my circumstances may be, everything on Christmas Day seems somehow different and more special than on any other day of the year. Ours was a very traditional Christmas. It was back in the time when relatives lived close by, and on Christmas Day we all came together.

On Christmas Eve, falling asleep had always been a problem for me as a young boy. I was convinced that I lay awake all night, although the truth is that I probably was asleep within an hour. One year, as I was approaching that age of doubt, I remember lying there, trying to do the math. Was it really possible that Santa could visit every home in the world in one night? I had to sadly conclude that it was not, and that began to shake my faith and lead to a change in my thinking that I was not ready to accept. And then a wonderful thought came to me—there are some things we will never understand, and it is best not to worry about them, but just leave them in the hands of those who know. That thought gave me a warm, comforting feeling of reassurance, as I drifted off with visions of sugar plums dancing in my head.

It would still be dark—adding to the wonder—when our parents would wake us on Christmas morning, and we would quickly don our bathrobes and rush into the living room (when given permission) to see what Santa had brought. The reason for the early morning start was to allow time to open our presents and then get dressed and drive over to our grandparents' home, where all the aunts and uncles and cousins would congregate around another tree and open more presents. But the most anticipated moment, for me at least, was Grandma's wonderful cooking. She would be in the kitchen when we arrived, and the house would already be filled with the delicious aromas of her culinary labor. In the early afternoon, we would all sit around the huge dining room table, and Grandpa would give thanks for all our blessings and for the special gift of this day.

In my later years at home, I was allowed to participate in the midnight candlelight service at our church on Christmas Eve. The first year was when I was a Boy Scout, and our troop was responsible for watching the candles to avoid a fire. I felt very grownup to be out after midnight, and it also did wonders for my sleeping problem. As I grew older, I had other parts in the service, such as singing in the youth choir and reading scripture. But what I enjoyed most were those years that I would just sit with my family and friends, listening to the music and the retelling of the Christmas story and enjoying the warm glow of the candlelight. On one especially memorable year, we came out of the service to find that it had begun to snow. There were shouts of "Merry Christmas" in the still night air as we all hurried home to celebrate another Christmas with our families.

It was around the time in my life when I had rationalized my belief in Santa Claus that I had yet another Christmas epiphany. I am sure that, in my early years, it was the anticipation of receiving the gifts (and the food) that evoked the Christmas spirit in me. But the day came when I experienced a startling revelation as a young boy—I discovered the joy of giving. I had been able to save a few coins, and my grandmother drove me to a drugstore, where I purchased a bottle of perfume (or so I thought) for my mother. I could hardly contain myself until she opened my carefully wrapped gift. I suspect that I did lie awake a bit longer on that Christmas Eve, so intense was the anticipation of my mother's response. And she did not disappoint me. My heart soared as I watched the expression on her face when she opened my present. I thought I detected a tear in her eye, as she reached over to hug me, and I was convinced at that moment that I had discovered the secret of the true spirit of Christmas—the joy of giving.

By the time I had left the Duke campus behind me and turned down into the dark, quiet woods toward home, the thoughts of Christmases past, aided by the music on my tape deck, were beginning to work their magic. A nearly full moon, much like on that night coming home from medical school, was shining down through the trees, illuminating the natural gothic arches that the branches formed high above the road. Memories of the past and the anticipation of soon being home with my little family for another Christmas were truly lifting my spirits. And thoughts of being with our children caused me to reflect again on the lesson I had learned as a young boy—that the true spirit of Christmas is to be found in the joy of giving. In recent years, I had tried to share this revelation with Sarah and John, in what they referred to as "one of Dad's lectures." But they listened indulgingly, and I comforted myself in believing that the "lesson" was taking—and it probably was.

As I turned off the wooded drive and entered the residential area of Duke Forest, I had the uneasy feeling that my Christmas spirit was again starting to fade. For one thing, it didn't seem like nearly as many homes had their Christmas lights on this year. Maybe they didn't have the spirit either. But that was their problem, and I knew it would be different for me when I turned on to our street. Our home would be cheerfully lit with the candles we had put in all the windows and the floodlight illuminating the big wreath on our front door. Delicious smells from the kitchen would greet me at the door as Sharon put the finishing touches on our supper. The children, who were now in their teens, would be home enjoying one of our many Christmas tapes. Surely then I would have the Christmas spirit.

But as I turned on to our street, it seemed to be the darkest in the neighborhood. Not a single Christmas light was on at our house. As I walked in through the back door to the kitchen, Sharon greeted me with a smile and a cheerful "Hi, hon."

"I would have thought someone could have turned on the Christmas lights," I replied. (Why couldn't I have at least said "Hi" first?)

Her smile faded, as she brushed back a lock of hair from her forehead with the back of her hand. The kitchen counter was covered with a row of heavy sacks of food that she had obviously just brought in from the car.

"I'm sorry," she said with a faint sigh. "I was trying to get the last of the Christmas shopping done, and all the stores were so crowded that it took longer than I had planned. I'll go turn the lights on now."

"No, that's okay. I'll do it," I offered in my meek and inadequate reply.

I was chastising myself and resolving to be more pleasant when I walked into the family room and suddenly lost my resolve. Sarah and John were stretched out on the carpet, and the loud blast of their rock music grated against my ears.

"Hi, Dad!" they both shouted cheerfully above the din.

"Why in the world are you listening to that stuff when it's only two days until Christmas?" I demanded. "We have lots of beautiful Christmas tapes, and you can listen to that noise all the rest of the year."

Sarah got up and walked out of the room with a hurt, indignant look on her face. John leaned over and turned down the volume on the stereo.

"Where are the Christmas tapes?" he asked.

"What's bugging Dad?" Sarah asked her mother as she walked into the kitchen.

Sharon gave her a tired, patient smile. "I think he's just trying to get us all into the Christmas spirit."

"Well he sure has a funny way of doing it," Sarah said as she went off to her room to listen to music on her radio.

We were quiet at dinner that evening. Afterwards, I went off to my study to stay out of my family's hair. I figured they had had quite enough of Dad's Christmas spirit for one day.

The following morning, Christmas Eve, I went back to the eye center to see a few postoperative patients and discharge some who were still in the hospital. After the last patient was seen and we had exchanged holiday wishes, I decided to stay in my office for a while to finish up some work that I had not completed the night before. There were still a few gifts in the room that patients had brought in during the week that I had yet to take home. For the most part, they were jars of pickles and preserves, homemade candies and cookies, and tins of nuts. Set among them was a brown cardboard box that offered no clue as to its contents, but which I recognized without opening it. I had been receiving similar boxes for many years and knew what this one contained, and who had sent it—the Peanut Man.

———

It had been more than a decade since he first came to our clinic. There was nothing remarkable about his appearance or demeanor. He was in his mid-sixties, a man of average height and somewhat greater than average weight. However, he was not fat, and while he did not cut the physique of an athletic man, neither did he give the impression of one who is idle with his time. His thin, gray hair was cut short, and ruddy cheeks accentuated his otherwise pale face. His manner of dress was also nondescript and suggested, if anything, that clothes were not high on his list of priorities. He always wore a white, short-sleeved shirt, regardless of the time of year, and his dark trousers were typically polyester. All of this was consistent with his personality, which was quiet, but still warm and friendly.

He had spent most of his working years as a night watchman in a factory. This gave him time for his avocation and true love, which was tinkering and which seemed to fill up most of his spare time. His favorite activity, and the thing he probably did best, was taking antiques (or just any old odds and ends) and turning them into useful and attractive household items. But what he truly seemed to enjoy the most in life was sharing his creations with others. He loved to give.

I first became a recipient of his generosity rather early in our relationship, when he came into the office one day and handed me a most unique lamp. It had begun as a shallow, cast-iron frying pan. He had drilled a hole in the center of the pan, into which he fitted a metal pipe topped off with a light bulb attachment and a lampshade. I can truly say that it was one of the nicest gifts I had ever received from a patient thus far in my young practice. I was especially taken by the fact that he had made it himself. In retrospect, I may have gone on about it too much, because it turned out to be only the first of many gifts, of ever increasing value, that he would give me over the years.

It was not much more than a year later when he came in with an enormous table lamp. This one was made from an old-fashioned lantern, the type I could envision a conductor swinging from the back of a caboose. He had somehow attached the bulb fitting on top of the lantern and run the electrical cord down one of the metal supports that held the glass lamp.

Within the base of the lamp, he had fitted a smaller light bulb, which could be turned on individually to simulate the original glow of the lantern. All of this was mounted on a well-finished block of wood to which he had attached a metal plate with my name. Needless to say, I was overwhelmed.

In those days, my examination room and private office were one and the same. At the office end of the room, I had a corner table, above which hung a watercolor painted by my brother, Chuck. It is a still life of old farm implements from our days in Oklahoma and included a lantern. I wondered if that painting had been the inspiration for my patient's beautiful lamp. In any case, I set the lamp on the corner table beneath the painting, where it remained throughout my years at Duke. When I moved to Yale and had a larger desk, I used it as my desk lamp, and it remains a treasured possession to this day.

I suppose it gave my patient satisfaction to see his lamp in a special place each time he came in for his office visits. At least it did nothing to deter his continued generosity.

The next present was not a lamp (which was fortunate, since I was running out of tables). It did, however, upstage his previous gifts. It was a huge, antique floor-model radio in a beautifully finished wooden cabinet. He had removed the old, internal works, which had long since given up the ghost, and replaced them with a new radio. He even managed to attach the modern radio behind the front of the original console so that it could be operated with the same knobs that were used when the old radio was brand new.

For a man who was now in his seventies, this struck me as a remarkable accomplishment. Just to get it into the office, which he did with the help of a friend, was no mean feat. He stood beside his latest creation with perspiration on his brow and a sense of pride and satisfaction in his countenance. Frankly, I didn't know what to say, but I called in everyone in the clinic to admire it. The ruddiness of his cheeks spread across his entire face as he bowed his head in a blush and a smile with each new accolade. I am sure he was embarrassed by all the attention, but he also seemed pleased.

I soon learned that his talents were not limited to restoring old objects. One day he came in with what was clearly the most impressive of all his gifts to date and required the help of two extra men to bring it into the office. It was a brand-new, handmade wooden cabinet, measuring approximately two feet in height by three feet in width and depth. He had made it all by himself and finished it with a beautiful, hand-rubbed, natural wooden exterior. Large doors on the front opened to release the wonderful fragrance of new wood from within. By this time I was running out of superlatives to express my admiration for his talents and my gratitude for his generosity. But I did my best, wishing to myself that he did not feel the need to continue bestowing such lavish gifts on me. I had to confess, however, that it was a timely gift, since it was just what we needed for John's room, which we were finally getting around to converting from infant's room to that of a young man of eight.

The following Saturday afternoon, John and I went over to the office to bring his new cabinet home. That was bad judgment on my part. The thing weighed a ton and was clearly a job for two, if not three, grown men. But John was big for his age and willing to give it a try. As we carried it down the back stairwell of the eye center, an edge of the cabinet caught on one of the stairs, bringing our forward momentum to a sudden halt. The cabinet stopped, but John did not. His head careened forward into the cabinet with a sickening thud. He was good-natured about it, but I'm not sure if he ever felt that the new cabinet in his room was worth the swollen lip he had to pay for it.

About the time I thought my benevolent patient could surely not outdo himself again, he did just that, presenting me with the biggest surprise yet. He did not appear to be carrying anything that day, but after his examination he asked if we might have a word in private. Sharon stepped out of the room and closed the door. He was silent for what seemed like several minutes. I noticed tears were beginning to well up in his eyes and I realized that his emotions were making it difficult for him to speak.

"Doc," he finally began in a raspy voice, "me and my wife don't have no children, and when we die there won't be no close relatives. We don't have much, but we do own our home and some land, and I reckon it's worth something. So I have written in my will, that after I'm gone and after my wife is gone, whatever is left is to go to the Duke Eye Center. Maybe you can use the money to help other people."

Now it was my eyes that were welling up with tears. I couldn't have spoken at that moment, even if I had known what to say. But I think—I hope—that my silence spoke to him more loudly than words. I finally regained my composure enough to thank him as sincerely as I knew how. We both laughed a little to conceal our true emotions, shook hands for a rather long time, wiped our eyes, and walked out of the room together.

During the decade that he had been coming to the eye center, I was able to control his glaucoma with medications, but had watched his vision gradually decline from cataracts. Not long after the visit in which he announced his most generous gift, I told him that the time had finally come to have cataract surgery. We had been discussing this possibility for several years, so he seemed mentally prepared. But I was not prepared for what he would say next.

He told me that he could not afford to have the surgery at Duke. His wife had been ill, and they had already built up a significant medical debt. Even with Medicare, he could not afford the co-payment. Since he had been so kind to me over the years, I naturally wanted to do all I could to help him, not only medically, but also financially. I told him I would be pleased to waive my surgical fee. Unfortunately, however, I had no control over the additional operating room and hospital charges, and he said even that was beyond his means. I couldn't believe that there was not some way I could help one of my kindest, most generous patients. I suggested that we talk with our social worker to see what additional assistance might be available, but at that point I began to feel him withdraw, defensively.

He informed me that he would take advantage of the Veterans Administration Hospital, where he was entitled to free medical care. The VAH was part of our teaching program, and all the surgery was done by our residents in training under the supervision of a Duke faculty member. I told him that I would at least arrange to assist with his surgery. He thanked me for that and left the office. Little could I have guessed as he walked out the door that day that it would be the last time I would ever see him at the eye center.

I did assist with his surgery, which fortunately went well, and saw him with the resident at the VAH once or twice during the early postoperative course. After that, however, he seemed to always come on days when I wasn't there. Months passed, and he had begun to slip to the back recesses of my mind when a brown cardboard box arrived in the mail. I suspected that I knew who had sent it, and this was confirmed when I glanced at the return address. There was no note attached, but when I opened the box, I was not surprised to find six jars of peanuts.

During the years that my generous patient had been coming to the eye center, he often brought similar boxes of peanuts in between his bigger gifts. He explained that the men's class at his church roasted and sold the peanuts to raise money for various community projects. I suppose, therefore, that he not only helped prepare the peanuts, but also purchased them with his own money to assist the needy and then gave them as gifts to bring happiness to still more people. His generosity at the eye center was not limited to me. He also brought jars of peanuts to Robin and Sharon and all our staff, as well as our residents and fellows, and soon they also began showing up at the VAH. So familiar were his jars of peanuts to all of us that he eventually became known as the Peanut Man.

Peanuts have always been one of my weaknesses, and those from the Peanut Man soon became my absolute favorites. I must confess, therefore, that I was pleased to receive his most recent gift. But I would have much preferred for him to bring them in person, rather than mailing them. I had always assumed that he would eventually come back to the eye center so that I could continue to care for him. But months and then years passed without a word. I tried to arrange to see him at the VAH, but whenever I went, he was never there. And yet, like clockwork, the boxes with six jars of peanuts would show up each Christmas and several other times throughout the year.

One day I received a letter from a friend of the Peanut Man. He informed me that his friend was having financial difficulties because of his wife's continued illness. He also said that he feared his friend was going blind, but couldn't afford to come back to Duke. I sent the friend a letter of thanks and then wrote a long letter to my patient, telling him how much I missed him and that I wished he would come back to the eye center, where I would gladly see him without charge. He never replied. I tried to call him, but his phone had been disconnected. I tried again to reach him at the VAH, but still to no avail.

More years passed, during which time I never saw him or heard from him. I sent him a card each Christmas and additional letters during the year, imploring him to come back, so I could at least do what I could to help him, since he had done so much for me and so many others. But still there was never a word, and I had no way of knowing if he was even alive, except that the peanuts continued to come.

I was mystified. Had I done something wrong? Had I offended him? Should I have insisted on doing his surgery all those years ago? Should I have offered more financial help? Or had I offered too much?

For the hundredth time, those questions went through my mind as I sat in my office that morning on Christmas Eve. I glanced back over at the brown cardboard box among the other gifts and noticed, for the first time, that there was something different about this one—there was an envelope carefully taped to the side. I peeled it off from the box and removed the letter it contained. As I held it in my hand, it momentarily gave me a feeling as though it was a message from beyond the grave. I took a deep breath, leaned back in my chair, and began to read.

Dear Doctor Shields,

I am sorry I haven't written sooner. My wife has been sick and she needed me. She died just before Thanksgiving.

I am OK. I don't see too good any more, but good enough to get around and to write this letter. And I guess I owe you some explaining.

When I gave you those gifts, I didn't expect nothing back. At first you were real good, 'cause you seemed happy with what I gave you and that made me happy. But then you tried to give me things back and that wasn't what I gave my things to you for.

I asked my preacher about it and he explained it this way. It's harder to be a good getter than a good giver. Lots of people like to give, cause it makes them happy. But if there wasn't good getters, then giving wouldn't be no fun. He said we all need to work on being better getters, especially at Christmas time, 'cause that's when we get the biggest gift.

When God sent Jesus on the first Christmas, it was his gift to us. What we're suppose to do is say thank you, God, thanks a whole lot, and then take that gift and love it every day of our life. And I guess one way we can do that is to make other people happy by being good getters of their gifts.

So I hope you understand. I'm pretty old now and may not be able to make it back to Durham. But don't worry about me. I'll keep those peanuts coming long as I can. And you just keep enjoying them.

Merry Christmas,

"The Peanut Man"

P.S. You probably didn't think I knew about that name, but I kind of like it.

The Peanut Man had a way of bringing tears to my eyes, and at that moment I was thankful to be alone. I looked over at the table in the corner of my office, where his lantern lamp still stood. It had been there for over a decade, trying to tell me something that only now I was beginning to understand. When he gave me those gifts, he wanted nothing in return, except my gratitude and the joy they brought me—that was how he derived his joy. And when I tried to return his generosity with offers to help him, he withdrew because that defeated his greatest source of joy. The best thing that I could have given him in return was simply to receive and appreciate his gifts—to be a good "getter."

And that made me think—did I have it wrong all those years? Is it possible that Christmas is not primarily about giving, but about receiving? When I gave that first present to my mother so many years ago, I felt a happiness that I had never before experienced. And I became increasingly convinced, over the years that followed, that in the act of giving I had discovered the true essence of the Christmas spirit. But now I began to realize that something even greater had been happening in the exchange of that gift. My mother had discovered it (possibly at that very moment)—that the true spirit of Christmas comes in the joy we bring to others by how we accept their gifts. It was her precious gift to me—the look in her eyes that morning told me that I had done well, my gift was received with a grateful heart, and I was loved.

And the corollary, of course, just as the Peanut Man's preacher explained, is that the proper attitude at Christmastime and throughout the year—the true spirit of Christmas—is to accept and be grateful for the greatest gift ever given.

———

That night the four of us went to the candlelight service at our church. We sat in the back, as was our custom, and enjoyed once again the old carols and the reading of the scriptures. At the end of the service, all the lights were turned out, and for a moment it was quite dark. Then a child lit a single candle in the front of the sanctuary. It was barely visible from where we sat, but we watched as the candle was used to light the one beside it. And as the flame was passed back to the candles that each of us held, the room became increasingly brighter. It was to remind us that Jesus came into the world as a light in the darkness. And as he touched lives with his message of love and hope, the light spread, and now, two thousand years later, it shines in all parts of the world.

By the time the flame reached the candles in our row, the sanctuary was awash with a warm golden glow. But I felt that the true warmth at that moment was coming from within me as I sat there with Sarah on one side and John on the other, the flickering candlelight illuminating their beautiful faces.

As we walked out of the church that evening, it was not snowing. In fact it was still rather balmy. But somehow that now seemed just fine. Maybe it was like that on the first Christmas. Anyway, the stars were twinkling beautifully in the clear sky high above, as though they were reminding us of the Christmas gift. And I, for one, felt a profound sense of gratitude for that and for the love of my family and for all the gifts that fill us with the spirit of Christmas throughout the year, if only we will receive them with a grateful heart.

Ω

14.

Kristi

The winds of change blow hot and cold through our lives. They can bring new opportunities and new joys—a new job, a newborn child, a new home, or a new chance at life. But they can also bring fear, anxiety and heartbreak—leaving the familiar and trusted for the unknown, watching our children go out the door, or saying good-bye to loved ones, sometimes for the last time. And not infrequently, the winds can blow both ways at once, leaving us with confused and bittersweet emotions.

Sharon and I sat together quietly on the couch in our family room. Sarah and John were now off at college, and we had been empty-nesters for a couple of years. The call from Yale had come unexpectedly. Life in Durham and my work at Duke were good. I assumed that I would complete my career there. We had a new chairman at Duke Eye Center, Dr. David Epstein, who was a good friend since our days together at Harvard. He was doing a great job, and I was comfortable working for him, although it was likely that my remaining years at Duke would simply be a continuation of what I had been doing for the past quarter century. Yale was offering a change.

There had been previous offers from other schools, but the time had never seemed right. The children were still at home, and moving would be disruptive for them. I had work at Duke that I wanted to complete, and we were all very happy with our life, our friends, and our church in Durham. Now things were different. I was in my fifty-fifth year, which is a bit old for a major life change, especially one as demanding as chairing the department of a world-class university. But if I was ever going to make the change, it was now or never. And positives for Sharon and me were our happy memories of life in New England and the many friends we still had there.

One of the first things I did was to ask the children how they felt about it. John was always ready with sage advice. He asked if it would mean more work. I assured him that it would, and after a moment of thought, he simply said, "Don't do it." I should have listened. But the family was uniformly supportive, and so I agreed to be interviewed for the position. My first visit to Yale should have served as a harbinger of things to come. The plane could not land in Connecticut due to heavy fog, so we flew on to Boston, where I rented a car and drove to New Haven, arriving well after midnight. On that long drive, my mind was flooded with conflicting thoughts, especially of what and whom we would be leaving behind. We would miss our friends and colleagues, and I would surely miss my patients. Many of their faces appeared in my mind as I stared ahead into the dark New England night, but one face was especially vivid. Like so many of my patients, she had become very special to me over the years, and leaving her would be difficult. But as I reflected back on her life over the past couple of years, it occurred to me that maybe she and I had learned something together about accepting the changes in our lives.

—

Her name is Kristi, and she is one of God's special people. She is gentle and serene, with a love of music and tenderness for all those around her. She greets life with the faith and enthusiasm of a child even though she is now an adult. These special gifts derive, at least in part, from her medical condition, Down syndrome.

Within every cell of our body, there is a cluster of twenty-three pairs of minute structures called chromosomes. These structures are composed of thousands of genes, which form the blueprint by which each new life is created. When scientists separate the chromosomes from the cell and magnify them, they look like twenty-three pairs of worms, with each pair joined at the middle. Each set of chromosomes has a slightly different appearance and is assigned a number. At the moment of creation, the first cell of a new life receives one chromosome of each pair from the mother and the other from the father. So incredibly precise is the uniting of these chromosomal pairs that a perfect baby is born in the vast majority of cases. But there are times when something goes wrong.

Most birth abnormalities are due to one or more defective genes, which may lead to a disorder at birth or to a disease later in life. Less often, the genetic defect may be more extensive, with loss of a portion of a chromosome. In extreme cases, one chromosome may be missing, or there may be three instead of two. The latter situation occurs most commonly with chromosome twenty-one, which is referred to as trisomy twenty-one, or Down syndrome.

People with Down syndrome have a characteristic appearance. They are typically short and stocky and have a slanted appearance to their eyes. They have variable degrees of mental deficiency, but an endearing personality of gentleness, kindness, and serenity. I was privileged to care for many patients with Down syndrome during my practice, but none embodied these special traits more beautifully than Kristi.

"Hey, buddy!" she said as I entered the examination room. That was her traditional greeting.

"How's my girlfriend?" I replied. That was my standard response, and we never varied our script.

She always wore an infectious smile, which I could not help but return. She was now in her mid-thirties, but still possessed the same childlike charm as when I first met her more than twenty years earlier. She was quite short, with the plump little body of a preadolescent. For as long as I had known her, she had dressed simply in T-shirts or knit pullovers, jeans or slacks, and comfortable tennis shoes. Her straight, dark brown hair was worn in a pageboy style and framed a round face with squinty eyes that were magnified behind thick, horn-rimmed glasses. She had a short, turned-up nose and thick lips that seemed to be frozen in her serene smile.

"How's your wife?" she proceeded with our script. Although she had never met Sharon, she never failed to inquire about her as a traditional part of our greeting.

"Fine," I replied, looking down at her medical record that I was holding.

"How are your kids?" she continued the script.

"They're great."

"How's Dr. Blasini?"

"He's doing fine. He asked about you the last time I saw him." That brought an even bigger smile to her face.

"How's Robin?"

"She's fine. She'd love to have you go back to see her before you leave."

Now it was my turn to ask about her family, as was our custom. But on that particular day, I sensed that something was not right. The events of recent months and the look in her eyes seemed to say, "Don't ask."

I first began seeing Kristi when she was a young teenager, and she always came with her father. He was also of short stature, but carried himself with an air of dignity and confidence. He had a thin moustache and well-groomed hair and was always neatly dressed in a dark business suit. He had a serious but pleasant demeanor that spoke of intelligence and success.

Kristi and her father had a very special relationship. He was extremely firm with her, in much the same way that an owner is with a pet. If she didn't respond promptly or appropriately to my requests during an examination, he would sternly admonish her. He often seemed overly harsh to me, but I never doubted that he loved his daughter and was doing what he felt was necessary to prepare her for the difficult life that lay ahead. And she obviously loved and respected her father, with a devotion that reminded me of a dog to its beloved master. She never appeared to mind his rebukes, but almost seemed to welcome them as a sign that he truly cared about her. He was clearly the most important person in her life, and in those days, he was her family.

Kristi was greatly in need of strong family support. Not only was she limited in her mental capacity, but she was also nearly blind. She was born with congenital cataracts, which had been surgically removed at an early age, leading to the need for her thick cataract glasses. While the surgery had been successful, it left her with scar tissue in both eyes that eventually led to glaucoma and marked damage to her optic nerves. Her vision was now at a level that allowed her to only discern the largest E at the top of the eye chart with either eye. However, she had adapted remarkably well to her limited vision, as young people often do, and she functioned so well in her daily life that a casual observer would never have guessed that she was dealing with such a visual handicap. But I feared for her, because the glaucoma was threatening to rob her of the precious remaining sight on which her future so depended.

The pressures in her eyes were several times higher than was safe to prevent further, complete destruction of her optic nerves, which would mean total and permanent blindness. She was using pills and several drops to control the pressure, but medical therapy simply wasn't sufficient. With some patients, I would have wondered if the medicines were not being used as prescribed, which is a fairly common reason for failure of medical therapy. In Kristi's case, however, I never doubted that she was taking her medications faithfully and appropriately. For her it was a religion. She had compulsively memorized the time for each pill and eye drop down to the minute, and her father confirmed that she would sooner miss a meal than forget one of her medicines.

We were left with no choice but to recommend surgery, and there were two ways that this could be approached. One was the traditional cutting operation, in which a new drainage channel is created inside the eye. In Kristi's situation, however, this approach was fraught with a high risk of complications, including internal bleeding, which I had learned to respect all too well from my experience with little Benjamin. The alternative was the laser procedure that we had used successfully for Craig. We had been studying this procedure and felt comfortable that it offered the best hope for Kristi. It had the advantage of avoiding actually cutting into the eye, and it was performed in the clinic area with a large laser unit that occupied an entire room. A disadvantage, however, was severe pain from the powerful laser, requiring local anesthesia, in which a needle is inserted behind the eye to deliver the numbing medicine. This was obviously very difficult for young people, and often precluded the use of the procedure for them. We weren't sure how Kristi would deal with it, but felt it was worth a try.

Our glaucoma fellow that year was a wonderful young man by the name of Dr. Marino Blasini from San Juan, Puerto Rico, where he subsequently returned to establish a very successful practice and to become a revered teacher at his university. He is a compassionate physician whose concern for his patients is magnified by his rather volatile Latin American emotions. After some discussion, we agreed that it would be best for Marino to give the anesthesia, and then I would do the laser surgery. I knew that he dreaded giving the injection to Kristi, but he marched resolutely into the room where she bravely waited with her father while I went to see a patient in the adjacent room.

I grimaced when I heard the inevitable crying next door, but I cowardly waited until it had abated before returning to her room. Kristi was standing with her face red and swollen and covered in tears. She was hugging Dr. Blasini, who also seemed to be on the verge of tears. Her father sat quietly with a firm, emotionless expression. Marino told me that Kristi had been a real trooper, and that the numbing medicine was quickly doing its job. It didn't take Kristi long to get control of her crying, which soon turned to laughter as we assured her that there would be no more pain. Her infectious smile was back, and the three of us began to laugh while her father continued to sit quietly. Our mirth was short-lived, however, when Sharon came in with a serious, worried look on her usually cheerful face. She walked over to Marino and me and quietly reported that she could not get the laser to turn on. We looked at each other with expressions of shock and disbelief.

Marino and I hurriedly excused ourselves, leaving Kristi and her father with Sharon. I suspect that both of us were praying there would be a simple answer to this apparent dilemma. But there was not. We spent nearly an hour and several phone calls trying to get the laser to work, but all to no avail. It had never happened before—the laser had always been such a reliable workhorse. Of course, we learned an important lesson that day, which we should have already known—never give the anesthesia injection until you know the laser is working. But why, of all days, did we have to learn it today? Marino was beside himself, and I didn't feel much better.

"Oh my God! Oh my God!" he kept repeating. "I just can't believe this is happening. What are we going to tell Kristi and her father?"

We finally went back in to their room to disclose the bad news to both of them. Kristi began to cry again, and her father firmly rebuked her, saying that she had to behave more maturely. But it must have been terribly hard that day for a teenage girl whose mind was even younger and who was afraid not only of more pain but of a possible life of blindness.

Kristi and her father returned on subsequent days for her laser surgery, and with more crying and hugging, Marino was again able to give Kristi her numbing injections. Thankfully, the laser procedures were successful in controlling her pressures, at least for the next several years. Those experiences appeared to bond Kristi and Marino. After he moved on from Duke, she never failed to ask about Dr. Blasini, and my assurance that he was thinking about her never failed to bring her biggest smile.

One day, several years later, when Kristi was in her twenties, she came in for her routine office visit by herself. She had come in a van that was owned by the group home where she was now living. She seemed proud and a little excited to tell me about her new situation, in which she had her own room and friends next door. They were teaching her special things, and she would soon have her own job. She would be earning money and taking care of herself. But I feared that her outward enthusiasm was being tempered by an inner dark cloud of doubt and fear. Her next words explained it.

"Dad travels a lot," she explained. "He's not here much, so it's best for me in my new home." She paused. "It's real nice. Maybe you can come see it sometime." Then there was a longer pause. "My dad misses me. He's gonna send me letters and presents and come see me all the time." There was almost a pleading tone in her voice as she spoke those last words, as if she were trying to convince not me, but herself.

So the months and years passed, and Kristi continued to come in alone for her regular visits. Each began with our traditional greeting—her asking about my family and Dr. Blasini, and me inquiring about her life and especially her dad. She always had something to tell me about him—where he had been, what he had sent her, when she had seen him last. But as time passed, I began to notice that her stories, particularly those of their times together, were sounding repetitive, and I feared that she was leaning on memories to sustain her hope.

One January, she told me that her father had not been able to come home for Christmas, but that he had sent her a present. It was a small, plastic camera, which she had learned to use. She had brought it with her that day and asked if Sharon could take a picture of us together. And so, on a bleak, winter day, Kristi and I stood side by side in the examination room, trying to give Sharon our best smiles.

During those years, another tradition began to evolve. After I would finish my examination and talk with her for a few minutes about what I had found and what it meant, I would sit at my desk and write the findings in her chart. One day she walked over to me while I was writing. She just stood beside me silently and patted me on the back in her gentle, affectionate way. I didn't think too much of it at the time, since I always patted her on her back or hand when I first came in the room, as I did for many of my young (and old) patients. But for us it became a ritual and it expanded. She would often give me a little hug and sometimes wrap her arm around my neck, which tended to make my writing difficult. They were sweet, entirely innocent gestures, but I am afraid that I failed to read the deeper meaning in them.

It eventually became clear that Kristi and her father rarely corresponded anymore. He was not a cruel man, and I am convinced to this day that he was doing what he felt was best for his daughter. As a mother bird must one day push her children from the nest, I suspect that he was gradually weaning them from each other so she could eventually survive on her own. She had friends and good care in the home where she lived and also love and support in the church she attended. But all these things simply weren't the same as having a family.

Something else was also beginning to happen during those years. The pressures in Kristi's eyes were going back up, despite returning to the use of our strongest medicines. It eventually became clear that she would require more surgery. Fortunately, in the intervening years, a new type of laser had become available, which was small and portable and could be used in the operating room with the patient asleep. This meant that Kristi would not have to endure the painful needle sticks behind her eyes that she so dreaded with the old laser, and her tears turned to a relieved laughter when I explained this to her. However, the new approach meant that she would have to go through the procedure of being scheduled for operating room time, which was handled by Robin. And so it was that Kristi and Robin became buddies.

Robin's office was just down the hall from our examination rooms. Beside her desk she had a large bulletin board that was overflowing with photographs of our residents and fellows and especially their children. Being on Robin's bulletin board was something of a badge of honor, and our young physicians continued to send her updated pictures long after they had left Duke. Kristi seemed to be enchanted by the board, particularly when she found the picture of Dr. Blasini and his two sons, who had been born shortly after Marino and his wife returned to Puerto Rico. Robin's warm, friendly personality must have won Kristi's heart, and Robin had a hard time getting her to leave that first day. In fact, she only left reluctantly after Robin promised that she would see her again soon and would get a picture of the Blasini family for her. Another bond was clearly in the making.

When Kristi returned the following week for her surgery, she refused to go to the operating room until she had seen Robin, because she had something to give her. It was a photograph of herself standing alone in her room. I suspect that one of her housemates took it for her. She was standing straight and serious to the left side of the picture, the remainder of which revealed the Spartan contents of her room—a simple bed, a small dresser with a mirror, and an empty wall. Robin, in her typical congenial way, made a big fuss over the gift and then studied her bulletin board carefully for the best place to put it. Finally, she pinned it right beside Dr. Blasini's picture, bringing out a huge smile in Kristi, who then went off happily to her surgery.

In the months that followed, we saw Kristi quite often. The new laser operations were not successful and had to be repeated in both eyes. Eventually, however, her glaucoma again came under control, and I was thankful that she still had her limited but useful vision. Gradually we settled back into her routine of periodic visits. But on no visit did she ever fail to ask about my family and Dr. Blasini and now Robin, whom she always went back to see, ensuring that her picture was still on the board.

As the years passed, and Kristi entered her thirties, I continued to ask about her father, but eventually she seemed to give up trying to pretend. One Christmas she told me that she had heard nothing from her father that year. But she didn't seem particularly sad. Something new had happened in her life—she had heard from her mother. Through all these years, this was the first time she had ever mentioned anything about her mother to me. I had always assumed that her parents were separated, but had never received any indication as to whether her mother was even alive. It seemed ironic that, in the same year that her father had apparently chosen to make his final break from Kristi, her mother should come back into her life.

Her mother had sent her a Christmas present that year. It was a key ring, on which Kristi had already placed her one and only key, which went to her room. Attached to the key ring was a large, plastic picture holder into which her mother had inserted a picture of herself. She was a slender woman whom I judged to be in her early sixties. Her gray hair was long and straight, and she wore no makeup on her tan, weathered face. Around her neck was a single strand of brightly colored beads, which clashed somewhat with the flowery, full-length cotton dress that stopped just above her ankles to reveal brown leather sandals. She was standing beside a man who had long, straight hair as well and a beard that was in need of trimming. His loose cotton shirt was open nearly to the waist, revealing several chains against his hairy chest, and his pants were baggy and wrinkled. He too wore leather sandals that seemed to have come from the same craftsman as those of his partner. The two struck a relaxed, pleasant pose in front of a vintage Volkswagen van.

Kristi seemed to be extremely proud of her newfound family. She explained to me that her mother and her husband were now living in California. She had not been able to write to Kristi all these years because she was doing a lot of moving and her life had been difficult. But things were now straightened out for her, and she promised that she would write regularly and hopefully see her someday. A look of hope came back into Kristi's eyes as she shared all this with me—a look that I had not seen for many years.

Not long after that Christmastime visit, Kristi brought Robin another gift. It was a picture that she had drawn with crayons on a large sheet of newsprint. It featured a number of people with a small girl in the middle.

She pointed out several people in the picture, including Robin and Dr. Blasini. But closest to the small girl, who was obviously Kristi herself, was a man on one side, dressed in a neat suit, and a man and woman on the other side. The couple both had long hair, and the man wore a beard.

Robin made her usual fuss over the picture and then looked around her office with some bewilderment, wondering where she would put it. The newsprint was nearly equal in size to her bulletin board, and her cabinets and other wall hangings left very little additional space. But she found a spot on a wall near the floor, where she taped the picture as Kristi looked on approvingly. Robin didn't leave it there, but kept it rolled up in her desk, ready to tape back each time that Kristi was scheduled for an appointment. One day she had to scurry to put it up at the last minute when Kristi came in unannounced. She had something special to tell us, and I had never seen her so excited.

She had received a letter from her mother, inviting her to come to California for a visit. Her mother did not have enough money to help pay for the trip, but members of Kristi's church had given her enough for a bus ticket. Kristi then became very serious and explained that she might not return, since she believed that her family would probably want her to stay and live with them. She hoped that Robin and I would be okay, and she promised that she would always remember to write.

Kristi did write. We received a postcard from Oklahoma and another from Arizona. In her large, block letters, she assured us that she was all right. The people with the bus company were apparently doing their job well in watching out for her. But the postcard from California was disturbing. Her mother had not been there to meet her at the bus station when she arrived, but she hoped to see her soon. That was the last correspondence we received from Kristi. Several months passed before we received a call from her home that Kristi was back in Durham. And so it was that the two of us were back together again in the examination room on that particular day when our traditional greeting was cut short by a look in her eyes, which seemed to say, "Don't ask about my family."

Her sweet, serene smile and concern for other people were still there. But something had changed. There was now an element of maturity about her that comes from experiencing pain and of knowing emptiness. I never learned whether she found her mother or what transpired between them if they did meet. I only know that it must have been a very painful experience for Kristi—so much so that she chose never to speak of it.

I wasn't sure what to say next, so I simply proceeded with the usual examination and then sat down to record my findings. True to our tradition, Kristi quietly walked over and stood beside me. There was the usual pat on the back, and then her little arm wrapped around my neck. She gave me a big hug that pulled me off balance, and I smiled as my pen scratched across the page of her record. But my mood changed to concern as she touched her cheek to mine, and I realized that her face was wet with tears. And then she kissed me on the cheek, and I felt the emotions welling up in me as I looked toward her and something caught my eye.

Down by her side she was holding the key ring that her mother had given her—the one with the plastic picture holder. But the picture of her mother had been removed, and in its place was the one that Sharon had taken of Kristi and me. A wave of emotion momentarily overcame me, and I reflexively turned away. It wouldn't do for a patient to see her doctor cry. I took a deep breath, regained my composure, and then turned back to face her with the best smile I could muster and gave her a big hug.

Fortunately, Robin came into the room at that moment. She had not been sure if she should tape Kristi's picture up that day, considering the recent events, and decided to solve that problem by visiting her in the examination room. Robin must have sensed that emotions were hanging heavily in the room, and she always had a way of relieving tense situations with her wonderful sense of humor. She asked Kristi what she was holding, and when she showed her the key ring and the picture, Robin made some light comment, questioning Kristi's taste in men. That brought a big laugh from all three of us, and Kristi hugged Robin.

"You guys are just like my family," Kristi said.

"Well, listen now," Robin responded. "You don't have to wait till the next time this guy brings you back. You come see me any time. And I could sure use a new one of your drawings for my office."

This brought the biggest smile of the day, and Kristi promised to comply. As she left the examination room that day, she stopped at the door and turned to look at me with a very thoughtful expression on her face.

"Next Christmas," she said, "will you send me a Christmas card?"

I promised.

———

Her tears puzzled me. Were they from joy or sadness? Sharon had always been genuinely supportive of my career. When we left Oklahoma thirty years earlier, everyone assumed that we would return to our home state, where I would establish a private practice, and we would have a quiet, comfortable life among family and old friends. But when Sharon saw that the academic bug had bitten me and when we received an offer to stay at Duke, she never hesitated in her encouragement to take advantage of the opportunity. She knew all too well what this meant—starting a new life far from home, living on the more modest income of an academic, and the disruption at home from my frequent traveling (she even bought me a new suitcase to celebrate the occasion). And over the years, she never complained about any of it, but seemed to take pride in my accomplishments and was my greatest source of inspiration.

And now I was again asking so much from her. We would be leaving the life that we had spent the last twenty-five years creating in Durham. We would be leaving dear friends, our life at Duke, the support of our church—all that had become so familiar and comfortable to us. But most of all, we would be leaving Sarah and John, who would remain in their respective colleges in North Carolina. I guess we were all having second thoughts when the call came from the dean at Yale. Sharon's tearful response to the call convinced me that it was all wrong, and I told her that I would call him back and say that we were not coming. I don't know that I ever interpreted her tears correctly, but she bravely insisted that I not call back. And so began several bittersweet months of preparations to leave and painful good-byes.

We never fully realize how important people and places are to us until we are about to lose them. During our final months in Durham, we had many quiet, poignant, and sometimes tearful farewell dinners with old friends. And there were parties that were both embarrassing and emotional. Our chairman and good friend, David Epstein, hosted a party in the department for Sharon and me and presented us with a handsome Duke captain's chair. There was the usual ribbing, but also many kind words. Dr. Machemer, our former chairman, and his wife hosted a lovely dinner for us in their home with all of our faculty colleagues, where there were more jokes and gifts of Duke memorabilia. But the most special party of all was in Robin's apartment with all the eye center staff. There were lots of little gifts, many of which were jokes, such as UNC merchandise (lest we forget), and then Robin brought out the surprise of the evening that will forever be my most cherished memory of Duke. It was a large, framed picture consisting of a circle made up of all my glaucoma fellows with their names and dates at Duke on little brass plaques beneath their pictures. Inside the circle was a picture of me, along with one of Robin and my dear friend and partner in the glaucoma service, Dr. Rand Allingham. As we left Robin's apartment that evening, I certainly felt emotionally drained but profoundly grateful.

Finally, all the dinners and parties were over. The movers had come, and our house was empty—the home where Sarah and John had grown from infants to young adults. On our last night, we stayed in Sarah's apartment in Burlington, which is about thirty miles from Durham and where she was attending Elon University. While Sarah and her mother were having some quiet time together, I went back to the eye center for the last and most difficult time. I said personal good-byes to David and Rand and to Sharon, who had been such a faithful nurse for so many years, and to my other friends and colleagues. And then I went back to Robin's office. Neither of us knew quite what to say, but made nervous jokes and looked at her bulletin board for one last time. Finally, we could put it off no longer and quickly said good-bye, promising to keep in touch (which we have), and I hurried down the hall with tears in my eyes, praying that I would not bump into anyone else.

Before driving back to Sarah's apartment, I had one last stop to make. I drove across town to Kristi's home. I had sent letters to all my patients, including Kristi, letting them know that I was leaving and who would take over their care. But I felt that I should say good-bye personally to her and had put it off to the last minute. Driving over, I wondered how she was taking it. We had become like family to her at the eye center, and I had been part of that family for twenty years of her life. Did she feel that yet another member of her family was deserting her? I worried about how another major change in her life might be affecting her, and knew that I had to be gentle, but strong and supportive.

When I arrived, the middle-aged caretaker of the home met me in the driveway; we had spoken earlier about the visit. She escorted me into the house and back to Kristi's room. And there she sat on the edge of her bed. But she didn't seem at all sad. She actually appeared to be quite excited. She wanted to show me everything in her room—her bed, her dresser and chair, and the pictures on the walls, all of which she had drawn herself. One picture in particular caught my eye. It showed a little girl in the middle, with two doctors on one side and a nurse on the other, with a second woman who seemed to be standing beside a bulletin board. I stood in front of the picture, feeling my emotions welling up. And then Kristi, in her tender, perceptive way, took my hand and stood quietly beside me.

We looked at the picture together for a few moments, before she softly spoke.

"Don't worry, old buddy. I'll take care of Robin and Sharon. And I'll write to you, so you won't feel lonely."

I looked down at her serious, angelic face, and we both broke out into huge smiles and then began to laugh. I was the one who was going to be strong and supportive for her, and yet it was Kristi, with her childlike faith and confidence in the good things in this world, who assured me that everything would be okay. And I knew she was right.

Ω

15.

Raymond

Yale University and Duke University share a number of striking similarities and equally striking differences. They are both private universities that were originally affiliated with religious denominations (Yale with the Congregational Church and Duke with the Methodists). Each began under a different name (Collegiate School and Trinity College, respectively) and acquired their present names from generous benefactors (Eli Yale and James B. Duke). Today, they are approximately the same size, with just over ten thousand students, of which half are undergraduates and half are in graduate programs. Although one is in the North and the other in the South, both have diverse and eclectic faculties and student bodies, and each ranks among the top universities in the world for academic excellence. They even share the same school color—"true blue." The young president of the nascent Trinity College was a Yale graduate, who also introduced football to the school and was its first coach. When Trinity played the University of North Carolina for the first time in 1888, the student body chose to honor their popular president and coach by adopting the color of his alma mater. In a sense, then, Duke blue is actually Yale blue.

The biggest difference between the two universities is their longevity. Yale University was founded as Collegiate School in 1701, a full three-quarters of a century before our nation declared its independence and more than two centuries before Trinity College became Duke University in 1920s. When Yale was opening its doors to the early classes in Connecticut, the Piedmont region of North Carolina, where Durham and Duke would one day stand, was still virgin forest with only scattered farms. As a result, Yale has a decided edge on Duke when it comes to history. It is uncommon to read any aspect of American history without encountering a Yale alumnus. One of innumerable examples is Eli Whitney, who lived in Hamden, just north of New Haven, where we also found our home. Many people equate Whitney with the South because of his quintessential America invention. The fact is, however, that he graduated from Yale in the late eighteenth Century and shortly thereafter went to Georgia for a summer to tutor the children of Nathaniel Greene, a former general in Washington's Continental Army. As it turned out, he actually spent that summer inventing the cotton gin (albeit with vital assistance from Greene's wife, Kitty) and then returned to the North for the remainder of his illustrious career.

Two pages of history at Yale that were especially meaningful to me were Mory's and Jonathan Edwards. As a young boy growing up in Oklahoma, before the days of television, our family had a record player and about a half dozen old single records. One of those was a recording by Bing Crosby singing "The Whiffenpoof Song." It told of a place called Mory's, the Temple Bar, a man named Louie, and something called the Whiffenpoofs. I had no idea what any of it meant (I assumed the Temple Bar had something to do with a religious group) and was totally unaware that it all took place at Yale University. At that time, I had only a vague understanding that Yale was a school and no clue as to where it was. Nevertheless, the song became one of my childhood favorites, and I believe that I knew all the words by the time I was eight years old. About two decades later, during our navy years in Connecticut, Sharon and I visited the Yale campus one weekend and stumbled across a small, two-story, white-frame house, the only indication as to its identity being a brass plaque on the door with a single word—Mory's. By this time in my life, I had learned a little of the history—that a family named Moriarity once ran a drinking establishment on Temple Street that was very popular with the men of Yale (not exactly a religious group), and that it was later moved to York Street and renamed Mory's by its new proprietor, Louie. As I peeked through one of the windows (it was closed that day and off limits to the public, anyway) at the old oak tables and the walls covered with centuries of Yale history, I felt fortunate just to have come this close to a "shrine" of my boyhood memories. Little could I have guessed then that three decades later, I would become a member of Mory's and enjoy many Monday evenings listening to the Whiffenpoofs—Yale's premier men's a cappella group—serenade the diners "with their glasses raised on high."

Jonathan Edwards would have undoubtedly disapproved of the merry making at Mory's. An early graduate of Yale, in the class of 1720, back when the school was still primarily dedicated to training ministers, Edwards became acknowledged by many as the preeminent theologian of the eighteenth century, at least on this side of the Atlantic. He served as pastor in Northampton, Massachusetts, for twenty-one years, although his greatest fame derived from his prolific writings, which are studied by scholars and theologians to this day. Tragically, his life and illustrious career were cut short when he died of a smallpox inoculation in 1758, the same year that he was installed as president of the College of New Jersey (now Princeton University). Many decades later, back in Connecticut, his alma mater honored him by naming a residential college after its distinguished alumnus. During our years at Yale, there were twelve residential colleges, where undergraduate and some graduate students lived, dined, and socialized. Members of the Yale faculty can, upon invitation, become a fellow of one of these colleges. A dear friend since our days together at Harvard, Dr. Martin Wand, had been an undergraduate student in Jonathan Edwards College and facilitated my invitation into the fellowship of JE. The fellows (men and women) gather every Thursday evening in a venerable, wood-paneled room of the college to enjoy libation, dinner, and stimulating conversation. It is a remarkable group of people, representing scholars from all walks of academia, most of whom are internationally recognized in their particular field of higher learning. The friendships were warm, the conversations were enriching, and those Thursday evenings at JE are among my fondest memories of our years at Yale.

If longevity is the biggest difference between the two universities on Yale's side of the ledger, it is probably fair to say that the biggest difference on the Duke side can also be summed up in one word—basketball. In fact, that proved to be a bit of an embarrassment for me shortly after we arrived at Yale. As I was working out my contract with the dean of Yale School of Medicine, my colleagues at Duke suggested that I ask for season tickets to the football and basketball games. That seemed to make sense, especially with basketball, for which it was almost impossible to get Duke tickets at any price. What I failed to realize at the time, however, was that the difference between Yale and Duke basketball is about as great as that between the longevity of the two schools. In any case, the dean seemed more than happy to grant my request and not only gave us two sets of season tickets for the football and basketball games, but also passes for any other sports event at Yale that we cared to attend. And so, shortly after our arrival, Sharon and I proudly took our special tickets to a Yale basketball game—and that was when reality set in. Much to our surprise, there seemed to be more people on the court than in the stands. It wasn't long before I learned, to my dismay, that I was the butt of a joke going around the medical school—the guy who actually asked for season tickets to Yale basketball games. But we enjoyed the sports at Yale, especially the football games in the fall—as long as the weather was good.

My daily commute from our home in Hamden to my office on the Yale campus was a bit longer than my old drive through Duke Forest, but it was every bit as scenic and far more historic, thanks in large measure to Eli Whitney. I could have taken the interstate and cut off a few minutes, but I much preferred the more peaceful back roads down Whitney Avenue, past the site of the inventor's factory, where a white frame house still stands that once provided lodging for single male workers. Near the house is a red barn with gray colonial trim, which was once the transportation center for the factory. On the other side of Whitney Avenue, Lake Whitney runs picturesquely beside the road for about a mile before roaring over a spillway and into a stream that flows under a covered bridge and past a stone building, which once held coal to power the factory. The combination of it all—the lake and the spillway, the covered bridge and the historic buildings—provided a picturesque drive that changed in appearance and mood with each season.

The banks of the lake are lined by tall, stately evergreens, intermingled with a variety of deciduous trees. In the spring, while the latter trees were just beginning to show their buds, the far bank from the road would burst forth with the pink blossoms of mountain laurel, Connecticut's state flower. On calm mornings, the profusion of color would reflect in the placid water, providing a double dose of springtime beauty. Throughout the summer, the shoreline was shaded by the evergreens and the deciduous trees, whose dark green leaves eventually turned to the rich reds, oranges, and yellows of fall. As the cool temperatures of early autumn met the warmer lake water, steam would rise from the surface, some days reaching high into the crisp morning air, creating lovely and often dramatic scenes, especially where the water went over the spillway and under the covered bridge. And then the New England winter would invariably set in. Many people consider this to be the least desirable of the seasons, but for Sharon and me it was a time of magical beauty. The lake freezes, and the gently falling snowflakes fill the air, caressing the boughs of the evergreens and outlining every intricate bare branch of the deciduous trees. Warm lights glow through the windows of snow-covered homes beside the road as people hunker down for the long winter nights in much the same way as they must have done in the days of Eli Whitney.

Immediately south of the Whitney factory site, the land suddenly rises dramatically in steep, rocky slopes that were carved out by glaciers during the last Ice Age. Today it is called East Rock, with its counterpart to the west representing the extent of the glaciers' effect. In some areas, the slopes of East Rock are densely wooded, and a road winds up to a plateau, from which Long Island Sound and the distant shore of Long Island can be seen on a clear day. During one of my first morning drives to work, the sun was just coming up over the escarpments, turning the clouds a brilliant orange. And at the very moment that I was passing the south end of Lake Whitney, the clouds parted, allowing a shaft of light to pierce the morning sky and illuminate a small portion of the lake below—exactly where two swans were swimming! I almost had a wreck. I never saw anything like that again, but I accepted it as a welcome to our new home and was often reminded of it as I passed the spot on my way to work over the many years that followed.

And so we began our transition from Duke to Yale. All seemed to be going well at first, and I enjoyed the beautiful drive to work each day and was captivated by the history and traditions of Yale. And I was looking forward to getting started with my new responsibilities and to meeting the new patients who I would be privileged to care for at Yale. Memories of the tearful good-bye with Kristi and so many other patients at Duke were still very fresh in my mind. I missed them, but could not suppress an anticipation of what interesting and challenging new patients I would soon be encountering. As it turned out, the first encounter came much sooner than I expected, and from a source that I could never have imagined.

———

My new office at Yale was like nothing I had ever had at Duke. For one thing, I had never had an office with a window, and now I had two enormous windows that arched gracefully at the top and looked out across Cedar Street to the stately Sterling Hall of Medicine, which was the epicenter of the medical school campus. It was also a very large office. At Duke, I barely had room for a desk and a chair. Now I had room at one end of the office for a large desk and an entire wall of bookshelves. At the other end there was a couch, two chairs, and a coffee table, where I could meet with small groups.

The movers had arrived late Friday afternoon and filled my big, empty office with boxes of books and other items. And so I decided to come in early the next morning while no one was around to start unpacking. I had just arrived and was standing in the silence among stacks of boxes, wondering where to begin, when I was suddenly startled by the shrill ring of the telephone. I didn't even realize that a phone had been installed until the ring brought my attention to it on the desk behind more boxes. I couldn't imagine who would be calling me. Sharon was the only one who knew I was there, and she didn't have the office number yet. My first thought was a wrong number, and I considered not answering it. But as I picked up the receiver, I could never have guessed in a hundred years what I would encounter on the other end of the line.

"Dr. Shields?" It was the voice of a man, and it sounded distant and shaky.

"Yes," I responded tentatively.

"This is Raymond. Raymond Langford."

'Raymond Langford?' The name was vaguely familiar, but I couldn't for the life of me put a face with it nor remember when or where I had known him. Up to that point, I had only met a few people in Connecticut and felt sure that he was not one of them. This was a name from somewhere much further in the past. I was at a loss for what to say as several awkward seconds of silence ticked by.

"Do you remember me?" There was almost a pleading quality in his voice.

"Uh, y-yes," I lied, hoping for a clue or an epiphany at any moment. But none came, and he seemed to realize that I was struggling.

"I was your patient at Duke. You operated on me a long time ago."

'Raymond?' Slowly, it started to come to me—like a blurred picture on a screen that is slowly coming into focus. At first, the developing image had more to do with an emotional feeling from somewhere in the past than with any specific details. And there was something unpleasant about the feelings that were trying to draw a picture from my memory: a feeling of frustration—of having failed someone. Gradually, the vague image of a middle-aged man began to materialize—a rather nondescript person with gray, thinning hair and a slight frame with stooped shoulders, but a kind face and gentle eyes. At least he had been middle-aged when we first met over twenty years ago. The image was now starting to become clearer in my mind. He had usually come with his wife and daughter, their only child. I seemed to remember that the two women were always criticizing him for one thing or another. But he never appeared to mind. He would just smile, as though to say, "Isn't it nice to have people who care about you?" Most of their criticisms seemed rather trivial to me, except for one with which I had to agree—and then I began to remember the source of my frustration.

Raymond had a chronic form of glaucoma, for which I had recommended the standard treatment of medicated eye drops. The purpose of glaucoma medication is to lower the pressure in the eye, which will otherwise progressively destroy the optic nerve that connects the eye to the brain. This progressive nerve damage eventually leads to visual impairment that begins in the mid-periphery of a person's vision, but slowly spreads outward to the far periphery and inward to the center of vision, eventually resulting in total and permanent blindness if the pressure is not properly controlled. Because the progressive loss of vision is gradual and often imperceptible to the patient, a visual field test is performed periodically, in which the patient is asked to identify lights illuminating the periphery of a bowl-shaped instrument. The sad truth about glaucoma is that any loss of visual field is irreversible, and the most that doctors can hope to do for their glaucoma patients is to preserve the remaining vision by keeping their eye pressures under control. Of course, the medicines don't work if the patient doesn't use them as recommended, and poor compliance with prescribed treatment, as I had experienced years before with Sir Rex, is a major reason why many glaucoma patients lose their sight.

As my memory of Raymond continued to crystallize, I could almost see his visual fields. With every visit, they were getting progressively worse, despite the fact that his pressures were usually at a good level when we measured them in the office. I became suspicious that he was not using his drops faithfully between appointments, and this was confirmed by his wife and daughter, who would fuss at him about it on every visit. But he would just smile and say, "God will provide." Raymond was obviously a man of considerable faith, which I respected, although I felt constrained to suggest that maybe it was God who provided the medicines and that he expected us to use them. He would only laugh good-naturedly and reply, "Yes, I'm sure you're right. I'll try harder." But he never did—at least not for any sustained period of time. His wife and daughter would report that he was good for a few weeks after each appointment, but would then slip back into his old ways as other things in his life seemed to take priority. And I would watch with increasing frustration as his loss of vision continued to progress with every visit. I tried everything I could think of—cajoling, pleading, even berating. And through it all, he would sit quietly, looking me straight in the eyes and nodding in agreement to everything I said with his sincere, gentle smile. But nothing changed. We talked about what might be keeping him from using his drops, and he would just shake his head and smile, as though he honestly had no answer. We wrote out schedules and talked about linking the use of his medicines with meals or other daily activities. Still nothing. Of course, a logical solution would have been for his wife or daughter to put the drops in for him. But when I suggested this, they retorted with an assortment of reasons why that wasn't possible. It was as though, despite being constantly fussed at by his family, Raymond was otherwise on his own. This puzzled me and added to my frustration.

When laser therapy for his type of glaucoma became available in the early 1980s, I performed that on Raymond. For a while it successfully lowered his eye pressure and stabilized his visual fields. After a few years, however, the benefit of the laser procedure wore off, and repeated treatments were not effective. So his progressive loss of vision began again, despite my repeated admonitions to use his drops. He was now approaching blindness in one eye, and I thought surely that would motivate him to be more faithful in complying with my recommended treatment. But nothing changed. It became a ritual that I would read him the riot act during every visit, and he would just nod his head in agreement and smile. He no longer said that God would provide, but we both knew what he was thinking. And through it all, he was such a good-natured, gentle, well-meaning person that it was almost impossible to get mad at him. And I guess that was what frustrated me the most—I wanted so much to help him, but was failing.

It finally became clear that medical therapy was not going to save Raymond's sight, so I reluctantly recommended the basic glaucoma operation, despite the potential risks involved. We were fortunate that the surgery went well, and for nearly a decade, his pressures were well controlled in both eyes without medication, and his fields of vision remained stable. But then, as happens all too often, the small channels that I had surgically created inside his eyes to allow release of the excess fluid began to scar closed. The pressures in his eyes started going up again, with resumption of the progressive loss of his fields of vision. I suggested that we repeat the surgery, which is not an uncommon practice, but he was hesitant.

A lot had changed in Raymond's life since I first began caring for him. I had watched him go from middle-aged to an elderly gentleman who even looked and acted older than his true age. His wife continued to come with him, since he was now unable to drive, but I no longer saw their daughter. They didn't seem inclined to talk about her, except to say that she had gone somewhere "out West." Raymond had long since retired, and he and his wife had moved into an assisted-living facility. I recommended that we resume his eye drops, and he said he would—but he didn't, which was one thing that had not changed. When I again brought up the question of repeat surgery, he nodded agreeably and said he would think about it, but it never got beyond that. And then one day he missed his appointment. We tried to reach him, but the people at the facility where the Langfords had been living could only report that they had moved and left no forwarding address. And so, for my last years at Duke I no longer saw Raymond, and he gradually began to fade from my memory—until that Saturday morning in my new office.

All of those memories about Raymond and his family, which spanned nearly two decades, had washed back over me in a matter of seconds. The image was now clear, and I felt more comfortable in resuming the conversation.

"Well, Raymond, it's good to hear from you. It's been quite a while."

"Yes sir, it has been a long time. And it's good to hear your voice too."

Then there was another long pause as I began to wonder about the purpose of his call. I probably should have kept quiet and let him speak, but the uncomfortable silence finally prompted me to continue.

"So, how's the family?"

After more silence, he began, hesitantly.

"Well, the missus died last year."

"Oh, Raymond, I am so sorry."

"Yes, sir," the words seemed to be coming hard for him. "She was a good wife, 'ceptin' I never could seem to make her happy. She didn't like that retirement place we moved to. So we moved to a different place in a new town where we didn't know nobody. And we hadn't been there long, afore she got sick and died. We only had one room in that place, and I didn't have nothin' to do all day. So I finally got rid of most of our stuff and bought me a bus ticket."

"A bus?" I wanted to make sure I was hearing him correctly.

"Yes, sir." Another long pause followed as I waited for a logical explanation—but none came.

"So, where did you go?"

"Well, nowhere exactly. I just been livin' on the bus."

Now I was becoming truly incredulous and at a loss for words.

"At first I went out West," he finally continued, his voice increasingly plaintive, "to try to find our daughter. But I didn't know where she was and never did find her. So I just kept a-goin'."

"Well, Raymond, don't you have family somewhere?" I asked.

"No, sir. It was just me and the missus—and our daughter somewheres. We didn't even have any friends, really."

"So, Raymond, are you all alone?" I asked reluctantly.

"Oh, no, sir, I ain't never alone."

I didn't quite know how to process that response. Had he met someone on the bus? Knowing Raymond, that seemed highly unlikely. Then I remembered his words from years past—"God will provide"—and I suspected that I understood the meaning of his statement, which he proceeded to confirm.

There was that good-natured laugh of his, which I also remembered, as he said, "I reckon you know what I mean. I've always known that the Lord is with me wherever I am, and he will provide."

I could only smile. But he still had not told me why he was calling.

"Raymond, is there anything I can do for you?" I asked.

"Well, yes, sir, that's why I'm callin'. I tried reachin' you at the Duke Hospital, but they said you had moved up north to Yale. They didn't have no number for you, but I called Yale Hospital and got this number." Again, there was a pause as one part of the puzzle began fitting together. "Problem is, Dr. Shields, that I can't see too good no more. You remember I'm blind in my left eye, but I could still see to read through a little hole in front of my right eye. 'Cept that went away, and now I can only see to the side, and I can't see to read no more, and it's pretty hard to find my way around."

What Raymond was describing is typical of the progressive loss of vision from glaucoma. As the mid-peripheral loss of visual field closes in centrally, the patient is left with only a small central island of vision, with which they may still be able to read. But then that central island will disappear—often rather suddenly—leaving the patient with only a peripheral island of vision on their temporal (outer) side. The side vision may be good enough for a person to find his or her way around, but not sufficient for reading. Gradually, as the glaucoma inexorably progresses, even the side vision gets smaller and eventually disappears, and then the patient is truly blind in that eye—which, for Raymond, meant total blindness.

"Raymond, where are you now?" I inquired, becoming increasingly alarmed.

"I think I'm up in New Hampshire somewhere. I was trying to get to New Haven, but I must have got on the wrong bus."

"Well, at least you're not too far away. Do you think you could get down here?" I asked.

"Yes, sir, that's what I want to do."

"And you let me know just as soon as you arrive, do you hear?"

"Oh, yes, sir, that's exactly what I'm gonna do," he replied emphatically.

Based on his poor track record of compliance with anything I had ever suggested in the past, I had an uneasy feeling that the frustrations were about to begin again. And then, as though he was sensing my concern, he spoke in a slow, firm voice.

"And, Dr. Shields, don't you worry about me. I'll be okay. Just remember, I ain't never alone."

And with that, the line went dead.

———

I sat at my new desk for a long time that morning as a myriad of questions flooded my mind. How does a person "live" on a bus? I supposed that he had all his earthly belongings in a suitcase. But where did he clean up and change clothes? I had images of Raymond bending over a sink in the men's room of a bus stop, of sleeping on the bus or on a bench at one of the stops, and of finding what he could to eat along the way. The whole thing was crazy. It would be challenging enough for a young person with all their senses, but for an elderly man—I calculated that he must have been approaching his eighties—with limited sight, it just seemed beyond imagination. I tried to think what it must be like to be old and all alone and watching the world become darker with each passing day. It must have been frightening to wander around in the shadows of unfamiliar places, having to depend upon strangers for directions and never knowing if those strangers would help him or possibly rob him of his few remaining possessions—or even his life. I held out no hope that he was using his glaucoma medicines. But the biggest question that I kept asking myself that morning was what I should or could do to help him. For twenty years,

I had tried to help him—and had failed. And now it was as though I was being given one last chance to make up for the past.

I waited in hopeful anticipation that he would call again. For days, each time the phone would ring, my first thought was that it might be him. But days passed, and then weeks, with no word. This was before the days that cell phones were in common use, and I assumed that Raymond had called from a pay phone, so I had no way to track his call. There were any number of bus lines in New England, but none were able or willing to confirm the name of a rider. I tried going to local bus stations a few times, just to see if he might be wandering around in the waiting areas. Of course, I wasn't sure if I would still recognize him, but no one even came close to fitting his description. I learned of several shelters and other charity programs in the New Haven area, but none of them had any record of a person by his name. They promised to contact me if they received any word of him, but I never heard back from any of them.

I never heard from Raymond again and was left to only guess what might have happened to him, a blind man wandering around so far from home. Had he tried to find his way to New Haven? Had he actually made it, and had we been within in a few miles of each other? Or had he taken another wrong bus and wound up somewhere even farther away? Had he been accosted by someone along the way in a bus station or on a bus? If the police had found his body, they most likely would not have known whom to contact. My hope and prayer, of course, was that some kind person had befriended him and helped him find appropriate care. If he was alive, though, why did he never call again? Was it because he was now totally blind and figured there was nothing else I could do for him?

I never learned the answers to any of these questions, and as time passed and the demands of my new job continued to mount, thoughts of Raymond once again gradually slipped back into the shadowy recesses of my mind. But there were times when vivid memories of him would suddenly reappear, and with them the old feeling of frustration and guilt. Raymond was certainly not the only glaucoma patient to have difficulty complying with recommended medical therapy. I had my share of such patients at Yale, and on more than one occasion, as I looked into their eyes and tried to encourage them to use their drops, I had the feeling that I was staring into the kind, gentle—if not frustrating—eyes of Raymond. And I couldn't help but smile inwardly. Although he had frustrated me and even made me a bit angry at times, I found myself over the years thinking less about his unwillingness to take good care of his health—as misguided as that was—and more about the gentle and trusting way he lived his life. I never saw him show anger, even when those closest to him seemed harsh and uncaring. It was as though he had a way of seeing the good within each person, even when it did not always seem obvious on the outside. And I will always remember his last words to me—that he was never alone—and I rather suspect that it was this faith that allowed him to find peace and hope, even when he seemed to be all alone in a world that was turning dark.

It has now been many years since that Saturday morning telephone call and my final, brief, inexplicable encounter with Raymond. Even if he survived the harrowing experience then, the passage of time has undoubtedly taken him to where the light is hopefully shining once again. And, whatever happened to Raymond, I am quite confident that he passed from this life with a smile on his face and with the firm conviction that he truly would never be alone.

Ω

16.

Martha

We had only been at Yale for a few months when she came into my life. And the timing was quite fortuitous, as I was already starting to feel the stress of my new responsibilities. Yale University is widely regarded as one of the top institutions of higher education in America, if not the world. During our final year at Duke, Yale was number one in the national rankings. But no sooner had we moved to Yale than it promptly fell to number two (interestingly, a position it shared that year with Duke), causing me to ponder any cause-and-effect relationship. Of course, my presence at either university had absolutely nothing to do with its success or failure (at least not its success), but I couldn't help wondering whether this coincidence was an omen of things to come.

The ophthalmology department at Yale once enjoyed a strong national reputation, although it had begun to struggle in the years before our arrival. Traditionally, Yale School of Medicine had focused more on research than clinical care, and this was a sustainable fiscal model when funding for research and reimbursement for clinical care were plentiful. But times were changing on the national health care front—competition for research dollars was increasing, and reimbursement for clinical care was declining. To remain solvent, medical schools across the country were being forced to make major adjustments, largely by expanding their clinical programs to compete with the private sector.

When we arrived at Yale, the research section of the ophthalmology department was still strong, with several world-class scientists (in fact, the official name was—and still is—the Department of Ophthalmology and Visual Science), but the clinical section had not kept pace with the times. As a result, the department was losing money—lots of money. And being deeply in the red made it difficult to recruit and retain top faculty and to expand facilities and programs, all of which are necessary to create a strong department and a balanced budget. This is probably why people more qualified and wiser than I had already turned down the position. But I was naively confident that it was a solvable problem—a little reduction in overhead here and little increase in revenues there, and we would soon be in the black. I had not been in my new position long, however, before I began to realize that it was not going to be so simple. And I soon found myself lying awake at night wondering how in the world we were going to turn the situation around. I was becoming increasingly depressed about the prospects for our department and, in truth, starting to feel a bit sorry for myself. And it was in this frame of mind that I had the good fortune to meet Martha.

———

She is one of the most remarkable people I have ever had the privilege of knowing. There seemed to be an inner strength about her that spoke of confidence and the ability to cope with whatever life threw her way. She was never arrogant or boastful about it, but simply carried off her persona with disarming modesty and a casual demeanor, as though it was really no big deal. In short, she was indomitable. I loved her sense of humor, which she seemed to turn up as a defense mechanism whenever life became too challenging. As to her physical appearance, she was really quite striking. Her big blue eyes sparkled when she laughed and accented her perfectly coiffed honey-blond hair. She was always impeccably dressed and carried herself in a dignified, almost regal manner. And there was one more thing about Martha—she stood all of three feet and one inch tall.

Just twenty-four days after the first cell in a mother's womb divides to start the creation of a new life, buds begin to protrude that will become the limbs of the little person—first the arms and then the legs. Before long, bones begin to develop in the arms and legs and the hands and feet. Between the long bones of the arms and legs are cartilage segments, called epiphyseal plates, which are critical for the normal growth of the bones.

For most of us, the development and growth of our bones, as well as of the other parts of our body, follow a predictable pattern in accordance with the genetic blueprint in that very first cell. But occasionally something goes wrong in the blueprint, which can lead to developmental abnormalities. If the defective gene happens to regulate the epiphyseal plates, the long bones may fail to grow properly, leading to a group of disorders called skeletal dysplasia. In addition to short stature, these individuals may have other developmental abnormalities, such as a small chest with restrictive lung disorders, cleft palate, and myopia (nearsightedness) with retinal detachment. And it was with such a defective genetic blueprint that Martha entered the world.

On the day she was born, Martha was given last rites—twice. She was very small, very frail, and very ill. In addition to her short stature and a cleft palate, she had a small chest, which restricted her breathing, and she seemed to struggle for every breath. The doctors were perplexed by her condition and its origin. There was no family history of similar problems, although they knew that her young mother had grown up in an area of New Jersey with bad air pollution. They also knew that she had been x-rayed for cramping, which led to the discovery that she was pregnant. What influence these factors may have had on Martha's apparent genetic abnormalities was never known. They finally gave her a diagnosis of spondyloepimetaphyseal dysplasia—a very big name for such a very small child. The doctors did not give Martha's family much hope that she would survive through infancy, and indeed, only one week into her life, she was again given last rites. But there was one fact that no one could have foreseen at the time—within this small, fragile frame resided a remarkable fortitude and will to live.

Two years before Martha's birth, war was raging in Korea, and an attractive young co-ed was beginning her junior year at Duke University (long before our arrival). For her, the war was not the statistics that appeared every night on the evening news, nor the protests that were occurring on some college campuses. The war for her was much more personal. She and Tom had met shortly after he transferred to Duke from the Military Academy at West Point. They had a lot in common. Both felt a certain sense of entitlement and yearned for all the happiness and pleasures that life had to offer. And they soon decided that they wanted to spend their life enjoying those pleasures together. Tom had graduated the previous spring, and they were married one week later. But it was a short honeymoon, because he had to report to active duty in the army, leaving his young bride to complete her studies at Duke. That fall, in a tear-filled reunion, he told her that he would soon be deploying to Korea. The reunion would be their last. Just before Christmas break, the letter arrived, and her life came crashing down around her. She told her parents that she did not have the will to return to Duke, but they insisted.

The best man at their wedding had been Tom's closest friend at West Point. He began making frequent trips to Durham that spring, first to console his friend's widow and then to court her. In her tragic and lonely state of mind, she was vulnerable to his advances and promises of possible happiness. Just before she graduated, they were married in a brief ceremony. But things began going poorly at home almost from the start. His drinking and difficulty holding a steady job led to frequent fights, and she was becoming increasingly ill, especially with stomach cramps. The doctor's could not pinpoint the cause of her problem and finally ordered an X-ray, which revealed, to everyone's surprise, that she was pregnant. And so it was, with the country still at war, her true love dead, and her marriage in peril, that Martha's mother began the ordeal of bringing her daughter into the world.

She had hoped that a baby in the family would make her husband more responsible and bring the two of them closer together, but it seemed to have just the opposite effect. When the young couple learned that they had a seriously ill child, Martha's father seemed to take it as a personal failure and became even more withdrawn from his family. Years later, Martha would say that she never really knew her father, remembering meeting him on only three brief occasions. One thing her parents agreed on when she was still an infant was that they were not capable, physically or emotionally, of caring for a child with so many serious problems. As it turned out, the matter took care of itself for the first two years of her life, since Martha was in the hospital far more than she was home. But then, at the tender age of two, when she was finally able to come home for good, her parents placed her in a home for "crippled children."

It was the worst thing that could have happened to the small, sick, struggling child. As she later told it, most of the children in the home were "grossly retarded." Her family and doctors apparently assumed that Martha's many developmental abnormalities also included her mental capacity. But that was not the case. People with Martha's condition typically have normal intelligence and many can anticipate a full lifespan. She eventually made friends with two children at the home who also seemed to possess average intelligence. Billy had suffered from encephalitis early in life, and his head was grossly enlarged and misshapen. Andrew was partially blind. His mother had been a prostitute, living on the street with her son. The state took him from her and placed him in the home. For the next five years of her life, Billy and Andrew were the only exposure to relative normalcy that Martha would know on a daily basis. Aside from that, growing up among seriously abnormal children, witnessing death on a regular basis, and seeing how unkindly people were treated in the home created a state of constant emotional trauma for the already ill child. It may have actually been her chronic sickness, however, that got her through those trying years, since she was too weak to be fully aware of her surroundings. In her fifth year of life, she was again given last rites. But that indomitable spirit within the frail frame prevailed once more. And then one morning in her seventh year, Martha woke up and suddenly realized that she felt better than she could ever remember. She describes this as a "significant turning point" in her life.

Although she continued to live in the home until she was ten and a half years old, Martha now realized that she was capable of learning, and a world of knowledge and beauty began to open up before her in the books that she devoured. During all this time, her mother had continued to visit her on a regular basis and was beginning to understand what Martha was capable of achieving. She wanted desperately to give her daughter every opportunity, but she was now divorced, raising four boys, and dating the man who she would eventually marry. With all of this in her life, she still felt that she was incapable of caring for Martha at home. So she tried putting her in a foster home, which lasted for one year, and then placed her in a Catholic school for girls, where she stayed for two years. Martha describes the latter experience as being almost as difficult as that in the home for crippled children, because of the "bad language" and "other things" that went on there. In the meantime, her mother remarried, and her new husband was a kind, understanding man, whom Martha would come to like very much. And so, when she was almost fourteen years old, Martha finally came home to live with her family.

But life continued to be rocky for Martha. The local school system wanted to put her in a class for "retarded children" and later in a class for children with "learning disabilities." Her mother refused both and began homeschooling, even though it got Martha in trouble for truancy. Over the years, Martha developed close bonds with her brothers and stepfather and came to feel especially close to her mother, whom she admired greatly and for whom she has profound gratitude for helping her achieve her potential. She was finally able to graduate from high school with respectable credentials and then matriculated to a college in Rhode Island, where she earned her bachelor degree in social work. With that, Martha moved to New Haven to become a social worker and counselor and to start her own life. And it was there that our lives would eventually become entwined.

———

How does a person respond to a life that has thrown them so many curve balls? In addition to her short stature, which made tasks that are simple for most people monumental for her, Martha had already undergone surgery for her cleft palate, had restrictive lung disease and asthma, and wore heavy, thick glasses for her myopia. Could she be faulted if she was bitter, despairing, and withdrawn? But that was not Martha's way. She was determined to make the most of her life. She rented an apartment—a very small one—and furnished much of it with children's furniture, which was more comfortable for her. She shared her apartment with a menagerie of cats and kittens—the "loves of her life." She also bought a car that was specially equipped, since she couldn't reach regular floor pedals. She was totally independent, and there seemed to be nothing that she could not handle. But what was most impressive was that she did it all with good humor and a true verve for life. She would later tell me the secret of her happiness.

At some point along her road of life, she had developed a personal philosophy for living. She said that a person can dwell on the parts of their life that they don't like and be miserable, or they can take an inventory of their blessings and find happiness in focusing on them each day. Although her physical status could have led her down the road of misery, she chose to pick the parts of her body that she loved and was proud of and to build her happiness around them. She loved her honey-blond hair and her lips and her smile. But the part of her body that Martha loved the most was her eyes.

She loved her eyes not so much because of the good vision they provided—although that was critical to her success and happiness—but because she felt that they were the prettiest part of her body. And indeed they were pretty. They were deep blue and accentuated by long eyelashes, and they sparkled with her animated talk and laughter. But most of all, they seemed to say that here, within this small, fragile frame, was a giant of a person who loved life despite the unkind turns it had given her and who lived it to the fullest. And yet, tragically, it was this one part of her body—the part she loved the most—that she was about to lose.

She was at work when it began. For several months, she had been noticing what seemed like bugs flying around her, but when she turned to see them, they would disappear. She didn't think too much about it until one day at work, when she looked up at a calendar to affix the date to a letter she was writing and suddenly noticed an unusually large number of the dark spots. She would later learn that the spots are referred to as floaters. Along with the floaters, she began seeing flashing lights. She realized that the problem was coming from her right eye, and now she was concerned—indeed, she was scared. She left work early and drove home, hoping that the symptoms would go away with a little rest. But they got worse—more flashing lights and more dark spots. And then, as though someone was pulling a curtain closed in front of her right eye, everything began to go white. Now she panicked. With the aid of her good left eye, she called the emergency room at Yale–New Haven Hospital. After telling the person on the other end of the line what was happening to her, she was put on hold for what seemed to her like forever. But eventually she heard a young voice coming over her phone and introducing herself as the Yale ophthalmology resident on call for the evening. Martha explained her situation with as much calmness as she could muster, and was then told by the resident that she needed to be seen immediately. And so, driving through late afternoon shadows with both hands on the steering wheel and struggling to see her way with only one good eye, she managed (with considerable effort and much prayer) to make her way to the hospital. And thus began Martha's long odyssey with Yale Eye Center.

The resident was waiting for Martha when she finally arrived at the ER. She took her back to an examination room, where the resident examined Martha's eyes and informed her that she had a retinal detachment of her right eye. Martha did not know what a retinal detachment was or how serious it could be, but she would soon learn.

The retina—analogous to the film of a pre-digital camera—is a very delicate tissue in the back of the eye that is essential for vision. Just in front of the retina, the eye is filled with a clear gel, called vitreous. In some eyes, this vitreous gel will contract, pulling away from the retina and becoming partially liquefied. It happens most often as a function of aging, but can also occur in younger people, especially those with significant myopia. It is the contracted body of gel, floating in the liquid portion, that can produce the floaters and flashing lights. If the contracting vitreous does not separate cleanly from the retina, it may tear a hole in the delicate tissue, leading to a detachment of the retina from the underlying vascular structure. As the retina progressively detaches, it gives the impression of a shade being pulled down or a curtain being closed in front of the eye. If the detached retina is not surgically repaired promptly, irreversible damage to the retinal cells will result in permanent loss of vision. And that was the situation in which Martha found herself in the ER that night.

The resident immediately called the retina surgeon, Dr. Ray Gariano, who was not much older than the resident, having completed his retina fellowship and joined the Yale faculty within the past year. But he made up for his youthful lack of experience with an intense compassion for his patients, sound clinical judgment, and gifted surgical hands. Although it was now late in the evening, he told the resident that he would come in as quickly as possible. When he walked into the examination room about a half hour later, Martha looked up at a tall, handsome young man with warm, caring eyes and must have felt that her knight in shining armor had arrived. Through all the years that I knew Martha, she always spoke of "Dr. Ray" in almost romantic terms, and I think he ranked right up there with her cats.

Dr. Gariano confirmed the diagnosis and told Martha that it would be necessary to schedule surgery as soon as possible. The actual diagnosis was giant retinal tear, meaning that the hole in the retina was quite large and that the detachment would be more difficult to repair. He also noted that she had an elevated pressure in her left eye, but the most immediate concern that evening was to get her to the operating room promptly and reattach the retina in her right eye. He used the traditional, time-tested technique, in which the fluid is drained from behind the retina and a band is placed around the outside of the eye to bring the detached retina into contact with the underlying vascular layer. The operation went well, and the early postoperative course was quite encouraging. But as with so many events in Martha's life, good fortune was again to be denied.

Following a successful surgical reattachment of the retina, there are potential complications that can eventually reverse the favorable outcome. One of the more common of these is scar tissue, which grows on the surface of the retina and then contracts, causing recurrent detachment. And this is what happened in Martha's eye. The condition is much more difficult to treat than the initial detachment, because the strands of scar tissue on the retina must be removed in order to achieve reattachment. This is accomplished with an operation called vitrectomy, in which delicate instruments are inserted into the eye through the vitreous to remove the scar tissue and reattach the retina. It offered the best chance for saving the sight in Martha's right eye, but once again, fate seemed determined to deal her a bad hand.

Although the vitrectomy procedure was technically successful, scar tissue continued to grow in Martha's eye and her retina detached yet again. And so, for the third time, she was taken to the operating room. This time, all the stops were pulled out. In addition to another delicate peeling of the scar tissue and reattachment of the retina, a laser was used to "spot weld" the retina in place, and the back of the eye—where the vitreous had once been—was filled with silicone oil in an attempt to hold the retina in place. But it was simply not meant to be. The retina remained only partially attached, and her beloved eye—the part of her body that she had loved the most, and an eye which had 20/20 vision just a few months earlier—could now barely see the motion of a hand immediately in front of it.

Of all the challenges that Martha had faced in her trying life, she would later describe the loss of sight in her right eye as "the most bitter pill" of them all. It was not just that she had lost the vision of one eye, but that, in her mind, her eyes were no longer beautiful. She felt that they were now darker, and she was troubled by a slight drooping of the right upper lid. The part of her body that she had loved the most and was most proud of had been taken from her. It was as though she had lost a loved one, and she treated it with all the phases of such a loss—grief, depression, anger. Even for a person of her great fortitude, this was almost too much—the final straw. She had kept a diary since childhood, and in her anger she put three volumes in her bathtub and burned them. She would tell me later that she had thought about suicide and had hoped that her car would "go up a tree."

But Martha had been through too much to let any setback detour her from the path that she had chosen for her life, and the passage of time gradually began to work its balm. She found that she could function adequately with one good eye, and the loss of her right eye actually made her even more appreciative of the sight she had. As she slowly returned to her normal pattern of life, she once again took inventory of the things that she loved and that brought her happiness: her hair, her smile, and, of course, her cats—and even her eyes, which she finally decided were still beautiful. So, with her power of positive thinking and a healthy dose of good humor, she once again became the cheerful, seemingly carefree person who found happiness in each new day. And one of the things that gave her special joy was seeing her beloved Dr. Ray on frequent visits to his office. The condition of her eyes, at least her retinas, had been stable for some time. However, Dr. Gariano had become increasingly concerned about the high pressure in Martha's left eye. He finally started her on a glaucoma drop, but felt that she should now be followed in the glaucoma clinic. And so it was that a very special woman came into my life during our first spring in New Haven.

—

Glancing at her medical record before entering the examination room, I saw that her name was Martha and that she had been followed in our retina service for a retinal detachment of the right eye, which had lost sight despite three operations. The record also indicated that she was thought to have glaucoma and had been started on an eye drop. What the record did not prepare me for was the person I would find sitting in the examination chair. She sat erect and dignified, but her head barely reached the top of the chair, and her legs extended straight out in front of her with her feet just beyond the edge of the seat. Such encounters can be embarrassing, and we have a tendency to look away and pretend that nothing is out of the ordinary, which usually only makes the moment more awkward. But there was something about Martha's demeanor that quickly assuaged any uneasiness. She had a warm, comfortable smile and extended her hand while introducing herself in a very natural, matter-of-fact way. I could not resist returning her smile, and the firmness of her handshake told me that here was a truly special person. From then on, I never thought much about her physical stature, although I never ceased to marvel at how courageously she lived her life.

After a few pleasantries, we got down to the business of examining her eyes. A check of her visual acuity confirmed that the right eye was now essentially blind, with only the ability to see a moving shadow when a hand passed just in front of the eye. Thankfully, the left eye still checked out 20/20. The next step was to examine her at the slit lamp, and I wasn't sure how we were going to accomplish that, considering her size. But this would be my first of many lessons in how she adapted to achieve whatever needed to be done in her life. Without hesitation, she slid forward to the edge of the seat, grabbed the handles of the slit lamp, pulled herself up to the chin rest and waited for me to begin the examination, as though to say, "Okay, buddy, let's get on with it."

The examination revealed that she did indeed have glaucoma in her left eye—her only good eye—but that it was still in a relatively early stage and under reasonable control, and I was optimistic that we could preserve the good vision that she had left. So we discussed a treatment plan, which would involve office visits every three to four months. As we said good-bye on that first day, I had an impulse to help her down from the chair, but something told me that would not be necessary or appreciated. Sure enough, she turned herself around in the chair, slid over the edge of the seat until her feet landed on the footrest, and then stepped down onto the floor, taking her papers and sauntering out the door with a "toodle-do." At the reception desk, where she was to exchange the paper for a return visit card, she gave a good-natured call so the receptionist would look over the edge of her desk to see Martha patiently waiting for her. As I watched her walk out of our reception room that day with independence and dignity, I could not help but smile and shake my head at this demonstration of indomitable spirit.

And thus began a long friendship. I looked forward to her visits, during which I learned more each time about this amazing person. I loved her sense of humor and her positive attitude and was fascinated by all the things she was doing in her life. On one occasion, when Sharon was visiting our family in North Carolina, I asked Martha if she would like to have dinner at Mory's, where she had never been. She seemed excited at the prospect, and I told her that I would pick her up at her home. She was now living in a small house and asked me to come in while she got her coat. As I stood there looking around her tiny living room, the scene was one that will forever be in my memory. Most of the furniture was designed for children, except for a couple of regular-sized pieces for her guests. And on every chair, especially the small ones, sat one or more of her menagerie of beloved cats and kittens. We had a delightful evening, and I learned much more about this special lady and her remarkable life. I felt good that her glaucoma and vision were stable and that her life seemed to be on an even keel—until that day when it all came crashing down again.

If any good thing can be said to have come from the tragedy of Martha's right eye, it was to prepare her for what was about to happen in her left eye. Almost two years to the day that she had begun losing sight in her right eye, she noted the first floater in front of her left eye. This time she knew not to hesitate. An immediate call was placed to the eye center, and she again found herself driving through the evening dusk, with her only eye fixed on the road ahead as it gradually faded from view. Miraculously, she made it and was met at the ER door by her Dr. Ray. His examination confirmed our worst fear—she had a retinal detachment of her left eye. Because she had known to come in promptly this time, it was not as far advanced as the detachment in the right eye had been. But being all too aware of the poor outcome in the right eye, each of us undoubtedly harbored a sense of disbelief and fear that evening, which we tried to hide behind a positive discussion of the next step—another trip to the operating room.

By this time, Martha's visual world had essentially gone into the shadows. It is hard to imagine what thoughts must have been going through her mind. She had never known a day that was not a challenge, but she had met each with resolve and courage, and she had created a good life for herself against all odds, even after the loss of one eye. But now, what would happen if she lost all her sight? How would she carry on? Who would take care of her? What would she have left to live for? I don't know if any of these thoughts were going through Martha's mind that night. I can only report that there were no hysterics, no crying, and no asking, "Why me?" But she was very quiet. It was as though a veil of serenity had come over her. She seemed to be at peace—as though she had reached deep inside herself to find some great inner strength. For whatever reason, she seemed to believe that everything was going to be okay, and amazingly, it seemed that she was comforting and reassuring all of us, instead of the other way around.

Technically, the operation was a success. The retina was reattached. But Martha's world remained dark. Her left eye—her only hope for good vision, her only hope for a semblance of a normal life—was covered with a thick gauze patch as we all waited anxiously for it to heal. Remembering all too well what had happened to her right eye, in which the first operation had also appeared to be successful until the complications of scar tissue thwarted the outcome and resulted in permanent blindness, we knew that it was too soon to breathe any sigh of relief. Those were anxious hours and days for all of us. And yet Martha remained the most confident and optimistic of us all. It was as though some new inner strength had taken hold of her since the loss of her right eye, when she had almost given up. She now seemed to possess a confident assurance that not only would everything be okay, but also that she could cope with whatever the future held for her. In fact, amazingly, as she lay in her hospital bed, in her dark world, there was a constant smile on her face, and she talked enthusiastically about her plans for the future. She talked about a trip to Italy. For several months, she had been saving her money for the trip. Italy was a place that she had always wanted to see, and she saw no reason why she should not go and see it. Of course, even under the best of circumstances, going to such a faraway, foreign place is a daunting prospect. And in her case, how would she manage all the challenges of travel with such physical limitations? How indeed would she manage if the sight in her left eye did not fully return? And what would she do if a problem arose with the eye or with any of her other medical problems when she was so far from home? But none of these concerns seemed to bother Martha. She saw no reason why she should not enjoy a full life like anyone else.

The time finally came to remove the patch from her left eye. As Dr. Gariano carefully peeled the tape from her delicate skin and wiped her red eyelids with a moist cotton ball, Martha gingerly opened her eye, and the first thing she saw was the gentle, caring face of her beloved Dr. Ray. Her smile was now from ear to ear. But the view was blurry and distorted. The eye needed more time to heal, and we all knew that we were not yet out of the woods. They were tense days and weeks that followed. Martha went back to her little home, where she had a friend who helped her with daily chores and brought her to the eye center for her frequent appointments. At first, she had to be led into the examining room, but eventually she was able to ambulate on her own as her vision slowly returned. And through it all, she remained light-hearted and good-natured, and to the casual bystander, she did not seem to have a care in the world. At a time when we should have been bolstering her spirits, she was actually making us laugh and feel better with her constant good humor. But as her vision continued to improve and she could read farther down on the eye chart with each visit, there were unmistakable moments when her demeanor would become quiet and introspective, and she would momentarily close her eyes with a look of profound thankfulness on her petite face, and one could only guess what she was thinking (or praying). And then the day came when she read every letter on the 20/20 line. It was a time for celebration, and there were many moist eyes in the clinic that day. Of course, Martha was elated, but she seemed to take it all in stride, as though to say, "Aw, shucks." It was not for lack of gratitude at her good fortune, but just that she had believed all along that it would happen. And that spring, less than six months after facing a possible life of blindness, Martha went to Italy.

———

I continued to see Martha on a regular basis for well over a decade until I retired and left Yale. Although we struggled at times to control her glaucoma, her retina remained attached, and she retained 20/20 vision in her precious left eye. But other medical problems were taking their toll. She was having increasing pain from arthritis and requiring ever-stronger medication. Her legs were gradually giving out, and she finally became confined to a wheelchair—a very small one that had been designed for a child. But there was one thing that never changed—her indomitable spirit. She simply never gave up. She actually went back to school to obtain her master's degree in public health. And she continued to work for as long as her health would allow. Her attitude toward life never seemed to waver—she was determined to make the most of each gift that she was given and to find happiness in every day. One day, when she came in for her routine visit, she introduced me to the gentleman who had brought her. He was of average height and seemed to have an unusually kind and caring nature about him. She said that he was a friend and that over time, their friendship developed into an especially close and lasting one. Their relationship was particularly important for Martha, because her Dr. Ray, to whom she had become so attached, had left Yale and Connecticut not too many years after saving her sight.

The loss of Dr. Gariano was a major blow to both Martha and me. He had been an important part of our department, and I hated to lose him. But he had meant even more to her. Not only had he saved her sight—and possibly her life—but he had been a great emotional support for her. During all the years that I continued to care for her, rarely a visit went by that she did not mention his name—usually in an almost dreamy way. But she was not being negative or feeling sorry for herself—that was not her way. It was as though she was remembering a very positive and beautiful part of her life and finding happiness in keeping it alive in her memory. She always remained true to her philosophy for happy living—to find the things that she liked about herself and her life and to find her happiness in them. And it was not possible to be around Martha for long without having her philosophy of living rub off on you.

———

We never balanced the budget at Yale, although I spent many sleepless nights and miserable days trying to do it. I hated having to let people go and reduce salaries and cut back on the size of our facilities, all in an effort to reduce overhead. But even that did not bring our budget into the black. And I hated letting the dean and Yale down by failing to accomplish what I had been hired to do. Those were the most challenging years of my professional career, and yet, as I look back on them, I realize that they were also some of the best years of my life. I don't know to what extent Martha, and other patients like her, influenced my thinking. In fact, it is obviously wrong to even compare my problems to those that Martha has had to deal with throughout her life. There is no comparison. But maybe that is the point. If a person like Martha can find the silver linings among the blackest clouds, no matter how thin those linings may be, can't we all do the same?

I certainly had much to be thankful for during our years in New Haven. Yale University is a very special place, and I loved the Gothic architecture, the history, and the traditions. I loved the dinners at Mory's and the Thursday evenings with the fellows at Jonathan Edwards College. And I loved the many warm friendships that we enjoyed in New England—the rekindling of old friendships from our days at Harvard and the many new friendships we established in Connecticut. The old southern myth that people up North are less friendly was certainly not our experience. It may be a slightly different type of friendship, but it is every bit as warm and lasting. I especially loved working with the bright, young people at Yale—the undergraduate students at JE, the medical students, the residents, and the fellows. They were an oasis for me—an escape from the administrative hassles—and I took pride in watching them move on to their next level of education and eventually out into the world to become the new generation of doctors and leaders.

But most of all, I loved the special relationship with my patients. They taught me so much as I observed the ways they lived their lives with courage and dignity. They will forever hold a special place in my heart, but none more so than Martha. It is hard to imagine a life more challenging than hers. And yet she chose not to focus on the negative parts of her life, but to find the things about her life that she loved and that made her happy and to focus on them. And Martha was one of the happiest people I ever knew.

Ω

17.

Blessing

Waiting for spring is arguably the most trying aspect of the New England seasons. Even for aficionados like Sharon and me, who delight in the magical splendor of a snowy winter's day, there comes a time when we too join in the old refrain from the Good Book: "For everything there is a season." It is somewhat like the sparkling white, bejeweled wedding dress that shares in the "oohs" and "aahs" on its appointed day and then, relegated to the closet and the ravages of time, fades to yellow and loses its sparkle, leaving only distant memories of its past glory.

In November, when the first snow often arrives, it is greeted with general enthusiasm as people rush from their firesides to gaze out the window into the dark night air to ooh and aah over the softly falling snowflakes as they are illuminated by the lamplights. In December, the snows are still welcomed and appreciated by most, and there are few who do not long for a white Christmas. But by January, with the excitement of the holidays behind us and the prospect of a long winter ahead, the number of snow enthusiasts is dwindling, and most people are simply hunkering down with the realization that this is just the way it is. And by February, a good word for snow is hard to find, and there is either silence on the subject or the inevitable grumblings. By late February in the Carolinas, the crocuses are beginning to make their perennial appearance, soon to be followed by the daffodils and the dogwoods and all the colors of another spring. But up in New England, late February only promises more winter, with snows that often extend well into March. And by now the snow, like the faded wedding dress, has lost much of its splendor. It stands in large, dirty mounds, waiting to melt with the spring thaw. And the streets are brown with the dirt and sand that were deposited over the winter to help motorists. And the busy passageways in businesses and homes are brown with the same dirt that has been brought in on our shoes. And people are just ready for spring.

There was one winter during our years at Yale when the snow came unusually early and threatened to never leave. In fact, the first snowfall that November was so early that I had not yet gotten around to performing my annual task of raking the fall leaves. So I waited, with a trusty rake close at hand, for the snow to melt and allow me to fulfill my autumn duty. But that snow was followed by another—and another. November gave way to December, and the leaves remained hidden beneath a recalcitrant bed of snow. We certainly had a white Christmas that year—and a white January and a white February. By March, the snows of November were still on the ground, and there had not been a single day in over four months in which our world was not covered by layers of snow and ice. Finally, in late March, the sun melted the last traces of that long winter's snow, but it was not until early April that I was finally able to get out with my rake—which must have thought I had completely forgotten about it—and begin raking the leaves of a long ago fall.

It felt strange to be raking fall leaves when the green shoots of spring flowers were making their appearance in our yard. Overhead, buds on the trees looked down on this curious spectacle, and I couldn't help but wonder if they were contemplating, as their ancestors lay lifeless on the ground, that this would be their fate before the year's end. But I had another concern. For over four months, our grass lay buried beneath the thick mat of leaves and heavy layers of snow and ice, and I wondered what I would find as the rake pulled back the first parcel of leaves. Would the grass have succumbed to the constant pressure and lack of sunlight and be brown and dead? But to my delight, I found tender, green shoots of grass, ready to burst forth for another spring and summer. And that set me to thinking (raking provides ample time for thought) about how the resilience of this grass was an apt metaphor for the indomitable nature of the human spirit. Like the burdens of winter, the exigencies of life—illness, injury, failure, worry, loss, loneliness, heartache—are sometimes so overwhelming that death seems to be the only answer. And yet that is when so many people seem to find an inner strength that allows them to persevere and rise above their afflictions and find the sunshine of a new day. Over the years, it was my privilege to observe this strength in many of my patients—Ronnie,

Kristi, and Martha, to name a few. These and many others taught me about the resilience of the human spirit, and I was blessed to have been touched by each of their lives. But of all these blessings, none was greater than that of a young man I would meet at Yale. And to say that he blessed my life seems especially apropos—because his name was Blessing.

———

He was twelve years old when we first met, and my initial impression was that here sat the saddest person I had ever known. He seemed so small in the large examination chair. Copious tears were flowing down his dark brown cheeks. They were not so much tears of sorrow or self-pity. They were coming from eyes that were red and irritated and painful—actually, he was in great pain. Not only were his eyes the source of his misery, but they were also failing to provide him with any useful sight. His left eye had long since been totally blind, and his right eye, as the result of a recent series of tragic events, offered only shadows of light. And to add to the pathos of the scene, he seemed to have no family; the person with him I assumed to be a friend or caretaker. And then there was the name. Who would name a child Blessing? Especially under the present circumstances, it could not have been more incongruous—like a bad joke.

So there he sat—small, blind, in pain, crying, alone, and with a name that seemed to mock his sad state of affairs. I remember so vividly having conflicting feelings that day. One was abject pity. I recall wondering what hope the future held for such a child. And yet, at that same time, I had a surprisingly positive feeling about my young patient. There was something special in his demeanor. In the midst of all his misery, there was a gentleness, an acceptance—almost a sense of humor. He seemed to be telling the rest of us not to worry, that everything would be okay. There was clearly a decided ambivalence in my feelings at that moment—pity for his physical state, but wonder at an apparent strength that seemed to lie just beneath the surface.

And I was not the only one to notice these admirable and endearing qualities in this young man. He had been coming to our department under the care of my colleagues since the tender age of seven, and had long since established himself as a favorite of all the doctors and staff. Since much of his time at Yale was spent in the glaucoma clinic, he came to be especially close to the three women who ran that section of our practice. They had taken Blessing under their wings and made him a special part of our extended family. And since the glaucoma clinic was also where I worked, these three women had quickly become very special to me as well. Their names are Corinne, Gail, and Ann, and they eventually filled the spot in my heart that I had left back at Duke when I said good-bye to Robin and nurse Sharon. All three were ophthalmic technicians, a profession in ophthalmology that has gradually replaced nurses in most eye clinics. Although they were close to each other and worked great together, each had her own role in the glaucoma clinic and her own distinct personality.

Corinne was the senior of the three, just a few years younger than me. It seemed that she had been at Yale forever and had countless stories to tell, not to mention the wisdom that comes with years of experience. But there was nothing stodgy about her. To the contrary, she was totally unpretentious and given to loud bursts of laughter at the least provocation. Besides our closeness in age, she and I had other things in common, including being obnoxiously boastful grandparents and possessing a mild stammer, which in her case was quite endearing. Corinne was the supervisor of the technicians and had somewhat the aura of a mother superior. We were all respectful and a bit deferential to her, but the truth is that she was just one of the family.

Gail was the most professional of the three. By that I mean she went about her work in a methodical and efficient manner, which at first gave the impression of being a bit aloof. Part of this may have come from the fact that her primary job was to perform our visual field exams. This involves working in a dark, quiet room and constantly admonishing the patients to pay attention to the little flashes of light coming from all directions and occasionally chastising them for poor performances. But Gail was anything but aloof. Although it took me a little longer to get to know her than the other two, her warmth, caring, and friendliness soon came through. And the patients adored her. As with Corinne and Ann, she knew all of them by their first name, and I think they considered it a badge of honor if Gail gave them good marks on their field exam. In fact, the patients adored all three of these very special women and would invariably ask about them if one happened not to be around on the day of their visit.

And then there was Ann. She was the youngest and most petite of the three. The first thing that impressed me about Ann was her smile—it could brighten the cloudiest day. Her husband, Rick, also worked at the medical school as the head of the audiovisual section. He wore a full beard and was as large and burly as she was petite. They had met when she was taking scuba lessons from him. Rick and Ann were not blessed with children, but like George and Margaret of an earlier era, they were blessed with each other. They loved to travel together, and although Rick was the professional photographer, Ann was the designated photographer on their journeys and would invariably come home with hundreds of pictures. They also enjoyed all the holidays together, including Saint Patrick's Day and Halloween. The former is especially popular in the Northeast, what with the large Irish population, and no one could outdo Ann and Rick in the wearing of green and being in the middle of all the festivities. On Halloween, they always came to our home, not for treats, but to treat us with their elaborate costumes and good cheer. One year, I came to the door to find a towering Darth Vader and a lovely little Princess Leia. Sharon took a picture of the three of us together, using Ann's ever-present camera. Those are special memories, but my fondest are of working with Ann in the clinic. Her primary role was as coordinator of our clinical trials, in which we evaluated new treatments for glaucoma. She not only coordinated these activities with precision, but treated our volunteer patients with such warmth and good humor that I think they actually looked forward to the long days they spent with us. Ann also spoiled me. She worried about me not eating lunch and always made sure that there was a supply of cheese crackers and Fig Newtons in my office. It is probably obvious that she held a special place in my heart, but all three of these women were very special to me, and the four of us were like a little family—and Blessing was like one of our children.

When Blessing first arrived at the Yale Eye Center in the seventh year of his life, he was already completely blind in his left eye—that is to say, he could not tell day from night. With his right eye, he could just barely perceive the largest letter on the eye chart, especially if he was allowed to get a little closer to it. Sadly, however, even this was not to last. Like Benjamin, Craig and Ronnie, he had been born with congenital glaucoma, and it was this that had robbed him of all sight in his left eye and was threatening to do the same in the right. The pressure in that eye was dangerously high, and it was only a matter of time before it would destroy the few remaining nerve fibers that connected his eye to his brain, plunging him into a world of total darkness for the remainder of his life. He was under the care of one of my colleagues in the glaucoma section, who knew that surgery to lower the pressure was the only hope of saving what little vision Blessing had left. He also knew that financial resources were a problem at home, and made arrangements for Blessing's surgery to be done at little or no cost.

The first operation my colleague attempted was to create a drainage channel within the eye that would allow the fluid (aqueous humor) to drain out and relieve the pressure. This was similar to the surgery that I had performed on Benjamin decades earlier, and sadly, the outcome was not much better. Almost immediately, the drainage channel closed, the pressure went even higher than before surgery, and little Blessing suffered severe pain and tearing even to the point of causing nausea and vomiting. There was no choice but to take him back to the operating room and try a different surgical approach. This time the surgeon went inside the eye in a very delicate operation that is designed to restore the normal channels of aqueous drainage. Again, there was a rocky postoperative course, but eventually the pressure came down to a level that was just barely acceptable, and the vision returned to what it had been before the first operation. It looked like Blessing might be out of the woods—but his saga had only just begun.

For a year, he enjoyed his limited vision and freedom from pain, and life returned to a semblance of normal. He went back to school and could read large print and make out most of what was on the blackboard if he sat in the front row of his class. But his return to the relative normalcy of childhood proved to be a double-edged sword—he was, after all, a young boy who wanted to be like his friends and enjoy being out-of-doors and playing games. One day, as he was playing basketball at school, he broke for the basket and hollered for the pass. He saw the ball coming, but with only one weak eye, he lacked depth perception, and the ball approached him as a blur. It went through his hands and hit his eye—his right eye. The world went black and the pain returned. More days were spent in the hospital trying to control the pressure in his eye, which was again at a dangerous level, and waiting for the bleeding in the eye to resolve. Gradually the blood did clear and the pressure came back down to a barely acceptable level, and his vision was almost as good as before. It looked like he had dodged the bullet, and he returned to school for another two years. But the worst yet was waiting for him at the next turn.

A water gun seems like such an innocuous toy. What child has not played with one, usually without incident? The worst that most often happens is a pet becoming the annoyed victim of a squirt and the irritation of getting wet. But for Blessing, it represented the end of his life as he had known it. It happened on a Sunday afternoon when he was in the third grade and playing with some friends in the backyard—and someone had a water gun. At close quarters, a water gun can exert considerable force. And the force exerted its full impact on Blessing's right eye. Again, he was plunged into darkness and pain, but the outcome was not to be as fortunate as with the basketball injury. This time the pressure in the eye was low—dangerously low—which signaled torn tissue inside the eye. The tissue was his retina. Like Martha, he had suffered a retinal detachment, in his case as the result of the blunt injury. He would later describe it as being "half-underwater." He could still see above, but the lower half of his vision was distorted. Gradually, the distortion expanded upward, eventually taking his remaining vision—"as though I was drowning," he recalled, a metaphor prophetic to what lay ahead. And so he went back to the hospital and the operating room. The retinal tear was especially large, and its repair required removal of blood and the vitreous gel that fills the back of the eye and the injection of silicone oil into the eye to hold the retina in place. And because the pressure was likely to go back up after the surgery, a plastic tube was positioned inside the eye to facilitate drainage of the aqueous humor.

The postoperative course was a tragic, downhill spiral for Blessing. The vision in his only seeing eye was now barely sufficient to perceive a bright light, and the pressure was back up to a dangerous level, causing severe pain and threatening to take away his last thread of sight—his last connection with the visual world. The drainage tube wasn't working—it was clogged with the silicone oil—and he was taken back to surgery to clear the tube. For a while, the vision improved and the pressure remained low, but only for a few months. Then one day he came in with a pressure that was too low because the tissue over the external part of the tube had broken down and exposed the tube, running the risk of allowing infection into the eye, which could be the final blow. So it was back to the operating room to remove the tube and repair the torn tissue. For one week he remained in the dark with a patch on his only seeing eye, but when the patch was removed, the darkness remained. Blessing would never see again.

It was at about this time that I was first asked to see Blessing in the office. Fortunately, the pressure in his right eye remained just barely acceptable with the use of medicated eye drops, but his vision was "still messed up," as he described it, tears were constantly running down his cheeks, and he was hurting. The pain was coming mostly from his left eye—the eye that had no vision at all. The pressure in that eye was very high and was causing swelling and painful blisters on the front clear window of his eye (the cornea). He was having terrible pain, and the tearing wouldn't stop. We tried several types of drops to lower the pressure and to reduce the blisters, but it provided only partial relief. Finally we decided to perform the same laser operation on Blessing's left eye that I had done for Craig many years earlier. Of course, it had no chance of bringing back sight to the eye, but by lowering the pressure, it would hopefully relieve the pain and at least allow him to keep his eye. Fortunately, it worked, and he became physically comfortable and able to begin the long process of adjusting to his new life in a world of darkness.

Over the next several years, Blessing and I began to develop a special relationship. It was a very difficult time for him. Although he was no longer having pain or the constant tearing, he was now having to face something much more painful—the pain of knowing that he would never see again. The vision in his right eye was limited to the bare perception of light and shadows, and we had the sad duty of telling him that it was not going to get better. For a young boy who only wanted to be like other boys—to play ball, to run, to someday drive a car—accepting his blindness was the bitterest pill of all. Like all too many patients that I have known over the years, Blessing went through the stages of loss—shock, denial, anger. He would later tell me, "I was angry at God, but you can't be angry at him forever." Gradually, that inner strength that I had glimpsed when we first met began to reappear as he entered the stage of acceptance and started to learn how to cope with the life that would be his from now on. It was fortunate that he had begun to learn braille in the first grade, because now he would have to rely on it.

Once Blessing resigned himself to it, he quickly learned the ways and means of living with blindness and would eventually acquire a service dog named Tommy. I was heartened to see the progress that he was making and most of all to see the return of his indomitable, positive spirit. Although I continued to worry about what hope the future held for him, I was encouraged by the intangible resilience that he showed in every aspect of his personality. He simply would not allow people to feel sorry for him, because he constantly exhibited so much joy in his life. He was always cheerful and upbeat with a smile and kind word for everyone. In some ways this only made it worse, since everyone wanted the best for him and yet feared the worst. As the years passed and my administrative responsibilities continued to occupy more of my time, I had to relinquish Blessing's care back to my capable colleagues. They kept me informed as to how he was doing, but our paths did not cross again for several years. And when they did cross next, it was in the unlikeliest of places.

—

On a balmy summer evening in early August, the birds were performing their final serenade of the day, and twilight was beginning to cast long shadows across a small, remote parking lot. A lone, nondescript building sat in the middle of the lot. Low and box-like, the only clue to its identity was a cryptic sign over the entrance—The Space. Just inside the entrance, the still, warm air was heavy with the fragrance of incense. At the top of a short rise of stairs, a pretty young woman with long, straight hair and no makeup took my money. She suggested that I might want to spend some time in their gift store. This prompted me to glance down at my watch, fearing I might have miscalculated the time. There would be a bit of delay, she explained with a smile and a shrug that seemed to say that this was not only commonplace, but as it should be.

The gift store seemed more like a used clothing shop. All the merchandise appeared to have enjoyed a former life and was rather casually displayed on a variety of unmatched wooden and metal tables that seemed to be of the same vintage as their contents. There were strings of beads, tie-dyed shirts, little bowls that I assumed were for burning incense, and, of course, incense. In my blue blazer and tie, I suddenly realized that I was the oddity in the room. The few other browsers were a generation or two my junior and were dressed in decidedly casual, if not slightly exotic, attire. It was uncomfortably quiet in the room, but the others paid no attention to me, as though I wasn't even there, for which I was grateful. I am only vaguely familiar with the concept of Bohemian culture, but at that moment I felt like I was being introduced to it from a front row seat. For a fleeting second, I entertained the idea of making a purchase, but just as quickly realized that there was absolutely nothing I could take home to Sharon. So, after what I hoped was a respectful duration of time, I quietly left the store in search of the performance hall.

It was in the basement. More precisely, it *was* the basement. And the décor appeared to carry out the prevailing theme of the building. The seating had obviously been obtained from used furniture stores (or maybe even local trash sites). There were vintage chairs and couches of all descriptions, with a colorful array of pillows, blankets, and afghans, many of which covered defects in the upholstery. They were arranged in some semblance of a plan. At least they all faced more or less the same direction, which was toward a stage at the far end of the room. It was raised about a foot off the floor and held several musical instruments. For a moment, I thought I was the only one in the room, but then realized there was a handful of people scattered about, quietly hunkered down in the overstuffed seating. I was about to select my own seat when two more people entered the room and immediately brightened my mood—it was Ann and Rick. They were dressed, of course, in appropriate, casual attire and seemed to fit right in, as they did wherever they went. Ann flashed her radiant smile as we approached each other and exchanged pleasantries. She had been my source of information about this place and the evening's event. Earlier in the week, she showed me a small clipping from a local newspaper, announcing a concert at The Space. I had never heard of it, and the names of the performers meant nothing to me, except for the last one on the list—Blessing Offor.

I had known that Blessing was interested in music, but did not realize that he had begun performing in public—and in point of fact, aside from some gigs with a friend in restaurants, tonight would be his solo debut before a real audience. It was hard for me to imagine that small, blind, friendly but somewhat shy boy getting in front of an audience, and I was a bit fearful as to how it might go. Before the evening was over, however, I would not only have reason to totally rethink my concerns about his future, but would begin to have remarkable revelations about his past.

The gift store crowd gradually filtered in to the performance hall and settled down in the vintage chairs and couches, filling possibly half of the room. Ann, Rick, and I found a couch together near the front and waited rather anxiously for the show to begin. Eventually, a young man who had been sitting in the audience stood up, walked to the front, and welcomed us to The Space. I was relieved when he announced that the first act of the evening would be a new face on the scene who was performing alone in public for the first time. I had hoped that Blessing would be first, since I was not keen on sitting through the other performances in order to hear the one person for whom I had come out this evening. As the emcee introduced Mr. Blessing Offor, all heads turned to see the entertainer coming in through the back door. And at that moment, I was in for one of the surprises of my life.

As I turned to look, I had to blink and look again. What I saw was not the little boy I had once known. He was now a young man—a sturdy, handsome young man with a sparkling white smile and an air of confidence in his stride. He wore stylish sunglasses that hid his blind eyes, and beneath his T-shirt a muscular torso suggested that he had been spending hours in the gym as well as with his music. Could it possibly have been such a long time since I had last seen him? It seemed like only a few years—maybe five. But in that time, he had gone from a small, shy boy who evoked a sense of pity to a confident, well-built, handsome young man who exuded charisma.

To a subdued but polite applause, he approached the front of the room with a red-tipped cane in his left hand, while gently touching the elbow of a young woman who walked beside him to his right. With the tip of his cane, he felt the edge of the stage, stepped up onto it, and with some assistance from his companion, located and seated himself in a chair behind his keyboard. Then he was left all alone on the stage, and there was total silence in the room.

He did not seem to be in any hurry to proceed. He felt his keyboard and played a couple of random chords. Then he shook his head, smiled, and let out a nervous little laugh. Then there was more silence. I was starting to get nervous—was my impression of the new Blessing premature?

"Wow," he finally uttered with another laugh and shake of his head. He played a few more chords, took a deep breath, and then proceeded. "I'm a little nervous tonight." This elicited a faint, but sympathetic laugh from the audience. "But I really want to thank you for coming. It means a lot to me." He seemed to be warming up—a few more chords were now coming together as a theme. "I've been working on some songs, and this first one I guess is how I see my life. I hope you like it."

The theme on his keyboard now developed into a full melody as he began his song. At first, his voice was a bit quiet and a little shaky—I could tell he was nervous, and so was I. Quickly, however, he seemed to gain confidence as his volume strengthened and a full, rich, yet soothing voice filled the room. He was not only an accomplished instrumentalist and vocalist, but we were amazed to learn later that he also wrote the lyrics and music for all his songs. I immediately loved his style. It was not the loud, ear-splitting sounds that characterized so many of his genre, in which volume seemed more important than content (to me, at least). It was soft and sincere, with nearly perfect elocution that was easily heard above the accompaniment on his keyboard. And the words threatened to bring tears to my eyes. They spoke of finding the light in a world of darkness, of finding a way through seemingly hopeless odds, and of emerging with all the joy that life has to offer. It was obvious (at least to the three of us in the front-row couch) that these sensitive words came from a life of experience and from the heart.

As the last note drifted out of the room, the audience broke into a thunderous applause, in striking contrast to the tepid response that had first greeted him. But none were clapping (and shouting) louder than Ann, Rick, and myself, and I hoped they did not see the tear in my eye. Blessing played and sang several more songs. By the end of the performance, he had the audience in the palm of his hand. The emcee must have realized that we all needed to catch our breath and announced that there would be a brief intermission.

He was immediately surrounded by well-wishers, and we stood back until the others had their say and moved on. Then Ann went up to him and identified herself.

"Oh, Ann, I'm so glad you're here. Thank you for coming!"

"And, Blessing, Dr. Shields is here too," she said.

"Dr. Shields, I can't believe you came!"

"Wouldn't have missed it for anything, Blessing. You were just wonderful tonight."

There was an attractive, middle-aged woman standing quietly beside Blessing, whom he introduced as his cousin, Cecilia. She was as open and warm as him, and we all hugged and laughed and then posed for a picture (with Ann's camera, of course). Then we bade farewell to Blessing, saying that we looked forward to his next performance and promising not to let so much time pass until our next time together. Ann and Rick were going on to some other event that evening, which amazed me, since it was approaching my bedtime and I was heading home. Outside the building, a lot of the people from the audience were standing around enjoying the cool summer breeze. As I began walking through the crowd toward my car, I saw Cecilia sitting alone beside an old lawn table. Our eyes met, she smiled, and something told me that I should walk over and speak to her. As we shared a few remarks about our common admiration and affection for Blessing, it occurred to me that I knew so little about his past, and she seemed willing to tell me. So I pulled up a rusty lawn chair beside her, and this is the story she told me.

Blessing was born in a small village in Nigeria, the youngest of six children. His parents worked hard to provide for them—his father as a carpenter, who made furniture and owned a small furniture store, and his mother as proprietress of a local grocery store. The other five children were all healthy and attended public schools. But Blessing's congenital glaucoma set him apart from the start. He never had useful vision in his left eye, and the limited vision in his right eye was feared to be a barrier to his education. His parents wanted all their children to have every opportunity in life, so they sent Blessing, at a very young age, to a private school, where it was hoped he would have the best chance to succeed against his handicap. The principal of the school had lived in New York and began giving English lessons to Blessing. But he was struggling with his studies due to poor eyesight, which seemed to be getting worse. An ophthalmologist in a larger city nearby told the family that Blessing was going blind from his glaucoma and that he could perform surgery to save his sight. But the price that the surgeon required for the operation was exorbitant—far beyond the family's ability to ever pay. And it was for this reason that Blessing's father made the difficult decision to send his son to America.

His father had a brother by the name of Chigozie, who was a student at the University of New Haven, and Blessing was to live with him so that he could get proper eye care at the Yale Medical Center. Blessing was only five and a half years old when he had to say good-bye to his entire family—the only support he had ever known and the only home he had ever known—to get on an airplane for the first time, all alone, and fly halfway around the world to a foreign land, where he had only rudimentary command of the language, to live with people who he barely knew. One can only imagine what goes through the mind of a small, nearly blind child, who must have felt that he was being abandoned by all the people whom he had ever loved, and who was suddenly all alone, facing the fear of the unknown. And yet, even at that tender age, he was buoyed by the inner strength and resilience that would characterize the remarkable person he was destined to become.

Uncle Chigozie took good care of Blessing. The public school system was reluctant to accept him at first because of his poor vision (and possibly his limited English), but his uncle insisted, and with the help of a state agency called BESB (Board of Education and Services for the Blind), he was able to enter the first grade in the fall, where he quickly showed that his intelligence and determination were sufficient to overcome any of his handicaps. His uncle also arranged for Blessing to start taking piano lessons, but the boy preferred to be outside playing with the other children in the neighborhood—in other words, he was a typical young boy. Sadly, it was his desire to have a normal childhood that eventually ended any hope of a normal, sighted life. First came the major setback after the basketball accident, and then the water gun incident, which severed the last thread of hope. And yet, through it all, he persevered—through the loss of vision, the depression and anger, and the adjustment to a life without sight. And most remarkably of all, he was able to do it and still keep up with his studies and his music, and Cecilia told me that he was on track to graduate from high school within the next two years.

As I drove home from The Space that evening, my mind was awash with all that I had learned about Blessing within the past few short hours. In a way, I guess I wasn't surprised, because it was all in keeping with the strength of character that I had always seen in him since that first day, years ago, when I had encountered a small, struggling child. But I couldn't help feeling a powerful sense of almost giddy elation as I now saw that this strength was carrying him toward a future that held great promise. And, indeed, the years that followed would justify my optimism.

—

During his junior year at Hamden High School, Blessing was invited to perform with a local recording artist in a program called Concert for Kids, sponsored by the Hamden Education Foundation. The two young people sang a duet to a packed auditorium and raised four thousand dollars in ticket sales. Blessing's career was now well on its way. He was increasingly in demand for concerts, but never let his music and performing interfere with his academic achievements.

The following summer, he was again featured in a concert, but this time he had not only top billing, but also his own band, which included two young men on strings, a drummer, and a female vocalist, while he continued to sing and play his keyboard. It was an outdoor event at a park, where the audience sat on blankets and folding chairs on a lawn that sloped down toward a covered pavilion for the performers. The crowd was several-fold larger than had been at The Space the previous summer and was no less enthusiastic about Blessing's music. This time, all four of us were there—Ann, Corinne, Gail, and me. As we sat listening to the music, I wondered if my companions were marveling, as I was, at the contrast between the talented, successful young man up on the stage and the little boy we had once known—I suspect they were. When his part was over, we all congregated near the side of the stage for adulations and more hugs and laughs and, of course, more pictures (need I say whose camera we used?).

During the previous academic year, Blessing had sent a letter to his friends in which he shared with us his determination to make music his career, composing and performing piano and vocals. He also aspired to parlay his success into establishing programs in Nigeria for children with special needs. To those ends, he was hoping to record a professional demo CD in order to display some of his original songs. He would send the CD to colleges and record producers and sell them at concerts and performances. But the cost of such an enterprise was considerable, and he was asking if we could help by contributing to the "Blessing of Music Fund." Of course, each of us was delighted to be a part of his future, and the CD became a reality. That evening at the outdoor concert, I proudly purchased a copy of Blessing's first CD, which is among my treasures to this day.

After graduating from high school, Blessing could have easily forsaken higher education to pursue his musical career. But, true to his principles and discipline, he recognized the importance of a good education, and, possibly with the help of his demo CD, he matriculated that fall to Belmont College in Nashville. Needless to say, he majored in music, which included piano, saxophone, organ, voice, and composition. As I thought about him in Nashville, I was taken by a sense of irony that two of my favorite musicians (and two of my favorite people) were in the same town—Ronnie Milsap and Blessing Offor. The two of them are so much alike. In addition to being remarkably talented musicians, both rose against formidable odds, including blindness, to achieve success and happiness in their lives. And both have such warm, friendly, good-humored, positive, uplifting personalities that they just make you feel good to be around them. I had hoped that the two might meet during Blessing's years in Nashville. It didn't happen—I guess they were both so busy—but if they ever do meet, I bet they will become the best of friends.

When he was back in Connecticut for Christmas break during his sophomore year at Belmont, the two of us went out to dinner one evening to catch up on his life. Blessing was now twenty years old and had not been back to Nigeria since he had left nearly fifteen years earlier. Uncle Chigozie had moved to Florida, where he was practicing law, and Cecilia was now a nurse in Denver. While in high school, Blessing had met a wonderful woman by the name of Lisa, who worked with students who had special needs. She apparently saw the same extraordinary qualities in her young client as the rest of us did, as well as his need for a home, and eventually invited him to live with and become part of her family. It was into their driveway that I drove on the evening Blessing and I were scheduled to meet for dinner. He introduced me to his extended family, who obviously had as much pride and affection for him as if he were one of their own. I also met his service dog, Tommy, and the three of us piled into my car and headed off.

As we settled into our seats at the restaurant, with Tommy lying at his master's feet and flames crackling in a stone fireplace close by, there were two questions on my mind that I had been wanting to ask Blessing. The first had to do with the origin of his name. I could still remember how it had struck me when we first met eight years earlier. I had never known anyone with such a name, and it seemed not only quite unusual, but also almost a mockery of his pitiful physical state at the time, which seemed to be anything but a blessing. Over the years, however, I became increasingly impressed not only by the pride he took in his name, but also by how he was developing into a person for whom the name seemed quite appropriate—he was truly a blessing for himself as well as for all who knew him. And yet, I had never asked him how he came to have such a special name.

The question elicited a big laugh, with a flash of his sparkling white teeth. He had obviously been asked it many times before, but didn't seem to mind telling the story again.

"I am the youngest of six kids," he began. "The other five all still live in Nigeria."

He paused for a moment with a pensive look on his face, as he must have been thinking about how long it had been since he was last with his brothers and sisters.

"Christianity is a minority religion in Nigeria," he soon continued, "but my parents are strong Christians, and that must have influenced the names they chose for each of us kids. My oldest brother is called Ebere in Ibgo, the Nigerian language, and that is the masculine form for the name Mercy. He is just now graduating from our country's national service. I have a sister who is also named Mercy, but hers is the feminine form in Ibgo. She's in nursing school. My older sister is already a nurse, and her name is Peace."

It was obvious that Blessing took pride not only in the names of his siblings, but also in their accomplishments.

"Then I have a brother with an MBA who is now in business. His name is Emeca, which means 'things God does.' And my other brother, who is closest to me in age, is called Chidi, and that means 'God lives.'"

I was most surprised when Blessing told me what Chidi does.

"Chidi is an ophthalmologist."

And I couldn't help but wonder how his younger brother's illness might have influenced that career choice.

"So then I came along"—Blessing laughed—"and they must have been running low on names by then. I'm not even sure if they were planning on me, but they looked on everything as a blessing from God. And so they named me Ngozi, which is the masculine form of Blessing."

Then there was another pause, a pensive expression, and a barely perceptible shake of his head, as he must have been thinking about the irony of his name and the agony he had caused his family when he was a child.

"Well, you sure have lived up to your name," I suggested after a respectful pause.

He demurred.

"And that kind of leads into the other question that has been on my mind," I continued. "What is your secret, Blessing? How have you been able to accomplish all that you have done, and with such a positive attitude, despite the hurdles that life has put in front of you?"

This query did not elicit a laugh, or even a smile. He only nodded, with a thoughtful look on his face that signified his understanding of the gravity of the question. But he seemed to be as willing and as prepared to answer it as he had the first one.

"I think my blindness is part of God's plan for me," he began slowly, as though carefully considering each word. "When I could still see some, I wasn't very focused—I just wanted to be outside playing with the other kids. When that was taken away from me, I began to focus more on my piano lessons and composition. In high school, I think I had a different perspective than my classmates. Instead of seeing those four years as the most important in my life at the time, I saw them more as part of a continuum of life. I think I was a little more mature and focused on making the most of that time in order to prepare myself for the future phases of my life. So I see my blindness as a blessing that has shown me God's purpose for my life."

Now I was the one shaking my head in thoughtful amazement at having received yet another profound lesson from one of my patients. Our food arrived at about that moment, and we ate in silence for a few minutes. But I could tell that Blessing was not through with his answer to my question. As he chewed on his steak, he seemed to be considering how to express his next thought, and then he swallowed and continued with what he explained was his theme in life.

"If we accept our lot in life as a gift, rather than a curse," he began slowly, as though each word was an integral part of his life's theme, "with gratitude rather than anger, then I believe it will become a blessing and will guide us to find our purpose in life and our happiness."

After leaving Belmont College, Blessing moved to New York, where his musical career continued to flourish as a singer, songwriter, pianist, and saxophonist. He began opening for several major bands and released his second CD. In 2010, he was named one of four musicians worldwide to receive the International Young Soloist Award, and he performed that summer at the Kennedy Center Millennium Festival in Washington, D.C.

It is a long way from The Space to the Kennedy Center, a long way from a small village in Nigeria to the bright lights of Manhattan, and a long way from a small, frail child with little apparent hope for the future to an accomplished young man with a future that seems to have no limits. Of course, his story is not complete—in fact, it has only just begun. But I believe I know how it will end. I am confident that whatever Blessing accomplishes in his musical career and in his life, he will be a smashing success, because no matter what the future may hold for him, he has found the secret of making the most of it, and in so doing, enjoying true happiness.

Ω

18.

Arthur Murdoch

During the last Ice Age—beginning about eighty-five thousand years ago—glacial flows crept down from the north across the land mass, a portion of which we today call Connecticut. Like a mammoth scouring pad, it abraded and engulfed layers of Earth's hard, primal crust as well as the softer elements that had formed over millions of years in our planet's continual evolution. For thousands of years, the debris lay suspended and entombed in the dormant glaciers—some pieces as big as a house, and others finer than sand. Then, around eighteen thousand years ago, the ice began to melt and recede, returning its contents to the land from whence it had come. And so it is that today we have one of New England's most iconic landmarks—stone.

My shovel had only pierced a few inches into the soil when I felt the all too familiar clunk. It had become a standard part of the ritual in our ongoing efforts to convert the ancient, virgin land around our new home into gardens. The next step in the ritual was to tap around the source of the resistance with my shovel to determine its size. Smaller stones could be easily dug up and tossed into a wheelbarrow for disposal later in the wooded area behind our formal backyard. The larger ones required more effort and a special piece of equipment—the gardener's equivalent of a crowbar. Our neighbor had told us, when we first moved in, that this is a standard and indispensible tool for all New England gardeners. It is basically a heavy steel rod that measures about five feet in length and an inch in diameter. The working end flares out in a spade-like configuration for prying under and dislodging the larger stones, which ranged in size anywhere from that of a cantaloupe to a good-sized watermelon. I would carry these stones to the junction of our lawn and wooded area, where I gradually created a modest stone wall. Although the stones were a nuisance, digging them up and building the wall provided a satisfying sense of historical connection with the pioneers of this area, who had done the same—albeit on a much larger scale—back in the seventeenth and eighteenth centuries. In most cases, their stone walls and foundations are the only remaining evidence of those early settlers, and we were fortunate to have some excellent examples within walking distance of our home.

Our house was perched on the side of a small mountain, which afforded a nice view to the next ridge about twenty-five miles away. The land just over the crest of our mountain was largely unsettled—at least in recent times—and had some great hiking trails. Having had to give up running in deference to my knees and hips, hiking these trials soon became my favorite form of exercise. A short walk through our neighborhood led to a country road that wound between two mountain ridges. Except for a few modest homes set back from the road, the land still looked as it must have to the early settlers when they first made their way through the dense forests. Although they are gone now, evidence of their existence and labor lives on in the stone walls that line the road and stretch up the mountain slopes among the trees and rocky terrain. Remnants of their homes and barns are also to be found in the fragments of stone foundations that now share the land with the wild shrubs, flowers, and ferns. Considering the effort required just to create our modest little gardens and stone wall, I could only imagine the toil of those pioneers, who cleared the stones from their fields to plant their crops and then used the stones to build their walls and foundations. As the road took me deeper into the woods, past more reminders of my predecessors' labor, I couldn't help but wonder whether they too had enjoyed the beauty and fragrance of the wild roses, the flowering trees and vines, and all the flora that greeted me throughout the summer along that old country road.

Before long, my walk would bring me to narrow hiking trails that left the road and wound up into the mountains on either side. From that point, the last remnants of civilization were left back on the road, and the nearness with nature became palpable. In early summer, wild blueberry and blackberry bushes and patches of strawberries lined the narrow paths, first sporting their bright blossoms and then their sweet, colorful fruit— which was best left for the birds. Large swaths of mountain laurel literally turned the hillsides a brilliant pink at their appointed time in the spring and then shaded the trails for the rest of the summer with their densely leafed branches. At some places along the trails, small streams ran across or beside the pathway, supporting a variety of lovely mosses and ferns on and around the ever-present stones. In the fall, brightly colored leaves covered the trails and drifted atop the streams or collected in pools amid the rock clusters. It was necessary to keep a close eye on the rocky trails to avoid stumbling, but I paused often to gaze into the deep, dark woods as they rose up toward the ridge on one side of the trail and fell back into the valley below on the other. The mountain slopes were graced with tall, stately oak, ash, elm, maple, and other trees amid a heavy ground cover of mountain laurel, shrubs, dried leaves, and giant clusters of the primordial stones. Off in the distance, the gobbling of wild turkeys was frequently heard, and it was not uncommon to encounter a deer standing on the trail or bounding across it.

For a short distance, the trails were typically steep and a bit strenuous (for me at least), but the crest was soon reached, and then the paths leveled out and followed the ridge of the mountains for miles. Near one of my favorite ridge trails, a large, flat rock reached out from the mountainside, facing south and providing a place for rest and remarkable vistas. Lakes sparkled between adjacent ranges of mountains, and dense forests covered the ridges and valleys, belying the bustling activity that was occurring just beneath their boughs and giving a sense of remoteness from civilization. Just beyond this tranquil scene, East Rock jutted above the landscape, providing a gateway to the New Haven skyline. Sail boats and ships were often visible on Long Island Sound, and on a clear day, it was possible to see the coastline of Long Island, over thirty miles from my lookout. I enjoyed many peaceful hours on that rocky perch, often watching a hawk lazily circling overhead and occasionally finding it hard to leave until the sunset had winked its final burst of glory.

Walking the old ridge trails offered a remarkable sense of serenity. The only sounds were those of the birds and the wind in the trees. It was rare to pass another hiker, but I had a feeling of companionship with my predecessors who must have traversed these paths long ago. Although the trails today are maintained by a local hiking club, I could imagine that they were once used by the Native Americans of the area as they journeyed to neighboring villages or local hunting grounds, and by the early settlers as they made their way to visit at a nearby farm or to trade in the closest settlement. While nearly all evidence of past civilizations is to be found in the valleys, the high ridges most likely offered the straightest and smoothest routes of travel before roads were cut through the lowlands. However, there was very little evidence that the higher elevations were ever used for any other aspects of their lives, and it was that assumption which created such a surprise one day when I came across a most unexpected sight.

It was barely visible through the trees along the mountain ridge. In fact, it could have been mistaken for just another tree trunk in the forest, as it was tall and straight. But there was something decidedly different about its composition—it was made of stone. Curiosity compelled me to leave the trail and make my way among the trees and thick underbrush toward this odd sighting (had I stayed on the trail a bit farther, I would have discovered a small side path that led to the site). In any case, I soon found myself in a small, grassy clearing of which the principal occupant was the object of my interest—a stone chimney. It was obvious that it had once been part of a home, but now it stood all alone, like a sentinel reminder of a time in history long past. There was no indication as to where the boundaries of the house had once existed. Judging from the orientation of the chimney and its hearth, I assumed that the main living area must have been the grassy area that was now occupied by a medium-sized tree.

For a moment, I stood entranced by the scene, wondering what type of family could have once lived in such an unlikely, remote setting. But then my eyes were caught by another object, and I began to realize that the chimney was not the only remnant of the life that had once inhabited this mountain ridge. To one side of the presumed home site—the side toward the edge of the ridge—there was a rectangular depression in the ground, measuring about five by ten feet, that had been carefully lined with stones of smaller size than those used for the chimney. Steps had also been created from stones at one corner, which provided access to the flat surface of the depression, about two feet down. Although the surface was now overgrown with weeds, I felt rather certain that I must have been looking at what was once the family's garden. And then, before I was able to fully process the significance of this discovery, I was drawn to yet another stony structure, which was in some ways the most intriguing of all.

Just beyond the garden, at the very edge of the mountain ridge, a low, intricate, rather artistic wall had been created from even smaller stones. On the near side of the wall, the ground was flat, but immediately to the far side it dropped off precipitously for several hundred feet to the valley down below. While the chimney and garden site had once served obvious utilitarian purposes, this third finding seemed to tell of another side to the family who had labored so diligently with the earth's bounty of stone—it must have been where they took their rest. Although trees had now grown up on the mountain's steep slope, partially blocking the view beyond, I could imagine the family sitting together in the evenings on the grass beside their stone wall, gazing out across a beautiful vista and watching the sunlight sparkling on the lakes, creating long shadows in the valleys, and finally disappearing behind the distant horizon.

It was not a path that I traveled often, preferring the trail that led by the flat rock overview, but I made it a point to visit the old "homestead" at least once every summer. As the years passed, it became an increasingly intimate place for return visits, as though I had some kinship with those who had once lived there. I was beginning to think of them as old friends, even though I knew absolutely nothing about them. My efforts to learn something of their history were uniformly unproductive, and I began to fabricate stories in my mind as to what the facts of their life might have been. Each summer, I would approach their home site with some fear that I might find the setting changed since my visit the previous year—especially that the chimney, which seemed to be balanced rather precariously, might have tumbled down during the past winter. But, with each new year, it was still standing, despite the ravages of wind, rain, snow, and ice, and everything was much as I had left it the previous fall. Except for one summer.

I didn't immediately notice it. My first concern, on the initial visit that summer, was the chimney—still standing—and the old garden site and the stone wall, where nothing seemed to have changed either. Then I became aware that something was different. It was a small garden, not in the old garden plot, but several yards away from it, rather near the edge of the mountain ridge. Someone had dug up a small portion of the grassy turf, maybe two by four feet, and planted a few varieties of flowers—zinnias, marigolds, and some others that I couldn't identify. So now the mystery of my "friends" homestead had acquired a new dimension. I was not their only visitor. Of course, I knew that other hikers were aware of the site. Although I had never actually encountered any of them, there had been evidence from time to time—a cushion, an empty water bottle, and the like—that people had stopped here during their treks to relax and enjoy the view. But this little garden, with its fresh flowers, meant that someone had more than just a casual interest in the place. My imagination was again set in motion about this curious, remote spot in the mountains, now attempting to postulate who the mystery gardener might be. The most likely answer was some young hikers who liked to leave things better than they found it (in accordance with the camper's mantra). But whoever it was had to transport the plants, tools, and probably water up the steep trail—and do it fairly regularly, since the little garden seemed to be well maintained. I later learned that there was an easier approach to the home site from the other end of the trail, although climbing it was no simple feat either. Whoever the gardener was had a serious commitment to their project.

My curiosity about the garden prompted me to make more visits than usual to the old homestead that summer. Each time I found the little plot to be well kept up, and each time I wondered again who the gardener might be. There was never any other sign that someone had been there, except for the well-cultivated and weeded soil and the happily growing flowers. I finally resigned myself to the likelihood that I would never discover the identity of the mystery gardener—until one day, when it was revealed to me in a way that I could never have anticipated.

It was a pleasant Saturday afternoon, rather late in the summer. The sun was warm on my back, and there was a cool, gentle breeze which suggested that autumn was just around the corner. I had decided to make one final visit to the home site and its little garden before my hiking season came to an end. As I left the trail for the narrow path into the clearing, I paused to once again take in the pleasantness of the surroundings, with which I now had a very comfortable familiarity—the chimney, the old garden site, the stone wall by the ridge, and the new little garden. But as my eyes turned toward the latter sight, I was startled to discover that I was not alone.

He was on all fours by the edge of the little garden with his back to me. My first impression, from the appearance of his dress, was that he might be a vagrant. Atop his head was a dilapidated straw hat, beneath which thin shocks of white hair extended half way down his neck. A faded denim jacket with holes in both elbows hung loosely from his fragile frame, and his cotton trousers were even more frayed than his jacket and were covered with dirt. His feet were bare except for well-worn leather sandals. He continued to work on his garden, seemingly unaware of my presence, and I was not sure what to do next. He was obviously rather elderly, and I didn't want to startle him for fear of having to perform CPR in this remote place. But as I stood there silently for several long seconds, my dilemma was solved for me in the most bizarre way. Without turning around or even stopping his work, he spoke in a soft, casual manner.

"Hello, Dr. Shields."

At first I thought I surely must have misunderstood him. But then he turned to face me, with a faint, wry smile and a piercing gaze straight into my eyes. For a moment I feared it might be me who would require CPR as I gasped in recognition of the person before me.

———

The letter was buried in a pile of correspondence on my desk. It had been a long day with a busy clinic, and I was hoping to finish up some office work before heading home. The pile consisted mostly of journals and advertisements with a few letters that my secretary had opened for me. I was moving through the stack quickly, since most of the items were going directly into the circular file. But then I came to a curious-looking letter that caused me to slow down. It was hand-written in rather sprawling cursive on lined paper. My first impulse was to set it aside for another day, but the opening line caught my eye and pulled me in to read the letter in its entirety.

> Dear Dr Shields,
> I need your help. I have been coming to Yale's Eye Clinic for 22 years, and I suppose I would be blind by now if it wasn't for your doctors there. I want you to know that I am very grateful for what has been done for me. But now there are bad problems. They don't listen to me anymore. My eyes are getting worse, but no one will listen to me or take my problems seriously. I try to explain, but they tell me everything is OK, but I know it isn't. They send me to different doctors and they all say the same thing. I believe there may be a conspiracy. They all say I am doing fine, but I am not, and I think they know it. I live in constant fear that I will soon be blind and no one will listen to me or help me. What can I do? I know you are in charge there and I am in desperate need for help.
> Will you please help me!!
> Arthur Murdoch

I read the letter several times, trying to decide what to make of it. Mr. Murdoch was obviously quite disturbed. I had total confidence in all the members of our faculty and knew that there must be some misunderstanding. Nevertheless, curiosity got the best of me, and I went to our record room and pulled his medical record, which was about three inches thick. Sure enough, he had been seen by nearly every doctor in our department. Aside from early cataracts, no one could seem to find anything wrong with him. The record showed that virtually every ocular and neurological examination and test for vision loss had been performed, all of which had turned up nothing. But he would always come back sooner than his appointment date, always with the same concern that he was going blind. And always his vision was the same, and nothing serious could be found. After several episodes like this, his doctor at the time would suggest another opinion from a different doctor. And so it was that he had been seen by nearly all of our doctors—except me. I guessed that I would have to be the next on his list, although I didn't hold out much hope that I could do any more than my colleagues had already done.

As I drove home that evening, Mr. Murdoch was obviously very much on my mind. We had been taught since medical school to always listen carefully to our patients. Many times the diagnosis becomes apparent just from their description of the symptoms, even before an examination is performed. But it is also well known that there are patients who can lead you "down the primrose path," as we used to put it. Some people suffer from a morbid concern about their health—an obsession about any unusual bodily or mental sensation—which is commonly known as hypochondriasis. A more important lesson that I had learned over the years, however, is that even hypochondriacs can be sick—in other words, always take a patient's complaints seriously, because you never know when they may be telling you something that will disclose a true physical problem.

The next day I spoke with several of my colleagues who had cared for Mr. Murdoch. Their responses were uniformly the same—a smile, a roll of the eyes, and a shake of the head. He was clearly an enigma, and no one knew quite what to do with him. After multiple extensive examinations and diagnostic procedures, looking for every conceivable ocular and neurological cause of visual impairment, absolutely nothing could be found to justify his fear that he was going blind. When I spoke with the doctor who was currently caring for Mr. Murdoch, she seemed overjoyed that I was willing to take a look at him. Her enthusiasm in transferring his care to me was not exactly reassuring, but I felt that I had to give it a go.

I listened to the phone ring for quite a few times and was just about to hang up (with some degree of relief, if truth be known), when I heard the sound of the receiver being lifted at the other end. Then there was further delay and the fumbling sound of someone struggling to get the phone to their ear. But finally a weak voice came over the line.

"Aye?" came the faint and plaintive greeting.

"Mr. Murdoch ..."

"Who's speakin'?" The voice was suddenly stronger, interrupting me before I could explain who was speaking. It conveyed a hint of irritation—or was it fear? In any case, it took me back a bit, and I had to pause for a moment to judge how to proceed.

"This is Dr. Shields at the Yale Eye Center. I received your letter and would be happy to see what I can do to help you."

There was another long, uncomfortable pause, and I was trying to think of what to say next when he continued our conversation.

"All right," he replied in a calmer, steady voice, as though to say, "You have stated the facts, now what do you plan to do about it?"

"I would be pleased to see you in my clinic and to try to find what we can do to help you," I proceeded. Again there was no response from my new patient, so I continued. "I can have my office call you to arrange an appointment at your convenience."

"All right," he slowly responded in what seemed to be his standard repartee, although this time with an inflection that suggested approval of my proposal.

"Very well then, and I look forward to meeting you," I concluded. I was about to hang up, not really anticipating any further response, when he surprised me with his own closing remark.

"And I thank ye for callin'," he spoke in an almost friendly tone, and then hung up his phone. It was the first full sentence I had heard him utter, and I felt sure that I detected a faint Irish brogue.

Our appointments scheduler told me that when she had called Mr. Murdoch, he insisted that his appointment with me was quite urgent, so she scheduled it within a few days. I must confess to being a bit apprehensive that day as I prepared to meet him for the first time. Corinne came out of his examination room, having just performed her usual procedure of updating the medical history and checking his vision. She gave me an all-too-knowing smile and shake of her head as though to say, "Okay, pal, let's see what you can do."

As I walked into the dimly lit room, I found a diminutive man who looked older than his seventy-five years sitting in the examination chair. His head was down and turned to one side, revealing shocks of gray hair with faint remnants of red from earlier days. The hair was parted in the middle and came down just over his ears. It was hard to see his face, but it seemed surprisingly smooth, if not a bit pasty, and rather delicate. He wore a starched white shirt that seemed a size too big for his fragile frame and tan cotton trousers that were a bit worn in the knees. His feet, which just reached the footrest, were bare except for a pair of vintage leather sandals. He didn't look up as I approached him, nor when I extended my hand in greeting. But he somewhat reluctantly and reflexively offered me his hand, which was moist, fleshy, and limp. It was clear that there would be no small talk, so I decided to proceed with his history and physical examination.

"So, Mr. Murdoch, can you tell me what the problem seems to be?" I began, in my usual manner of obtaining the medical history.

For the first time, he looked up at me with his pale green eyes that pierced into mine. There was something distinctly discomforting about his gaze, and even more so about his response.

"Well doctor, I'm goin' blind now, aren't I." It was spoken more as a statement than a question, and was delivered in a soft, even monotone that hinted of passive-aggressiveness, as if to say, "You're the doctor—why are you asking me such questions?" And yet there was more in it. On the one hand, it suggested a trace of fatalism, as though he truly believed what he was saying, while at the same time seeming to express the supplication of one truly looking for help.

"We don't know that, Mr. Murdoch, but let's have a good look at your eyes, and then you and I will talk about it and see what we can do."

He gave me the look of "Yeah, I've heard all that before, but do what you have to do." And so I proceeded with the examination. He did have mild cataracts, which had been documented many times before, but they were having little or no effect on his vision, which was almost perfect. The remainder of the examination was completely normal, as I had suspected. However, the pressure in his eyes was a little on the high side of normal, and the appearance of his optic nerves was a bit out of the ordinary, although probably just a variation of normal. Neither finding was really enough to make me consider glaucoma, and I would have written them off as normal in any other patient—but the discoveries gave me an idea for Mr. Murdoch. It would do no good to tell him that he was fine—he had heard that many times before and had consistently rejected it as failure of the medical profession to understand him. I had the advantage over my colleagues of access to all the prior studies that had been obtained, which ruled out nearly every physical cause of visual impairment. I also had the advantage of having learned over the years that we must always treat the whole patient, even when it may not involve any physical part of them—and that there are times when "little white lies" can be strong medicine.

After completing the examination and making some notes in his medical record, I turned on the lights and took a seat on my examination stool beside Mr. Murdoch. I looked straight at him and began my analysis with a look of grave concern.

"Mr. Murdoch, I am afraid we have a serious problem. The pressure in your eyes is higher than I would like to see, and I am concerned that it may be damaging the nerves in the back of your eyes. We call this glaucoma, and it can lead to complete and permanent blindness."

I paused for a moment to see how he would respond to what he had heard so far. He looked up at me, locked his eyes on mine, and gave a slow, knowing nod, as though to say, "I knew there was a problem; now give me the whole story."

"The good news is that we have many ways to treat glaucoma and prevent the blindness. First, we will have to get some more tests, and then decide on the best course for you. But as long as you and I work closely together, you should never go blind."

"All right," he responded, which I interpreted to mean, "Let's get on with it."

I gave him some papers to take to the checkout desk, where they would schedule his return visit in a few weeks for the additional tests and further discussion. I wasn't at all sure that he was buying my pitch, but as he stood up to leave I flattered myself in thinking that I saw a faint smile momentarily cross his lips. As he left the examination room, I patted him gently on the back, and Corinne gave me her quizzical look, as if to say, "What have you done now?" I must confess to feeling a bit smug at that moment, like I had won the first round. But if I had known then what lay ahead, my smugness would have evaporated in humility.

The tests were all normal, as I had suspected. I explained to Mr. Murdoch that this was good news, but that we still faced a serious problem. It would not be necessary to start treatment yet, but we would have to keep a close watch on him. Somewhat to my surprise, he accepted this plan, provided that he could come back frequently, and we agreed on visits every three months. And thus began a doctor-patient relationship that I would never have anticipated.

Over the years, I have been repeatedly reminded of how often our initial impression of a person can prove to be so far off the mark once we come to know them better. More times than not, our mistaken first impression of a person is on the negative side—ill temperament, aloofness, arrogance, boorishness, and so on—only to find that they are really quite tolerable, if not delightful, after we have taken the time to become truly acquainted with them. And so it was with Mr. Murdoch. During the months and years that followed, as we met for his appointments, I marveled at the transition in his personality—or at least in my appreciation of it. He was like an entirely different person. I saw him change from a withdrawn, suspicious, passive-aggressive person to an open, friendly, delightful individual whose company I came to genuinely enjoy, including his charming Irish brogue.

For a person who had once been so reticent to enter into more than the most minimal of conversations, he now surprised me with his willingness to talk and share all his thoughts and feelings. And what he talked about the most was his life's history, which we discussed on nearly every one of his office visits. I learned that he had grown up in Ireland, where he had been an altar boy in the local Catholic church. I learned that he had come to America with his family when he was a youth, and that he still lived—alone now—in the same family home in Connecticut where he had grown up. I learned that he worked part-time as a custodian in the Catholic church of his hometown, and that he had never married (I suspected that I knew the reason for the latter, but we never discussed it). I felt that I had come to know Mr. Murdoch rather well, until the day came when he would remind me of another important lesson—more often than not, we know very little about what is truly inside a person.

Throughout those years, I often felt a bit guilty about "treating" Mr. Murdoch under false pretenses, but I kept reminding myself that I was treating something just as important as a physical disorder. His fear of going blind was just as real to him as it is to a person with a true sight-threatening disease, and he needed someone who would take his fear seriously and do something to help allay that fear. Had I not given him a specific focus for his fear and the assurance that it was being addressed, I suspect he would have simply continued going from one doctor to the next, as his anxiety mounted and his quality of life deteriorated. What I had failed to take into consideration, however, was that his fear of blindness was only one aspect of a much bigger and more serious problem. I guess I had been so blinded by the positive changes in his attitude that I had failed to detect the subtle warning signs that his underlying condition was getting worse—until the day came when everything began to fall apart for him. And even then, our friendly relationship and the trust we seemed to have in each other caused me to initially be deceived into believing his stories.

It began the day he told me that he was leaving his church, because he was being "abused" by the priest.

"Physical abuse?" I asked.

"Nay, 'tis more the verbal," he clarified, although he didn't wish to elaborate. Over the years, he had hinted of abuse in his church back in Ireland, but it was a subject I tried to avoid.

In any case, he felt that he had no choice but to resign his custodial position and transfer membership to another church. This was a time when the news media was replete with stories of sexual abuse in the Catholic Church, especially with young boys, many of whom were now grown men. There was a great deal of soul searching on the part of many who had known about such events, but had failed to take appropriate action. Although I wasn't sure how seriously to take Mr. Murdoch's story, nor how deeply I should get involved in it, I didn't feel that it was right to do nothing.

"Is there someone in your church that you can talk with about this?" I asked.

"Aye, there are abuse counselors in the parish," he replied.

"It seems to me that you should talk with one of them, Mr. Murdoch."

"Aye, I believe that would be wise. And I thank ye for the advice."

And he did follow up on my suggestion and even called me the next day to give me the name and phone number of the counselor, who was in a town some distance from his (he explained that he could no longer trust anyone in his hometown). But there was another problem. It would be hard for him to travel to the counselor's town for a meeting, and it seemed that someone in his hometown was blocking the counselor from coming to see him there. This is when I began to get suspicious of something that I had been missing. I asked Mr. Murdoch if he would mind my calling the counselor, and he actually seemed pleased and relieved to have me do so.

I was able to reach the counselor without difficulty, and we had a pleasant conversation. He had not yet met Mr. Murdoch and knew very little about him, but assured me that there was no one in his hometown who was preventing him from calling on him there and that he would be pleased to do so. We both agreed that all such matters had to be taken very seriously, considering the climate of the times, and the counselor assured me that he would follow up and keep me informed.

At about this time, Mr. Murdoch began feeling the need to come in for office visits more frequently than usual, with numerous phone calls in between. He was obviously becoming increasingly disturbed, and the direction of our conversations was becoming increasingly disturbing to me. The problem in his old church had, in his mind, spread throughout his hometown, and he felt that everyone was talking about him. But what seemed to concern him the most was the effect it was having on my colleagues and me.

"Dr. Shields, I canna' tell ye how sorry I am for causin' all this trouble for ye and the other doctors," he told me one day.

"What trouble is that, Mr. Murdoch?" I asked.

"Everyone in me town is sayin' ugly things about you doctors here at Yale, and I know they are na' true. 'Tis only because they're all out to get me, and I'm so sorry for ye."

"What things are they saying?" I asked with growing concern about the direction of our conversation.

"'Tis not so much ye, but some of your other doctors. They think Dr. [name deleted] is a queer," he responded with grave concern.

That particular colleague of mine had left Yale and moved from Connecticut more than a decade earlier and there was clearly no question regarding his sexual orientation. I finally realized that Mr. Murdoch was suffering from a disorder that I was not qualified to handle. Over the years, I had been aware that he was being seen by several other physicians at Yale in cardiology, gastroenterology, pulmonary disease, and dermatology. Although he carried a long list of diagnoses, I didn't know if any of them were any more real than his tentative diagnosis of glaucoma. But one thing was now clear to me—the physician that Mr. Murdoch needed most right now was a psychiatrist.

I was hesitant to suggest this to Mr. Murdoch for fear of losing his confidence, but in the course of reviewing all the doctors who were seeing him, he volunteered the fact that he had been going to a psychiatrist for many years. It was not a Yale doctor, but a private practitioner near his hometown, which he had not previously shared with me. But there seemed to be some concern about that doctor, because he was in poor health himself and semiretired. He had Mr. Murdoch on a couple of medications and had told him that he did not feel he could go much further in treating him. With Mr. Murdoch's permission, I called the psychiatrist, who confirmed everything that his patient had told me and shared with me his diagnoses, which were much as I had suspected—depression and paranoia. He also said he felt it was time to transfer Mr. Murdoch to the care of another psychiatrist, who could possibly prescribe stronger medications. I offered to help find a psychiatrist affiliated with Yale, which he appreciated, and we promised to keep in touch.

During our increasingly frequent office visits, it was obvious that what Mr. Murdoch needed most was to talk about his social problems, so I would briefly exam his eyes, assure him once again that his "glaucoma" was under control, and then listen. His paranoid ideations were becoming increasingly disconcerting, until one day they reached a crescendo when he announced that he was selling his home—the only home he had known since his childhood.

"But Mr. Murdoch, where will you go?" I asked.

"Aye, 'tis a pity," he responded, accurately reading more into my question than I had expressed in words. "'Tis the home of me family. I will miss it, sure I will. I'll miss me gardens. They were planted by me parents, and I have kept them ever since." He looked off dreamily for a moment, and then his face clouded. "We should never have moved back in town!" he exclaimed with a burst of anger that I had not seen since we first met."

"Back in town?" I asked. "You mean you haven't always lived where you are now?"

"Nay," he responded with a touch of hesitation in his voice. He paused and looked down pensively, as though he was trying to think of what to say next.

"I was but a wee lad when me family came from Ireland," he finally continued, now looking up at nothing in particular, "but I saw the way they treated me father and mother. Shameful, it was. We could nay go on living so. And me father took us to where we would be safe—away from those shameful people. He built the house with his bare hands, he did—board by board, stone by stone."

In all the years that we had talked about his life, Mr. Murdoch had never mentioned any other home than where he was then living, which he referred to as his family home. But then again, many things had changed in the past few months, and I couldn't help but wonder if this was not just another trick that his mind was playing on him. One thing, however, seemed clear—the memory of this long-ago time was bringing him a moment of peace, if not happiness, as I detected a dreamy look in his green eyes and a faint, wistful smile on his lips.

"Aye, they were happy times, they were," he said, seemingly to himself. "They could nay hurt us there. We were happy just being together— improvin' our home, growin' things in our garden, readin' in the evenings by the firelight. On pleasant nights, we would sit outside and enjoy the cool breezes and watch the sun go down. Aye, those were happy times." For several long moments, he appeared to be lost in his reverie, but then it was as though an ominous cloud moved in to again darken his mood, and he quietly shook his head in despair.

"Then came that awful day," he continued, now with a decided tone of anger in his voice. "I say it was them that did it, but me father would never speak of it again. The smoke was still hangin' the day we left our home forever. We found a house on the edge of town—a new town. For a while it was all right. They left us alone. But the town grew up around us, and the people were just like all the others. We never should have come back to town," he repeated to himself.

For the first time since we had met years ago, I saw that mixture of anger and fear with which he had initially greeted me. But I knew his feelings were not directed at me. They were directed at all the people in his hometown, who he was convinced were out to get him—and not only him, but the people he cared about as well. And I knew that this conviction was just as real to him as was his fear of going blind.

"I canna' go on this way," he repeated, now with a softer tone of resignation and despair.

He shook his head slowly, there was a long silence, and I wished I knew what to say.

"But Mr. Murdoch, where *will* you go?" I repeated my question, this time with a more pragmatic intent.

"Well, maybe I'll find a room somewhere, or maybe an apartment," he responded somewhat casually, as though that was one of the lesser of his problems. "I donno' where, but I'll find something. All I know for sure is that I canna' stay in that town nay longer."

I am not sure which of us was lower at that moment. He was obviously in the depths of despair, and I felt terribly inadequate in my ability to help him. I could only suggest that he discuss it with his psychiatrist and that we keep in close touch and maybe schedule our next visit even sooner than normal. He agreed to that, and we shook hands and said good-bye. But as

I watched him walk out the door, I could not have imagined then that it would be the last time I would ever see him in my office.

When he failed to show for his next appointment, we called his home only to learn that the number was no longer in service. Neither the abuse counselor nor his psychiatrist was able to help us. We also learned that he had missed his other medical appointments at Yale, and no one seemed to know how to reach him. We sent letters, hoping that they would be forwarded to his new address, but there was never a response. I considered the possibility that he might no longer be alive and checked the obituaries every day. As weeks drifted into months and then nearly a year passed, I gradually gave up hope that we would ever find him, and he slowly slipped into the recesses of my consciousness—until, that is, the day that I faced my mystery gardener on the mountain ridge.

———

"Mr. Murdoch!" I exclaimed, having partially regained my composure.

"Aye, 'tis me," he responded with a somewhat sheepish smile. "Ye'll pardon me if I do na' rise, but 'tis a slow process at me age."

That comment relieved a bit of the tension, and I smiled as I knelt down beside him. We silently looked at his garden for several long seconds, neither knowing quite what to say. Then it began to dawn on me—the destroyed home, the garden, the overview. Could it possibly be? Had it not all just been in Mr. Murdoch's mind?

"Is this it, Mr. Murdoch?" I finally asked, hoping that my skepticism and incredulity were not too obvious.

He didn't answer, but just kept looking down at his garden. At first I thought he didn't understand my question. But then he slowly looked up and shifted his gaze over to the old chimney. He stared at it for some time, as if he were searching for an answer within it. Then he turned his eyes over toward the old garden plot with further contemplation, and then to the wall beside the ridge. There was a distant pensiveness in his gaze, but also a sense of puzzlement, as though he did not quite know how to answer my question.

"Aye," he finally answered in a rather quiet, uncertain tone, with that dreamy look in his green eyes.

There was something about the nature of his brief response that seemed to caution against further discussion of the topic. And besides, there was another matter that was much more pressing at the moment.

"So, where have you been this past year?" I asked.

Now he turned his gaze directly toward me with a faint, almost apologetic smile.

"Oh, I found me a little apartment," he replied rather nonchalantly. "No one knows me there, and I am quite content, I am. There is a doctor in the town who is takin' care of me, including me glaucoma." He spoke the last phrase looking directly into my eyes with a knowing smile, causing me to wonder if he had known all along.

"But Mr. Murdoch, why did you leave and not let anyone know where you were?" I implored, finally coming to the heart of the matter.

His smile faded to a look of deep gravity, and he turned his head away from me before speaking.

"Och! I could nay let them hurt ye and the other doctors. Them and their vicious rumors." He almost spit the words out with venom.

So that was it. Even in his time of great personal anguish, he had been thinking about the welfare of others. In retrospect, I should have figured it out. But at that moment, I realized how little I truly knew about this man and how many questions remained unanswered. How much of what he had told me over the years was real, and how much of it was only unfounded fears within his troubled mind? How long had he suffered with those fears? Did they go all the way back to his youthful days as an altar boy in Ireland? And did he drift between reality and fantasy? Were there times when he knew that our many visits to manage his "glaucoma" were really to treat something very different?

And what about this old homestead on the mountain ridge? Was it really what he believed it to be? I had heard another version of the home's history that seemed a bit more plausible, and I couldn't help but wonder if this remote place was not just a harbor in his mind from those he feared. His fear that people around him were intent on hurting him and those he cared about seemed to be the overriding negative force in his life, and I had no doubt that it was every bit as real to him as any physical threat. And yet I could not help but marvel at the realization that within his mind, even though it was in agony and twisted by gross distortions of reality, there was still the capacity for charity and genuine concern for the welfare of others.

As quickly as his burst of anger had come did it vanish, and he actually laughed as he turned to me with one last request.

"Well, now, Dr. Shields, will ye be so kind as to help an old man to his feet?"

I returned the laugh and performed his bidding. We stood there for a moment, both of us a bit ill at ease. Then I extended my hand and, unlike that first time we had met, he looked me straight in the eyes and gave me a firm and warm handshake. I asked that he promise to call me if I could ever help him in any way. He just smiled.

I stood there beside the old chimney, as he slowly trudged down the path that led to the easier way off the ridge. I watched him depart until his straw hat and white hair vanished beneath the horizon of the trail. And then I was again all alone in my familiar, tranquil little old spot where I had spent so many pleasant summer moments. Over the years, I had entertained my own fantasies about the history of the old homestead, and now, as I stood there in the quiet solitude of the place, I wondered for a moment if this bizarre encounter had not been just another of them. Mr. Murdoch was getting to me, and I had to laugh at myself. But one thing was clear—this old chimney and its stone companions would forever harbor the most poignant memories for me. I would come back next spring and maybe find my old friend tilling his little garden for another season—or maybe just find his memories.

That winter was an especially harsh one, with days on end of heavy winds, snow, and ice. Spring came later than usual, and I was not able to get out for my initial hike of the new season until early May. But on the first warm weekend of spring, I laced up my hiking boots and headed out for the old country road, past the stone walls, the wild roses, and flowering trees and up the trail toward the mountain ridge. In most years, my first hike of the season would have been along the trail that led to the rocky overlook. But in that new season, something compelled me to take the path up the opposite side of the road toward the old homestead. As I neared it, I sensed that something had changed. The view through the trees that had greeted me for nearly a decade was not there. I quickened my pace and rounded the side path into the clearing—and there it was. Over the winter, the chimney had collapsed and now lay in a pile of stones. The ground around it was strewn with leaves and branches, covering the old garden plot and much of the stone wall and completely obliterating any evidence of Mr. Murdoch's little garden. It wasn't entirely unexpected, but I couldn't help feeling a bit of remorse—and a sense of loss. For a moment, I entertained the idea of trying to clean it up a bit—at least moving some of the larger branches. But as I thought about the history of the land—how life had come and gone in its natural cycles—it seemed best to leave it undisturbed and allow the cycles to continue.

My sense of loss was not just for this little piece of land and its stones. I had the feeling that this final act in the passage of a bygone era might also be an omen for the loss of a friendship. I had not heard from Mr. Murdoch or anything about him over the winter, not since we had shared this very spot six months earlier, and I had a feeling that I would never see him again. In truth, I hoped that he would not return here, since finding the final remnant of the old house in ruins might only have added to the pain in his life. Of course, I did not even know if he was still alive. He would have been in his mid-eighties by then. Maybe he actually did pass during the winter along with the old chimney. In any case, I never saw or heard from him again.

In one sense, old chimneys and old friends are much alike—in the end, their greatest blessings may be the memories they leave us of days gone by. In my mind, the old stone chimney is still standing on that mountain ridge, just as it was for the majority of summers that I visited it during our years in Connecticut. Now, back in North Carolina, I often think of those mountain trails, the country road, and the stone walls, and I am reminded of the sturdy New Englanders who settled the land and who still live there today. Like the durable stones, they too have weathered life's adversities and left us with reminders of the resilience and goodness of the human race. I never knew if Mr. Murdoch passed away during that harsh winter of destruction, but he is surely gone by now with the passage of many more winters. And yet, like the old chimney, his memories still return to me at times, and they bring me a sense of hope, especially when I become discouraged about the way we humans tend to treat each other. They remind me that within the human heart there is still a remarkable capacity, even in the midst of personal suffering, to reach out in charity to those with whom we share this life.

19.

Dave and Iola

One of the most iconic and ubiquitous features of the classic New England village is the venerable Congregational church. For me, the image that evokes the most poignant memories of our days in Connecticut (with the possible exception of a weathered stone wall) is that simple white frame structure with its plain glass windows, standing tall and dignified beside a village green, with its steeple reaching high above the surrounding treetops. Many of these churches claim their descent from the pilgrims and Puritans who came from Europe in the seventeenth Century, bringing with them a simple faith, a fierce independence, and reform movements not only in their religion, but also in such social issues as abolition of slavery and women's suffrage. These early Congregationalists were also responsible for the establishment of many of today's institutions of higher learning, including Yale University.

Although still commonly referred to as Congregational churches, today they represent a denomination of Protestantism called the United Church of Christ, or UCC, which was formed in the 1950s through a merger of several denominations. Sharon and I knew very little about the UCC when we first arrived in Connecticut, but an amusing turn of events led us to eventually join one of the churches. We were temporarily living in a rental house and had been attending a church on the Yale campus, but woke one Sunday morning to find our neighborhood covered in a foot or more of newly fallen snow. The plows had not yet come by, and driving seemed ill-advised. There was a UCC church about a block from our house called Spring Glen Church. We had not paid it much attention—for one thing, it was of newer construction and lacked the historical interest of the older Congregational churches—but it was convenient, and so we decided to give it a try on that snowy morning.

A bit before 11 a.m., the time that we were accustomed to church services beginning, we trudged through the snow and entered the sanctuary to find the service already in progress. As we located some empty seats and settled in, we wondered why people seemed to be staring at us. The answer came less than five minutes later, when the minister gave the benediction and everyone got up to leave. That was when we learned that their service starts at 10 a.m. As we sheepishly turned to leave, less than ten minutes after arriving, we introduced ourselves to the minister, a kind, fatherly gentleman by the name of Bill Hobbs. The following Sunday, we decided to give the church another try—this time for the full hour. As we left the service and again spoke with Reverend Hobbs, I was impressed that he remembered our names. "Well," he said with a twinkle in his eye, "you made quite an impression last week."

Bill and his wife, Barbara, paid us a visit shortly after our embarrassing first encounters, and we quickly became good friends and joined their church. Sadly, however, it was not long after that before Bill developed a serious illness that forced him to resign and eventually took his life. That great loss was partially assuaged by the arrival our new minister, a fine young man who became known as Pastor Andy. He was about the same age as our daughter, Sarah, and he and his wife, Gwen, had two girls who were close in age to our granddaughter, Allison. When Sarah and Allison came up to visit us, the three little girls enjoyed playing together, and we all became good friends. We were very fond of Pastor Andy and enjoyed his timely and provocative sermons. But there was one in particular that will forever stand out in our memories.

It was the first Sunday of a new year, a time designated in the Christian calendar as Epiphany. And so, befitting the season, Andy began his sermon with the story of three men who offered gifts to an infant child. But the men were not magi—they were musicians. And the gifts they offered were not gold, frankincense, and myrrh—they were gifts of music. The child's name was Charles Matthew, and he was the sixth and youngest child of Dave and Iola Brubeck. At the mention of their name, Sharon and I turned to each other and shared knowing smiles. Andy proceeded to explain that Dave Brubeck, the legendary jazz genius, had been on his way to a recording session when their son was born, and between the hospital and recording studio he formulated a piece that would become known as "Charles Matthew Hallelujah." But he needed help completing it, and when he reached the studio, the three other members of the Dave Brubeck Quartet did just that, with their saxophone, bass, and drums. When she heard the piece, Iola said it sounded like each band member was presenting her new baby with a gift of music.

Of course, Andy was using the story that morning as a lead-in to the familiar Biblical story of the three wise men and their gifts to a newborn child, and that led to a discussion of how we too can share gifts with others of what is good, kind, loving, and peaceful in us. It was an appropriate message for a new year, encouraging us all to do a little better in the coming months than we had done in the past. But, I have to confess, what registered the most with me in his sermon was the knowledge and respect that Andy obviously possessed for Dave Brubeck. I would later learn that he was one of Andy's heroes, not only because of his monumental contributions to the world of music, but also for his courageous stands on many controversial social issues. At the conclusion of his sermon, Andy suggested that each of us ponder what we can give in the coming year as he played a recording of Charles Matthew Hallelujah. As the music filled the sanctuary, I closed my eyes and found my mind wandering back to memories of recent times—some good, and some very bad.

———

Western Connecticut, with its proximity to New York City, as well as its pastoral landscapes and charming towns and villages, has long been home to many of the rich and famous. These include captains of industry, world leaders, athletes, and stars from every aspect of entertainment. Since Yale Medical School is one of the major health care providers in the area, I had the privilege of meeting and caring for a few of these special people. But of them all, the one whose relationship I would come to cherish the most was Dave Brubeck. He had been coming to Yale long before my arrival, and I did not even realize he was on our schedule that morning until Ann whispered in my ear that someone very special was in the next room. In the few seconds between reading his name on the medical record and walking into the examination room, my mind raced back through the decades in which his had been a household name. During my college and medical school years in the 1960s, he was already a living legend (eventually to be proclaimed so by the Library of Congress) and a major part of the music that was being enjoyed on campuses around the country and the world. And in the decades and generations that followed, his music and performances never lost their enthusiastic following, as evidenced by his popularity in Pastor Andy's generation.

What impressed me the most as I walked into the examination room that morning was his disarmingly warm friendliness and humility. In the years that followed, I would come to realize that these were attributes that truly exemplified his nature. But at that moment, I was a bit intimidated by both his reputation and his physical stature. Although he was approaching eighty and his dark, wavy hair had turned white, he still stood tall, straight, and dignified, and his signature horn-rimmed glasses framed soft but piercing eyes. We spoke briefly, mostly about his medical history, and then I proceeded with the examination. He had early cataracts, but his vision was still good, and we agreed to meet again in about six months. Ann had remained in the room with us and, not surprisingly, had her camera. So we all posed for a picture, and it was then that I became aware of one more important aspect of Dave's life—the woman beside him. He had introduced me to Iola when I first entered the room, but it was not until she stood beside him in the picture that I began to suspect what her role in their life and in his success might be. And over the years, as I was privileged to become better acquainted with both of them, it was increasingly apparent that the love they had shared for more than six decades was truly at the core of the Dave Brubeck story.

———

An air of excitement filled the old auditorium on the campus of the University of the Pacific. Where generations of students had once sat, the current classes were now joined by their professors, alumni, and friends from the college town of Stockton, California. They had all come to see and hear their university's most celebrated and beloved favorite son, Dave Brubeck. During the question-and-answer portion of the evening, someone from the audience asked him where he had met his wife. In his quiet and unassuming manner, he simply smiled and pointed to a door in the back of the auditorium. "Right there," he said.

It had been several decades earlier in 1940 when, as a young undergraduate in his junior year at what was then called the College of the Pacific, Dave's attention had been drawn to that same door just as an attractive freshman entered the auditorium wearing a stylish dress. Her name was Iola Whitlock, and that stylish dress, as she tells it, was beyond her means at the time, but had fortuitously come to her when the intended recipient failed to claim it. Dave may have been impressed by the dress, but it was obviously the person in it who won the young man's heart. Although a year would pass before their first date, he wasted no time after that and asked her to marry him that same evening. He told her that he could only make one promise—that she would never be bored. Now, after more than seventy years with the world's most celebrated jazz composer and pianist—whose proposal she accepted that night—Iola can look back on the moment and, with a wistful laugh, attest to the veracity of Dave's promise.

Dave and Iola were married in 1942 as war was raging around the world. Shortly before the wedding, Dave enlisted and was soon heading overseas to serve in Patton's Third Army, leaving his young bride behind with the thousands of others who waited and prayed for the safe return of their loved ones. Iola had majored in speech and radio and was able to find work after graduation at a local radio station. The small station had a low-power transmitter, but it was enough for Dave to hear her each evening in his barracks before his unit deployed to Europe. While overseas, he volunteered to play piano for the Red Cross girls, who were there to entertain the troops. He was such a hit that his colonel asked him to form a band. The military was strictly segregated at the time, but because the band was "unauthorized," Dave was able to form one of the first racially integrated bands in the US armed forces. This was among the first of many courageous stands to which Pastor Andy had referred that Dave would take throughout his lifetime.

After the war and further study in music at Mills College, his career began to take off with creation of the Dave Brubeck Quartet, which gained great popularity in nightclubs and on college campuses around the country. However, as in the army, his band included an African American, which created a problem in the fifties and sixties, when integration was still a heated issue. Dave cancelled several concerts during those years and even a television appearance when there was resistance to his integrated band. One of those occasions, which he and Iola later shared with me, occurred in my hometown of Enid, Oklahoma, and had a rather amusing twist. There was only one hotel in the town at that time, and Dave was told by the desk clerk that they could not accommodate his African American band member (although labels were undoubtedly less politically correct in those days). Dave's repeated attempts to achieve a reprieve in their policy were futile, and he and his band mates soon found themselves standing outside the hotel, wondering what to do next, when a Cadillac pulled up. A man stepped out of the car and asked them why they were standing there. Dave explained, and the man asked if they minded if he went in and talked with the hotel folks. Dave said it would be fine with him but didn't really know what more could be said that he had not already tried. The man went in and soon returned to tell the group, "You all can go in now." Dave was amazed and queried what he had said to produce such a miracle, to which the man responded, "I just told them if they didn't want to lose their little old hotel, they'd better let the men stay the night." (He apparently owned the building.)

Our daughter, Sarah, plays the piano and has a gift for composition but never learned to read music, and she was delighted to learn that Dave Brubeck also could not read music in college, despite majoring in the subject. However, his ability with counterpoint and harmony more than compensated for this deficiency, which may have actually been an asset in developing his unique style of music with its unusual time signatures. In 1959, the quartet recorded *Time Out*, an album that included "Take Five" and "Blue Rondo à la Turk," which quickly went gold (and eventually platinum) and was followed by a dizzying number of additional recordings in the 1960s. During that decade, Dave also created and directed an all-jazz format radio station. Disbanding the quartet in the late sixties allowed him to focus more on orchestral and choral works, including oratorios, cantatas, and operas. But he was never far from his beloved jazz, especially when three of his sons joined him in the 1970s. He later reformed his quartet, which was his primary creative outlet, and continued to produce albums and perform in concerts worldwide as accolades and honors came with increasing frequency well into the twenty-first century.

—

My career, in the meantime, was not going nearly so well, as I continued to struggle with the dilemma of how to balance the books in our department at Yale. It was clear that reducing our deficit would require a multipronged approach, including charitable donations. Accordingly, one of my first efforts upon joining the department was to copy what I had learned at Duke by creating an advisory board of influential and well-connected people, many of whom were patients of Yale Eye Center. Some were prominent business people, while others were well known for their role in politics, athletics, and especially entertainment. As I came to know Dave and Iola better during periodic visits for their eye examinations (I was now caring for both of them), I mustered the nerve one day to ask them if they might consider serving on our board. They politely explained that Dave's hectic schedule would likely preclude them from regular attendance at the meetings, but that they would be pleased to do what they could to help. This was truthfully more than I had dared to expect, and to say that I was overwhelmed and grateful would be a gross understatement. It not only bolstered the prestige of our board, but also opened a new level of friendship for me with Dave and Iola—although there would come a time when that friendship would be put to the test.

The advisory board floundered during the first few years, largely from my failure to provide the members with a specific direction and challenge. Then a dynamo of a man, Mr. Rocky Cingari, whose family owns a chain of supermarkets in the area, took over as chairman of the board and helped us identify macular degeneration as the target of our fundraising. This was the turning point. Macular degeneration is a leading cause of visual impairment in the elderly, and we had excellent scientists working in the area but needed more funds to expand our research. It was the perfect focus for a major fundraising effort. We were fortunate to have as our honorary chairperson for the multi-million-dollar campaign Lieutenant Governor M. Jodi Rell, who would later become one of Connecticut's most popular governors. In the spring of that year, our advisory board held a kickoff dinner for the campaign at the Marriott Hotel in Stamford (one of our board members, Mr. Joe Kelly, was regional manager of the Marriott Hotels). It was a small but festive affair with many prominent citizens of the state in attendance, including Lieutenant Governor Rell. But what thrilled me the most was that Dave and Iola were able to join us, and I took great pride in introducing them to the other members of our board.

With that delightful evening behind us, it was now time to get down to the task of raising the money. At our next working meeting, it was proposed that one way to do this would be through a gala dinner event. Joe Kelly kindly offered use of the Stamford Marriott for the venue, and since we had the good fortune of having Dave and Iola on our board, it was suggested that we might feature his quartet as the highlight of the gala and call it "An Evening with Dave Brubeck." As they had warned me, the Brubecks were not able to attend our working meetings because of Dave's incredibly busy touring schedule, and so it befell me to call and ask if he might be willing to help us make our dinner a success. And much as Ronnie Milsap had done in a previous era, Dave graciously agreed to perform with his quartet for the charity event. Unfortunately, however, the challenges that were to follow in organizing the gala were also far too reminiscent of our earlier problems with Ronnie's concert.

The first step, of course, was to pick a date that would work with Dave's schedule, and we finally settled on an evening in the fall of 2001. That was when our problems began. In retrospect, we probably did not give ourselves enough time to do all the necessary planning. The one bright spot for me, however, was our development officer, Mr. Chris Pates, a wonderful young man who immersed himself in every detail of preparing for the gala. But despite his best efforts, early September came and we were nowhere close to being ready. He and I had a rather solemn meeting one afternoon to review the numbers. We only had about one hundred people scheduled to attend—far below our goal. While this wasn't a bad number, it certainly wouldn't qualify as a gala and would not be worthy of a performer with the stature of Dave Brubeck. I must confess to being rather depressed as I contemplated yet another failure in my efforts to find answers for our department. But within a week, all my seemingly big problems were suddenly put into their proper perspective—on the day that the world was forever changed.

I was in the clinic seeing patients. It was a beautiful September morning with a clear blue sky. All the examination rooms were filled, the waiting room was overflowing, and I was already behind schedule and a bit harried when Gail approached me. I had never seen such a serious expression on her face. Had I heard what was happening? My first impulse was that there must be a problem in the department. It seemed that a week rarely went by without some crisis that required my attention. No, the problem was not in the department. That gave me a moment of relief until Gail proceeded to describe a plane hitting the World Trade Center. Well, that was pretty bad, but I envisioned a small, private plane going out of control and was about to go on to my next patient. And the towers had collapsed! Now I noticed that the entire clinic was engulfed in an eerie silence as patients whispered among themselves about the fragmentary information that was coming in from New York City, Washington, D.C., and a field in Pennsylvania.

In the operating room, one of our doctors was just starting his third case of the morning. He was irritated by an undercurrent of whispering that was detracting from the surgery and demanded to know what was going on. As one of the nurses whispered the news to him, hoping the patient would not hear, the surgeon's hands began to shake uncontrollably. He was a skillful surgeon who rarely let anything ruffle him in the operating room. But he was suddenly faced with the unthinkable. His wife and daughter were in New York, where their child attended a special school. He steeled himself to complete the operation, ordered all other cases for the day to be canceled and rushed out of the operating room and to his car. As he approached New York, listening on his radio to the unfolding grim reports, the traffic became increasingly congested and finally came to a halt. Cars were not being allowed to enter the city, and the young surgeon became one of the hundreds of thousands who were trying to find out something about their loved ones in New York. Thankfully, before the day was over, he would be reunited with his family. Thousands of others would not be so fortunate.

The dean called an emergency meeting of the department chairs at noon. He briefed us on the information that was available. The situation in New York was still in such a state of confusion that the extent of the casualties and fatalities was completely unknown. But it was anticipated that the conflagration might lead to thousands of injuries that could overwhelm the ability of even the New York hospital system to cope. Since Yale–New Haven Hospital is within an hour of New York, we were advised to prepare for the possible overflow of casualties. We left the dean's office in shocked silence as we returned to our departments. I briefed our faculty and staff and then began to formulate contingency plans. Very few patients were coming in for their afternoon appointments, and we let most of our staff go home early, since everyone wanted to be with their families as more tragic details continued to unfold on our television screens. I spent the rest of the afternoon trying to make sure that every possible preparation had been made to deal with any trauma cases that might come to our hospital. But as afternoon turned into evening, it became increasingly apparent that we would not be receiving any of the injured victims—because so few had survived.

A few days later, Chris and I again sat solemnly in my office. The unthinkable events of recent days were still casting a cloud of shock and dismay over all of us. But like everyone else, we had to move on with our responsibilities. And for us, that meant deciding what to do about our gala dinner, which was now only a few weeks away. Nothing had improved on that front since our last meeting, and now we had the added detractor of a country in mourning. It also happened to be the three-hundredth anniversary of

Yale University, and plans had been in the works for months to stage an extravagant celebration in the fall. But under the current circumstances, celebration seemed inappropriate, and the school had scaled back the plans for commemoration to a few subdued and dignified observances. And it seemed that we should follow suit by rescheduling our dinner for a better time. I called Dave, who completely agreed with our plan to postpone the evening of his performance. He graciously offered to consider an alternative date sometime in the spring and said that Iola and his scheduling people would help us work that out.

If it can be said that any silver lining could possibly be found in such a horrendous national tragedy, it was that the delay worked wonders in allowing us to better organize our fundraising event. The first step, of course, was to notify all the attendees that the original date had been cancelled. At least we thought we had notified everyone. The day after the dinner was to have been held, I received a rather unpleasant call from a friend who said that he and his wife had dressed up and driven more than an hour to the Marriott, only to learn that the gala had been cancelled. Needless to say, I felt terrible and apologized profusely (and am happy to say that we are still friends). But aside from that glitch, plans for the revised event seemed to be well on track. Each member of the advisory board was carrying out their assigned task admirably—the dinner menu, wine, flowers for the tables, party favors, entertainment during the reception, an elaborate, printed program full of sponsors for the event, and, of course, ticket sales—and it was all under the capable coordination of Chris Pates, who was leaving no stone unturned. The highlight of the gala remained the evening with Dave Brubeck and I knew that this would guarantee success no matter what else happened. In fact, ticket sales were progressing beyond anything we could have dared to hope for, and it looked like we were going to make it this time.

———

The strains of Charles Matthew Hallelujah still rang in my ears as we filed out of church on that special Sunday morning. When we reached Pastor Andy to shake hands, I told him how much we enjoyed his sermon and then could not suppress a smile when I asked if he would like to meet Dave Brubeck. It was the first time I had seen Andy lost for words, and he could only stare at me as though I was making an inappropriate joke. I hastened to explain our plans for the gala and the Dave Brubeck concert and told him that we would be honored to have him and Gwen as our guests. Not surprisingly, he was overwhelmed at the prospect of meeting one of his lifetime heroes, and I left the church that morning feeling very good. Not only had I been able to share something good with a friend (wasn't that the theme of his sermon?), but everything also seemed to be on track for our gala, and I felt confident that it was going to come off without a hitch. I should have known better.

On the morning of the gala, Chris had to go to the hospital emergency room. He had literally given himself an incapacitating headache by working such long hours and worrying about every little detail. But by that afternoon—somewhat heavily drugged—he was at the Marriott making sure that everything was perfect. He worked with the people from Dave's band to set up the sound system and ensured that everything else was in order for the evening concert. Sharon and I came a bit early to check on things, but by then Chris had been there for several hours and there was really nothing left to be done. Thanks to him, it looked like nothing could possibly go wrong. And everything did go smoothly—at first.

As the guests started to arrive in their party finery, the evening truly began to take on a festive air. Our attendance figures had grown to over three hundred—a three-fold increase from the past fall—which would fill the large Marriott ballroom. During the reception in an adjacent room, a chamber orchestra from Yale provided soft background music, and servers passed among the guests with flutes of champagne and hors d'oeuvres. There were many dignitaries in attendance, including Governor Rell and her husband, as well as several other state and municipal officials. There were also luminaries from the sports world, such as Bobby Valentine, then the manager of the New York Mets. But, of course, the greatest excitement occurred when Dave and Iola arrived, and everyone wanted to meet them and have their picture taken together. Off in a corner, I saw Pastor Andy and Gwen standing alone and brought them over to meet the Brubecks. I know it was a seminal moment for Andy to meet one of his heroes, and I think it was also rather special for Dave to meet a minister who had actually incorporated his music into one of his sermons.

Then it was time for everyone to move into the ballroom for dinner. As the guests found their assigned seats, Chris and I shared a smile from across the room—everything was going perfectly. Sharon and I had arranged to sit at the same table with Dave and Iola, but Dave excused himself just as the food was being served to go back stage to be with his band, which was scheduled to come on right after the dessert. And it was about then that the problem began. The advisory board had chosen to present awards to some community leaders who had been especially generous in their philanthropy (we called it the Person of Vision Award). Each recipient had been asked to make a brief acceptance speech—a few minutes each—before the Brubeck concert would begin. Now, in fairness, I have to admit that I was part of the problem. After a word of welcome, I gave a presentation about the impact of eye disease and how the proceeds of the evening would support research in macular degeneration. In retrospect, I should have made it shorter, because all the awardees who followed seemed to take my lead and go beyond their allotted time—way beyond. As the evening dragged on and the dessert plates and coffee cups were cleared and the time for the concert to begin had long since passed, a growing sense of restlessness seemed to pervade the room. I looked over at Chris, whose face was ashen and totally devoid of its earlier mirth—I had no doubt that his headache had returned with a vengeance.

With no end in sight, I finally decided that I had to go back stage and explain the situation to Dave and his band members. As I entered their room, the tension could have been cut with a knife. Four distinguished gentlemen of world-class stature in their profession sat in their tuxedoes looking at me through nonplussed eyes. My discomfort and embarrassment must have been obvious as I poured out my most contrite apologies and assured them that it would not be much longer (or so I desperately prayed). But Dave just laughed and told me not to worry about it. And it was at that moment that I learned another very important character trait of Dave Brubeck. Although he had every reason to be upset, and may have been so inwardly, his outward demeanor was only one of kindness and consideration for the feelings of others. He seemed to sense my anxiety and was trying to put me at ease, which I found to be rather amazing. His warmth and good humor rubbed off on all of us, and I could sense a notable relaxation of tension in the room. Fortunately, it was not too long after that before the acceptance speeches finally came to a merciful end, and the Dave Brubeck Quartet was introduced to a thundering ovation. The band performed as though nothing untoward had happened—truly the magic of classic Brubeck. Despite the late hour, it was obvious that everyone in the ballroom that evening was reveling in the special moment that they were privileged to experience. And I, with a sigh of relief, realized that I had just been privileged to learn yet another special quality of a very special person.

———

In the years that followed, I continued seeing Dave and Iola when they came in for their periodic eye examinations. And between those visits, I followed their remarkable life with growing wonder. Here was a man who was at the top of his profession when I was still a youth. And now, nearly six decades later, as I was beginning to contemplate my retirement, he was still going as strong as ever. His schedule of concerts, award presentations, and other events, both nationally and internationally, would have been enough to challenge a person half his age, and yet he never seemed to lose his youthful enthusiasm for sharing his gifts with others. When once asked, "How long will you keep this up?" he responded, "I guess the answer is as long as I can. As long as you want to listen, I'll keep playing." But as I came to know the two of them better, I became more convinced that my early impression of them had been accurate—one of the essential elements in Dave's professional longevity was Iola.

During the early years, Iola traveled with Dave to some of his concerts, but that changed when their six children began to arrive and it was clear that her primary responsibility was in the home. It is a tribute to Dave and Iola that their family not only remained close and loving, but that four of their sons followed in the family tradition and became professional musicians of note in their own right: Darius on the piano, Chris on bass and trombone, Dan on drums, and youngest son Matthew on cello. Their only daughter, Cathy, also emulated her parents in their passion for humanitarian work. She organized benefit concerts by the quartet and, with her husband, founded the organization called Jazz4Life, dedicated to aiding children in distress in the United States and throughout the world. One of the darkest moments in an otherwise joyous family life was when their second son, Michael, died of a sudden heart attack. Michael loved music of all types but had a special gift for poetry and one Christmas presented his father with a book of his poetry. Dave set one of the poems to a choral piece titled "Once When I Was Very Young."

After their children were all grown, and with a burgeoning number of grandchildren and great-grandchildren, Iola traveled with Dave 100 percent of the time, not only as his closest companion and soul mate, but also as his personal secretary, manager, lyricist, coauthor of many artistic works, and collaborator in establishing educational and humanitarian programs. In the 1960s, the two of them developed a jazz musical, *The Real Ambassadors*, which was based on their experiences during foreign tours on behalf of the U.S. State Department. In more recent times, Iola coauthored with Dave a mini-opera, *Cannery Row Suite*, based on characters in John Steinbeck's American classic, which debuted at the Monterey Jazz Festival in 2006. Iola also contributed a column to every issue of *The Dave Brubeck Quartet Newsletter*, which provided a more personal side to their remarkable story—some of which Dave would be too modest to disclose in full on his own. There was a time in 2007, for example, when Dave injured his left ankle on a piece of iron, threatening to derail completion of a solo piano album, *Indian Summer*, a nostalgic collection of old standards going back to the early days. At Iola's advice to "give it a try," he did indeed complete the work. But it was Iola who told the rest of the story. The piece of iron was a metal bar sticking out from beneath the mattress in their motel room, and the injury was quite nasty, requiring cleaning and treatment at a nearby clinic. Then, after completing the recording and returning home, the pain became so intense that he went to a hospital the following day and was immediately admitted for intravenous antibiotics and surgery for a serious infection. He was hospitalized for six days but given a five-hour pass to go to New York to receive a lifetime achievement award from the London Symphony Orchestra!

Education and social issues seemed to rank right beside their love for music and creativity. Their advancement of civil rights, which had begun during Dave's army tour in World War II and continued into the early days of his career, remained a lifelong passion for them, along with the promotion of international relations and social justice. In the late 1960s, Dave produced *The Gates of Justice*, a cantata that mixed Biblical scripture with the words of Dr. Martin Luther King Jr., and in the early 1970s, he wrote a cantata, entitled *Truth Is Fallen*, in protest to the Vietnam War and dedicated to the memory of those who fell at Kent State and Jackson State. In 2000, the University of the Pacific established the Brubeck Institute in honor of their two distinguished alumni, Dave and Iola. In addition to promoting music, creativity, and education, the institute built on the Brubeck's dedication to social issues that spanned not only civil rights, international relations, and social justice, but also the environment. And it was the latter that Sharon and I were privileged to experience firsthand on another special Sunday morning.

A decade had passed since we first made our inauspicious entrance to Spring Glen Church, and we now felt comfortable and at home as we sat in our pew that morning waiting for the service to begin. A casual perusal of the bulletin suddenly caught my attention when I noted that this was to be a special service devoted to our care of the environment. The opening responsive reading was a series of related statements by prominent individuals such as Rachel Carson: "Those who contemplate the beauty of the earth find reserves of strength that will endure as long as life lasts." But what really woke me up that morning was when I saw what would follow the readings—a cantata entitled *The Earth Is Our Mother* by Dave Brubeck.

In 1854, Chief Seattle spoke to his people about the sacredness of their land, which the president in Washington proposed to buy. His words were later paraphrased by an ecologist at the University of Vermont. "How can you buy or sell the land?" he asked. More than one hundred years later, Dave Brubeck asked the same question through the chief's words. A young man in our church choir sang the solo that morning in his sonorous, baritone voice with an enchanting choral and orchestral accompaniment. "Every part of the earth is sacred to my people," he began against the backdrop of dance-like Native American music. The mood then became more unsettled. "Will you teach your children that the earth is our mother?" In the middle of the cantata, a hymn-like chorale observed that "the earth does not belong to man. Man belongs to the earth. Man is merely a strand in the web of life." The section ended with an anguished cry, envisioning a world we have destroyed. "Where will the eagle be? Gone! The end of living! The beginning of survival!"

In the silent interludes between pieces, I'm sure a pin could have been heard to drop—we were all in the spell of these powerful words and equally powerful music. "When the last Red Man has vanished in the wilderness and his memory is only the shadow of a cloud moving across the prairie, will these shores and forests still be here?" As I listened to the words, I understood why Dave loved them so much that he would enshrine them in a musical forte. He had combined elements of jazz, classical, and Native American musical styles, and although I lacked the knowledge to appreciate it, the experts claimed it incorporated sonorities and textures not often heard in Brubeck's music. All I knew was that the beauty of the music was worthy of the deep significance of the words. "Preserve the land for all children and love it as God loves us all," Chief Seattle said to those who would buy the land. "As we are part of the land, you, too, are part of the land. We are brothers after all."

The music that morning left such an impression on me that I could not resist sending one of the bulletins to Dave and Iola. And I soon received a very thoughtful letter back from Dave in which he expressed his gratitude and his delight that the music had found another receptive audience. And to me that letter revealed yet another of Dave's admirable character traits. Here was a man of international stature, who was showered with awards and who rubbed shoulders with the famous and powerful of the world and yet did not seem to consider himself as superior to others, but treated all people with equal warmth and respect, and who, despite a dauntingly busy schedule, took the time to write a personal letter to me.

As I came to know Dave better, I was increasingly in awe of the recognition he continually received from all sectors of our society. In addition to multiple lifetime achievement awards, honorary degrees, and having been named a living legend by the Library of Congress, he was honored by his country as both a diplomat and an entertainer. In 2008, he was presented the Benjamin Franklin Award for Public Diplomacy by Secretary of State Condoleezza Rice, who noted that she had grown up on the sounds of Dave Brubeck because her dad was his biggest fan. In 2009, Dave and Iola returned to Washington, D.C., to join a small group of distinguished Kennedy Center honorees. Here they met President Barack Obama, who told Dave he attended his concert in Honolulu at age ten and had been a jazz fan ever since. And then he was toasted by former President Bill Clinton. But in his typical humble manner, Dave's later reflection on the experience was "I kept thinking this couldn't be happening to me." And as Iola tells the rest of the story, it almost didn't.

After a lengthy formal luncheon, Dave and Iola had gone back to their hotel room to rest up before dinner at the state department that evening. Dave had stretched out for a nap while Iola began unpacking their suitcases, and that was when she discovered the problem—Dave's valet with all his formal attire was missing. By now it was late Saturday afternoon, and they had to settle for whatever they could get at a local tux rental. The jacket was a size too small, and the shirt fit but had built-in cufflinks that scratched his arms and caused bleeding. The pants were so tight that they could not be buttoned, and there were no suspenders, so they had to be held up by tightening the cummerbund. And it was under these circumstances that Dave received one of his most distinguished awards, but with his typical grace and dignity. It was stories like this that reminded me once again of how fortunate I was to enjoy the friendship of two very special people.

———

It was a perfect New England fall morning. The air was cool and crisp, with only a gentle breeze to ripple the leaves. The sky was a brilliant blue, and the warm sunlight sparkled off the orange, yellow, and red leaves that still clung to their branches. The fallen leaves lay in colorful array along the roadside, covering much of the green grass and snuggling up against the old stone walls. As I left their town of Wilton below and began climbing up the winding road toward the Brubecks' home, I passed neatly maintained farms and stately colonial homes that were set back amid ornamental trees and grassy, leaf-strewn lawns. I had been invited to have lunch with Dave and Iola that day, although the truth is that I sort of invited myself. Their cataracts had progressed over the years and had finally required surgery, which was performed by one of my colleagues, since I was no longer operating. Fortunately, they were both doing well in that regard, but Dave had been having a problem with his heart and explained that it would be difficult for him to keep his scheduled appointment in New Haven for his eye examination. So I offered to come to their home with my little black bag and examine their eyes there. Of course, I had an ulterior motive—I truly cherished their friendship and welcomed any opportunity to spend a little more time with them. In any case, they seemed pleased to accept my offer and graciously invited me to come in time for lunch.

As I rounded the last bend in the road, close to the top of the mountainous drive, my GPS informed me that I had reached my destination. Before me stood an oriental-style wall with an arched entrance that opened into a courtyard with luxurious gardens through which a stone walkway led to a lovely home of understated elegance. A woman opened the front door and escorted me through the house to where Dave and Iola were enjoying the beauty of the day on their deck. Although he would be celebrating his ninetieth Birthday in less than a month, Dave stood as tall, trim, and dignified as ever. He wore dark slacks and a starched white shirt with an open collar, and I had a feeling that this was about as casual as he ever dressed.

The three of us sat around a small table in their sunroom, enjoying the warmth of the light as it filtered through the glass panes. Just beyond the windows, the view dropped down some distance to their beautifully landscaped backyard. Because the house is built on a rather precipitous slope, the front entrance is on the top level, and the rooms gradually step down until they reach the deck and sunroom in the back. Iola pointed out a picturesque brook far below that ran through several pools, which Dave had designed with a series of dams. The brook continued to meander through the backyard before heading on down the mountain slope amid the rocks, grass, flowers, and multicolored trees.

We had a light but delicious lunch of soup and sandwiches, served by the same woman who had met me at the front door. But it was the conversation that was most delightful. With a little encouragement from me, Dave and Iola told stories of their life together with typical humility, good humor, and verve for life. I felt sure they had told the stories hundreds of times before, and yet they seemed to tell them to me with no less enthusiasm. As I sat there enthralled in the moment, I could not help but envision a young couple who had met seventy years earlier in a college auditorium, and whose feelings for each other had only grown dearer with the passage of time. And I couldn't resist asking Iola how it was that their marriage had remained so fresh and strong through all the years. She thought for a moment, and then, with a twinkle in her eye, responded, "Well, he was gone a lot." We all laughed, knowing that any separation for them had only made the heart grow fonder. But one thing was clear. Dave had kept the promise that he had made to her so long ago—Iola was never bored.

We finally moved to another room where the subdued light was more conducive to eye examinations. I took the instruments out of my black bag and proceeded. It only took a few minutes, because they were such cooperative patients and thankfully were both doing very well. We then sat in that room and talked a bit longer until I feared that I might be overstaying my welcome and stood to leave. Iola said good-bye to me there, and Dave walked me to the front door. In fact, he walked with me along the stone steps through their gardens and stood in the courtyard as I backed my car out onto the road. And that image of him standing there, always respectful of the feelings of others, remains in my memory as a reminder of the consummate gentleman who I was so privileged to know.

The sun was now low in the sky and casting long shadows across the road and over the surrounding meadows as I slowly wound my way back down the mountain toward the town in the valley below. As I passed through a quaint village, I glanced across the green and noticed the familiar scene of a simple white frame church standing tall, straight, and dignified. And it once again conjured up images of the sturdy New England people with their strong faith and unflinching devotion to the principles of freedom, justice and equality. And it occurred to me that no one I had ever known epitomized those values more than the two people who I had just left back on the mountain slope. Dave and Iola Brubeck surely fulfilled the admonition that Pastor Andy had given us in his sermon many years earlier—to share our gifts with others. Not only have they given the world a treasure trove of music that will last as long as there are hearts that soar with the sounds of beauty, but they have also inspired thousands of devoted followers with the joy of creativity and instilled in the minds of countless more the values of education, human rights, social justice, and concern for the environment. And yet, for me, they have given something even more—they will forever be a reminder to walk humbly, to respect the dignity and feelings of all people, and to revel in the beauty of each day that we are given to live.

Ω

20.

Susan

She had the voice of a mature woman but the face of a young, innocent child—and a span of thirty years separated the two.

It had indeed been thirty years since a young couple from western North Carolina brought their five-year-old daughter to my office at Duke. The scenario was one with which I had become all too familiar—distraught and anxious parents, a bewildered and frightened child, months and years in happy anticipation of parenthood, the promised joys of a beautiful baby, and the thrill of watching their child grow and flourish and succeed in life.

And then all the hopes are dashed in that moment when they are told "something is wrong." Then come the questions, the denial, the anger. "Why my child?" "What did we do wrong?" "Why can't the doctors do more?" And finally, slowly, the resignation sets in. "Our child needs for us to be strong, and we will do whatever it takes."

And all the while, the little child doesn't understand. For all their short life, they have known the frequent and distressing trips to doctors, where people poke at and shine bright lights into their eyes. And it hurts, and all they want is to be left alone, to hide from the dim world in the comfort of their parents' arms. But maybe they do understand some things. Maybe they sense the anxiety of their young, troubled parents. Or maybe they just feel the added intensity of their love.

Their name was Gantt, and it didn't take long to recognize that Mama Gantt was the driving force of the family. The look in her eyes told you that she was all business—at least on this day. She was full of questions. She wanted to know everything about her daughter's condition. And if anything didn't make sense, she wanted to know why. It was quite apparent that you didn't cross Mama when it came to her family—especially her daughter, Susan.

If Mama Gantt was the pragmatist of the family, Daddy was the romantic dreamer. He stood back with Susan, quietly holding her hand. While Mama's eyes projected resolve and even a hint of anger, his were gentle and accepting, as though to say that everything would be okay. Susan clung to her daddy's leg, and he laid his hand softly on her shoulder with an occasional pat. It was a role that was obviously familiar to both of them: Father trying to reassure his daughter—and maybe himself.

Susan was a precious little girl, petite and demure. She had a sense of serenity about her, with soft brown bangs on her porcelain brow, and eyes like those of her father, that were gentle and trusting. But it was her smile that seemed to tell the story—a sweet, natural smile, which suggested an understanding of the goodness of life, an understanding that was far beyond her years. Her beauty, revealed through that smile, was clearly more than skin-deep. And it was her skin that told of her problem—because Susan had been born with a condition called Sturge-Weber syndrome.

It is one of a group of disorders that involves the skin, the brain, and the eyes. In Susan's condition, an abnormal accumulation of blood vessels, called hemangioma, affected these three parts of her body. On the skin, the hemangioma typically involves one side of the face, creating a bright red birthmark. In some people, the hemangioma is swollen, causing further disfigurement of the face. However, in Susan's case, it was nearly flat, creating only the slightest asymmetry in her smile, which actually added to its beguiling appeal.

In the brain, the condition frequently causes seizure disorders, of which she suffered. But of course, it was the problem with her eyes that had brought Susan to Duke that day. The abnormal blood vessels grow in both the front and back of the eye, leading to increased pressure within the eye and a form of glaucoma that is very difficult to treat. It often cannot be controlled medically, in which case surgery is required. But the surgery is risky, because it will sometimes cause the abnormal vessels to rupture, filling the eye with blood and destroying the last chance for sight. That is why her ophthalmologist back home had referred Susan to Duke.

Despite the family's faithful use of the eye drops and pills for Susan's glaucoma, the pressure remained too high in the affected eye, which would soon be blind if we didn't do something more. We had no choice but to operate. I didn't relish the thought of operating on such a delicate eye. Memories of little Benjamin still troubled my mind and gave me an uneasy foreboding of Susan losing her eye. But we had no choice.

Mama Gantt, of course, wondered why the medicines didn't work and why there weren't others that we could try. She wanted to know why we didn't have a better operation, one that wouldn't be so dangerous for her daughter. In truth, I had the same concerns. But that was the best we could do in those days, and I tried to put a positive face on the situation for the family, despite my own fears and reservations. After many more questions, and when Mama was convinced that she had left no stone unturned, we all agreed to proceed with the surgery.

We were very fortunate. None of the potential complications occurred, and Susan's early postoperative course went smoothly. We kept her in the hospital for five days, until the time came for her to go home. It is amazing how emotionally attached we can become to people in such a short time. As Susan and her parents left that day, it felt like I was saying good-bye to old friends. I would have preferred that she come back for at least a few postoperative visits, but the long drive posed difficulties for the family, and they had a good ophthalmologist at home. So we all agreed that he would resume Susan's care.

Her doctor sent me a few follow-up reports, and I was heartened to learn that she was continuing to do well. Eventually the correspondences stopped, and as the years passed I assumed that I would most likely never see Susan or her family again. I gradually relegated her to that part of my memory where dwell the ships that pass in the night. The Gantts had become for me like one of those fleeting, chance encounters we have with others, where both sides pause briefly and then move on, never to see each other again. Some may be truly fleeting—cars passing at an intersection, driver's eyes locking for a moment, and maybe for that moment wondering who the other is, where she is going, and how her life is. And then the traffic light changes. Other encounters last a bit longer: an introduction at a party, brief small talk, and then they look away, or a stranger in the park with whom you share for a moment the beauty of the day.

For doctors, these encounters can be longer and more meaningful, but they, too, eventually come to an end when the patient returns to their referring physician. All these encounters linger in our memory for a while—and then, like the last afterglow of the day, they fade into darkness.

My memory of Susan might have eventually gone the usual way of life's brief encounters had it not been for a picture. Before her surgery, our photographer had taken a picture of Susan, which clearly showed the red birthmark down the left side of her face. Because it provided such a classic example of Sturge-Weber syndrome, I used it in many lectures over the years and in each edition of my textbook. As a result, I never forgot Susan, although it was more by her picture that I came to remember her than by the brief moment when our paths had crossed.

It was and remains a very special picture to me. While it provided a classic example of the disease that Susan bore, it spoke of much more to me. The five-year-old in the picture was a beautiful little girl, with sparkling eyes that radiated the same joys of life and hope for the future as any young person. But it was that smile of hers which captivated me. In a way, it haunted me. It had the simplicity and innocence of a child, but with something much deeper—a maturity, perhaps, and a sense of character that said, "Here is a special person who is going to do special things with her life."

Many times over the years, in fact over the decades, as I looked at that picture and her smile, I wondered where she was and who or what she had become. Had she overcome the stigma of her birthmark and her seizures to move on in her life and find happiness and success? Had the maturity and character that I saw in her youthful smile blossomed into a woman who was making a difference in her world? Or had the burden of her chronic infirmities caused her to become withdrawn and cynical about life? I didn't really expect to ever know the answers, but the phone call to my office at Yale that early fall afternoon was about to bring back a flood of memories and the answers to many questions.

———

"Hello, Dr. Shields, this is Susan Gantt. Well, actually, it's Susan Griffie. I'm married now."

Susan Gantt? Could it really be? The picture of a five-year-old girl immediately came to my mind. But this was the voice of a grown woman with a beautiful southern accent. Talk about a voice out of the past—thirty years to be exact.

"Are you still there?" she asked. My surprise had left me momentarily speechless.

"Oh ... ah, y-yes! Yes, I'm here, Susan. You just took me by such surprise."

"I'll bet I did. It's been a long time. Do you remember me?"

"It sure has been a long time. And, yes, I do indeed remember you."

Her photograph had immediately flashed before me, and I found myself marveling that the picture now had a voice after all these years. So many questions flooded my mind. But at that moment, I guess I was mainly wondering why she was calling after so many years.

"You're probably wondering why I called," she said, as though reading my mind.

"Well, yes, but I'm so glad you did," I hurriedly replied, beginning to regain my senses.

"Well, I wanted to know what kind of operation you did on my eye. I give motivational talks about how I have learned to cope with life's problems and I like to be accurate with my story. Did I tell you that I have a son? Well, I do. His name is Christopher. He's so cute, but he's a little overweight, and the kids at school tease him about it. You know how kids can be. Well, anyway, I've been able to help him, because I know what it's like to be teased. I think God does everything for a purpose, don't you? He gave me my handicap so I can understand how to help other people. And that's what I want to do with my life."

So I had been right about the depth of character that I had seen in Susan's smile all those years! I guess I wasn't surprised, but I felt a warm sense of satisfaction. The little girl whom I had contemplated for thirty years had indeed grown into a special woman. I don't recall that I ever answered her question about the surgery, and I'm not sure that she was really interested, but from that moment on, a new friendship blossomed. No longer were we a doctor and his little patient—we were two adults, bonded by something from their distant past. I told her about the picture that I had kept all those years and had used in my lectures and textbook. She seemed pleased, and we ended our conversation with my promise to send her a copy of the latest edition of the book. And she responded with the sweetest letter.

> Dear Dr. Shields,
>
> I am writing to you today because I want you to know that I received your wonderful book yesterday. I was so shocked that you sent me a book! Your beautiful, wonderful book. I am so very grateful and I thank you ever so much.
>
> I don't usually hand write letters anymore because of my penmanship, or lack of, but it just seemed like

the thing to do at the time. Normally, I would be on a computer, typing.

Words can't express how I appreciate what you have done for me as a friend and as a doctor. I believe you were a master vessel as God is our great Physician.

I am sending you a few pictures of myself and my family. I thought you might want to see what I look like now.

Susan

She had enclosed two pictures of herself: one with her makeup, which covered the birthmark, and one without. I think I liked the natural one best, because it was more like the Susan I had known for the past thirty years in that childhood photograph. Either way, she was still pretty, with the same sparkling eyes and beguiling smile, which had matured over the years but still expressed a youthful optimism for the good that life has to offer.

We exchanged Christmas cards that year and then began exchanging e-mails early in the new year, although she proved to be much better about it than me and provided the bulk of our correspondence. Her e-mails had a folksy and humorous touch that often made me laugh. It was like we had been friends forever.

It has been quite a while since I have heard from you. I received your Christmas card. It was so nice of you to send it. Did you get mine? I never heard from you. Usually you write back ... I sent you some pictures. You must be pretty busy, huh? ... Is the weather nice there? Or is it still cold?

Her chastisement for my delinquency in writing amused me and brought back visions of Mama Gantt keeping me in line. I couldn't help but wonder if Susan had acquired that same strength of character that I had seen in her mother. In any case, I responded promptly and promised to do better in the future with my correspondence. And her entertaining e-mails kept coming.

I have been planting flowers. Christopher planted SUNFLOWER SEEDS in my BACKYARD. I hate sunflowers! But what can you say to a seven-year-old, especially when he already planted them? I figured they wouldn't come up anyway. I was wrong. They came up just as pretty as you please! If I had planted seeds, they would have rotted! You understand I am laughing as I type this, don't you?

Yes, I understood. And I was learning more about this complex person. She obviously had a good sense of humor. And she loved the many beautiful things in her life. I suspect that she even liked sunflowers.

I love it when it's warm and sunny. I planted my flowers. They are coming up nicely. The old-fashioned kind like my grandmother had. Sweet Williams, sweet peas, Flox, hollyock—I guess I spelled that right? HAH! Anyway, they are multicolored. Flowers are my delight in summer.

What I enjoyed most in her e-mails was the expression of concern that she obviously had for others. This seemed to further support my impression of the special person I had seen in her smile over the years, and I was anxious to learn more about how she was incorporating her compassion into the motivational talks.

I don't know how the elderly and poorest of people get their medicine. I truly believe they either go hungry or buy their medicine. And I believe they choose food over their medicine. Because on their income there is no possible way they can have both. We are a poverty-stricken nation, and most just look away from it. It hurts my heart. But I am only one person. Oh well, so much for my sob story. Have a wonderful day.

She also had a pragmatic side that caused her to worry about the daily frustrations of her own life, and yet she was able to keep things in perspective and laugh at herself and remember the source of her blessings.

Scott [her husband] and I are working on trying to get my kitchen remodeled ... I wish I could just walk out of it and buy a new one! But I am blessed and have to be grateful for what God has given me. Things can always be worse. I am just glad my house is brick. Well, enough complaining for me. I hope you have a super great day and a little extra sunshine in your day!

She always brought sunshine into my life with her precious e-mails. In fact, sometimes they were almost too much for me.

My heart is so full of special places for special people. I suppose you will always be one of those people. Though I gave my heart first to Jesus Christ as a girl, then to my husband. These are the loves of my life. God has blessed me so. But as a child, I will always remember a little girl in a BIG place with a kind doctor. One never forgets those things. I hope in all your years of being a doctor, you got a blessing out of your work, because it seems to me you had your work cut out for you. I hope you are blessed.

At that moment, I felt very blessed to enjoy such a special friendship. In fact, our e-mail correspondence had only heightened my desire to get to know Susan better, and I decided that I should do something about it. Sharon and I had begun planning our annual summer trip to North Carolina and our traditional week at the beach with all our family. I told Susan that I hoped we could get together during that time. She embraced the idea, but had her own family plans for the beach to deal with first.

The days are longer and so sunny here. I am finishing up my laundry as I type, because we are leaving for Myrtle Beach Sunday morning. Scott and I are taking two of my sister's children, so we'll have quite a handful! Christopher will be eight years old tomorrow. I can't believe how fast the years go by.

Unfortunately, her time at the beach proved not to be very relaxing. But what concerned me most was that her seizures were giving her trouble, which she hadn't shared with me before. And yet, despite all her problems, she seemed to have a remarkable capacity for taking everything in stride.

We are back from the beach. We got back last Sunday. I got back from a vacation and now I need another! I have never taken three children with me before ... We got there on Sunday, and it rained until Wednesday. But we found things to do ... On the way home, I had a seizure, and then on Tuesday and Thursday as well. Oh well, enough about me ... How are things your way?

By this time, our family was at the beach, and I was wondering if my scheduled visit with Susan was still realistic, considering her medical condition. But she seemed to have long since learned to take all her problems in stride and wouldn't hear of changing our plans. Her only concern was that she didn't know how to direct me to her home.

I am looking forward to you coming. I am horrible about giving directions. You will have to get the directions from Scott. I will let him give you directions. Perhaps if you call sometime, or even if you don't want to call, you can get Scott to fax you the directions, but you could probably do better talking. I don't know. Let me know one way or the other. I am so looking forward to seeing you.

Scott and I spoke, and he gave me good directions. And so I began my much-anticipated journey. It was a warm summer morning as I left the family at Sarah's home and headed out under an overcast sky, with low-lying mist still clinging to the fields beside the road. There were very few cars out that morning, and I felt relaxed and contemplative as I drove down the highway. It had been nearly a year since Susan's phone call. Our correspondence since then had sent mixed messages as to the person my little patient had grown up to be, and I was wondering whom I was really going to meet. Had my earlier impressions of her been correct? Would that smile still be there, and had I interpreted it accurately? I especially wondered about her motivational speaking. She had never mentioned it again since our initial phone conversation. Where did she give her talks? And what was her message? Well, I would find out soon enough—and that thought seemed to give me a strange sense of unease.

Scott's directions were excellent. I only made one wrong turn and arrived at her home just before the noon hour, right on schedule. She lived in a neat little red brick home, with a well-kept yard and a carport full of the things that indicated a young boy lived there. Following Susan's instructions, I entered through the carport and knocked on the side door.

318

I felt a bit apprehensive as I waited for the door to open. But in a moment, it did, and there she was—after thirty-one years.

For an instant, I stood there trying to reconcile the little girl I had known for the past thirty-one years, largely through a single photograph, with the young woman who now stood before me. Her carefully applied makeup concealed the birthmark, and the only evidence that I could connect with the past was the slight asymmetry of her smile. She was as beautiful in womanhood and she had been in childhood.

"Dr. Shields, I can't believe you're here!"

"Hi, Susan."

Then came the inevitable moment of awkward silence as we both wondered whether we should shake hands, hug, kiss, or just smile at each other.

"Let's hug," I finally suggested. And we did. And then we laughed. And the ice was broken.

Susan was dressed in a neat black outfit, probably her Sunday best. In my slacks and sport shirt, I wondered if I should have dressed up more. She was probably wondering if she should have dressed down more. But it didn't really matter.

She showed me her new kitchen and her flowers and pictures of Christopher, and then the conversation turned to lunch. We both agreed that it should be someplace quiet where we could talk. Since Susan didn't drive because of her seizures, her knowledge of getting around town was limited, but Scott had given her directions to an Italian restaurant. And so we headed out.

Our drive to the restaurant became just the first of many experiences that the day held in store. To my amusement, Susan seemed perplexed that I kept asking her when to turn or stay straight. Soon I grasped that she wasn't quite sure either.

"Do you know what street it's on?" I finally asked.

"No. But Scott said to turn right at the police station."

"Do you know where the police station is?" I inquired.

"It's around here," she replied, looking in all directions. After driving in circles for a few minutes, we finally located the police station.

"So, where from here?" I asked.

"I don't know. You're on the wrong side of it." I looked at her with a quizzical smile. "Scott told me how to go from the street over there."

So we got on the right street.

"You're going the wrong direction," she informed me, with a hint of frustration in her voice.

I turned into a drive to get us headed properly and tried to suppress my laughter. But soon we were both laughing, and before long we arrived at the restaurant.

As I opened her door, we saw a little green frog just inside the door-frame of my car. Susan insisted that we get it out of the parking lot, lest it be injured. I tried to pick it up, but every time I did, it jumped and I jumped and Susan laughed. Then she tried, and soon we were both down on our knees trying to catch the little green guy, to the puzzled glances of other diners who were crossing the parking lot. The frog finally got away from us and hopped beneath another car, and we gave up our quest.

Inside the restaurant, Susan told the hostess that we wanted the quietest table, and we were taken to a nice little corner. She then asked the hostess to turn down the overhead music, which, somewhat to my surprise, was done.

I seemed to be learning many things about Susan—her frustration when things didn't go as planned, her compassion for a little frog (her father's influence?), and her assertiveness in letting her wishes be known (Mama Gantt?). I wondered what else would be revealed about her that afternoon, and it wasn't long before I learned that this was only the beginning. She was willing to talk, and for nearly two hours, over our lunch, her life unfolded before me.

—

"Well, I guess you want to know everything," she began.

I smiled and nodded across my salad.

"Okay. Well, let's see. I was born in this little town called Forest City, which isn't far from here, near the mountains. Everything was fine at first. I guess I was too young to know that I was different from the other kids, or just didn't care. It was mostly me and my mama and daddy and my older sister, Stephanie. I got along okay in school for the first three years. But then, just before the fourth grade, we moved to a new town, and that's when the trouble started.

"This new town was cliquish and not accepting if you hadn't been born there. So I never did feel like I belonged. In the fourth grade, there was this girl who was sick a lot. I don't know what her problem was, but the other kids were so mean to her. When the teacher left the room, they would tease her until she cried, and then they would laugh and seem so proud of themselves. I wanted to make them stop, but what could I do?

"The next year, the sick girl didn't come back. So now I became the target of the kids' abuse. They called me all sorts of ugly names when the teacher was out of the room, like 'red face' and 'two-tone' and 'seizure girl.' They just wouldn't let up. I tried to be brave and ignore them, but I eventually broke down crying, which of course is just what they wanted. And they played such mean tricks on me. Like one time they took all the screws out of my desk, so it collapsed when I sat down. Another time, they stole some candy and put it in my desk and then accused me of stealing it. And the saddest thing was that the teacher never believed me or stood up for me. She made me stand in front of the class and eat the candy she found in my desk. And then she forced me to eat a whole bag of candy, which almost choked me."

This must have been painful for Susan to relate—it was certainly painful for me to hear. But it wasn't entirely unexpected, and I was looking forward to the part where her life began to take a turn toward the positive.

"How did your parents deal with your problems at school?" I interjected.

"Mama was tough."

"Tough?" I asked.

"She sure stood up for what she believed. She would go to school and bawl out the teachers for the way they treated me."

"And your father?"

"Oh, Daddy was real different," she laughed. "He told me I should make allowances for other people's behavior. To try to understand them and forgive them. He told me that I should be better than them."

We sat quietly for a while as we ate our lunches, and she seemed to be thinking about where to resume her story.

"My childhood was awfully unhappy. I never really had any friends. But my senior year in high school was the worst year ever. I gained weight and went up to 155 pounds. That's a lot for someone who is only five foot one. I was sick a lot that year and had a lot of seizures at school, and I was ridiculed for it. In a way, though, it was my best year. I had had enough of it all. My meds were changed, and I saw a difference in myself. I lost some weight, and that made me want to lose more. I changed my diet habits. I cut everything I ate in half. I wouldn't eat bread or anything sweet. This almost killed me, because I was a sweet freak! I loved sweets and candy. But I wouldn't touch it, even if it was offered to me. I wouldn't even chew a piece of chewing gum! I drank only grapefruit juice. I was so determined to lose weight. And you know what? By that spring, I had lost thirty-two pounds. And by July, I had lost fifty-five pounds!"

Now the story was heading where I had hoped it would. Her strength of character was beginning to show, and I couldn't wait to hear how she used it in her motivational speeches. She had obviously maintained her weight over the years and seemed proud of it. And she must have seen the delight in my face at the positive turn of her story, because she continued in that vein.

"I used to sing in our church choir. When I was fifteen, the choir director noticed that I had a pretty good voice, so he arranged for me to sing a duet in a church program with this boy who was a little older than me and sang real good. Mama refused to come to the program. She didn't want to be embarrassed. 'I don't want Susan to be laughed at again,' she protested. But, of course, Daddy believed in me and couldn't wait to hear me perform. And Mama reluctantly came with him. And you know what? Everyone at the program couldn't believe how well I sang! Even Mama was proud. That was the beginning of one of my greatest joys to this day. Daddy became my agent, and for the next few years, I sang solos all over the place. It was wonderful!"

"So," I ventured to ask, hoping to keep her moving toward her motivational secrets, "are you more your mother's girl or your father's?"

She thought for a while and then said, "My Daddy."

But I wasn't so sure. She clearly had the compassion and gentleness of her father. She had his tendency toward the dreamer, the philosopher. But she also had her mother's pragmatism and strength—and perhaps anger—and I suppose she needed that to make it in the world in which she had found herself. I just smiled and looked into her eyes.

"Yeah, and Mama too," she added with a sly smile, as though she were reading my mind.

"You have been fortunate to have such supportive parents," I offered.

She thought about that for a moment, and then her countenance fell to a frown. "But even they don't take me seriously."

I was sorry to see the story resuming a negative direction, but had to ask what she meant about her parents.

"Well, for one thing, I really wanted to go to college. You know, that one over in the mountains."

"Appalachian State?"

"That's it! But they wouldn't let me go. They said it wasn't practical, because I couldn't drive. But freshmen weren't allowed to have cars on campus anyway. I don't know. And then there was the music. Daddy just dropped it after I graduated from high school. I never knew why."

We had finished our lunch. The table had been cleared, and I was starting to get concerned again about the course that Susan's story was taking. She obviously had more to tell, and I wanted to hear it all, so I suggested that we go back to her house and continue our visit there.

Driving back to the house, we were silent for quite a while. I suspect that both of us were thinking about what direction our conversation should take. My burning question centered on her motivational talks and how she had turned a tragic childhood into something positive that gave guidance and hope for her listeners. So far, there had been no mention of this—nothing had been said about motivational speeches since our first conversation nearly a year ago. So, with some hesitation, I finally broke the silence.

"Susan, what about your motivational talks?"

There was another long silence as she was obviously thinking about what to say.

"I visited my high school awhile back," she began slowly, with a touch of pain in her voice. "They acted happy to see me, especially the guidance counselor. But she didn't seem very enthusiastic about my ideas to help other students. I suggested that we start a Sturge-Weber support group. She would agree with me up to a point and then always end with 'but ...'" Then came another thoughtful silence.

"So you haven't been able to give your motivational talks?" I asked.

"Well, I gave a testimonial in church once. But that isn't the same. I try to help Christopher. Maybe I told you he is a little overweight, and the kids tease him about it. I told him what Daddy told me about trying to understand and forgive people and to be strong. But I don't know."

Clear frustration put an edge in her voice and maybe a touch of anger, and for a while we again drove in silence.

"No, I've never actually done a motivational talk," she finally continued. "But I hunger to—to make a difference in the lives of other people. I want so much to tell my story, because maybe it would help someone else." There was another long pause. "But nobody seems to want to listen."

Just then, we reached her home and drove silently into the driveway. When we got inside, she suggested that we sit in their living room to talk.

"So, Susan," I said after we were comfortably seated, "why don't we pretend that I am your audience, and you tell me what you would say in your motivational talk? I really do want to hear."

"You really do?" she asked.

I nodded. Although it had yet to be fully revealed, I remained confident, or at least hopeful, that I had not been wrong about the depth of character and the special person that I had seen for the past thirty-one years in that picture and in her smile. But she didn't seem to know where to begin.

"Well, I would begin by singing," she finally said after a thoughtful pause.

"Would you sing for me?" I asked.

"Do you really want to hear me sing?"

"I would love to."

"Well, you'll have to come into our music room, 'cause that's where our tape recorder is."

And so we moved to the music room because, as she explained, she needed the tapes for her accompaniment. As I settled down into a large leather easy chair, Susan selected the tape and announced that her first song was called "The Galilean." With her head raised and eyes closed, she lifted her hands with palms toward heaven and sang as though I was an audience of thousands. It was beautiful and moving, and I couldn't resist applauding as her final note drifted away.

She seemed pleased and announced that her next song was very special to her. She said it was her song. I guess she meant it was her signature song. It was titled "Hurt By Hurt" and tells how we build walls around ourselves, one hurt at a time, and how Christ can lead us to tear down those walls, one at a time. She sang it with the feeling that can only come from one who has truly lived with the hurts and the walls and the spiritual conviction to overcome them. It gave me goose bumps.

"Gosh, Susan," I finally said, after a respectful pause, "that is as good as any motivational talk I ever heard. Maybe you have been speaking to others through your music without realizing it."

But instead of a happy response to my suggestion, her countenance again fell, and she just shook her head. "Yeah, but nobody even wants to hear me sing."

"Don't you sing in church?" I almost pleaded as I sensed another door closing on my hopes for her.

"No," she said, with a sad expression. "We have a spiritual group instead of a choir, and they do all the singing, and I'm not part of it. I do teach Sunday school class, though. I've been doing that for fifteen years. This fall, I'll be teaching the fifth grade."

I was struck by the irony—it was in the fifth grade that she first encountered personally the indifference and cruelty that people of all ages can have toward the burdens that others must bear. Maybe I could dig out something here that would provide the answer—and the silver lining—to Susan's story. So I took one last chance.

"Pretend that I'm your class," I ventured. "What would you say?"

Susan gave the question considerable thought. Then, with a deep breath and an expression of firm resolve, she began. "I would tell you to be yourself. To believe in yourself. To be strong." (Her mother?) "To be forgiving and understanding." (Her father.) "To never let go of your faith. To remember that you are never alone." (Christ in her life.) "I would tell you not to judge others by first impressions—not by the outside. Take time to find out what is on the inside, because that is what counts."

Listening to Susan's beautiful words, I could not help thinking about the children in her Sunday school classes over the years. How many of them had something about themselves that they didn't like? How many of them thought they were too tall, too short, too fat, or too skinny or hated their red hair or freckles? What if just one of them had heard Susan's message and today felt better about who they are and accepted others for who they are? And that made me wonder how often we each touch the life of another person in something we say or do—something that may affect someone or even alter the course of that person's life—without ever realizing the influence that we have had.

But my thoughts apparently hadn't reached Susan; she remained dejected, and a somber mood clouded the room. She was still obviously frustrated and angry—no longer because of the taunting of her childhood, but now because of her inability to tell her story as an adult, which she yearned to do. And yet I felt that she just didn't realize how many lives she might have already touched.

"Susan," I began, hesitantly, "I wonder if maybe you're not giving yourself the credit you deserve. I think you really have a beautiful message and I suspect that more people have heard it than you may realize. Just think, if only one child in your classes over the years has taken your words to heart, you may have made their life better. And you may have touched the life of someone you never even met by the way your students are kinder to that person."

There was a long silence. She seemed to be in deep thought, and I was worrying that I might have said too much. But then she began to tell me one more story.

"I taught a vacation Bible school class once. It was a real large group of children from the first to the fourth grade. I like to use humor and different approaches in my teaching, and this one day I did something very different. I didn't put on any makeup and I wore old, torn clothes. When the children came into the room, I was at the front of the class, with my back to them. After they were seated, I turned around, and they all gasped. I asked them what they thought had happened to me. A lot of hands went up, and they all thought that somebody had beaten me up. 'How did it happen?' they wanted to know. I told them I was a homeless person and slept in the park last night. They were horrified! Then I laughed and said, 'Just kidding! I didn't sleep in the park last night, and I wasn't beaten up. This is the way I was born. It's a birthmark.'

"Well, you can imagine the nervous laughter. It took them a while to grasp what had just happened. Then I explained the reason for what I had done—that we shouldn't judge people by first impressions, by the outside. We should take time to look at what is inside. That's what counts. God doesn't make mistakes. He has a plan and purpose for all of us. We only have to accept who we are and what we are given and make the most of it. And we should look at other people the same way."

Susan gave a slow, luxurious sigh. Gazing off somewhere into the distance, she seemed to be in deep, contented thought. And then, slowly but undeniably, I saw it appear. There it was—what I had looked at through all those years and wondered about its meaning. It was still there, and it was true.

The smile.

Ω

21.

Becky and Roger

Those annoying strings of callback messages, which had once greeted me at the end of each clinic day, were now only distant memories—a reminder of how far communication technology had come in my four decades of practice at Duke and Yale. The frustration of the time-consuming "phone tag" that followed, as the caller and I went back and forth trying to reach each other at a mutually convenient time, should have been enough to make me jump on the bandwagon of any newer and better way of communicating. And yet, for some reason, I was (and still am) always one of the last to embrace the latest technology, only recognizing woefully behind the curve how much it improves our lives. I was among the last of my colleagues and friends, for example, to own a cell phone, although now I cannot imagine how I ever got along without it. But even cell phones are limited by the necessity of connecting with someone on the other end of the virtual line (that is if you are as old-fashioned as me in using the cell phone—or whatever it is called today—as a phone), and the ability to communicate without involving the human voice has, I suppose, been the greatest advance in communication technology.

The first liberation from the telephone tag was, of course, the facsimile, which soon became known as the fax. Again, it took me longer than most to recognize the value that this technology provided in being able to communicate almost instantly with a colleague. But when Robin and I finally figured out how to use it efficiently, I was convinced that we had reached the zenith of communication technology and frankly felt a bit smug to have mastered it. Not long after that, however, I was at a meeting, sitting at a table with colleagues from around the country, talking about the best way to continue our communication after we returned home, and I was rather proud to agree that the fax was our best bet. And then someone at the table said the word— "e-mail." I had never heard of such a thing and remember being a bit irritated that some newfangled idea was being introduced just when I was getting comfortable with the existing technology, which seemed at the time to be good enough. My first thought was to dismiss it as a passing fancy that I doubted would ever make prime time—so much for my prognostic talents.

At the time, I did not even have a computer in my office. We had bought a primitive one for Sarah and John to use for games, which I felt was the extent of its value. Robin had a computer at her desk, and when we eventually and reluctantly began to utilize e-mail for some communication, I would dictate my messages for her to send out, and she would give me hard copies of the messages we received. During my final years at Duke, I finally obtained an office computer, but used it sparingly until I moved to Yale, where I no longer had Robin's assistance (she was surprised to learn that I was now actually sending and receiving e-mail messages all by myself). And, as with the cell phone and fax, it was not long before I wondered how I ever functioned without it. I had, at last, entered the cyber age and joined the throngs in cursing e-mail each day as a double-edged sword. It was great to have such a quick way to send a message, no longer having to play phone tag, but it was also a nuisance to sit in front of the computer for an hour or more every day, going through the long list of messages.

I must confess that e-mail is about as far as I ever got with electronic communications. Social media—Facebook, YouTube, Twitter, and the like—were only vaguely understood concepts to me. I tried to rationalize this by claiming they were too impersonal and that I preferred communicating with my friends one-on-one. But the truth is that I just never cared to make the effort to learn all the newfangled things. With time, however, I did come to appreciate the profound impact that such electronic networking could have on our global society. It was brought home most compellingly in 2011 with what became known as the "Arab Spring," which would have such a dramatic effect on much of the Middle East by the end of that year. And although those were the types of events we heard about most often on the news, I also came to appreciate how equally powerful social networking could be for individual interactions. And the most poignant illustration of this for me was when I had the privilege of meeting a remarkable couple whom I came to know as Becky and Roger.

—

Word of her impending arrival was greeted with a mix of emotions. It had certainly not been planned. In fact, it was a bit of an embarrassment, especially for her mother, who was closer in age to the grandmothers of the women with whom she sat waiting at the obstetrics clinic. She and her husband were both professors at the local university, and the years of pursuing their academic careers had delayed their marriage and their family. She was in her early thirties when their first child was born, a boy, and, before long, a second son arrived. But that was nearly a decade ago, and she had long since given up on her dream of having a little girl—until the day she visited her family doctor. The embarrassment phase eventually passed and was replaced with worry about the health of her child that was soon to be. But on the day she was told that she had a healthy baby girl, her only emotion was a giddy joy as she began to think about combing hair and ribbons and frilly dresses.

Her father, Professor Djalal, had been more sanguine from the outset, although his colleagues at the university noticed that he seemed to walk around with a perpetual faint smile on his face during those months of anticipation. He was a man of faith and always seemed to believe that everything happened for a reason and would eventually work out for the best. He was also in the minority in his particular faith. Indonesia is nearly 90 percent Islamic, and his family was Christian, a religion which accounts for less than 10 percent of the country's population. His family had been of the protestant faith for many generations since missionaries had come to the islands. It had been a tradition in the family to select biblical names for their children, and their two sons were named Daniel and Joseph. So when the new arrival came home, her father announced that she would be called Rebekah. And she soon became known as Becky.

As for the boys, the thought of having a baby sister in their house left them nonplussed, to say the least. Growing up in a Jakarta suburb near the coast and its equatorial climate, their leisure time consisted year-round of swimming, fishing, and all the activities that make up the typical life of a boy. At home, with three males in the house and a mother and wife who catered to their every need, it was truly a boy's paradise. What good could come from having a little girl hanging around? They would probably have to suffer the indignities of pink stuff and silly dresses and yucky smells. That sentiment lasted for a brief spell after Becky and her mother came home from the hospital, during which time the boys did their best to ignore their little sister. It was not long, however, before the power of feminine appeal in the form of a cuddly infant began to work its magic on the brothers. She had a round, sweet face with the typical soft brown Javanese complexion. Her large, dark eyes sparkled with inquisitiveness, and her black hair was a profusion of little curls. But it was her sunny disposition and loveable nature that won every heart in the home—including the boys'. In fact, they soon began to vie for her attention, with both brothers coveting the role of personal protector for their little sister.

As soon as Becky was able to walk, Dan and Joe began teaching her the joys of life from their perspective. It is not surprising, therefore, that dolls and tea parties gave way to balls and fishing poles. And much to her mother's dismay, Becky soon came to prefer blue jeans and T-shirts to dresses and ribbons. It was not long before she could keep up with the boys of her neighborhood in virtually every sport and outdoor activity. Becky had clearly become a tomboy, although her father would only smile and say that she was just "down-to-earth." Her formative years, however, were by no means limited to the vigorous life. She also began to demonstrate at an early age the intellectual inclinations of her parents. She was especially intrigued by computers, although she had only a passing fancy with children's computer games, which were in their primitive stage at the time—what she really wanted to know was how they worked. Her mother taught mathematics at the university, for which Becky also displayed an aptitude that she would eventually apply to a major in computer science.

Throughout her years of formal education, Becky retained the tomboy persona in her dress and athletic interests. As a result, despite her attractive physical features, she went unnoticed by most of her male contemporaries and really didn't seem to show much of an interest in them either. That is not to say that she did not have dreams for the future. In fact, her brothers would tease her about being "the dreamer," because she talked so often of her dreams—a happy home with a loving husband and healthy, beautiful children. But for the moment, she had all she wanted. She felt secure at home with the love of her parents and brothers. And she was more than content with her studies in computer science, which was in an exciting phase of rapid evolution. After earning her master's degree, she obtained a teaching position in her old upper school and soon became one of its most popular teachers. Life was good. The dream could wait. And then it all began to crumble.

Of the more than six thousand inhabited islands that make up Indonesia, one is called Timor, the eastern half of which is the independent nation of East Timor. It was called Portuguese Timor until Portugal decolonized it in 1975, after which Indonesia declared it to be a province of its own country. For the next quarter century, there were intermittent skirmishes as the people of East Timor struggled to gain their independence from Indonesia, culminating in the first new sovereign state of the twenty-first century. As a young man, Becky's older brother Dan had covered the story for one of the local television stations and gained distinction for his courage in reporting from the front lines. Even when he became a senior correspondent for the station, he continued to take occasional assignments to report firsthand on the recurring violence in Timor, putting his life on the line and causing his family grave concern for his safety. And indeed, he made one too many trips into the fray and was mortally wounded by a stray bullet while embedded with the Indonesian army. He was rushed back to Jakarta, where the family stood by his side in the hospital until the end. On the last day, when he was in and out of consciousness, it was Becky to whom Dan spoke his parting words: "Don't forget your dream."

The family was devastated. For Becky's parents, it was beyond what their frail constitutions could take. It had been more than a decade since they had retired from the university, and both had been in poor health for several years. The loss of their firstborn seemed to be the catalyst that led to their final decline, and Becky watched in growing dread as her parents aged and deteriorated right before her eyes. Her mother was the first to go. The doctor just said that her heart gave out. This was the final blow for her father. He became incoherent and had to be admitted to a chronic care facility. Within a month, he too had passed away. There was talk that he may have taken his life. But no one ever knew.

And so, in the course of less than a year, Becky had lost both of her parents and her oldest brother. For months, she lived in inconsolable sorrow, not knowing how to respond or even how to think about her life, but just going through the motions of teaching her classes and coming home every night to her empty apartment. Joe was living in a flat not far from her and tried to reach out to comfort his little sister, but he was suffering the same disconsolation as Becky, and for the first few weeks they mourned in solitude. Then one day he gave her a call and they began to find healing through sharing their grief. They would meet most evenings at one or the other's apartment, sometimes sitting together in silence, sometimes reminiscing, occasionally laughing, and often crying. But time gradually worked its soothing restoration, and they eventually agreed that it was time to move along with their lives.

It was Joe who observed that neither of them had been to the doctor in a long time and that a good general checkup would be a reasonable way to begin their return to the world of the living. Becky agreed and was able to schedule her appointment first. As she sat with the family's longtime physician, she explained that she was having no physical problems but just felt it was time for an "annual" checkup (actually the first in many years). He reviewed her records, which revealed her to be a healthy young woman, and then began his examination, chatting all the while that everything was just fine. He measured her blood pressure and pulse, listened to her heart, asked her to say "ah" as he stuck a wooden spatula back into her throat, looked into her ears with his otoscope, and then picked up his ophthalmoscope to look in the back of her eyes. He seemed to spend more time on the latter part of his examination and became rather silent as he did so. Finally, he set his instrument down and appeared pensive, as though he was searching for the right words.

"Becky," he began in a slow, fatherly tone, "everything checks out fine, except there is one thing that concerns me."

She took a deep breath and felt her body become tense. He asked her if she knew whether any member of her family had glaucoma. She did not know of anyone and allowed that she was only vaguely familiar with the term.

"Well, it is something in your eyes that can cause blindness. When I looked at the nerve in the back of your left eye, I saw some changes that suggest you may have it. I can't be sure, but I would like for you to be seen by a specialist."

When Becky heard the word "blindness," she blocked out everything else the doctor said. She could only think of living the rest of her life without sight. How would she be able to survive on her own? What would become of her dream?

A few weeks later, Joe drove her into Jakarta, where she was scheduled to be seen by an ophthalmologist who specialized in glaucoma. Those had been the most anxious weeks of her life, and she became even more apprehensive as she walked into the doctor's office, fearing what she might be told. And her greatest fear was realized when the doctor confirmed that she did in fact have glaucoma. He explained that the cause of the nerve damage in her left eye was a high pressure, which she had in both eyes. Without proper treatment, this could eventually lead to blindness. But then he hastened to tell her the good news. There was effective treatment in the form of medicated eye drops that would lower the pressure and prevent further nerve damage—and prevent blindness. With those last words, Becky felt that the greatest weight of her life had just been lifted from her shoulders. The doctor started her on one bottle of eye drops, which he later increased to two bottles, and told her that she would not go blind if she used her drops faithfully every day. And she did.

It was not long after her diagnosis of glaucoma that Joe took a job in Jakarta and moved to a new apartment about an hour away from Becky's. There, he met the woman that he would marry, and before long, Becky was informed that she was about to become an aunt. She loved her role as Aunt Becky and continued to enjoy her work as a teacher, and for a while, she was quite content. But gradually, she came to realize that she needed more, and Dan's words began coming back to her—"Don't forget your dream." Then one day it hit her with a sense of alarm as to just how much of her life was already behind her and how far she still was from her dream. She was approaching her fortieth birthday and was alone except for Joe and his family, who did their best to make her feel a part of them, but it wasn't the same as having her own family. She knew it was time to do something, but wasn't sure just what. There were two strikes against her chances of ever finding a husband. The first was her religion. As a Christian, she was in a small minority of the Indonesian population, which greatly reduced her pool of potential suitors. The second detractor was her age. In her country there was a cultural barrier to marrying "older women." As she reflected on her predicament, she concluded that her best chance was with a Western man, who would more likely be of the Christian persuasion and have more liberal views about older women. But how was she to meet such a man? She had never been out of Indonesia and knew that this was not the place to find a Christian, Western, available man. Then one day it dawned on her that the answer had always been right in front of her eyes.

For the past twenty years, Becky's life, aside from her family, had been devoted to her study and teaching of computer science. During that time, social networking had blossomed. She had not paid much attention to it, but was aware of its potential, including the opportunity to meet a special person. As she explored the various online dating and matchmaking sites, she was amazed to find how many there were. She studied each carefully and eventually settled on one that seemed to be secure and reputable and that would put her in contact with men in the Western world. Then she had second thoughts. Was this really the right thing to do? She had never been a fan of social media—they seemed so impersonal to her. And did she really want to put herself out there for all to see? On the other hand, what did she have to lose? And more to the point, what were her alternatives? So she began to type.

The next day, as soon as she got home from work, she went to her computer to see if she had any responses. Nothing. She checked the next day and the next, and still there was nothing. Days turned to weeks and weeks to months, and still she did not have a single response. She finally stopped looking on a daily basis, but continued to check frequently, refusing to allow herself to give up hope. But as the first full year approached, she felt an increasing since of despair. And yet she would not succumb to the possibility that her dream might, after all, be just that—a dream.

———

Rebekah (Becky) Djalal

Half way around the world, in New Haven, Connecticut, Roger Bass glanced at the name on his computer screen. Something caused his gaze to linger a moment longer than it had on the other names. Maybe it was the brief description that she had provided of herself—"down-to-earth." That brought a smile to his face. It was the same description that he had used for himself.

Roger was born and bred on a farm in the plains of eastern Colorado near the Kansas border. His early years had been similar to Becky's. He enjoyed the vigorous, outdoor life—swimming and fishing when he was young, and then working alongside his father when he was big enough to help on the farm. It was a contented life, safe in the love of his parents and sister. But, like Becky, he also had an inquisitive mind and knew that one day he would leave the farm, pursue higher education, and go wherever that might take him. After graduating from high school, however, he put his education on hold for two years to work for the Peace Corps in Cambodia. This proved to be one of the highlights of his life. He quickly came to love the people and to develop a special appreciation for Asian women. Upon returning to the United States, he never lost his warm feelings for those whom he had met there, although he could not have known at the time how profoundly those feelings would one day impact his life.

In the fall, he moved to Boulder and matriculated to the University of Colorado, where he obtained his bachelor's degree in history. His time in Cambodia, and the books he had read as a youth, convinced him that history would always be a part of whatever profession he pursued. But with few opportunities with an undergraduate degree in history and a burning desire to continue his education, he remained in Boulder to earn his master's degree. By that point in his life, he decided it was time to pursue something more practical, so he left his family and home state to attend law school at the University of Arizona. He discovered that he enjoyed the study of law and was especially intrigued with how he could integrate it with his love of history. But, having earned his JD, he still felt a restlessness and uncertainty about his future. More importantly, he didn't feel that he had completely satisfied his thirst for higher education. And so he took the big leap and left the southwest to pursue a PhD in sociology at Yale University.

For his doctoral thesis, Roger wrote about the sociological impact of the Cambodian massacres, a topic that he had been studying for the past ten years. Not only was the defense of his thesis highly successful, but the work was also subsequently published in book form. It was well received within the academic community, a readership that unfortunately is not very remunerative. He realized that it was finally time to go to work. With academic positions in history or sociology few and far between, he accepted a job with a law firm in a small town near New Haven. He found the work to be challenging and interesting and was content with his life. He didn't seem to notice how the years were flying by until one day he looked in the mirror and realized that he was not getting any younger—in fact, he was approaching his fiftieth birthday. He had dated off and on, but never developed any serious relationships. The love of his parents and sister had always seemed to be enough family for him. But with the passage of time, Roger's life took a turn that was sadly reminiscent of Becky's tragic experiences.

Like Becky, Roger's parents were older than most when he was born. One day he received a call from his sister, Linda, who was living in New York, that their father had suffered a heart attack. He met her at Grand Central Station and they rushed home together. But they did not make it in time. Three days later, they stood beside their mother as their father was laid to rest in the Colorado soil. They stayed with their mother a few more days, during which time they realized that she would not be able to stay alone in the old family farmhouse. The doctor said it was early Alzheimer's disease and that she would be better off in an assisted living facility. Roger and Linda complied and, with only a mild resistance from their mother, found suitable arrangements for her. Both hated to leave her there alone, but they had jobs back in the Northeast that they could not afford to lose. They called her almost every day, as she gradually showed less and less recognition of who they were. Early one morning, they both received a call from the home that their mother had passed away peacefully in the night. And so, after less than a year, the two siblings again stood together in the old Colorado cemetery, saying good-bye to their final parent.

Roger was now approaching his mid-fifties, but was still content with his life. His law practice kept him busy, and he enjoyed reading his history books at night and taking the train in to New York to visit Linda. She was living alone as a successful businesswoman. An earlier marriage had not worked out. There were no children. Four years earlier, she had given Roger a fright when she announced that she had breast cancer. But the surgery and chemotherapy had gone well, and she was approaching her "five-year cure" when she became aware of a pain in her abdomen. At first, the pain came and went, and she didn't think too much about it until it finally persisted and grew progressively worse. The medical evaluation revealed metastases not only to her liver but also in her spine. The doctors tried everything, including experimental chemotherapeutic agents, but nothing seemed to be effective. Roger came to see her virtually every day, taking the train in after work and staying until late hours, after Linda was asleep. Finally, he had her transferred to a hospice near New Haven, where he was with her almost constantly—until the very end.

Now, at the age of fifty-five and all alone, Roger realized it was time to get serious about looking for a wife. His past experience with dating in the local community did not give him much encouragement. Of the few available women he had met who were anywhere close to his age, none seemed to share his values or simple approach to life. As he mulled all this over in his mind, his thoughts went back to his days in the Peace Corps and the gentle Asian women he had met. They seemed to be the type with whom he would feel most comfortable. But how could he meet such a woman?

Over the years, Roger had become particularly facile with the Internet, both in his law practice and as a reference tool for studying history and sociology. He was also vaguely aware of websites that linked people together through social media and even brought them physically together through dating and matchmaking sites, although he had never had the slightest interest in them. But now he began to wonder if it would be worth a try. His first inclination was to laugh at himself for having such a crazy idea—this just wasn't him. But the more he thought about it, the more he convinced himself that it could do no harm. And so he browsed the Internet until he found a site that offered matches with Asian women and, without further hesitation, entered his information. In less than a week, he was looking at the name: Rebekah (Becky) Djalal.

———

Becky was tired when she came home from a day of teaching and thought she would skip the disheartening ritual of looking at her computer, which for a solid year now had given her nothing but disappointment. But more out of habit than anything else, she clicked it on and was about to walk away without even looking at it when her eyes froze on the screen and she had to catch her breath. She looked more closely to make sure it wasn't a mistake. But it was clearly on her site. A name—Roger Bass—and he was asking her if they might meet by e-mail. A westerner in a place called Connecticut—a lawyer, no less. And he said he was "down-to-earth." Becky suddenly felt giddy. She didn't know whether to shout or cry. She just sat down and tried to control her breathing. When she finally got her wits about her, she went back to her computer and, with trembling hands, began to type a response. "Yes, I would be quite happy to meet you." 'No, that sounds too formal,' she thought. "I would love to meet you." 'Definitely not—mustn't sound too anxious.' "Yes, I would be delighted." 'Not bad.' And with that, she clicked Send.

Roger had sent his message around 7 p.m. his time, just as Becky was rushing off to her first class of the morning. Since she did not see it until she got home that evening, by the time she sent her response, it was Roger who was leaving for work. He had a heavy courtroom schedule that day and would not have a chance to check his e-mails until he got home. Becky knew not to expect an immediate reply, but thought it might come later that evening. So she prepared her supper, ate a little faster than usual and went back to her computer. She checked it every thirty minutes or less until the hour of midnight was approaching—with no reply.

Reluctantly, she went to bed and was not surprised to find it hard to sleep. When she finally did drift off in the early hours of the morning, she had a vivid dream. In her dream, she saw a cozy white house surrounded by flowers on a quiet, tree-lined street. It was the type of home she would have expected to find in America from the movies she had seen. The front door was open, but when she went in, it was empty and no one was there. It was the same in each room she entered with an ever-increasing sense of foreboding. And then she awoke with an intense feeling of anxiety. She lay there, as the first rays of dawn filtered into her room, replaying the dream in her mind and trying to deny what she knew it meant. Had it all been a dream? Who could say what a year's worth of heartbreaks could do to a person's mind? She was almost afraid to get out of bed and check her computer for fear that it would be just as blank as she had found it all those months. At the same time, she felt an overwhelming compulsion to do nothing else. And when she did, her eyes welled up with tears as she saw what was on her computer screen.

> Hi Becky,
> Thank you for agreeing to meet me this way and allow me to introduce myself. I am Roger Bass and I live in Connecticut, which is in a beautiful part of America called New England. I am fifty-five and have never been married. I know that is unusual, but I recently lost my last close relative, my sister, and feel it is time to find a wife. My life is rather simple. I enjoy reading and quiet walks and occasional trips to New York for concerts. Oh, and I guess I should tell you what I look like. I am Caucasian, 5'10," and of average build, with brown hair that is start-ing to turn a bit gray. I can send a picture if you like (this is all new to me). Anyway, I would love to hear from you.
> Expectantly,
> Roger

'He would love to hear from me,' she repeated over and over in her mind. 'And he has never married and has lost all his close relatives.' She wanted to tell him that she knew exactly how he felt and that she also loved reading and walks and concerts. But would she look too anxious if she responded at this early hour of the morning? She decided to wait until she got home from school. That may have been the longest day of her life, and she remembers nothing of what transpired in the classroom, since she was constantly thinking of how she was going to word her reply. And when she finally sent it off that evening, she immediately decided it was all wrong and wished desperately that she could take it back. But it didn't seem to matter. Roger appeared to be genuinely pleased to hear from her. They shared pictures, and as Roger looked at Becky for the first time, he saw a woman dressed in jeans and a T-shirt with a sweet, round face, dark eyes, and black hair that accented her light brown complexion. 'Down-to-earth,' he thought with a satisfied smile. Thus began a series of daily e-mails in which they both marveled at how compatible they seemed to be with each other. But then, the unthinkable happened. It all came crashing down—literally.

Just as their correspondence was gaining momentum, Becky's computer crashed. She couldn't believe it. In all her years as a computer scientist, this had never happened. Why now? Was it a bad omen? Would Roger think she didn't care and move on to someone else? She had no other way to reach him. They had never shared mailing addresses or phone numbers, and she had not even bothered to write down or remember his e-mail address. She again found herself in despair, but holding tenaciously to her dream. Everyone in her department at school tried to help her fix her computer. They had to send for some parts, and it was a full week before she was back online. She immediately sent Roger an explanation and an apology, hoping desperately that nothing would have changed with him. His answer came back quickly. He had been concerned, but understood, and actually found it a bit amusing that this should happen to a computer scientist. She failed to see the humor.

They continued to correspond by e-mail for six months before they had their first telephone conversation. Who can say why they waited so long? Maybe it was just more comfortable this way, waiting until they felt sufficiently confident in their relationship. Maybe they were afraid that taking the next step would burst the bubble. But any reservations they may have had proved to be unfounded. Despite anxiety at both ends of the line when they heard each other's voice for the first time, it seemed just as natural as their e-mail correspondence had been. From that day forward, they spoke on the phone almost every day. And when the day finally came that they stood before each other for the first time, it also seemed perfectly natural, as though it had always been meant to be.

It was in the spring when Roger flew to Indonesia for his first ten-day visit. He was met at the Jakarta airport by Becky and her brother, Joe. The plan was for Roger to stay at Joe's home, although he and Becky were together almost every waking hour. Toward the end of the visit, Becky was sitting with Joe in his breakfast room while Roger packed his bags, and

Joe asked her if Roger had proposed. She said no, but that they did plan to marry. Joe, who had always been protective of his little sister, found this to be totally unacceptable—contrary to Indonesian culture. He insisted that Roger must propose. So Becky went to Roger's room and asked him if he planned to propose. Roger found this to be a bit amusing, but had to admit that it was a formality he had overlooked. "Well, will you marry me?" he asked with a smile, as he stuffed the last shirt in his suitcase. A momentary hesitation caused him to glance over at her, but she simply said "Okay" and went back to tell Joe that everything was taken care of. On Roger's fourth trip to Indonesia, Becky returned with him to the United States, leaving her native country for the first time. In February of that year, she became Mrs. Roger Bass. The dream was finally coming true. But she was now forty-one years old and he was fifty-six.

———

Despite the hundreds of hours that they had spent together on their computers and the telephone and in person over the past year, Becky had never asked Roger if he wanted to have children. Maybe she was afraid that it would chill their relationship. Maybe they were both too engrossed in getting to know everything else about each other. Or maybe they subconsciously felt that it was such a given that it didn't need to be discussed. Whatever Becky's reason may have been, it was definitely not for lack of interest. She desperately wanted to have children. It would be the final part of her dream—an essential part. So when she finally broached the subject with Roger and he told her that he felt the same way, she was overjoyed. Little could she have known at the time, however, that she was now embarking on her greatest challenge yet.

The obstetrician had not been encouraging. He told Becky that she was in pre-menopause and that hers would be a high-risk pregnancy. He recommended in vitro fertilization, or IVF. After a discussion of what this would entail, Becky and Roger left the doctor's office rather despondent. This was obviously not what they had hoped to hear. It sounded very complicated and unnatural, especially for two down-to-earth people. They decided that they would give the "natural" way a try first, and for a full year they waited expectantly—but without any success. Finally, realizing that time was running out, they returned to the obstetrician and announced that they were ready to take the IVF route.

They had been dismayed when the obstetrician told them what IVF would cost in the United States, and he suggested that they might want to look into having it done in another country. And so, once again, they turned to the power of the Internet, this time to learn all they could about IVF. Their study revealed that, indeed, the cost in many countries was less than half that in the United States, even when transportation and other travel expenses were factored in. This led them to explore their options in Indonesia, where Becky would have the support of Joe and his family, as well as her many friends there. They were pleased to find that several reputable IVF centers were available in Jakarta, and they soon agreed on one that was not too far from her brother's home. With Joe's help, they made contact with the center, and within a month, she had an appointment to be seen there for a complete evaluation and to begin the IVF process.

There remained one issue that greatly concerned both Becky and Roger. The only chronic medications that Becky was taking were her glaucoma drops. When they asked the obstetrician if this would be a problem during her pregnancy, he had suggested that it might be and that they should discuss it with their ophthalmologist. They had gone to several health care websites, most of which offered little or no information on the subject, while the rest were, at best, conflicting in their advice. When they asked her eye doctor if he thought it was safe to continue her glaucoma drops during pregnancy, he indicated that he thought it was. But Roger wasn't comfortable with that response. He had seen enough warnings in his perusal of the websites to put serious doubts in his mind. And so he again went to the Internet, this time to see where they might obtain a second opinion. And that led them to the Yale Eye Center. And that is how I came to know Becky and Roger Bass.

———

The chart read "forty-three-year old Asian woman with eight-year history of open-angle glaucoma." It went ahead to state that she was currently on two types of glaucoma drops and had tried the other available types with questionable benefit. The referring doctor suggested that her glaucoma might be progressing in her left eye. Of particular note was the fact that she wanted to become pregnant and would soon embark on a course of IVF.

On that first visit, of course, I knew nothing about Becky's remarkable past. What I saw before me was a pleasant young woman with a sweet, round face and light brown complexion that seemed to be free of any makeup. Her dark hair was in loose curls that also appeared to have received minimal attention. The most striking feature was her dark eyes that suggested at once both gentleness and intensity. I can't say if I noticed it then, but she was dressed, as she would be on all subsequent visits, in simple cotton slacks and a T-shirt. Roger was also sitting quietly in the room, looking every bit the part of the expectant father and supportive husband. They were both the type of people with whom you immediately feel comfortable, and I had the sense that we were going to get along quite nicely. But I had no idea that morning as to how intensely our lives would intertwine in the months ahead.

My preliminary examination revealed that Becky's original diagnosis of glaucoma had been correct. The optic nerve in her left eye was damaged and was causing early loss of peripheral vision, although she still had excellent central vision in both eyes. The pressure in each eye was borderline at best, despite the medications she was using. And that led to the main reason they had come in that day—was it safe to continue her drops during pregnancy, and if not, what were her alternatives? The one clear fact is that a certain amount of the medicine given in an eye drop gets into the patient's blood stream. This is because a percentage of the drop goes down small channels into the nose and throat (which is why we may taste our tears when we cry). The medicine is then absorbed by the mucous lining in the nose and from there goes into the blood vessels. While only a small amount of the medicine circulates throughout the body, it can be enough to cause serious problems in some people, especially those with certain preexisting conditions. And it can also get into the circulation of the baby who is developing in the mother, with the potential for causing birth defects or other problems. The exact risk of any glaucoma medication during pregnancy is unknown, simply because there have been no large clinical trials (for obvious reasons). But the general consensus is that it is best to avoid all of them during pregnancy—and that is what I had to explain to Becky.

She was trying to be brave, but I could tell that she was struggling mightily with her emotions. She would later tell me of her fear at the time that she had to choose between going blind or never having children. Either way, it seemed that her dream was once again in jeopardy. I could see the tears beginning to well up in her eyes, but I was also struck by her sense of firm resolve.

After handing her a tissue, I suggested that we talk about her options. The first thing to do would be to simply stop her drops for a few weeks to see what her pressures were without them. Sometimes, when a person has been on glaucoma medication for many years, the pressures don't change much when the treatment is stopped, and it had been a long time since she was last checked without drops. And if we found that her pressures were too high, which was a distinct possibility, we could then perform laser therapy in the hope of controlling her pressures without medicine during the pregnancy. At first, Becky was hesitant to stop her drops, knowing that they had kept her from blindness for the past eight years. I assured her that a short course without them would be safe and that we could proceed with the first session of laser treatment on her next visit if the pressures were too high. She looked over at Roger, who smiled and nodded his approval. And so we all agreed and tentatively scheduled the laser treatment for her next visit.

I can only imagine now what anxiety Becky must have suffered before that return appointment, fighting between thoughts of blindness and a life without children. I had so hoped to give her good news—but it wasn't to be. Her pressures were considerably higher than on the previous visit and were now clearly too high for the long term. She forced a faint smile, but her tightly pursed lips and moist eyes betrayed her inner trepidation. Roger took her hand and reminded her that she still had the laser option. I tried to reinforce that positive note, although I had my own inner reservations, knowing that the laser treatment is not uniformly adequate in every patient. But the procedure went smoothly in her left eye that morning, and we scheduled a return visit in one week to check the left eye and treat her right eye. As we said our good-byes, Roger maintained his calm, positive bearing, although Becky was just barely in control of hers.

Much to everyone's dismay, the next week did not bring any better news. The pressure in the left eye had not come down significantly since the laser treatment. I tried to sound hopeful, reminding them that it can take up to a month to see the full benefit of the treatment, but inwardly I was still nursing my concern. I thought back to another patient when I was just starting out in practice. That was before the days of the laser procedure, and I had performed glaucoma surgery on both eyes in anticipation of her pregnancy. It had been a stormy postoperative course, as is so often the case, and I fervently hoped we could avoid that for Becky. We went ahead with the laser treatment in her right eye that morning and then followed her closely as the pressures in both eyes seemed to grudgingly come down a few points. It was not the response I had hoped for, but with surgery as our alternative, I suggested no further treatment just yet. And more to the point, they were scheduled to leave for Indonesia the following week.

Roger and Becky found the facilities at the IVF clinic in Jakarta to be excellent, although they did not feel entirely comfortable with their physician. Something caused them to question his ability, and Becky began having second thoughts. But Roger gave her courage with his calming reassurance and stayed right beside her through every moment of the ordeal. For two painfully long weeks, Becky was required to remain at complete bed rest after implantation of the fertilized egg. However, it all seemed to be worth it on that joyous day when the doctor announced that she was pregnant.

I had never seen Becky so radiant as when she and Roger came in for her next visit and told me that she was six weeks pregnant. There was a moment of congratulations and hugs and then more good news when I checked her pressures—they were the lowest they had been since I first saw her. The eye pressure is typically lower during pregnancy, probably due to the hormonal influence, and I told them that this was most likely the explanation for the added good news, rather than any late effect of the laser treatments. Whatever the reason, there was nothing but smiles and laughter all around that day. For Becky, the fulfillment of her dream now seemed to be so close. And yet, her faith in that dream was about to face its greatest challenge.

I was in my office the afternoon that Roger called, three months to the day since our last visit. The subdued tone in his voice told me that something was wrong. And indeed, it was the worst—Becky had suffered a miscarriage. To make matters worse, the Indonesian doctor had implied that it was something wrong with one of them. Becky swore she would never go back there and was ready to give up. She didn't even have the will to leave their home, but wanted to go back on her glaucoma medication and asked if I would call in the prescription. With a heavy heart, I agreed to place the call, but also insisted that she come in for a follow-up visit within the month.

That visit was the quietest and grimmest the three of us had experienced together. Even Roger could not muster up his usual optimism, and I am afraid that I was adding nothing positive to the mood. Even the fact that her pressures were good, with resumed use of the eye drops, failed to brighten the gloom that hung over the exam room that day. Finally, with some hesitation, I brought up the question of adoption, telling them what a joy it had been in our family. They forced polite smiles and admitted that they had talked about it, but really were not sure what they were going to do at this point. Becky promised to continue her glaucoma drops and come back in a few months.

Roger gave Becky time to let her broken spirit heal and then talked her into giving the IVF one more chance. Once again, it was back to the

Internet, this time to find another part of the world where they might go for the procedure. Roger's search indicated that there were several reputable facilities in India. He and Becky looked at the various choices together and agreed on one in Delhi that seemed to best meet their criteria. They contacted the clinic and were pleasantly surprised to find that they could schedule an appointment within less than a month. So Roger went online and booked two tickets to Delhi, India.

It was the first time in India for either of them, and despite their knowledge of the world, they were not prepared for the poverty and squalor they saw as the cab drove away from the Delhi airport. They both expected things to improve as they got nearer the clinic, but were disheartened to find just the opposite. The clinic seemed to be in an especially bad part of the city. Roger thought there must be some mistake when the cab stopped and the driver indicated that this was their destination. As he looked around, everything seemed more run-down and dirty than in any area they had seen yet. Becky had closed her eyes a few miles back, unable to endure the sights as they drove from one sad area to another. And now, as she opened them and looked about, she had to fight back the tears. Roger squeezed her hand, and his silent smile gave her the courage to get out of the car. He checked the directions one more time to make sure they were in the right place. The faded inscription above a simple wooden door confirmed that indeed they were. He opened the door for Becky and they stepped into a small, dark hallway. As he closed the door behind them, the last rays of daylight were snuffed out—and so, it seemed, were their spirits.

A lone, bare light bulb dangled from a frayed cord midway up a narrow staircase, providing dim illumination in the only direction they could proceed. As they began their ascent, the first stair step gave an ominous creaking sound, and Roger stopped to test whether the next step could support them. Slowly, hand in hand, they moved up the stairs, and the air seemed to become increasingly stagnant and close, with a smell that bordered on the dark side of musty. The walls were dirty, and what little paint remained was peeling badly. About halfway up the stairs, Becky was suddenly overcome by a sense of panic. 'What are we doing here?' she asked herself. They stood for a moment, looking at each other, and Roger could sense his wife's trepidation.

"Becky, we can turn back anytime you want," he said in a soft, gentle voice. "But if we go back down these stairs now, will it be the end of the dream? Going up may be our best chance."

She closed her eyes and squeezed his hand, seeming to be weighing their two options. Then, taking a deep breath, she turned toward the door at the top of the stairs.

Walking through the door, they entered a small waiting room that was diffused with soft, warm light. The décor could not be described as up-to-date, but everything was very neat and clean. Just then, a middle-aged woman entered the room through the opposite door. The couple assumed that she was either the receptionist or maybe a nurse, and both were a bit startled when she introduced herself as Dr. Patel. Roger feared that the doctor might have sensed their surprise and, with an uneasy laugh, apologized for his chauvinism in assuming that Dr. Patel was a man.

"Well, you are not entirely wrong in thinking that," she said with a reassuring smile and in perfect English. "The other Dr. Patel is my husband. We are both physicians and run this clinic together. He is with another patient at the moment, but will join us shortly. So if you will come with me, we will get started on your interview."

Their initial impression of the first Dr. Patel was comforting and gave them both a renewed sense of confidence. As they walked through the clinic, the equipment all appeared to be state-of-the-art and everything was well organized and immaculate. The second Dr. Patel was equally pleasant and reassuring. Becky and Roger told him about their ordeal in Jakarta—the two weeks in bed and being blamed for the miscarriage. The doctor shook his head and implied that it was all quite unfortunate. He carefully explained everything that would transpire this time and then made arrangements to proceed the following day.

After the fertilized egg was transferred, Becky was asked to stay in bed for two days, and then the Drs. Patel told them they could return home. As they sat on the plane flying back to JFK airport, neither of them could believe it had all been so quick and easy. In fact, they wondered if it had been too quick and easy. Despite their reason for jubilance, neither of them could suppress their concerns, based on the past experience, and they could not help but wonder what the future might hold.

When I entered the exam room, I was a bit puzzled by the expression on Becky and Roger's faces—there was something sheepish about it. It was obvious that they had an announcement to make, but neither seemed quite certain how to proceed. They looked at each other and laughed, and Becky said, "You tell him." Roger turned his gaze to me and, with a contented smile, informed me that Becky was two months pregnant. That was the first I had heard about the trip to India. They shared some of the details with me, and we again had our little celebration. But then we were brought back to reality when I checked her pressures and found it to be dangerously high in her good right eye. She had followed my advice and stopped her glaucoma drops before the IVF procedure, but now the pressure was at a level that would not be safe for the next seven months. What benefit we might have derived from the laser procedure of two years ago had obviously been lost, and our treatment options were quite limited. Once again, I saw Becky's joy turn to fear.

Fortunately, during the two years since we performed the laser treatment with the traditional instrument, a new laser and technique had become available that offered advantages over the older protocol. We had only recently acquired the instrument at Yale, and I was still developing my comfort level with it. But it seemed to afford the best hope for Becky, and I recommended that we give it a try. The outcome was rather remarkable. Whether it was the laser treatment or the hormones finally having their effect, the pressure came down nicely in both eyes and remained so throughout her pregnancy. And so, at long last, Becky's dream seemed to be truly within reach.

I saw her in the office a couple more times during her pregnancy, with increasing optimism and joy as her eye pressures remained low and her obstetrical course continued on track. But the happiest visit of all was the day I walked in to the exam room and found a radiant mother holding her newborn son—and a proud, beaming father holding their newborn daughter. They had known that twins were on the way, and a C-section had been scheduled and successfully performed. Mother and children were all doing well. And they were two beautiful children with light brown complexions, dark curly hair, and big brown eyes. Roger introduced them as Megan and Joshua. I became so absorbed in doting over the two healthy children and congratulating their exultant parents that I almost forgot Becky was there to have her eyes examined. But that too was doing well, and we said good-bye for then amid hugs, laughter, and joy.

Over the next two years, I continued to check Becky on a regular basis. Her pressures eventually went back up, but we could now safely resume her medicated eye drops, and she did well from then on. They were always happy visits, with Roger and the children unfailingly by her side. It was wonderful to watch Megan and Joshua grow strong and healthy and to see their parents rejoicing in the love of their little family (even though Roger jokingly admitted that the children were undoubtedly reading the book on "terrible twos").

Shortly before leaving Yale, I had lunch with Becky and Roger. It was a week to the day since they had celebrated the twin's second birthday. Joe and his family had come over for the festivities and were caring for the children that day so their parents could enjoy a quiet lunch. We went to one of their favorite restaurants—a modest place, as might be expected of two down-to-earth people. During our meal, they filled me in on more details of their remarkable life together. As we sat there over three bowls of nourishing soup, I found it a bit difficult to reconcile their harrowing tale with the calm, contented couple across the table from me. And I couldn't resist asking Becky what it was that had kept her going through all those years of despairing heartaches and fears. She considered the question for a moment and then said with a thoughtful shake of her head that it was the dream of what she always wanted.

"And what advice would you give to other women in your situation?" I asked.

She looked pensive and distant for a moment, as though her mind was retracing all those events in her life—the challenges and the blessings— and with a confident smile, she answered, "You must dream, but you must also take action to fulfill your dream." Then, after a reflective pause and a glance toward Roger, who returned her smile, she added, "And never give up."

22.

Michael

The further along I went in my practice, and as I approached the end of my career, the more I realized how little I knew. It wasn't supposed to have been that way—or so I once thought. Throughout my formative years, as a medical student, intern, resident, and fellow, I had always been in awe of the vast knowledge that my mentors seemed to possess. Someday, I told myself, with hard work and years of experience, I too would join the ranks of those venerable senior physicians with their wealth of skill and knowledge. And I reasoned that narrowing my focus to a clearly defined field of medicine would enhance my chances of reaching that goal, which may have been one of my reasons for choosing ophthalmology. How could I not wrap my mind around every aspect of a discipline in which the related anatomy is only about an inch in diameter and constitutes less than one percent of the total body mass? Talk about naïve. One look around an ophthalmology library, with its thousands of books on the eye and vision, should have assuaged any notion of a simple discipline of medicine. Small clearly does not equate with simple.

The problem, of course, is that the more we learn about any subject, the more we realize how much more there is to know and ultimately how little we actually understand about the totality of the issue. And this is clearly true for all fields of medicine. As the years and decades passed, and my patients assumed that I should know everything about caring for their eyes, it became increasingly apparent to me how the gap between my knowledge and reality was only widening. This was frustrating for me and certainly for my patients when I was not able to preserve their sight. One of the most striking examples of this occurred late in my career, when I had reached that "senior status" and was expected to have all the answers. It was an experience that left me with a heightened sense of humility, but also with another reminder of how privileged I was to care for so many courageous and remarkable patients.

—

The most enduring image of him in my memory is of an overcrowded waiting room, which struck me as odd, since our schedule was not unusually heavy on that particular morning. At the time, our "waiting room" was actually the hall just outside a cluster of examination rooms, and the chairs against the wall were all filled. Stranger yet was that nearly all of the seats were occupied by young people, whom I judged to range in age from late teens down to around five years old. They appeared to be seated according to age, creating a stair-step effect, but the one thing they had in common was that each held a book in his or her lap and was quietly reading. As I walked by them, each in turn looked up and smiled with a courteous nod and then returned to their reading. There were nine of them in all, and the tenth chair was occupied by a pleasant-appearing, middle-aged woman, who also smiled and glanced approvingly at the children, of whom she was obviously in charge.

I was still puzzling over this unexplained occupancy of our waiting area as I entered the exam room of the first patient for the day. He was a middle-aged gentleman who gave an immediate first impression of being very friendly and open to conversation. We chatted for a few minutes, and I learned that he was the father of the nine children and the husband of the woman in the tenth chair. That alone would have been enough to make him and his family quite memorable, but the odyssey that began to unfold that morning would forever imprint in my memory the life of Dr. Michael Bell.

Surprisingly, both he and his wife, Colleen, were from small families, each having only one sibling. Michael grew up in Pennsylvania in a family that was somewhat mixed with regard to the religious alignment of the parents. His father was Catholic and insisted that the family worship in the

Catholic church, which they did until Michael reached the age of fourteen, at which time his father died. His mother had always been more of the Evangelical persuasion, and that is how she raised her two children after the death of their father. This dichotomy of religious experiences led to a degree of ambivalence in the young man's developing mind, which would manifest itself when he entered his years of higher education.

He was an unusually gifted student and decided that he wanted to attend the Massachusetts Institute of Technology and study theoretical physics. To his surprise and great disappointment, however, he was not accepted by MIT. This led to frustration and even a bit of anger—emotions that would resurface in later years—and, although he was accepted at the prestigious Carnegie Mellon University, he finally decided on the University of Pittsburg, where he began to pursue his interests in theoretical physics. During the first semester at Pitt, he also began to explore Eastern religions and drugs, much to the consternation of his mother, who expressed her feelings when he came home for the Christmas holidays. It was during those vacation days, as he spent time with some old friends from high school and church, that a major transformation occurred in Michael's thinking that would dramatically change the course of his life. As he relates it, he felt a "religious conversion back to Christianity."

Michael returned to the University of Pittsburg for the second semester, although with the intention of transferring at the end of the school year. That year of study was by no means lost time, as the scientific principles he learned would prove to be invaluable in the career path he would eventually follow to support his large family. But at that particular time in his life, he had decided on a radical change in his academic pursuits from science to religion. In the fall of the next year, he matriculated to the Philadelphia School of the Bible in downtown Philadelphia, and there he met Colleen. She was from a navy family and consequently had the perspective of having lived in various locations around the country and the world. They dated for a brief time before becoming husband and wife. Colleen dropped out of school so she could get a job and help put Michael though divinity school and eventually earn his doctorate in theology.

And so the young Dr. Bell was poised to embark on his career as a theologian and scholar. And it all got off to a very encouraging start. The years of hard work were rewarded with a teaching position in a prominent seminary, where he was able to pursue his major interest in Dutch Reformed Church in the seventeenth century. In addition to his teaching duties, he spent his days translating Latin and writing several books on his area of academic pursuit. It looked like he was well on his way to establishing his credentials and gaining recognition as a leader in his chosen field. But another aspect of their life was also beginning to develop, which was on a collision course with his career. Shortly after their marriage, Michael's mother had advised the young couple to wait on starting a family, a recommendation that they followed well beyond what she had in mind. After eleven years of marriage with no children, his mother was now asking why they were waiting so long and was encouraging them to move along with their life. So again, the young couple took her advice, and again they took it far beyond what she could have ever imagined. Michael and Colleen had always planned on having a large family—"as many as God would provide," they said. The number they had in mind was no more than six, and even they were surprised, but not disappointed, when it rose to nine. And it was around this time that Michael began to recognize the need to reevaluate his long-term career plans.

One thing I learned early on about Michael and Colleen was that their children are their first priority in life. They were committed to giving each one of them every opportunity for success and happiness, including the best available education. And this, of course, meant a considerable expense. Despite his excellent reputation at the seminary and his many academic achievements, Michael had not yet been able to obtain tenure, and even if he had, the income would have been insufficient to meet his family's needs. And so he eventually took on a part-time consulting position with a scientific firm, which primarily involved information technology. Michael had acquired some background in computer science during his year at Pitt, and this, combined with his innate ability in the field, made him a well-recognized asset to the company. Gradually, his consulting time expanded as his teaching hours at the seminary declined, until he finally made the decision to take a full-time position with a prestigious pharmaceutical company. And so it was that his life came full circle, as Michael transferred from religion back to science, although this time it was for financial reasons—to support his growing family.

Such a large number of children also created other challenges that would significantly influence the life of their family. Michael and Colleen had been considering overseas mission work between the completion of his teaching commitments and the beginning of his full-time employment in business. However, they were told by the administrators of the mission that they had too many children and that some would have to be sent to boarding schools. This was out of the question for Colleen. Even though the mission would cover expenses of private Christian schools, it was a totally unacceptable concept to her that their family be separated when the children were so young. At the same time, both Michael and Colleen were reluctant to send their children to public schools, but knew it would be difficult to put them all in private schools, even with Michael's enhanced income. And so Colleen made the decision to home school her children until they were ready to enter college. As I came to know those fine young people sitting out in the hall, I realized that she had made a sound choice.

The final decade of the twentieth century got off to a good start for the Bell family. The children were all thriving under the tutelage of their teacher/ mother. It is a tribute to both parents that each child not only adhered diligently to the rigid study guidelines that were laid out for them, but did so with cheerfulness and gratitude. Theirs was an environment of cooperative learning, in which the older children helped their younger siblings during the long hours of study, but it was also an environment of nurturing and love. And yet no one could have anticipated how the twentieth century would end for the family.

While Colleen and the children were putting in the long hours at home, Michael was working even longer hours to provide for his family. He had developed a reputation as an invaluable member of his company's team, even though he laughingly admitted that he "sometimes got in trouble for being too persistent." He was soon being recruited by other companies for his obvious talents, and one of those recruitments led to an offer that he couldn't refuse, even though it meant considerably more work and less time with his family. He now found himself attending late-night meetings and traveling around the country and the world. He became so busy and occupied with his work that he failed to notice the first signs of the shadow.

Much of his time was spent in front of a computer, and he began to notice that some of the words were distorted or fading in and out. At first he just chalked it up to fatigue from his long hours of work, but it seemed to be getting worse. One day he closed his right eye and found to his horror that he was suddenly engulfed in a world of shadowy darkness. He rubbed his left eye, hoping to wipe away a film, but the shadow persisted. He shook his head and squeezed both eyes tightly. When he opened them, everything was in focus—with his right eye—but when he closed that eye, the darkness returned. His heart began to race as he now considered the gravity of his situation. And thus began the long and tragic saga that would dominate the remainder of Michael Bell's life.

He slept little that night, and when fitful sleep did come, it was with recurring nightmares of terrifying darkness, from which he would awaken in a state of panic. The following morning, he walked into the office of a local optometrist, hoping upon hope that he just needed stronger glasses. But it was not to be, and his heart sank as he realized that no change in lenses eliminated the shadow in front of his left eye. The doctor determined that Michael had lost the central vision in that eye, and, of even greater concern, that there was also an area of darkness (called a scotoma) in the upper part of his right field of vision. He had not been aware of the latter loss, since it did not involve his vision when he looked straight ahead. But when he checked his peripheral vision with the movement of his hand, he was shocked to find that indeed the problem with his vision—whatever that might be—was in both of his eyes.

The optometrist could not explain the loss of vision, but felt that the nerves in the back of each eye (the optic nerves) looked a bit unusual, and he arranged for Michael to be seen by a prominent neuro-ophthalmologist in Philadelphia. He had to wait several excruciating weeks before he could get an appointment with the world-famous physician, during which time he was convinced that his vision was getting progressively worse. When the day finally came, he was given an extensive evaluation and was then told that his failing vision was due to a form of atrophy (or degeneration) of his optic nerves, a group of conditions that are commonly referred to as optic atrophy. Michael's mind now began to go into action. He had never been one to accept any decision or opinion without a thorough explanation and understanding of the facts upon which it was based. And never had that been truer than at this moment. How did the doctor know it was optic atrophy? What was the cause? And, most importantly, what could be done about it? Michael's characteristic persistence rose to a crescendo as he threw question after question at the doctor, who seemed to be increasingly irritated and even a bit defensive. Part of the doctor's problem was that, despite his vast knowledge, he really wasn't sure what was causing the optic atrophy. He explained that one of the most common causes is glaucoma, but that Michael's eye pressures were well within the normal range, and while this did not entirely rule out glaucoma, it made it less likely. The doctor finally told him that he thought the optic atrophy was congenital—something that had been present since he was born.

This didn't seem logical to Michael, since it had just begun to happen, but the doctor explained that congenital disorders sometimes do not become manifest until later in life. To make matters worse, the doctor said there was no treatment for his condition. And so Michael left the doctor's office confused, perplexed, and disheartened.

The doctor had told Michael that his condition might not get worse and that the best course was to wait and see what happened. So he tried to put it in the back recesses of his mind and returned to his demanding work schedule. But as the weeks and months passed, he could tell that the vision in his left eye was getting worse, and he was now becoming conscious of the shadow in his right eye. He let nearly a year elapse before he could stand it no longer and finally went back to the neuro-ophthalmologist in the hope that something more could be discovered about his condition or that maybe a new treatment had become available. No, he was told, nothing had changed appreciably, and it was still not entirely clear what was causing the optic atrophy. Michael was simply not willing to give up that easily, and he implored the physician—indeed, insisted—that surely something more could be done. The doctor nodded his understanding and looked back at the medical record. Then, without looking up, he said that he would like to send Michael upstairs to a colleague who specialized in glaucoma.

"But you already told me I don't have glaucoma!" he blurted out in growing frustration.

"Well, you don't have high pressures in your eyes, but some types of glaucoma can occur with normal pressure," the doctor responded, also with thinly veiled frustration. "Anyway, there is nothing else that I can offer to you."

Michael wondered why the doctor hadn't suggested this a year ago but was willing to try anything at this point, and so he went upstairs to schedule the appointment. As it turned out, the glaucoma specialist, Dr. Jonathan Myers, had been one of my last fellows before I left Duke. He now enjoyed an excellent reputation in one of the premier medical groups in Philadelphia. Michael was comforted by Dr. Myers's calm, reassuring manner and was especially relieved when he was told that he did indeed appear to have a form of glaucoma called normal pressure glaucoma. At least now he knew what was causing his problem and that something could be done about it. But, just to be sure, he obtained a second opinion from a prominent ophthalmologist in New Jersey, who agreed with the diagnosis. Dr. Myers had explained that, even though his pressures were within the statistically normal range, they were too high for the health of his optic nerves and that lowering the pressures even further should arrest the progressive deterioration of his nerves and prevent any further loss of vision. He started Michael on a medicated eye drop to achieve that goal and arranged for close follow-up visits.

It was at about this time that Michael was offered a high-level position in another prominent pharmaceutical company. It would not reduce his workload—it would probably mean longer hours and more away time, if anything—but it would mean a significant increase in his income, which the large family could clearly use. The hardest part of the offer, however, was that the company was headquartered in Connecticut, and his family would have to make the big move from their longtime home in Pennsylvania. They met together on several evenings, talking and praying about this momentous change in their lives. Finally, they agreed that the move was in the best interest of the whole family, and that is how I came to meet them on that first morning.

—

Dr. Myers's referral letter to me indicated that Michael's central vision in his right eye was still good, and although he could no longer see straight ahead with his left eye, it retained some useful side vision. On my initial examination, I agreed that the appearance of the optic atrophy in both eyes was consistent with glaucoma, and that the scotoma in his right field of vision was typical for that group of conditions. Michael was now using two different bottles of eye drops twice daily, and I would soon learn that no patient was ever more faithful in the use of their medications. However, although his pressures were good, I wanted to keep them as low as possible to hopefully ensure that he would not lose any more vision, and so I added yet a third bottle with a medicine that had recently become available and only had to be used once at bedtime. All in all, I felt comfortable with the diagnosis and was optimistic about Michael's future. Needless to say, he was delighted with this assessment, and we walked out into the hall together, where he introduced me to Colleen and their nine children.

I continued to see Michael on a regular basis and was pleased during those early months to find his pressures staying low with no definite change in his vision, although he felt that some days were better than others. I always knew, without looking at the schedule, when Michael was in the clinic by the long row of young people sitting in the hall, all totally engrossed in the books on their laps. They were endearingly friendly and courteous, always looking up from their book with a smile and a nod as I walked by. I was increasingly impressed with this remarkable family, not only for their quantity, but also for their quality. And yet, of all the memories I have of them, the one that will forever come to mind first when I recall the Bell family occurred on the Christmas just after we met.

Michael and Colleen agreed that Christmas should be celebrated without the exchanging of gifts. Whether this owed to the high cost of buying presents for such a large family or was in deference to the deeper meaning of the season, I never knew, although strongly suspected the latter. In any case, the parents did allow the children to celebrate by putting on their own Christmas pageant. As Michael explained this to me, I tried to envision how Sarah and John, or any average child, would respond to being informed that they would not receive any presents for Christmas, but—not to worry—the lack of gifts would be more than compensated for by the privilege of producing their very own Christmas pageant at home with their siblings. He must have seen the amusement—or amazement— in my expression, because Michael asked if my wife and I would like to see the pageant, which he was going to record on a DVD. Naturally, I said we would be delighted.

As Sharon and I settled into our couch in front of the television, we really didn't know what to expect. As the screen lit up, the first view was of a well-appointed living room in an upscale home. Then the actors came in from both sides, dressed in elaborate costumes. The sound quality made it a little difficult to hear, but it was obvious that each child was reciting lengthy, detailed lines. Michael would tell me later that they had been memorizing and practicing their lines for weeks to make sure that they did not let the others down when the big day of the performance arrived. As I sat watching the production, I again marveled at the remarkable values of these young people. Here they were, ranging in age from late teens to probably less than five, performing as though they were on a stage in front of a packed house of their own peers. They were not only giving it their best effort, but each one seemed genuinely happy and grateful for the privilege. It struck me as a testament to their parents, both of whom were dedicated to ensuring that each of their nine children had every opportunity to live a rich, meaningful life. And it was within this context that the events of the coming years would be cast in such a tragic light.

Michael had noted from the first time we met that his vision was better on some days than others, but within less than a year he was telling me that the bad days were beginning to outnumber the good. His sight was usually best when he first woke up in the morning and seemed to deteriorate as the day progressed. He was still able to go to work and manage his computer and keep up with his hectic schedule, but it was becoming increasingly difficult. As he described it, the vision in his good right eye seemed to be "breaking up," as though small pieces of a puzzle were being taken away each day. And even though he had no central vision in his left eye, the side vision was still critical to him, and he felt that it too was getting worse. In short, things were not going the way either of us had hoped.

I began seeing Michael with increasing frequency, and our formal testing confirmed that indeed he was having progressive deterioration of his side vision, even though the central vision in the right eye remained reasonably good. The continued loss of vision was puzzling, since his eye pressures remained quite low with the several bottles of eye drops that I felt certain he was taking faithfully. Eye pressure, however, can change throughout the day, so we brought him in more than once to measure his pressures every couple of hours throughout the day to make sure we were not missing a time when they were higher. These all-day sessions revealed consistently normal pressures, although some readings were borderline, and even low normal pressures can be too high for some people. Since he was now using the strongest pressure-lowering medicines we had, I recommended that we proceed with the glaucoma laser treatment, to which he readily agreed. This provided some additional pressure reduction in both eyes, and I was cautiously optimistic that his vision would now stabilize. But it was not to be.

The shadows continued to deepen. The routines of daily living were becoming increasingly difficult. And Michael's frustration was steadily growing over the inability of the medical profession to provide him with answers. I am quite sure that I was losing credibility in his estimation. For some time, he had been reading everything he could find related to his condition, and he would often bring in articles that he felt might be pertinent. He knew that the underlying cause of his progressive visual loss was not typical of glaucoma in many ways, and he had begun to question whether we had the correct diagnosis. I had to confess that I too was starting to harbor doubts, which did nothing to strengthen his confidence in me. We had many long sessions in the office, discussing his condition and what more we could do for him. Michael knew from his reading and our discussions that the only proven treatment for preventing the blindness from glaucoma was to get the eye pressure low enough to protect the optic nerve. However, he had also become aware that other types of medications, in addition to those that lower the pressure, were being studied in the hope of protecting the nerve. None of these had proven value, but we eventually tried them all, looking desperately for something that might save Michael's vision. They were all in the form of pills, and some made him so sick that we had to stop them, while he doggedly stayed on others for years, despite many unpleasant side effects. Whether any of these really helped, we never knew, but what was clear was that Michael was continuing to go blind.

We had a small group of glaucoma specialists in Connecticut who met for dinner a few times each year to discuss challenging cases. On one of those occasions, I presented Michael's case to my colleagues, admitting that I was not entirely sure that we were on the right track with him because of his continued loss of vision despite low pressures. A lengthy discussion ensued, as we considered the myriad ways in which different forms of glaucoma can present, as well as the other types of optic atrophy with which glaucoma can be confused. In the end, however, there was nearly unanimous consensus that Michael had an unusual form of low-pressure glaucoma and that all we could do to save his remaining vision was to get the pressure even lower—and this meant surgery.

A few days later, I discussed this with Michael, and he seemed some-what relieved—although still with a healthy dose of skepticism—that other experts agreed with his current diagnosis. He was especially pleased that something more was being recommended to stabilize his condition and readily agreed to the surgery in his left eye. We chose to operate on that eye first in order to evaluate the results in his weaker eye before subjecting him to the risks of surgery in his better right eye. And so I put him on my surgical schedule for a few weeks hence. As always, his family of ten was with him on the morning of surgery, all expressing understandable concern in their usual quiet way. Fortunately, I was soon able to come out of the operating room and tell the family that their father was doing well—at least for the moment.

The surgery did provide some additional pressure reduction in his left eye, although it would be months before we would know if this was going to stabilize his sight in that eye. In the meantime, he continued to notice progressive loss of vision in his right eye, and we had many discussions about the pros and cons of proceeding with the operation in his good eye. Michael was understandably reticent about surgery on the eye for which he was totally dependent for his continued livelihood. Although the postoperative course was continuing to go reasonably well in the left eye, he knew that this was no absolute guarantee for the same in his right eye and that potential complications of surgery could actually hasten his loss of vision. Furthermore, additional factors were now beginning to further complicate the picture.

When I had first met Michael, his general health was otherwise good, with the only additional condition being mild arthritis, for which he took occasional over-the-counter pain medication. In the years that followed, however, he began developing an alarming number of added disorders. He was waking up almost every morning with severe headaches, which would often persist for hours. This might have been related to the fact that he was not sleeping well. His nights were now being disturbed by obstructive sleep apnea (momentary absence of breathing), for which he had to wear a cumbersome device called a CPAP (continuous positive airway pressure). He also developed a condition called restless leg syndrome (an uneasy twitching of the legs when lying down), for which he was now taking medication. Each of these conditions, as well as their treatments, could be associated with his glaucoma and possibly aggravating it. He was seen by a host of medical specialists to determine what more could be done for his various disorders and to discover if he had any other medical problems. And unfortunately, there was much more.

A neurologist evaluated Michael and obtained an MRI, which showed a thyroid nodule and spinal hemangiomas (benign growths of blood vessels), but no cause for his optic atrophy. Of greater possible significance, a spinal tap revealed a slight increase in the pressure of his cerebrospinal fluid (fluid around the brain and spine), which was not high enough to concern the neurologist, but could have implications for Michael's glaucoma. A hematologist found borderline evidence of an unusual blood disorder, which again was not severe enough to recommend treatment, but could be related to the mechanism of his glaucoma. A gastroenterologist diagnosed irritable bowel syndrome, abnormal liver function, and low vitamin D, suggesting poor absorption by his intestines. A cardiologist discovered a mitral valve prolapse (a common disorder of a heart valve), and an otolaryngologist diagnosed benign positional vertigo (dizziness) for which a cervical (neck) collar was recommended. In short, Michael had acquired a staggeringly complex medical history. He had an excellent family physician, with whom we worked closely to coordinate all his diagnoses and recommended treatments. We never knew whether any of these added conditions were causing or aggravating his loss of vision, but we made sure that all were being appropriately treated just to leave no stone unturned. And yet the visual loss continued.

While a certain level of eye pressure is by far the most common cause of the optic atrophy in glaucoma, several other mechanisms have been recognized that may contribute to destruction of the nerve. One of the better understood of these is the blood supply to the optic nerve, often referred to as ocular blood flow. Disorders of ocular blood flow are especially common in patients with normal-pressure glaucoma, and Michael had shown evidence of this over the years by repeated bleeding of the nerve in his right eye. Most of the pills that he was taking for his glaucoma were believed to improve the blood flow, although firm evidence for this was lacking. At about the time that we had exhausted everything we could think to do for Michael, our new chairman at Yale, Dr. Jim Tsai, organized an International Ocular Blood Flow Symposium in New York City. It was to be attended by leading experts on ocular blood flow from around the world, and I saw it as an excellent opportunity to pick the brains of these experts in the hope of finding answers for Michael. Jim suggested that I present Michael's case at the meeting to further enhance this opportunity.

When I shared all this with Michael, he became quite enthusiastic and asked if he might attend the meeting. It is a bit out of the ordinary to have a patient attend one of our scientific meetings, but then there was nothing ordinary about Michael, and it was typical of him to want to be fully engaged in every aspect of his medical care. And so, as I stood before several hundred doctors and scientists in the venerable New York Academy of Medicine, I knew that somewhere out there in the darkened hall, one person was listening more intently than anyone else to my every word. Michael not only attended the meeting, but also talked with as many of the world experts as he could during the coffee breaks, and I am sure he grilled them for all the knowledge he could get. One of our prominent guest speakers, Dr. Joseph Flammer, was from the University of Basel in Switzerland, where he had one of the world's most complete laboratories for the study of ocular blood flow. Seeing the intensity of Michael's interest and concern, Dr. Flammer offered to give him a complete examination with his special instruments, if he wished to come to Switzerland. And, not surprisingly, Michael took him up on it.

I was impressed and delighted when I learned that he was planning to make such a long trip, and I shared his optimism that maybe it would provide new information that would allow us to arrest Michael's relentless loss of vision. Not long after he returned from Switzerland, I received a several-page letter from Dr. Flammer, detailing the results of all the tests and summarizing his opinions and recommendations. He began by agreeing with our diagnosis of low-pressure glaucoma and felt that an abnormality of blood flow to the optic nerve could be contributing to the progressive optic atrophy, for which he recommended an additional pill. He also suggested that another mechanism for the optic atrophy might be the pressure of the cerebrospinal fluid. This fluid not only bathes the brain and spinal cord, but extends along the optic nerve right up to the back of the eye, and pressure at that point might damage the nerve. However, there was also evidence coming out at about the same time that elevated cerebrospinal fluid pressure might actually protect the nerve from glaucoma damage, while a low pressure might make it worse. For the moment, therefore, his main recommendation for treatment was to maintain good pressure control, which we were already doing. And so we were left with no more definitive answers to Michael's conundrum than before his valiant trip to Switzerland.

But Michael was not ready to give up—far from it. He continued to read everything he could find and would send me long e-mails with a host of questions, some of which I could answer, but for others I had to admit that "We just don't know." I could feel Michael's frustration growing as his condition seemed to get worse by the day. When he came in for his office visits, I arranged to see him at a time when no other patients were scheduled, because we would often talk for two hours or more. Those conversations sometimes became a bit tense, as Michael would question my answers, which often seemed inconsistent to him and admittedly were vague at best—we simply didn't have all the answers, and I could only sympathize with his growing disappointment with my shortcomings. He would ask me why we did not "do something more," since nothing we had done so far seemed to be helping. But he and I both knew that "something more" meant surgery on his good eye, and when we discussed the risks, he would choose to think about it a bit more. We would always shake hands at the end of those marathon sessions and then walk out together to where the whole family was waiting patiently.

As Michael's frustration continued to grow and his confidence in me progressively waned, I suggested that we might want to get some more second opinions, which he had also been considering. He first went back to the neuro-ophthalmologist in Philadelphia, who had initially seem him more than a decade earlier and who now agreed that Michael had glaucoma but that there was nothing more he could do for him. He was also seen by a neurologist in Philadelphia, who performed an ultrasound examination to test Dr. Flammer's cerebrospinal fluid theory, which was said to be inconclusive. Still unwilling to accept a vacuum of answers as to why his life was being torn apart, Michael turned east to Boston and Harvard, hoping to find answers in that bastion of medical expertise. He was seen there by another neuro-ophthalmologist, who felt that the cause of the progressive visual loss was unclear, but confirmed the elevated cerebrospinal fluid pressure and arranged for an appointment with a neurologist who specialized in headaches. That visit failed to uncover an explanation for the headaches, and he was simply advised to try different pain medications. Finally, Michael was seen by a glaucoma specialist at Harvard, who agreed with the diagnosis of normal-pressure glaucoma and encouraged Michael to have surgery on his right eye, as the only hope for saving what sight remained.

Shortly after returning from Boston, Michael came into my office to announce that he was ready to proceed with surgery in his right eye. By this time, I was approaching retirement and no longer operating, so I asked Dr. Tsai if he would perform the surgery. Jim had already seen Michael on several occasions in his clinic at my request, so the two were familiar with each other, and Michael was comfortable with the arrangement. Jim performed a flawless operation, but when the patch was removed the following morning, our greatest fear appeared to be realized. The small island of central vision in Michael's right eye, with which he had still been able to see almost 20/20, was gone! The best he could do that morning was to perceive the motion of a hand within three feet of his face. We hoped upon hope that the vision would come back, but agonizing days turned into painful weeks, and still there was no improvement. This sudden loss of vision after glaucoma surgery, which can happen regardless of how well the surgery is done, is rare but obviously devastating when it does occur—and for Michael, it was catastrophic. His left eye, which had been the weak one for nearly two decades, was now his better-seeing eye.

The situation was now beyond desperate. Michael could no longer see well enough to continue his work. For the past several years, he had been negotiating with his employers for a disability pension that would allow him to continue supporting his large family. He had met resistance at first, which only compounded the frustration in his life, but was finally able to obtain a reasonable settlement, although the income would be far less than he had been making while fully employed. Michael was now retired, and I had feared for some time that he was starting to show signs of depression as the anxiety of impending blindness and its consequences on his family began to overwhelm him. He was gaining weight from physical inactivity, and his chronic headaches and inability to get a good night's sleep were obviously wearing him down. His cheerful, optimistic countenance, which I had known for so many years, was being replaced by a defensive, almost hostile attitude. And who could blame him? He was no longer able to drive and had to depend on Colleen (and the children) to take him wherever he needed to go. He worried about being able to provide for his children and to ensure a good education for each of them, much less to one day see them walk across the stage at graduation. But what had begun to weigh most heavily on him was the fear that his children might inherit his eye condition and someday be faced with the blindness that was now overtaking his life. And, tragically, that fear was about to be realized.

I received a call one afternoon from a colleague in the eye center who was doing a routine eye exam on the Bell's third son, Jed, now in his late teens. The doctor was concerned about the appearance of Jed's optic nerves and asked if I would come take a look. A cold chill ran through me when I heard those words. Could it be possible that Michael's children had inherited his condition? I hurried over to my colleague's exam room, quickly passing the long line of the Bell clan in the hall. As I entered the room and greeted Colleen and Jed, I was desperately hoping that I would find something totally different from his father's condition when I examined Jed's eyes. But it was not to be—although his pressures were normal, his nerves had some very subtle changes that could represent early glaucoma. Of course, Jed was much younger than his father had been when the problem was first discovered, but we did not know how long Michael might have been harboring subtle changes in his nerves before the diagnosis was made. In any case, I tried to project an optimistic outward appearance as I explained to Colleen and Jed that he could be starting down the same path as his father, although it was really too soon to tell. For now, we would just obtain a set of baseline studies and keep a close watch on him.

I feared that it might tip Michael over the edge when he learned of Jed's findings. And indeed, he was in my office the next day, wanting to know every detail of what I had found and demanding that we come up with better answers before his son wound up in his situation. I have felt the pain of many of patients over the years, but none more exquisitely than at that moment with Michael, and I struggled to think of what to say next. When the glaucoma specialist at Harvard had sent me his report, he suggested that we might have a colleague of his perform genetic testing on Michael to see what light that could shed on his condition. Since we had performed virtually every other diagnostic procedure, and especially in light of Jed's recent findings, genetic testing seemed to make good sense. Michael was totally agreeable with the suggestion and was soon on the road again, heading back to Boston.

Genetic testing was relatively new to the study of glaucoma in the early years of the twenty-first century, although new knowledge was coming out almost every day, and it promised hope for future methods of diagnosis and treatment. The first step in using genetic information is to identify the gene—or, more precisely, the mutation or change in that gene—that is associated with a disease. From the patient's standpoint, it usually begins with simply taking a blood sample, and that is what the genetics specialist at Harvard did for Michael after she had performed another thorough examination. What is then done with the blood, however, is anything but simple. The Human Genome Project, which had recently been completed, disclosed that there are twenty to twenty-five thousand genes that determine what we are and what can go wrong with us. But trying to find the gene that fits the disease is like looking for a needle in a haystack. At the time that Michael's blood was being analyzed, a few gene mutations had been discovered for certain types of glaucoma, but these represented only a small percentage of the total group of disorders. Some genes had also been found that seemed to be associated with other forms of optic atrophy, and there was a laboratory at Emory University in Atlanta that had developed a method for identifying mutations of those genes. Michael's blood sample was sent to that laboratory, and we were all amazed when the report came back indicating that he not only had a mutation for a gene, called OPA1, that was thought to be associated with a certain type of optic atrophy, but that it was a mutation which had never been seen before!

For the first time, it appeared that we might have a definitive answer to the dilemma of Michael's progressive blindness. But what did it really mean? Was it telling us that he actually did not have glaucoma all this time that we had been treating him for it? As it turned out, there were a number of papers in the recent medical literature concerning a possible association between normal-pressure glaucoma and mutations of the OPA1 gene. But, as with so much in medicine, there was more gray than black and white; in other words, the findings were inconclusive. Some writers suggested that there was a relationship, while others questioned this view. Nevertheless, the bulk of the evidence seemed to weigh slightly in favor of an association, and ironically, the most conclusive of those papers was coauthored by Dr. Myers, who had originally made the diagnosis of normal-pressure glaucoma in Michael.

The important question now was whether Jed harbored the same genetic mutation, and to our surprise and dismay, his report came back with the very same, previously unknown mutation as his father. We now had to have the other children tested, but there was a problem—it was a very expensive test that would cost several hundred dollars per child. On Michael's pension this was simply not possible. And since it was an uncommon test, performed in only a few medical centers around the country, it was not on his insurance company's list of approved diagnostic procedures, and they initially refused to pay the costs. But Michael was not one to let any barrier hold him back, especially when it involved the welfare of his family. By this time, we had enlisted the help of yet another neuro-ophthalmologist, Dr. Robert Lesser, a good friend and highly respected colleague. After many letters back and forth with the insurance company and through the efforts of Dr. Lesser, we were finally able to obtain approval for the testing. Three of the children elected not to be tested, but of the five who did, three more were found to have the family's unusual gene mutation.

Michael's next question was predictable—what could be done for the children to ensure that they did not one day end up in his current condition? And, sadly, that is where the story of medical genetics reaches a temporary roadblock for most inherited diseases. By itself, identifying the gene mutation in an individual only tells us whether or not the person is at risk of one day developing the condition. There are two other critical pieces to the puzzle that must fit into place before we can use the genetic information to formulate a definitive treatment plan for that disease. The first of these is to determine how the genetic mutation alters some biological process in our body to cause the disorder. In Michael's condition, for example, it might be that the mutation weakened his optic nerve to the extent that even low, normal eye pressure caused progressive damage and loss of vision. Or another theory might be that the mutant OPA1 gene produces a condition very similar to glaucoma that is not related to eye pressure. In any case, only after the function of the gene and the pathway of the disease process are understood can the final step be approached—finding a treatment to correct the abnormal gene or its consequences. Either of these latter two steps could take a generation or more of continued scientific exploration for a single disease.

And so we were left with a possible explanation for Michael's blindness, but with no idea of how to use this new information to formulate a better treatment plan for him or his children. The only treatment we could offer them at that time was to keep their eye pressures low, and we didn't even know if that really made a difference in their unusual condition. But there is ongoing research to find other ways of protecting the weakened optic nerve, and we have reason to hope that effective treatments will be discovered in time to help the Bell children. Michael seemed to be at reasonable peace with those thoughts, although I doubt that a day ever passes in which he does not continue to scour the literature for any new discoveries that might help his children and himself.

Shortly before I retired from Yale, Michael and I had lunch together after one of his morning examinations. Colleen and the children had dropped him off with the understanding that I would drive him back to the Yale Divinity School Library, where he was working on a paper. For more than a decade now, I had witnessed the suffering that had come to dominate his life—not only from the inexplicable, relentless loss of sight, but also from failure of medical science to provide him with answers. I had seen his frustration over the loss of his job, his independence, his ability to read and write and to provide fully for his family—but most of all I had seen his fear of what the future might hold for his children. And yet, as we took a table in the diner, I sensed an inner peace in him that I had not seen for a long time. His life, as he expressed it to me, had again come full circle, from the study of religion, through the world of business, and back to his religious studies, where he said his heart truly lay. And it was in this cycle of his life that he was able to find meaning to the events of the past years.

We sat in silence for a while, and his eyes appeared distant and a bit misty, as he seemed to be searching for a way to explain his feelings to me. Slowly, he began to relate the story of Saint Paul in the New Testament, and how he too had suffered from a malady, which he referred to as his "thorn in the flesh." While historians have never agreed on what that condition might have been, Michael believes it could have been related to his vision, since Paul noted in one of his letters that his followers would have "torn out your eyes and given them to me" if they could. Whatever his infirmity may have been, when Paul appealed to God for relief, he was told, "My grace is sufficient for you, for my power is made perfect in weakness." Michael tried to see his situation in the same light. Through all those years of frustration and anger, he had never lost his faith that there is a purpose in everything. He was able to see a rainbow through the darkest clouds—to see new opportunities emerge from the desolation of his own infirmities. He was now free to return to his true passion of religious study and writing, and he lived in an age when digital technology provided resources for the visually impaired that would allow him to pursue those interests. And for all of this, Michael was truly thankful.

As I drove back to the eye center after saying good-bye to Michael at the library, my spirits were buoyed by the realization that he was going to be okay—his inner strength and convictions were going get him through whatever trials the future might hold. Of course, he would never stop looking for medical answers, and he would forever be challenging his doctors to do everything possible for him and his children. I couldn't help but smile to recall him once telling me that he had sometimes gotten in trouble at work for being "too persistent." This was actually one of his strengths, and I was convinced that he would never stop seeking answers for the welfare of his family and himself. But now I also knew that he would, for the rest of his life, find fulfillment in each day by turning whatever challenges came his way into new opportunities.

23.

Joe and Donna

A headline in *The New York Times* caught my eye: "Turn 70. Act Your Grandchild's Age."

'Well, that certainly has my name on it,' was my immediate thought.

I was entering my fifteenth year at Yale and was scheduled to retire the following spring. Although we loved New England, Sharon and I were looking forward to our return to North Carolina and being near Sarah and her family. Before the retirement date, I would pass my seventieth year, which was one reason why the *Times* headline had caught my eye. And the article was not terribly comforting. "For most people," it stated, "the 70s represents the end, not a beginning. Average life expectancy is 78 years old." (And lower for men.) As one person was quoted in the article, "This one has the ring of mortality." Up to that moment, I had really not paid much attention to the fact that the winds of time had been blowing ever more swiftly with each passing year. Maybe I was too busy to notice. Maybe it was being around my young students and colleagues. Or maybe it was Allison—and that was the other reason why the *Times* article seemed to have my name on it.

Sarah's daughter, Allison, was nine years old and the light of our life, although it frightened me to realize how quickly she was growing up. After giving birth, Sarah had suffered a series of medical setbacks, and it was clear that Allison would be her only child. John was in Florida with his significant other, but still unmarried at the time. So Allison was our only grandchild, and yet we could not have felt more blessed if we had a dozen as beautiful, bright, and healthy as her. And Allison and "Papa" were inseparable buddies. Whenever we visited them in North Carolina, the two of us were together from sunrise to bedtime. The *Times'* admonition to act your grandchild's age was a reference to the many septuagenarians that are still active, such as Ringo Starr, who performed at Radio City Music Hall on this seventieth birthday. Well, I was certainly adhering to their advice, at least when I was with Allison. Despite the sixty years that separated our ages, I enjoyed playing games and reading with her, and I think it did allow me to temporarily ignore the passage of time.

And yet the thought of turning seventy and the impending retirement in the coming year was enough to give me sober pause. In all the previous phases of my life—childhood, higher education, the Navy, Duke, and Yale—there had always been the comfort of knowing that another phase lay beyond it. But with the retirement phase comes the uncertainty of what lies beyond and the question of how to make the most of the time that is left. I really wasn't concerned about the first part—I was content to leave that in the hands of a higher power. But the second was a serious question for me, and I was fortunate over the years to have role models, many of whom were my patients, who provided valuable guidance in the efficient use of that precious commodity—time. Two in particular will always stand out in my mind. One was a patient at Duke and the other at Yale. They never knew each other, and yet their lessons are remarkably similar. And they both certainly knew something about making the most of the time we are given—between the two of them, their combined ages totaled more than two centuries.

———

Sharon and I had found a nice little wooded spot in the North Carolina countryside, near Sarah's home, on which we were building our retirement home in preparation for the departure from Yale. And that, of course, involved frequent trips down South to check on the progress. We would usually fly into the Greensboro airport, pick up a rental car, and then head out on Bryan Boulevard.

As we drove under the green and white sign proclaiming the name of the highway, we always knew what the other was thinking—or, at least, whom we were thinking about. In truth, the sign could send our memories off in many directions—a reading of *The Night Before Christmas* on Christmas eve, a dinner party before a fishing trip, hours in the Duke student center, a meeting in Germany, a celebration of a civic icon, a funeral—but the most vivid memory for me will forever be of the day that a distinguished gentleman first walked into my office and into my life.

If there was ever a person who epitomized the confident, successful, powerful businessman, it was Mr. Joseph McKinley Bryan. He was truly larger than life in so many ways. My first thought was of the white-haired gentleman in the original Monopoly game. He had the same full face with a large, white moustache and heavy, white eyebrows, and although his hairline was receding, revealing a strong brow, he still had a good head of silky, white hair. Ruddy cheeks and a portly, robust frame suggested a man who was accustomed to a full and vigorous life. He was already well into his eighties, but he carried himself as a man much younger. His piercing blue eyes looked straight into mine as he gave me a firm handshake. He was rather intimidating on first impression, although I thought that I caught a twinkle in his eyes that belied a gentler nature. The latter impression would eventually prove to most accurately describe his true character, but on this first visit it was clear that he was there for business.

It took a little while for me to understand his speech pattern, which, in addition to being a bit gruff, was interspersed with frequent "hrumphs" and clearing of his throat as he tried to relate the reason for his visit. Fortunately, I had a letter of introduction from his ophthalmologist in Greensboro, which explained that Mr. Bryan suffered from both cataracts and glaucoma. It was felt that he would require surgery, not only for the cataracts but also for his glaucoma, since he was unable to tolerate any of the current glaucoma drops or pills. This was not uncommon in those days, when we were limited to drops that caused redness, discomfort, and blurring of vision or could aggravate systemic disorders, while the pills had a litany of side effects. And so, although the cataracts were already blunting his vision, the poorly controlled glaucoma was threatening irreversible blindness and clearly had to be addressed first. The laser treatment for his type of glaucoma had just recently become available, and I explained this option to Mr. Bryan. He then proceeded to grill me with a list of questions about the procedure, all of which were insightful and logical, suggesting a mind that was accustomed to understanding and going straight to the heart of any matter. I did my best to answer each question, and he finally seemed to be satisfied and agreed to be scheduled for the laser surgery.

Since it was a relatively new procedure, and I was initially the only one performing it in our area, we had set aside a half day each week to treat a fairly large number of patients with the laser operation. But something told me that I should not bring Mr. Bryan in with the rest of the patients, when I would have to move rather quickly from one to the next. And this proved to be a prescient decision. On the afternoon that we had scheduled him for his first session (we only treated one eye at a time), I had cleared my calendar of all other responsibilities. Even so, I was mildly apprehensive. I was still fairly young at the time, and I had learned that Mr. Bryan was a man of considerable stature in the state and beyond—failure was not an option. I did my best to appear professional and explained each step of the procedure as he sat down in front of the laser. I placed a drop of anesthetic on his eye and then applied a special contact lens, which contained a mirror that directed the pencil of intense laser light into his eye. As I focused the aiming beam and explained that we were about ready to begin, there were a few "hrumphs" and some clearing of the throat, and I strongly suspected that he was questioning whether this young doctor knew what he was doing. It was actually a relatively simple and easy procedure for both surgeon and patient, and I was confident that Mr. Bryan would soon realize this and relax. But the next few minutes would prove my confidence to be badly misplaced.

Over the years, I have gained the impression that men are more prone to fainting than women. In fact, it seems that the more virile and masculine they are, the more likely they are to fall. I have had healthy young men pass out while I was simply measuring the pressure in their eye—or just talking about examining their eyes. However, I had never experienced it during a laser treatment—not until that afternoon—and I couldn't believe that the first time was about to be with Mr. Bryan. The initial clue was the moist skin of his face, which I could feel with my hand that was holding the contact lens. And then his face began to turn a bit ashen, and I sensed that his breathing was becoming labored and he seemed to be going limp. I asked him if he was all right, but there was no answer. It was now obvious what was happening. I withdrew the contact lens and rushed around to the other side of the laser, just as he collapsed into my arms. I laid him down on the carpet and checked his pulse, which was rapid and shallow. Nurse Sharon, who always seemed to know when I was in trouble, rushed in and helped me raise his legs to improve the circulation to his head. Soon his eyes opened and he looked up at us with a bewildered expression. We were eventually able to help him into a chair, where he relaxed and regained his color and spirits. But the question now was how we should proceed. I had barely completed a quarter of the treatment when the problem began. I discussed it with Mr. Bryan, and he insisted that we finish the procedure right then. So, with Sharon by his side, we continued the treatment, stopping two more times to let him rest when he again began to feel faint. We finally completed the laser operation, which took considerably longer than any I had performed before, and I thanked my lucky stars that we had blocked off the afternoon for him. I assured him that it had gone fine and tried to assuage any embarrassment he might have by promising that his reaction was not uncommon. But he must have either known I was lying or wondered why I had not warned him about it in advance.

When he returned the following week, I was delighted to see that he was already having a good response to the laser treatment. And so we proceeded with the other eye, which went much more smoothly than the first, with only one break for rest in the middle of the procedure. Over the course of the next few months, the pressure in both eyes came down to a very safe and gratifying level. I am not sure which of us was more relieved by our good fortune, but it led to a warm relationship that would eventually disclose to me one of Mr. Bryan's greatest traits.

In those early days, with the advent of lasers and computers, we were entering a new age in our ability to both diagnose and treat glaucoma. Computer technology had already been applied to measuring the loss of peripheral vision in our glaucoma patients, and was now being evaluated as a more precise way to document damage to the optic nerve from glaucoma. An instrument for the latter purpose had recently been developed in Germany that seemed to hold promise. Compared to what we have today, it was rather crude, but it was a major advance for its time. It consisted of two cameras that captured simultaneous images of the nerve, much as our eyes see an object from slightly different angles. A computer then constructed a three-dimensional image from the disparate photos, as our brain creates depth perception from the information of our two eyes. It was a large, unwieldy instrument that took up the better part of an examination room, and the price tag of $100,000 was especially daunting in the early 1980s. In an effort to promote their instrument, the company had invited doctors from around the world to Germany for a demonstration. Since they were covering all the travel expenses, I decided to go and take a look at it, even though I knew there was no way we could afford to buy one.

Shortly before my trip to Germany, Joe Bryan came in for his routine follow-up visit. One of the things I was learning to appreciate about him was his inquisitive mind—he wanted to know what was happening in virtually every aspect of life. That day he asked me what was new in glaucoma, and so I told him about the new nerve analyzer. His next question, predictably, was how it worked and then what I thought about it. I told him of my pending trip to Germany, and he was silent for a moment.

"Hrumph. If it looks good, will Duke buy one?" he asked as he cleared his throat.

"No, sir, I'm afraid it is a bit beyond our budget," I explained and then shared with him the price.

There was another brief moment of silence as he seemed to be considering the matter. Then he proceeded in the demeanor of a man who was accustomed to giving orders.

"Hrumph. Hrumph. Well you go to Germany and check it out thoroughly," he instructed me with another clearing of his throat, "and when you get back, come see me, and we will—hrumph—talk about it."

I didn't quite know what to make of that, but I thanked him and promised to follow his directive.

My flight to Germany landed in Frankfurt. From there I would take a train to the charming city of Würzburg, where the meeting was to be held. The Frankfurt train station was an enormous structure of glass and steel from the early twentieth century, with throngs of passengers rushing to and from the various trains on numerous parallel tracks. It evoked memories of war movies, and I couldn't help but wonder what it must have been like when most of the young men were in German uniforms and the young women had tears in their eyes. It was almost surreal to think that I would have been an enemy in this station at that time, and yet now, thankfully, we were all friends.

I also found it reminiscent of earlier times that the passenger cars were divided into compartments with two rows of seats facing each other. I found one that was empty and settled in, but was soon joined by a young German man, about my age, who sat down across from me.

It turned out that we would be the only two in that compartment for the duration of the trip. We smiled and exchanged pleasantries in German with my limited command of the language. I got by the "Wie geht es Ihnen?" and the "Sehr gut, danke," but when he asked me another question in German, I had to admit that "Mein Deutsch ist nicht sehr gut."

He laughed and asked in perfect English, "Are you from the States?"

It has always been a source of embarrassment for me that, whenever I meet people in their county, they seem to have an excellent command of my language, but I have little or none of theirs. There are many reasons for this, although in the end I have only myself to blame for my linguistic deficiencies. But he was a friendly fellow and we had a pleasant chat—in English.

The reason for having the meeting in Würzburg was that our host, one of the world's leading glaucoma experts, Professor Wolfgang Leydhecker, was chairman of the Department of Ophthalmology at the University of Würzburg. It is a wonderfully European city, with the Main River running through the middle, ancient castles rising on hills to one side, and vineyards covering slopes in the opposite direction. The meeting began that afternoon with a reception in one of the vintage, historic buildings, and I was greeted by Professor Leydhecker—a distinguished-looking, elderly gentleman whose large frame was held in a perfectly erect and confident manner and whose ruddy cheeks were framed by a remnant of hair that was neatly combed straight back.

"So glad to finally meet you," he began in perfect English. "I am a big fan of your father's textbook," the latter offered with a bit of a twinkle in his eye.

I never knew if he was just pulling my leg or being truly complimentary. I was still rather young at the time, and the first edition of my book had only been out a few years. His reference to my "father's textbook" was obviously to imply that I was too young to have written it—or at least that was what I allowed my ego to presume. But he was a friendly, fatherly gentleman, and we got along quite well.

In the evening of the first day, our international group of doctors was taken to an old hospital in Würzburg, where Wilhelm Roentgen had pioneered the use of X-rays around the turn of the century. Another attraction of the hospital was a wine cellar in the basement. The vineyards outside Würzburg were part of a venerable wine industry, of which the hospital had long been a beneficiary. Our hosts explained that, during World War II, the patients were taken to the wine cellar to escape the Allied bombing. As we walked down the dark, musty corridors between enormous, intricately carved oak casks, I could only imagine what it must have been like in those days. Soon we came to a more modern, brightly lit room where we were treated to a wine tasting before dinner. I sat beside Professor Leydhecker, who amazed me with his in-depth knowledge of each German wine that we were served. It was a fitting ending to my first day in Würzburg.

The next morning, which was Saturday, the attendees gathered in a classroom of the University for an all-day scientific meeting to learn about the new imaging instrument. After several detailed lectures by experts on the device, we had the opportunity to look at one and work with it. It was really quite a monster, consisting of a sturdy, three-by-eight-foot table on which was mounted a slit lamp with the two cameras for the acquisition of the images. Enormous computers were positioned on and beneath the table for analysis of the data, and a printer at the far end of the table recorded the results. But it was revolutionary for its time, and we were all quite impressed. Some of the doctors at the meeting indicated that their hospital would be purchasing one, although I held out no such hopes for Duke.

On Sunday morning, Professor Leydhecker entertained us with a "house concert" in his home. I discovered that, among his many talents, he was an accomplished violist and had organized a remarkably good (at least to my ear) chamber ensemble with a few of his physician friends. It was a delightful and impressive morning, the likes of which I have never before or since experienced. After lunch with some of the group, I headed to the airport and was soon on my way home. Flying over the Atlantic, I had a lot to think about. It had been a fascinating and instructive three days. The instrument we had been shown was a prime example of the exciting advances in technology that were occurring in our field. I thought about how it might help in the care of our glaucoma patients, although I doubted that I would ever have the chance to find out firsthand. And that led me to thinking about my upcoming meeting with Joe Bryan and wondering what he had meant when we last spoke.

His office was on the eleventh floor of the seventeen-story Jefferson-Pilot Building in Greensboro, a spot he had occupied for over fifty years since arriving in Greensboro in 1931. A native of Ohio, Joe Bryan had not been born into a privileged life. In fact, he wasn't even able to finish high school or attend college. But after serving in the ambulance corps in France during World War I, he went into the cotton brokerage business in New York and, at age twenty-seven, was the youngest person to ever gain membership on the New York Cotton Exchange. He not only established himself as a successful businessman, but also began moving in the lively literary circles with such luminaries as F. Scott Fitzgerald and Dorothy Parker, with whom he would frequent Cole Porter's on Saturday nights. The most important person he met in New York, however, was Kathleen Price, whose father, Julian Price, was president of Jefferson Standard Life Insurance Co. in Greensboro. They were married in 1927 and moved to Greensboro four years later, where Joe went into business with his father-in-law.

Despite being the son-in-law in the business, it didn't take Joe long to establish his own credentials and prove his worth as a shrewd investor for the company. Radio was in its infancy, and Joe could see its potential for communication and for profitable investment. He cajoled his father-in-law into purchasing a struggling station, whose antenna and generator were atop the Jefferson building, and the rest is history. With the success of their first radio station, they expanded their communications holdings, including the first television station in the Carolinas, and in 1983 Joe Bryan received the prestigious Mike Award for his pioneering work in broadcasting. Today, Jefferson-Pilot is a thriving broadcasting enterprise that is especially well known for covering Atlantic Coast Conference basketball and football games.

Mr. Bryan officially retired in 1961, but he continued to go into his office every workday, where he would handle his personal investments and correspondence and enjoy a passion for which he would be most remembered during the final one-third of his life. In his ample, ornate office, with gifts and memorabilia from around the world, he sat behind a massive oak desk in a red leather chair. And that was where I found him as I stepped off the elevator on the eleventh floor and was escorted into his office.

He rose slowly and with some difficulty and motioned to the chair that I was to take in front of his desk. There was an awkward moment of silence (awkward for me, at least) as we both settled into our chairs. All our previous meetings had been in my office, where I felt comfortable initiating the conversation. But I wasn't sure of protocol on this day and sat quietly—and a bit uncomfortably—waiting for his lead as those piercing eyes remained locked on mine. In a moment, however, I saw the hint of a twinkle in his eyes and then a faint smile beneath his massive moustache.

"Hrumph. So how was your trip to Germany?" he began with the predictability of a man who is accustomed to going straight to the business at hand and then cleared his throat.

I was fairly certain that he did not want to hear all the social details of my trip, so I simply reported that it went quite well, thank you, and then began to discuss the instrument for which I had traveled to Germany. His expression was now entirely serious, and he nodded his understanding with each of my comments, never taking his eyes off mine. Of course, he wanted to know every technical detail, and I was glad that I had taken voluminous notes and committed most to memory. But then he asked me a question for which I was totally unprepared.

"How long will it take—hrumph—according to your business plan to pay off the initial cost and—hrumph—begin to make a profit?"

Well, I didn't have a business plan. In fact, that side of the matter had not even occurred to me, which is why I was never a good businessman. When he was running his company, Mr. Bryan understandably liked to make investments that paid off, and his remarkable success testified to his skill in making wise decisions. He knew that medicine was like any other business and that every major investment had to be viewed from the standpoint of its potential return. I was now becoming rather uncomfortable as I realized the large gap in my thinking about the new imaging instrument, and my response must have seemed weak and inadequate.

"Well, sir, I know that there is a great need for an instrument of this type," I began tentatively, praying that inspiration would come to bolster my feeble reply. "It will improve our ability to diagnose and follow our patients with glaucoma. I don't honestly know if this particular technology will prove to be the best. There will probably be better ones to come. But I think we need to start now with what we have so we can keep finding better ways to help our patients."

He showed absolutely no expression, other than the intensity of his eyes, which never wavered from mine, as he listened to my response, which did not even address his question. And then there was a long silence, and I was sure that I had blown everything. Did his silence signal his incredulity at the inadequacy of my planning, or was he simply extending the courtesy of waiting until he was sure that I had shut up? But what happened next is a moment I will always remember—the moment I learned that Joe Bryan, the onetime titan of business, was now the embodiment of the humanitarian.

Without changing his expression, he reached into his desk drawer and withdrew a piece of paper, which he handed across the desk to me. As I looked down at it, I stared in disbelief—it was a check for $110,000. Now I was truly lost for an appropriate response. My first thought was to point out that he had written it for more than the cost of the instrument. But he must have anticipated my dilemma and broke the silence with a brief explanation for the remarkable act that he had just performed.

"Hrumph. You will need a little extra for the setup of your new instrument," he said almost sheepishly, now with the twinkle back in his eyes and the smile beneath his moustache.

I never knew how serious he was about the business plan. As I came to know him better over the years, it was obvious that the driving force in this phase of his life was helping other people, and that was the passion he enjoyed in coming to work every day. But he was still a businessman, and he always wanted to be sure that every gift he made received the maximum return—not so much financially as in the degree to which it truly benefited others. And the latter would soon prove to be a problem with the remarkably generous gift that I had just received. At that moment, however, I could only do my best to express my most profound gratitude, which he received graciously and then stood to signal that our meeting was over.

Driving back to Durham, my elation over the unexpected gift was suddenly tempered by the realization of the problem I had created. Not only had I failed to consider a business plan, but I had also given no thought to where I would put the new instrument. It required a room as big as the one we used for our examinations, and we simply didn't have any available room in our clinic area. In the back of the eye center, not too far from our glaucoma clinic, there was a space for Robin and a few small faculty offices. Since I was the only faculty member in the glaucoma service at the time, we had a spare office that was used by our glaucoma fellow. It was just large enough to share with our nerve analyzer, and that is where we placed our $100,000 instrument. It was certainly not the ideal location, and I got a lot of teasing about it from the residents and fellows. I just hoped that Joe Bryan would not recognize the inappropriateness of it, but I should have known better.

Shortly after the instrument arrived and was set up (in the fellow's office), we had a small reception to show it off to the community and to honor our benefactor. I was very proud of it and was especially pleased to give Mr. Bryan a personal introduction to it. But as we walked through the clinic and he glanced in each room at all the other equipment and then back to the office area, I began to fear the worst. Sure enough, his first question was the location. He obviously wasn't pleased, and I don't think my efforts to assure him that the location would not influence the utilization or benefit of the instrument assuaged his concerns. But, being the perfect gentleman that he was, he let it ride and never mentioned it again. In truth, the nerve analyzer never did live up to the clinical value for which I had hoped, but it was extremely useful for research and led to a number of published scientific observations that helped advance our understanding of the field and the utilization of the more sophisticated instruments that would follow. I think this may have mollified Mr. Bryan to some extent, although I suspect that he always harbored some reservations about that first gift.

The bells were ringing high overhead in the chapel tower as our family stepped out of the Duke Chapel into the warm, friendly sunshine of a cool winter's Sunday. Sarah and John were in their early teens at the time and enjoyed our tradition after the morning service of visiting the student center on campus—more precisely, the Joseph M. and Kathleen Price Bryan University Center. It was a large stone structure, where we had once come to see Sir Rex Harrison perform. A popular feature of the center for our family was a painting of Mr. Bryan and his wife, Kathleen. She had suffered from Alzheimer's disease before her death several years earlier, and that is why her husband had funded not only the university center, but also the Joseph and Kathleen Bryan Alzheimer's Disease Research Center on the Duke campus, where pioneering research was advancing the understanding of that condition. But the reason why Sarah and John found the picture to be so captivating was that they had actually met the great man in his home.

It was a few days before Christmas. Our family had driven over to Greensboro to visit friends and had arranged to stop by Mr. Bryan's home on the way to deliver a loaf of pumpkin bread that Sharon had just baked. She and I had visited him there once before, and we read our kids the riot act about being on their best behavior and not touching anything in his stately house. It probably wasn't necessary, because they were typically well behaved, and more importantly, Joe Bryan loved children. He seemed to delight in showing them around his home, especially in the large, comfortable sunroom. There were two things in that room that we will always remember. One was a large painting of Kathleen. Joe took great pride in it and pointed out to Sarah and John that, wherever they stood in the room, she would be looking right at them. But what was most endearing to Sharon and me was a small, well-worn copy of *The Night before Christmas* resting alone on a table. For more than fifty years, this giant among the world's captains of industry had sat on the floor in his sunroom amid the children of the neighborhood and read this book to them on Christmas Eve.

As the years passed, Mr. Bryan's glaucoma remained well controlled, but his eyesight was failing as a result of his cataracts. He was approaching ninety years of age, and though his large frame was beginning to wear out, his mind was as sharp as ever, and he did not want blunted vision to slow him down. And so, with some fear and trepidation, I scheduled him for cataract surgery in one eye. My concern was not so much the difficult operation as it was the person who would be lying on the table in front of me—it was like operating on a member of my family. And, consistent with my previous experiences with Joe Bryan, my fears proved to be all too prophetic—and yet once again there seemed to be a guardian angel watching over us.

Surgical techniques were changing, and I had recently adopted one of the newer procedures. I could have used the older operation, with which I was very comfortable, but I wanted to offer him the best, so I proceeded with the newer technique. All was going well until suddenly—to my dismay—a piece of the cataract fell into the back of his eye onto the retina. This was a serious complication, and I couldn't believe it was happening now—with Mr. Bryan. It called for special measures to remove the fragment from the delicate retina, and I was fortunate that, in the operating room next door, was one of my retina colleagues, who was able to come over and help remove the errant tissue. The remainder of the operation went fine, and Mr. Bryan regained excellent vision in the eye—much to my profound relief. I don't think he ever knew that there had been a deviation from the standard procedure, but I sure never forgot.

After that experience, my relationship with Joe Bryan seemed to grow increasingly warmer. Sharon and I enjoyed several special and occasionally humorous times with him. She still laughs about a time in his home when we were getting ready to go to lunch and he wanted to ask her if she needed to use the ladies' room before we left. But being the proper gentleman of the old school that he was, he couldn't quite bring himself to use such indelicate words in front of a lady. So there were more "hrumphs" and clearing of the throat than usual as he asked her if she needed to go upstairs. She couldn't quite figure out why he would suggest a tour of the upstairs, just as we were about to leave for lunch, until the housekeeper whispered that that was where the ladies' room was.

On another occasion, we were having dinner in Greensboro with a small group from Duke who were honoring Joe for all his generosity. He had regaled us throughout the evening with stories of his life, such as his annual attendance of the Masters Golf Tournament in Augusta, for which he was a major benefactor and had been honored with the traditional green jacket. Another annual tradition for him was a fishing expedition in Canada with a small group of friends. He explained that he was actually leaving for that trip the following morning, and I asked the foolish question as to what time his flight left. Without the least hint of arrogance or condescension, he simply said it would leave whenever he got there. I should have known he had his own plane.

The Duke Eye Center had been growing, and a new wing had recently been added, which included our glaucoma clinic. The construction had been funded with a loan, leaving us with a sizeable debt that the university was understandably anxious to retire. Recalling that Mr. Bryan had given me the money for the nerve analyzer, our administration asked if I might approach him again for financial support. Aside from the charity concert with Ronnie Milsap, I had absolutely no experience with fundraising up to that point and hated the idea of going to my friend for more money, especially in light of the less-than-stellar results from his first gift. Nevertheless, I soon found myself once again riding the elevator to the eleventh floor of the Jefferson-Pilot Building. Although it had been several years since my first visit, nothing seemed to have changed, including the great man sitting behind the massive desk in his red leather chair. He motioned me to the same chair that I had occupied before, and after a few pleasantries, I began to explain our financial situation in the department. The lump in my throat was growing larger as I finally got up the nerve to ask if he might be willing to help us retire the debt. He listened very intently and courteously and—predictably—had many questions. When all the questions had been answered to the best of my ability, he thanked me for coming and, with a promise to consider my request, stood to indicate that our visit was over.

One of the many endearing traits of Joe Bryan was that he always sent a hand-written thank-you note after each visit. And so, right on schedule, a note arrived in the mail. In it he thanked me again for my recent visit and then explained that he would be willing to provide half of the funds to retire our debt if we could match it. Well, that was good news and bad. I was thrilled, of course, to have half of the necessary funds, but had no immediate inspiration as to where I would come up with the other half. The only possibility I could think of was a sizeable research account that I had built up over the years (which was probably an indication that I should have been doing more research). Although it would take nearly the entire account, it would be enough, and since I didn't have any other immediate plans for the money, this seemed like an appropriate expenditure of the funds. And so I happily reported to Mr. Bryan that I could match his generous gift, and thus the debt for our new wing and our glaucoma clinic was retired.

With these two sizable gifts, Joe Bryan had now contributed far more than anyone else to our glaucoma clinic. I was not only very grateful to him, but also had grown extremely fond of my special friend over the years and wanted to honor him in some meaningful way. And so, after obtaining approval from the university, as well as Joe's permission, the glaucoma clinic at Duke became officially known as the Joseph M. Bryan Glaucoma Clinic. The name was emblazoned in large brass letters on a wall of our waiting room beside an excellent portrait of him and a brass plaque that acknowledged his philanthropy and friendship to Duke University Eye Center. While it wasn't in the same league with the Bryan University Center or the Bryan Alzheimer's Disease Research Center, I was very proud to also have his name associated with our facility, and I think he was proud of it too. We had another reception in his honor, and this time I believe he fully approved of how his generosity was being used.

By now, the sands of time were beginning to run out for Joe, although he never seemed to notice or at least to worry about it. Maybe it was because he remained so occupied with doing what brought him the greatest pleasure, which was bringing happiness to others. He was now confined to a wheelchair and had difficulty coming to the eye center, so I occasionally drove over to his home in Greensboro to check on him. Actually, the calls were more social than professional. Thankfully, the vision in his eye with the cataract surgery was holding up, and he was having no particular problems with his eyes. The two of us would just sit in his library and talk. He invariably apologized for not being able to get up when I came in, and his voice had grown weak, but his mind seemed as sharp as ever. He always wanted to know what was going on in the "eye business." And I wanted to learn more about him, but whenever I would bring up his latest philanthropy, he would brush it off by saying, "I'm really just selfish. I like to see other people happy."

On his ninetieth birthday, a gala party was held to acknowledge his protean contributions to the wider community of North Carolina. It was such a large affair that it had to be held at the Greensboro Coliseum. The hundreds who attended the party probably thought we knew all about Joe's benevolence, but were surprised to learn that there was so much more. In addition to his high-profile gifts at Duke, he had supported other universities in the state, including a business school at one and public television at another. But his special interest was helping individual people in rural areas of the state, where he funded day-care centers, public libraries, summer camps for children, and grants for AIDS outreach, drug rehabilitation, domestic violence, and workshops for children from public housing. And the list seemed to go on endlessly. Although the affair seemed to embarrass and fatigue him, he was as gracious as ever and was heard to jokingly say after the party, "Well, let's start preparing for the hundredth." And he almost made it.

Joe reached ninety-nine years and two months before his great heart beat for the last time in the spring of the year. Robin, Sharon, and I drove over to Greensboro, where there was standing room only in the First Presbyterian Church as his admirers came to say good-bye to their true friend. In the homily, we were told that one of his last public appearances, just a month before his death, had been at the groundbreaking for a new complex at the North Carolina School of Science and Mathematics, which he had helped establish. We also learned that one of his favorite projects had been Bryan Park, a vast recreational complex that he funded in Greensboro. During his final years, he loved to be driven there and sit in his car watching the people enjoy boating, picnics by the shore, and golf. The previous fall, his statue had been unveiled at the park, and in characteristically humble style, his remarks included, "When it comes to giving, man must tip his hat to nature. She gives joy, beauty, and hope, and includes everyone." And I suspect that all of us sitting in the church that day felt that the same could be said of our friend Joe.

Someone had asked him during that final autumn of his life if there was anything he hadn't done that he wanted to do, and in typical conservation of words, he simply replied, "No."

But those closest to him knew that there was one unmet goal—he had really looked forward to driving on the last, unfinished segment of Bryan Boulevard.

———

As Sharon and I turned off of that final segment of Bryan Boulevard and onto I-40, we were quiet and may have been a bit melancholy about leaving the memory of our friend back there on his highway. But our thoughts and conversation quickly came back to the present as Sharon called Sarah on her cell phone to announce that we would be arriving in a few minutes. We then began discussing the main reason for our trip, which was the new house. Sharon had really been the driving force behind the project from its inception, and she was now reviewing with me the list of things we needed to check on during this trip. True to form, however, my mind was wandering. Thoughts of our new home were just another reminder that I would soon be retiring and leaving Yale and all the friends and colleagues whom we had come to cherish over the past fifteen years. My mind was especially preoccupied with the thought of bidding farewell to my patients at Yale with whom I had been privileged to develop such warm relationships. Memories of saying good-bye to those at Duke were still fresh in my mind, and I did not look forward to going through it all over again at Yale. And what promised to make this next set of farewells even more difficult than the first was the knowledge that there would be no more patients to replace them.

My momentary funk was soon lightened by reminding myself that I would be having at least one more visit with a most special patient shortly after we returned to Connecticut—someone who never failed to bolster my spirits. She would be returning to her home after spending the summer in Idaho. As she had done for many years, she would spend the fall in her Connecticut home before flying to Hawaii for Christmas, then to Florida for the remainder of the winter, back to Connecticut in the spring, and again to the mountains of Idaho for the summer. And what made this hectic schedule all the more remarkable was that earlier in the year she had celebrated her hundredth birthday.

———

One of my responsibilities at Yale for which I was particularly ill prepared was fundraising. It was clear that the sizable financial deficit in our department would have to be approached in a variety of ways, not the least of which was soliciting charitable donations, euphemistically referred to as development. Aside from Ronnie's concert and Joe Bryan's gifts, my experience in the world of development was essentially nonexistent when we moved to Yale. But, having observed the success of my colleagues at Duke with an advisory board of wealthy and well-connected patients to help with fundraising, I set out to assemble a similar board at Yale. It evolved over the years and proved to be one of my greatest joys, not only because of their help in raising money, but even more so because of the warm friendships that I came to enjoy with many special people on the board. One of their crowning achievements was the multimillion-dollar campaign that Dave Brubeck had helped to make a success. Although my role in the campaign was minimal, it gave our dean the idea that I knew something about development, which led to his request that I help with fundraising for the medical school. And that is how I came to meet Mrs. Donna Brace Ogilvie.

My first assignment as a fundraiser for the school was a series of visits with alumni and friends of Yale in Florida. Since it was in the middle of a cold Connecticut winter, I quickly came to realize that development work was not such a bad thing. And what made it even better was the delightful people that I got to meet. My job was not to ask them for money, but to "cultivate" (another euphemism in the development world) potential donors, which essentially meant schmoozing with some very nice folks. And the icing on the cake was that my partner on this and future trips was a young woman from the development office by the name of Sharon McManus, who would become the third Sharon in my life. What made her such a successful fundraiser was that she truly cared about people, and it showed. But there was one person who she seemed to be especially fond of and kept telling me about as we drove around Florida together. In time, I too would come to share Sharon's affection for this special lady, who we called Donna.

She was the last on our list of visits and, since it was winter, was living in her apartment in Florida. Sharon had explained in advance that Donna was in her early nineties and that her vision was severely limited by macular degeneration, so I was not expecting to meet the vibrant, attractive woman who greeted us at her apartment door. Her blond hair was perfectly coiffured (I would never see it otherwise), and despite her visual impairment, she looked straight at me through stylish glasses and gave me a warm, radiant smile. She was fashionably dressed in a pantsuit, and every aspect of her demeanor belied a person who had experienced more than ninety years of living. She gave us a tour of her apartment, including some low vision aides that she had acquired to help her cope with the macular degeneration. Then the three of us drove to a nearby restaurant, where I would begin to learn more about my remarkable new friend.

Unlike Joe Bryan, Donna was born into a privileged life. Her father, Donald Brace, and one of his college mates, Alfred Harcourt, created the highly successful publishing company of Harcourt-Brace. Donna recalls Sunday afternoons in her youth when famous authors, whose works were published by her father's company, would drop by their home for casual visits. She was introduced to such literary luminaries as Sinclair Lewis and Robert Frost. But as a young girl, she was less impressed with their credentials than with their manners, which she found to be wanting in some. Donna had learned at an early age from her father that privilege was not a thing to flaunt, but rather it was a responsibility that included giving back to the community.

During the Great Depression, her family was spared the tribulations of so many because of the continued demand for textbooks that were published by Harcourt-Brace. But she retained vivid memories of those bleak years, recalling successful businessmen who were reduced to selling apples on the street for five cents and others who ended their misery by jumping from windows. Although she was personally protected from the financial disasters of the day, those events had a lasting effect on her young, impressionable mind, and she would later devote her life to helping others wherever she could.

It is somewhat ironic that the multimillion-dollar campaign to raise money for research in macular degeneration is what led to my close friendship with Donna, who suffered from that very condition. It is not surprising that she was afflicted with it, however, since macular degeneration is the leading cause of visual impairment in the United States among people over sixty-five years of age. The macula is the central portion of the retina, which we use to look directly at an object (it is the part of your retina that you are using right now to read these words or when you read the "E chart" in the doctor's office). In addition to older age as a risk factor for developing macular degeneration, there are genetic factors, and shortly after completion of our campaign, scientists at Yale were the first to discover two of the genes for the disease. Unlike glaucoma, which first affects the peripheral vision, macular degeneration takes away the central sight, leaving the patient to get by with their side vision. One of the most striking illustrations of the effect it can have on a person's vision was provided by the American artist, Georgia O'Keeffe, who lived for ninety-nine years. One day in her early nineties, while driving back from her studio ranch in New Mexico on a bright sunny day, she noticed a "dark cloud" that seemed to follow her wherever she looked. It was her first recognition of the macular degeneration, which she later illustrated in a painting of a large black rock against a blue sky.

Donna's mother had lived to be 102 years of age and was legally blind from macular degeneration in her final years. So Donna was familiar with the course of the disorder and understandably interested in any advances that were being made in the field. As the three of us sat at dinner that evening, I told her about the work that was being done at Yale and elsewhere. We had an outstanding clinician-scientist in our department, Dr. Ron Adleman, who was involved in pioneering research in macular degeneration and was offering our patients the latest in the diagnosis and treatment of the condition. Although Donna was being seen by an excellent retina specialist in a private practice, we agreed that she should obtain a second opinion with Dr. Adleman when she returned to Connecticut in the spring, and I promised to arrange the visit for her.

Flying back to Connecticut after that first development trip in Florida, my thoughts of all the nice people I had met were largely overshadowed by the remarkable lady I had encountered on our final stop. Donna was not a gushy type of woman, examples of which I had known in the South (and a few in the North). Although I am quite fond of such people, I am never entirely sure where I stand with them. With Donna, one always knew. She was totally honest in a delightful and refreshing sort of way. Her knowledge of world events—both past and present—was broad and deep, and she was not in the least bashful about expressing her opinions on them. Despite her visual impairment and other physical limitations that the years were beginning to impose, her mind was still sharp as a tack, and she was not only intensely interested in everything that was going on around her, but seemed to have a zest for life that was undiminished by the passage of time. But what I would gradually learn about Donna was that her true joy in life—like that of Joe Bryan—was derived from bringing happiness to other people.

As tender green leaves began to adorn the trees and the flowers burst forth in their profusion of bright colors, heralding the arrival of another New England spring, I found myself looking forward to the next meeting with Donna. And on a warm, sunny day in late April, she arrived at the Yale Eye Center, accompanied by Sharon, who would be with her on all her visits. She looked as radiant as I had remembered, with her perfectly coiffured blond hair, stylish dress, and warm, friendly smile. We chatted for a while, but it was clear that she was there for a reason – to learn what we could do for her vision. A thorough examination confirmed the diagnosis of macular degeneration. There are two forms of the condition, referred to as dry and wet. The former is the more common and less severe form and involves a progressive deterioration of the macula. The less common but more severe wet form involves the growth of abnormal blood vessels under the macula, which leak and bleed. Sadly, Donna's was the latter type. Ron Adelman had been involved in developing laser treatments for the wet form, although the most it seemed to accomplish was preventing the vision from getting worse. More recently, he had been working with a newer treatment in which a drug is injected into the eye that causes the abnormal blood vessels to regress. With this treatment, it was possible to see improvement of vision in some patients, and Ron embarked on a series of the injections for Donna in the hope of recovering and preserving her eyesight.

By early summer, Donna had received multiple injections, but her vision had not improved. We had to accept the sad reality that her condition was too far advanced to achieve recovery of vision with the treatment, although it appeared that it may have kept her from getting much worse. Through it all, Donna retained her good humor and positive attitude, thanking us for our efforts and determined not to let this physical limitation prevent her from enjoying life to its fullest. A few weeks later, she left for Idaho to spend the summer with family and friends. Sitting on the deck of her mountain home, she made the most of her remaining peripheral vision and enjoyed watching moose lumber through the woods down below, boats sailing on a nearby lake, and the ever-changing colors of the distant mountain ridges. On warm afternoons, she enjoyed going for rides in the mountains with her family and sitting with them on the deck for a drink before dinner. If a person did not know better, they would never have guessed that Donna had such limited vision, because she was always commenting on the beauty of something around her. In short, she retained her zest for life, which was undiminished by the passage of time and the physical infirmities that came with it.

With the arrival of fall, Donna returned to Connecticut, and Sharon arranged for us to visit her and to take her out to lunch. It was a typical crisp New England fall day, with sunlight sparkling off bright yellow and orange trees against a clear blue sky. Donna's home was in the small town of Riverside in western Connecticut, not far from the New York border. It had been the family home since her father built it as a summer place in the 1920s. A decade later he converted it to a year-round home, and the family had resided there ever since. Following her mother's death in the 1970s, Donna and her husband, Jack, renovated the house and moved back in to it. Jack Ogilvie had been a highly respected surgeon and civic leader in the nearby town of Stamford. He was a Yale graduate, and the two of them honored their commitment to education by establishing scholarships for

Yale medical students, which to this day give underprivileged young people the chance to pursue their dreams. Donna lost Jack in the early 1990s and now lived alone, except for a housekeeper, in the stately home. Like Mr. Bryan's house, Donna's was impressive but not ostentatious, in keeping with the dignity of its time, and in striking contrast to the "McMansions" that were going up in the neighborhood. What was most striking was the rolling, wooded acreage on which the home was set. There was a pool in the back, beyond which the lawn sloped down to a picturesque creek that flowed into Long Island Sound. But in keeping with the modesty of its occupants, the garden still stood where Jack had once grown vegetables and flowers for the family.

With Thanksgiving not far away, Sharon had brought Donna a large pumpkin and a box of her favorite chocolates. True to form, Donna went on about how beautiful the pumpkin was, as though she could see it with 20/20 vision. Sharon had been to her home before, but it was my first time, and I was given a tour of the downstairs. A small library, where Donna spent much of her time, was packed with vintage books, many of which had been published by her father's company. Farther down the hall, a comfortable living room looked out over the back lawn. I could only imagine how it must have been when giants of the literary world sat in this very room on Sunday afternoons. And what memories Donna had of her life in that house! Her family was the first in Riverside to own a phonograph, and she loved listening to Charleston music on it. She also vaguely recalled their first radio, although she thought it was rather ugly. It was a floor model with a cloth front and wood slats. Donna remembered listening to a "famous Scottish singer" (she couldn't recall his name) who had a habit of crying when he sang. As a little girl, she felt sorry for him and would slip crackers to him through the wood slats—until her mother discovered what she was doing.

The most captivating feature of the living room was a large portrait of Donna's mother, which dominated the wall opposite the back windows. Judging from her dress and hairdo, the picture must have been painted in the 1920s. It portrayed a young, attractive, elegant woman, whom Donna described as "quite a lady." She looked in the direction of her mother's picture, and it seemed for a moment that her thoughts were in another time. Then she smiled, shook her head, and observed that her sister had been closer to their mother and more like her in many ways. The sister was her only sibling and was younger than Donna. She described her as "a bit of a renegade," having been expelled from prep school for riding through town on a horse. They had never been close, but there was a time in the 1920s when the two teenage sisters and their mother drove across the country to California and flew in a twin-engine plane over Los Angeles. Of course, flight was barely two decades old at the time, and Donna was scared to death, but was talked into it by her more adventurous sister and mother. And with a chuckle, she said, "I actually enjoyed it."

While her sister may have been more like their mother, Donna observed that she was more like their father and closer to him. She had obviously learned his lesson that privilege is not a thing to be flaunted, but to be accepted with humility and gratitude, and that it comes with a big responsibility to give back to others. And she began to put these lessons into practice at an early age. During World War II, when she could have been relaxing in the safety of her home, she chose to work as an airplane spotter and for the Red Cross. When she was in her second month of pregnancy, she was confronted with a crisis and did not hesitate to attempt artificial respiration for a wounded soldier—she tried, at least. And that was just the beginning of a life of service to the world around her. Despite her privileged life, she was always humble, modest and down-to-earth. "That is how we were raised," she said. "We never thought we were better than anyone else."

Although Sharon and I were supposedly taking Donna to lunch, it turned out to be the other way around, as we went to her yacht club and dined in the Brace Room, which was named after her father. It was situated on the sound, with sailboats bobbing nearby and a spectacular view across the water to inlets where stately homes lined the shore. The autumn sun glistened on the water and provided a sense of warmth as it came through the windows into the dining room. The conversation flowed effortlessly until Sharon or I would try to ask Donna about one of her charitable efforts, at which point she would abruptly redirect the discussion—she just didn't like putting herself in the spotlight. To her, giving was something that was naturally expected of those who are able and need not be fussed over.

There were times, however, when Donna was unable to quell the adulation of her admirers. For sixty-one years, she had worked as a volunteer in the Stamford Hospital, where Jack had practiced surgery. She had run the hospital gift shop, served as president of the hospital auxiliary, and performed any other service that the hospital needed. And so, as Donna was approaching her hundredth year, the hospital honored her with a gala dinner that was attended by several hundred of her coworkers from over the years and even patients who remembered how she always tried to help anyone in need. By this time, she was confined to a wheelchair, but she looked as radiant as ever, and her mind was obviously as sharp as anyone in the room. She accepted the adulation with her typical graciousness, but I could tell that she was uncomfortable being in the spotlight, and when a thunderous standing ovation seemed like it would never stop, I could almost hear her saying, "That's enough."

Donna was more comfortable working quietly in the background to help others. On one occasion, a young woman, who had once worked with Sharon, was dying of a brain tumor. Still holding onto hope, she would come up alone from Virginia for treatments in New York. Although Donna had never met her, she insisted that the woman stay at her home, where she took care of her and, probably more than anything else, gave her new friend the gift of knowing that there are those in this world who truly care about the welfare of others.

The day finally came when Donna reached the century mark, and a gala birthday dinner, worthy of the occasion, was held at the yacht club. It seemed that all the dignitaries from the surrounding communities were there, as well as representatives from all the organizations that she had supported for so many years. There were leaders from Stamford Hospital and Yale University, but also from Donna's prep school and her girls club, representing two of her greatest philanthropic passions—education and women. Of all her passions, her greatest may have been helping underprivileged women. In the 1940s, she began working for the Girls Club of America. When a separate organization, called Boys Club of America, tried to combine with the girls club and took their name, Donna helped to start a new organization called Girls Incorporated. The goal of the organization was to provide after-school training for underprivileged girls to give them a chance for a better life. I could see in her eyes that these types of encounters were Donna's greatest joy. And it was obvious that everyone in the room that night had benefited from Donna's generosity in one way or another and was thankful for the opportunity to express gratitude to a truly special lady.

Since she had just reached the age of one hundred, I couldn't help but wonder how Donna would survive and recover from such a hectic evening in which she was the constant center of attention. I think her family physician shared the same concern, because a few days later he disappointed her by suggesting that she should forgo her annual trip to

Hawaii for Christmas. However, she was able to go down to Florida to spend the winter in her apartment where she and I had first met nearly a decade earlier.

By now, there was little more that we could do for her eyesight, and it was increasingly difficult for her to come to New Haven. So, on a late spring morning, just three days before she was scheduled to leave for her summer in Idaho, I drove alone to her home to spend some time with her. We enjoyed a light lunch together in her dining room and then went into the library for a long chat until I sensed she was growing tired and that I might be overstaying my welcome. But before leaving, I had to ask her one more question.

"Donna, what do you want most for your family and friends to remember from your long life's experiences?"

She was silent and thoughtful for a long moment and then said in an almost matter-of-fact way, as though it was obvious, "To remember their responsibility to help others."

———

As we turned off the street into Sarah's driveway, Allison was waiting for us in the front yard. Although it had been just over a month since we last saw her, I was shocked (as I always was) to see how much more she had grown, not just in height, but in maturity as a young lady as well. She was clearly a barometer of time, reminding me of how each year was passing more swiftly than the one before. And I had no illusions that the retirement years would be any exception. There were times, as with all of us, that I wished time could stand still—those precious stages in the life of a child or grandchild that we wish would never end, special occasions with family and friends that we wish could just go on and on, and even now, as the winds of time blow ever more rapidly toward our final days. But, of course, we can no more control the passage of time than we can predict how much of it we have left. The best we can do, as I was once reminded by my friend Mark, is to recognize the beauty and wonder that surround us each day of our lives, to enjoy it to the fullest in that moment that we are given to enjoy it, and to remain fully engaged in life, despite the physical challenges that may come with the passage of time—as did Miss Nanny, Sir Rex, Dave and Iola, and Joe Bryan and Donna Ogilvie.

Joe and Donna were alike in many ways. Both enjoyed substantial wealth and seemed to enjoy even more the sharing of their good fortune with others. But I don't think that is the principal lesson I learned from them, as important as it is. What struck me most about both of them was that they never lost their zeal for life. Despite being increasingly slowed by the infirmities of age, they seemed to greet each new day as though it offered just as much opportunity, hope, and excitement as when they were young. And for them, I believe it truly did, because they continued to fill each day with what brought them happiness, which included bringing happiness to others, but also just enjoying the daily pleasures and beauty of life. So I guess the message is to find what brings us happiness and to fill our days—however many they may be—with those things and to enjoy them to the fullest and to never forget to be thankful for whatever blessings may come our way with each new day.

Epilogue

The rain has stopped, and a ray of warm sunshine now brightens the cabin interior, sparkling off an empty coffee mug. The yellow writing pads are full, and my old legs are a bit stiff from the hours of sitting as I recorded my memories. It feels good to stand and stretch. Outside, a majestic panorama is unfolding, framed by our cabin window. The heavy, gray clouds that earlier blanketed the entire sky are now giving way to billows of white and patches of blue. Only one lone stretch of dark clouds remains high above, and just beneath it, the source of my personal sunbeam has burst through with all its glory. Silver shafts radiate upward into the heavens like the spokes of a wheel, while a warm, golden glow suffuses the landscape down below. The air has cleared, revealing ridge after ridge of mountain peaks, the farthest being almost indistinguishable from the clouds and sky beyond. The distant ridges still appear blue, with white, smoke-like vapors hanging in the intervening valleys. Closer by, just beneath the glow of the sun, the next ridges of mountains are so brilliantly illuminated that they appear as hazy, homogenous silhouettes of golden orange. It is only along the ridges nearest our cabin that individual trees can be distinguished, outlining the peaks and finally coming into clear view. Autumn is approaching, and early touches of reds and yellows mingle with the greens as the sunshine reflects off the upper boughs and their leaves and needles. And I am reminded once again how precious is the gift of sight.

A package arrived the day before, but sits unopened beside the old oak table, as I know what is in it—or so I think. I have been receiving identical boxes for over three decades and can easily identify them from across the room. Inside will be six jars of my favorite peanuts. Although it has been more than two decades since I last saw the Peanut Man, he has continued to send the parcels on a regular basis, and they are always a most welcome gift. In fact, they remind me that it is past noon and I am a bit hungry, so now seems like a good time to open the box and take a handful of the salty delicacies as I prepare to go for a walk. Their wonderful fragrance fills the room as I open the box and find the expected six jars. But there is something else this time—a letter. In the past, the gifts arrived with no indication of who had sent them, although I always knew. The letter is typed on stationary from the First Methodist Church, where my benefactor and his colleagues cook their peanuts. However, it is not from him, but appears to be from the church secretary.

> Dear Dr. Shields,
>
> On September 22, Mr. W. T. came by to visit me and ask that I be sure and send you a case of peanuts in time for you and your family to have them by Thanksgiving. He told me he was going to have surgery on his knee, and he didn't expect to make it. He had been given a stress test for his heart and didn't do well. His doctor told him he couldn't recommend he undergo surgery; however, he opted to do it because he was having a hard time getting around, and he said he was lonely and ready to go join his dear departed wife. Well, I regret to inform you that he did survive the surgery, but passed away one week later. He was a much-loved gentleman in this community. And ... he thought the world of you. I knew you would want to know of this.

So the Peanut Man is dead—and I am reminded again of the passage of time. It seems fitting that I should receive the news of his loss with one last gift from him. His greatest joy came from giving to others and bringing them happiness. A flood of memories washes over me as I glance across the room at the lantern-lamp sitting on a corner table. He made it all by himself and gave it to me so many years ago when we were at Duke together. But the memory of him that is most indelible in my mind is the lesson he left with me—to be a good "getter." He taught me that one of the best ways we can bring happiness to others is to show genuine appreciation and gratitude for their gifts to us. I suppose the corollary is that each of us can also find happiness in our lives by recognizing the good fortunes that come our way and being truly thankful for them. At this moment, I feel especially fortunate to have known the Peanut Man, to have had the privilege of serving as one of his doctors, and to have received his generosity and his wisdom. And as I shake out a handful of peanuts and prepare to leave the cabin for my walk, I have a feeling that I am about to be reminded of many more reasons that I have to feel fortunate and to be grateful.

From the stone outside our cabin door, the path drops down about fifty feet and then levels off for a short distance of open trail before turning back and up into the deep, primal forest. The morning rain has left the woods feeling clean and refreshed and accentuates their many fragrances. Beneath my feet, the spongy pine needles and dried leaves emit their pungent aroma and provide a spring to my step. Hemlocks and hickory trees mingle with the tall pines along the pathway amid a thick undergrowth of mountain laurel and rhododendron. A carpet of ferns, trillium, heartleaf, and bright red-orange toadstools adds an accent of color to the wet, verdant flora. Sunlight sparkles down through the trees, playing off the leaves that flutter gently in the breeze. As the trail penetrates deeper into the forest, the way becomes darker with the addition of birch, basswood, and the mighty poplars that filter out more of the sun's rays. It is becoming not only darker, but also increasingly quieter. The songs of the birds, which were so plentiful around our cabin, are now barely audible in the distance, and the only remaining sounds are the rustle of the leaves high up in the trees, the crunch of my feet on the path, and my breathing.

The silence takes me back to another time when I stood in similar quietude on an old, abandoned railroad bed looking down over the edge far below at flowing water that was called Crystal Creek. I did not know it at that moment, but I was also standing on the precipice of being taught another lesson—the importance of listening. Closing my eyes, I can see a small frame building in the woods, with a young girl and her doll sitting together on the porch—Emily and Clementine? But, on closer inspection, I realize that the girl is actually a grown woman and the doll is a child, who is talking nonstop. The woman is listening intently to her every word, and her eyes are reflecting patience and acceptance. And then, just for a fleeting moment, those eyes—eyes that I have seen before—glance in my direction and lock with mine before her image fades into the deep, dark forest.

Being a good listener—like being a good getter—is something that I have had to learn and relearn throughout my life. Showing a person the courtesy of listening intently and respectfully to what they have to say not only tells them that their feelings and opinions are important to us, but also strengthens their sense of self-worth. Of course, careful listening and observation in all aspects of our lives are also critical to learning and to recognizing and appreciating all those good things that surround us each day. And, standing in the silence of these beautiful woods, listening to the memories of times gone by, I can't help but be reminded once again of the multitude of gifts that I have been so fortunate to receive from so many special people.

The trail is becoming steeper, and the trees are progressively shorter as they adapt to the changing elements. The wind has picked up, with a chill that prompts me to button my jacket. These high, remote areas can seem pretty austere, evoking a sense of eerie loneliness that is at the same time quite exhilarating. Not only are the trees smaller and already beginning to lose their leaves, but the flora beneath them is less abundant than it was back down the mountainside. What greenery there is, hoping to survive the coming winter, is lower to the ground, where it can conserve warmth against the ice and snow. It is an excellent example of how nature adapts to its surroundings and how it has learned to cope with whatever challenges are thrown its way. And that thought causes me to reflect again on how the same is true for much of the human race, examples of which I was privileged to witness in many of my patients.

There are very few fall flowers at this elevation, but I am surprised to look up and see one hardy exception. Beside the trail, a massive, sheared rock rises vertically far above my head, bearing no signs of life except for one small, pink blossom that is growing cheerfully out of a thin crevice. I am struck by the incongruity of such a delicate, lovely flower flourishing in this remote, hostile environment. How did the seed get up there? And how could it find enough soil to survive? I can't help but stop and admire the courage and fortitude of the little flower. And I can't help but think of how much it reminds me of Martha. Despite her petite stature and multiple medical challenges, she also had the courage and fortitude to blossom in a world that was hostile and unfriendly to her. She did it by not letting the negative aspects of her life overwhelm and destroy her, but by finding the positive things that she liked about herself and her life (maybe as the little flower found just enough good soil to flourish). And by choosing to focus on those good things, she found happiness and meaning in her life. Over the course of my career, I was fortunate to have many patients like Martha who taught me, in different ways, that true happiness comes not so much from what we have, but from what we make of what we have.

Blessing certainly made the most of what he was given. As a young child coming to America from Africa—alone, frightened, hardly able to speak the language, and barely able to see—he could easily have simply licked his wounds and let life pass him by. But instead, he chose to follow the same path as Martha. In fact, he chose to accept his lot as a gift rather than a curse, and to do so with gratitude rather than anger. He saw his blindness as a blessing, because it led him to focus on his music and his future and, as he put it, to find God's purpose for his life. And so, like Martha, he blossomed against staggering odds and is, I am quite convinced, destined for continued success and happiness no matter what new challenges may come his way.

As I continue along the trail, with Martha and Blessing at my side, we encounter another sojourner who seems to be their soul mate, despite substantial differences in his story. While Martha and Blessing never knew a day in their lives without physical limitations, Michael once had it all—perfect vision, perfect health, a promising career, success, and security—and then, inexplicably and relentlessly, it was taken from him. Who can say which is the bitterest pill—to have had something precious and lose it, or to have never known it? But what is clear is that Michael persevered through his great loss and emerged a conqueror by cleaving to the faith that there is a purpose in everything. Like Martha, he chose to focus on the positive rather than the negative aspects of his life—the things that he still liked about himself and his life—and to make the most of them. And, like Blessing, he was able to see his losses and challenges as opening new doors to new opportunities, as gifts rather than curses—and, in so doing, to find fulfillment in his life.

Most of us have never faced physical challenges to the degree that Martha, Blessing, and Michael have been forced to bear. And yet we all have known or will know times in our lives when the road becomes hard to travel—poor health, loss, unfulfilled dreams, animosity, failure, fear, despair. And there are times when these can seem just as overwhelming and disruptive to us as a catastrophic medical condition. At such times, it is easy to say that we should simply accentuate the silver lining of whatever our black cloud may be, but it is not always so easy to do—not for me, at least. These three remarkable people beside me are among my heroes because they have done it, and I would surely like to know their secret— where they found the inner resources to make the most of what they were given and to live happy and meaningful lives in the face of formidable odds. But when I turn to them for answers, I find myself standing alone on the trail. And so I move on.

Up the way, I think I see a group of people standing quietly beside the trail. As I draw closer to them, they appear vaguely familiar and seem to recognize me. I have the strange feeling that they have been waiting for me with something to say. Within the group is a middle-aged couple with two handsome young children standing beside them. The woman looks at me with her gentle but intense dark eyes and smiles as though to say that I should already know the answer. And maybe I do. Becky is reminding me that part of the answer I sought from my earlier companions is to have a dream—to know what we want to achieve in our lives—and to never give up on the dream. And Roger nods with a smile. But even though I can appreciate the wisdom of their message, I can't help being a bit dubious, knowing that dreams don't always come true. And that is when I notice the other two people in the group. They are both grown men and bear a striking resemblance to each other, although one is elderly, with thin, white hair, and the other is a young man, standing straight and proud beside the senior man—Benjamin's father? The elder gentleman seems to take great pride in the young man, who was such a little boy when I knew him. He gazes over at his son and then turns his eyes to me, and I realize he is reminding me that the answer to emulating Martha, Blessing, and Michael and to following Becky's admonition to pursue our dream is simply to do our best.

I have finally reached the furthest point on my walk and am ready to take a brief rest. Just off the trail, a large, flat rock cantilevers over the mountainside, much like my favorite perch on the hiking trail back in Connecticut. It offers a spectacular vista of the landscape, which has changed a bit since I left the cabin. The sun has dropped lower in the sky and now casts long shadows from the mountain ridges down the slopes and into the valley. Rising from the shadows on the far side, the trees are still drenched in a warm, golden glow of late afternoon sunlight. Overhead, the sky remains blue with only a few white, wispy clouds high above, and a lone hawk soars lazily in and out of the picture. As I sit gazing out over this awe-inspiring view, I have the sense that I am not alone. Beside me is a frail, white-haired woman, who is looking out at the same scene with obvious rapt enjoyment. I recognize how improbable it is that she could have made the rather demanding trek to this lookout point, but I am delighted to enjoy her company once again. Many years ago—a lifetime, it seems—Alice Fleming pointed out to me the beauty of a lovely spring day. Although we had passed the same way that morning, I had been so consumed by my busy schedule and the cares of the day that I totally missed the beauty around me. And the remarkable thing was that she was blind. That was when I began to learn that there is a "gift of sight" that transcends our physical ability to see—that allows us to enjoy the beauty of life in whatever our circumstances may be. Alice and I sit there together for a while, silently enjoying the moment in all its splendor.

Over the years, I have come to believe that this may be the most important secret to a happy life—to recognize and enjoy the beauty of each moment. All too often, I have let those moments slip by unnoticed or unappreciated, only to look back and realize, when it was too late, what I had and to regret not having enjoyed it more when I had the chance. It is a concept I once tried to teach Sarah and John—the old "carpe diem" watchword—but one that I should have spent more time practicing myself. As I glance over toward Alice, she is no longer there. In her place is my longtime friend and patient, Mark, who does not appear to have changed after all these years. He gives me that old smile, and I am taken back to the last time we were together in his backyard. Although he was dying of AIDS, he told me that he was happier than he had ever been at any time in his life. Like me, he had once allowed life's precious moments to be lost in the hurry and cares of the day. But now, for the first time, he was able to put those concerns in their proper place and actually see the beauty around him and enjoy each moment of it. I left him that day, for the last time, realizing that, if we can live each day in that way, when we come to the end of the day—or the end of our lives—we can look back without regrets, knowing that we made the most of each day.

It is time to head back. The temperature has continued to drop, and I am beginning to wish that I had worn a heavier jacket. But I am warmed by the thought of soon being back in our cabin, which will be filled with the aroma of dinner on the stove and with the love of our little family. And that thought reminds me that, of all the gifts I received from my patients over the years, the greatest were undoubtedly the lessons of love and of caring for and respecting others. My strongest memory is of a young mother who once showed me the purest form of love I ever witnessed. Although her severely handicapped daughter was unable to speak or show any signs of recognition, she cared for her child every day of her life with a love that was absolutely unconditional and without any thought of recompense. Walking down the trail, I can still see that young, frail mother standing in my office year after year holding her daughter as she became more and more difficult to manage. And yet I now see her child as a beautiful, healthy young girl (the advantage of uninhibited reminiscence), and I rather suspect that is how April's mother sees her daughter today through memory's haze and the power of absolute love. In any case, although I continue to fall pitifully short of the mark, she showed me the type of love that we should all strive to give each day to those who are nearest to us.

Just ahead, two young men are standing beside the trail sharing a good laugh. When they see me approaching, they look down and try to suppress their mirth behind guilty smirks. That causes me to chuckle as I remember all the antics of Barry and Craig when they were young boys. But as I see them standing side by side, I am reminded of how they too once showed me the power of love. There seems to be a fine line between love and hatred, and the two boys once slipped over onto the dark side of the line when one of their antics went badly awry. But love won when one of the boys was about to go blind, and his friend offered to give him his own eye—his only eye. I have no doubt that somewhere out there today, those two young men are still the best of friends, and I am grateful to them for reminding me once more that love can overcome the bitterest of feelings, if we will only give it a chance.

One of the most endearing forms of love that I was privileged to observe among my patients was in the elderly couples, whose mature love had withstood the test of time and grown stronger with each passing year and which only death could break asunder. There was one especially memorable couple, however, whose experience led me to question whether even death has such power. Pearl and Bud had been sweethearts since their youth. They survived the war years and Bud's injury, started a new life, raised their children, enjoyed many grandchildren and great-grandchildren, and happily grew old together. They weathered the infirmities of age, tenderly caring for each other right up to the end. And the end came on a day when Pearl returned to her hospital room, having just had cataract surgery. Despite his poor health, Bud had insisted on being there for her, and he was there with the family when she was rolled into the room. But his weak heart couldn't take it, and he left her at that moment after expressing his love to her one last time. As tragic as it was, and as much as my heart ached for Pearl and her family, I found myself feeling sorriest for those who go through life without ever experiencing such abiding love or faith in the promise that love never dies.

Dave and Iola had also been sweethearts since their youth. And despite becoming one of the world's most acclaimed jazz pianists and composers, Dave Brubeck remained faithful to Iola for their seven decades together, and like Pearl and Bud, their love only seemed to grow stronger with the passage of time. Through the way they lived every aspect of their lives, they not only provided me with yet another lesson in the power of love, but they also taught me to walk humbly, to care for the needs of others and for our environment, and to respect the dignity and feelings of all people. And as I continue down the path toward our cabin, I begin to feel the presence of other special people in my life who, in their own ways, taught me the same values of caring for and respecting others.

Returning to the lower level of the trail, where the trees are larger and now filter out much of the final rays of daylight, the view into the forest is becoming increasingly dim and is beginning to play tricks on my eyes. Among the tall trees, one trunk appears to be made of stone, like the chimney of an old house long forgotten. From where I stand, it is hard to tell, but an image from the past begins to form in my mind, and I now see an elderly gentleman kneeling near the chimney, as though he is tending to a bed of flowers. Of course, I know that they are both gone—the chimney on the ridge and Arthur Murdoch. But in my memory, they will always stand tall, reminding me of the resilience of the human spirit against life's adversities and of the remarkable capacity of the human heart to reach out in charity to the needs of others, even in the midst of our own personal suffering. I blink my eyes and there is nothing but trees, and yet it feels like I am not alone. An elderly couple is holding hands, and the man is looking at me with a satisfied smile. I was only starting out in my career when I first looked at those eyes and saw tears in them and didn't understand. But George Johnston planted something in me back then that I slowly tried to learn over the decades that followed—to never trivialize the cares and anxieties of another person, but to always give them the benefit of the doubt, as I would want them to do for me. I believe that that lesson, early in my career, helped me to better understand other patients that I would meet along the way, such as Mr. Murdoch. And just for a moment, I see him again beside the old chimney, and he nods to Mr. Johnston with an appreciative smile. And then I am alone again on the trail.

A twinkling of light down the way signals that I am coming back to the edge of the forest. The singing of the birds is becoming increasingly distinct, as though they are welcoming my return with their final serenade of the day. The melodious sounds once again bring to mind many of my patients, who found their purpose in life and their gift to others through the beauty of their music—the ageless and iconic compositions of Dave Brubeck, the newer but promising works of Blessing Offor, and many others. Two of those who will forever be close to my heart, like Dave and Blessing, are Ronnie and Susan, and I feel the presence of them both beside me as I continue down the path.

Not only was Ronnie Milsap robbed of his last vestige of sight at an early age, much like Blessing, but he also faced monumental challenges in his youth that could have left him bitter and resentful of the hand he was dealt. And yet he was able to see through the pain with a giving and forgiving heart, becoming one of our most beloved country music artists, while at the same time reaching out to others to help provide them with hope and opportunities for a better life. Susan's story, although on a different scale, is very much the same. She too suffered a painful childhood, being taunted by her peers for the medical conditions she was forced to bear. And yet she also rose above it to not only become a contented wife and mother, but also to dedicate herself to teaching others how to cope with their lot in life and to always judge others by what is on the inside. I can still hear the crystal beauty of her lovely voice as she sang for me in her home and on her CDs that I enjoy to this day. But soon the sound of her singing fades back into the serenading of the birds.

As I leave the woods behind and return to the open trail, the sun has set behind the mountains, and the sky presents its last performance of the day with streaks of orange across the distant clouds that slowly fade away to the gray of dusk. For a moment, I feel a disconcerting sense of loss, as though I am leaving my friends—and my life as I have known it—back on the mountain slope and am heading forward into a dim unknown. I suppose I am not alone in feeling this way as I leave my career behind and head into the final phase of my life. I have known some people for whom retirement was only a sad—and often brief—conclusion to their life, while others seemed to find it the most exhilarating and fulfilling time they had ever known, and I can't help but wonder which path I will discover. Of course, I know that I will miss my patients, and yet I have the feeling that they have left me with a wealth of gifts that—assuming I have learned their lessons—should provide sound guidance in whatever the future may hold. In fact, just down the open trail, I think I see one last group of my old patients who are waiting to walk with me.

They are all adults, but one is noticeably shorter than the others and still has her endearing quality of childlike innocence. She steps away from the group and reaches her hand out to me, and I can almost hear her say, "Don't worry, old buddy. It's gonna be okay." Kristi helped me once before to get through a major change in my life, and I am grateful for that memory and for the comfort she brings even now. As we stand smiling at each other, two more women step forward on either side of Kristi and put their hands on her shoulders. Both women also knew great change and uncertainty in their lives—Rei-Ying in China and Raimonda in Lithuania—but they each kept a flame alive in their hearts that gave them courage in the face of oppression and faith in better days to come. They look down lovingly at Kristi and then up at me, as though to confirm her assurance that everything will indeed be okay. And finally, an elderly gentleman joins the three women to complete their message to me. After all that time of searching for Raymond, there he is in front of me, and his words are predictable: "Indeed, don't worry. And remember, you will never be alone."

The image of my four latest companions lingers for a moment and then fades away to join the other sojourners of the day in the recesses of my mind. Now there are only four left—and what a remarkable foursome they are! Together, their cumulative lifetimes span nearly four centuries. And yet it is not so much the number of years they lived, but the way in which they lived them—especially in their later years—that has been such an inspiration to me. While many of us at this time in life are beginning to slow down and often becoming a bit melancholy at the thought that the best days are behind us and that there is little left to look forward to, these four woke up to every new day with youthful anticipation of what new adventure or pleasure lay around the next corner. As I stand waiting for their pep talk, they seem to pay me no heed, but begin walking down the trail ahead of me, as though I should know by now what to do. And so I follow.

Two of them walk side by side—a petite, matronly lady and a tall, distinguished-looking gentleman. Their arms are gently linked like those of two old friends, although their lives could not have been further apart— hers on a small farm in North Carolina, and his on the world stage. But they shared a common gift and now seem to be reminding me of it once again. Miss Nanny lived for 103 years, during which time she experienced the throes of segregation, the Great Depression, two world wars, and the civil rights movement. She had known loss, even of several children, and had become blind from cataracts in her nineties. But she never lost her zest for life, and at the age of ninety-six, she instructed me to proceed with her surgery so that she could continue to enjoy life to its fullest. And she did until the very end. Sir Rex Harrison seemed to have accomplished everything in his career by the time I knew him—numerous starring roles on the stage and screen and countless honors, including an Oscar and the distinction of knighthood from the Queen of England. He could easily have been relaxing in his Italian villa or on his yacht in the Mediterranean, resting on his laurels. But, like Miss Nanny, he never lost that youthful enthusiasm for what life might have to offer around the next bend, and he continued working into his senior years, making the most of his talents to the very end. What impressed me the most about both of these remarkable people is that they never seemed to grow old, because they never stopped living.

And finally, I recognize the other two in the group—Joe and Donna. In a way, they were like bookends to my career—Joe Bryan in my early days at Duke, and Donna Ogilvie in my final years at Yale. Although they never knew each other, they were so much alike in many ways. They both enjoyed substantial wealth, and yet the greatest joy they seemed to derive from their good fortune was sharing it with others. What impressed me most about both of them, however, was that they simply loved life. They were interested in everything around them and enjoyed all the beauty and adventure that life had to offer. And even when they were approaching their hundredth year and the infirmities of age were taking their toll, they greeted each new day with the same hope and excitement for what lay ahead as they had known in their youth, just as Miss Nanny and Sir Rex had done. And now the four of them stop and look back at me to see if I am paying attention, and then once again I find myself alone on the trail.

As I round the last bend and turn up toward the end of my walk, our cabin comes into view. Dusk has given way to darkness, but a light from the cabin window—the same window on which rain was pattering early this morning—shines like a beacon to guide me home. Traversing the final leg of my journey, I think I understand what Raymond meant by never being alone. I have an overwhelming sense of being surrounded by a host of special people whose friendship and wisdom I enjoyed and profited from throughout my life—people who taught me to hear and see all the gifts around me and to truly enjoy them, to make the most of each day we are given, to bask in the glow of the love of family and friends, to respect the feelings of all people and to be sensitive and responsive to their needs, to never lose a zest for life, but to greet each new day with hope and excitement for what may lie around the next bend—and to never forget to be thankful for it all.

As I reach the cabin door, something causes me to pause and look back down the trail and up the mountain slope, which is now bathed in moonlight, and to reflect once more on how my life has been enriched by the people whose paths I have been privileged to cross in my sojourn through life, and to be truly thankful to all of them for their gifts of sight.

Ω

Acknowledgements

In the course of writing *Gifts of Sight*, as a novice author in the nonscientific realm, I was extremely fortunate to receive the support and advice of many thoughtful people to whom I wish to express my most sincere gratitude. Two very special and long-time friends, Mr. Louis V. Priebe and Mr. J. Bruce Hoof, did their best to help find a home for the book, in the course of which they introduced me to Dr. Michael J. Easley, Mr. David Dary and Dr. Wayne J. Pond, each of whom were very kind with their time and advice. A special thanks to Mr. Frank Delaney for his friendship and guidance over the years, and to Ms Hunter Darden for her suggestions. My partner and friend at Duke University, Dr. R. Rand Allingham, reviewed portions of the manuscript for certain technical details, and my wife, Sharon, read every chapter and was my greatest source of encouragement. I also thank the people at Westbow Press for their professional assistance. But most of all, I want to thank my patients who inspired me to write this book. Only a few of their stories are included, but they all know who they are and how special they are to me.

CPSIA information can be obtained at www.ICGtesting.com
Printed in the USA
BVOW041502120413

318033BV00002B/3/P